D0192173

FACT
AND
ARTIFACT

FACT AND ARTIFACT

WRITING NONFICTION

SECOND EDITION

LYNN Z. BLOOM

UNIVERSITY OF CONNECTICUT, STORRS

A BLAIR PRESS BOOK

PRENTICE HALL, ENGLEWOOD CLIFFS, NJ 07632

Library of Congress Cataloging-in-Publication Data

Bloom, Lynn Z., 1934–
    Fact and artifact : writing nonfiction / by Lynn Z. Bloom.
      p. cm.
    Includes bibliographical references (p.) and index.
    ISBN 0-13-338807-7 (pbk.)
    1. English language—Rhetoric.   2. Exposition (Rhetoric)
I. Title.
  PE1429.B53   1994
  808´.042—dc20   93-21424
                                         CIP

Cover designer: Louise Fili
Production Coordinator: Bob Anderson
Photo researchers: Joelle Burrows and Lori Morris-Nantz
Cover art: Robert Mapplethorpe, *Calla Lily, 1988.* Copyright ©1988
    The Estate of Robert Mapplethorpe.
Don Marquis, "The coming of archy" from Archy and Mehitabel. Reprinted by
permission of Bantam, Doubleday, Dell Publishing Group, Inc.

Blair Press
The Statler Building
20 Park Plaza, Suite 1113
Boston, MA 02116-4399

© 1994 by Prentice Hall, Inc.
A Paramount Communications Company
Englewood Cliffs, NJ 07632

All rights reserved. No part of this book may be
reproduced, in any form or by any means, without
permission in writing from the publisher.

Printed in the United States of America
10 9 8 7 6 5 4 3 2 1

ISBN 0-13-338807-7

Prentice-Hall International (UK) Limited, *London*
Prentice-Hall of Australia Pty. Limited, *Sydney*
Prentice-Hall Canada Inc., *Toronto*
Prentice-Hall Hispanoamericana, S.A., *Mexico*
Prentice-Hall of India Private Limited, *New Delhi*
Prentice-Hall of Japan, Inc., *Tokyo*
Simon & Schuster Asia Pte. Ltd., *Singapore*
Editora Prentice-Hall do Brasil, Ltda., *Rio de Janeiro*

TO
MARTIN BLOOM
BEST CRITIC, BEST FRIEND

AND TO
WRITING STUDENTS, STUDENTS WRITING,
FRIENDS AND COLLEAGUES ALL.
YOUR VOICES RESONATE
ON THESE PAGES, IN MY HEART.

PREFACE

The photograph on the cover of this book metaphorically represents the essence of *Fact and Artifact: Writing Nonfiction*. Although the calla lily is unmistakably representational—the "fact," if you will—the photographer's selection, design, and rendering of this natural object transforms the natural fact into a distinctive artifact. The photographer's vision is as recognizable as his signature, Robert Mapplethorpe; the process represented is so dynamic that it becomes impossible for the viewer—another active contributor to the process—to separate the artist from the artifact.

So, too, do the various processes of writing nonfiction transform the "facts" about people, places, performances, processes, and controversy into the artifacts that are essays, portraits, reviews, narratives, satires, parodies, reports, scientific papers, and other works. Although *Fact and Artifact* concentrates on these processes and variations, the book is equally concerned with the ways and contexts in which writers work and with style, revision, and audiences of readers.

Fact and Artifact is an advanced composition book for people who value good writing, who take their work seriously, who want to write better and to have fun in the process. Whatever their diversity of backgrounds, interests, levels of skill, and reasons for writing, these advanced writers have progressed beyond the expectations of the conventional freshman English class. *Fact and Artifact* will not tour again that familiar territory. The book will, however, help to empower writers stimulated by a course or a job or inspired by a desire to have a voice, to share a vision or a viewpoint, to move an audience, perhaps to change the world.

Fact and Artifact is process oriented and student centered. Student voices, lively and varied and provocative, dominate the dialogue that the book encourages among students, their teachers, and the professional writers whose works are quoted here. The second edition includes many more student writings than the first, by students from all over North America and from China— younger and older; straight and gay; single and married; black, white, Asian, Hispanic; marginal and mainstream. The student writings in *Fact and Artifact* are so good that I have been accused of making them up. I didn't; they appear as they were revised and edited by the students themselves, identified by their real names.

What's New

During the decade that has passed since I wrote the first edition of *Fact and Artifact,* a great deal has happened in the dynamic fields of composition, literary theory, and teaching writing. I've revised the book throughout to accommodate new scholarship on reader-response theory; issues of gender, class, and multiculturalism; critical thinking; and dialogue within and across communities of writers in various disciplines.

Moreover, nonfiction, always loved by the reading public, has gained new respect among teachers, critics, and publishers as a distinctive, though diverse, category of writing, encompassing many of the forms explained in *Fact and Artifact.* I myself have continued to learn as a writer, experimenting with and publishing all the types of writing discussed in *Fact and Artifact,* including biography, criticism, reviews, "how-to" works, satire, poetry—and, recently, risky personal essays.

Chapter 1, "Writing in Context," has been expanded to take into account the fact that everyone writes in a complex of contexts: intellectual, personal, cultural, social, and political. The discussion ranges from practical concerns about good places and times to write to questions of whether to collaborate or not.

Chapter 2, "Style," has likewise been expanded to incorporate many more examples of student writing and new and theoretical considerations of voice, authority, and discourse communities. The virtues of clarity and conciseness are balanced against "the joys of excess."

Chapter 3, "Re-Vision and Revision," reinforces revision as the heart of the writing process. The new emphasis, on re-vision (re-seeing) and on revision (rewriting), acknowledges that writing improves through the combination of both activities. Its prominent location reflects its prominent emphasis in *Fact and Artifact.* New also are ten drafts of student Mary Ruffin's essay "Mama's Smoke," from start to finish.

Chapter 8, retitled "Writing About Processes," expands the emphasis of the first edition, on how-to writing, to include "Special Modes of Process Writing," including the relation of process and place, process and portrait, process by analogy, process as philosophy of life, and process as parody.

Chapter 9, "Writing About Science," now includes material on interviewing scientists and on writing natural history.

Chapter 10, "Writing About Controversy," has been reconceived to include discussions of critical thinking, assertive argument, and ways to conduct intensive, long-term research from primary and secondary sources.

Chapter 11, "Publishing," is now expanded to illustrate editing and proof-reading through the stunning example of Ning Yu's prizewinning "Red and Black," a tragic-comic tale of how he learned English in Communist China. In the first edition I insisted on discussing publishing, despite the objection, "How can you expect students to do *that?*" What was avant-garde then can be reasonably expected of advanced composition students today, particularly those with desktop publishing capability.

What's Familiar

In this edition of *Fact and Artifact* I've kept and updated what students and teachers liked in the first edition. This includes emphases on style, revision, publishing, and student writing. Chapters 4–10, as in Chapters 3–9 of the first edition, discuss the processes of writing essays, portraits, reviews, narratives, satires, parodies, reports, scientific papers, and other works. The processes described are derived from the ways real writers actually write. They are flexible and versatile; writers can adapt them to suit their individual emphases, angles of vision, desired aims. *Fact and Artifact* helps writers recognize the possibilities of various types of nonfiction by showing forms and variations on forms, as practiced by excellent professional and student writers. Each chapter concludes with a brief checklist for review and a list of nonfiction books that offer not only good reading but also good models. As with the first edition, *Fact and Artifact* is designed to be used in a variety of contexts—workshops, collaborative writing groups, larger classes, or by writers working alone.

By design, *Fact and Artifact* is understated, friendly and collegial. By the time advanced wrtiers have extracted from it what they want, they should have developed enough imagination and critical judgment to fill in the broad outlines of these chapters in their own ways. Advanced writers will continue to advance; this book is only the beginning.

The Community of Contributors

We're in this wondrous enterprise together, as writers and risk takers, teachers and students alike. The published authors whose work I've included are acknowledged in the citations; the student authors are acknowledged in the text, and forever in my heart. I am particularly grateful to the following students who critiqued draft verions of *Fact and Artifact*, first and second editions: Sarah Aguiar, Don Aker, Della Anderson, Bard Bloom, Laird Bloom, Audrey Guengerich, Kathy Heenan, Leslie Moore, Tom Moore, Susan Orton, Kelly Shea, Jeff Wood, and Ning Yu.

Among colleagues nationwide whose publications and conversation inform and reinforce my own work are Chris Anderson, Bill Bernhardt, Bob Connors, Lisa Ede, Peter Elbow, Rebecca Faery, Paula Feldman, Elizabeth Flynn, Diane Freedman, Rosemary Gates, Rick Gebhardt, Pat Hoy, Lee Jacobus, Andrea Lunsford, Richard Marius, Peter Miller, Don Murray, Linda Peterson, Tom Recchio, Mary Ann Rishel, Mike Rose, Mimi Schwartz, Louise Z. Smith, Mark Smith, Nancy Sommers, Kurt Spellmeyer, Priscilla Tate, Joe Trimmer, and Ed White. The reviewers of *Fact and Artifact* have made material contributions to this edition: Laura Brady, West Virginia University; Sandra Clark, Anderson University; Susanna Mason Defever, St. Clair County Community College; Mary Fuller, Miami University; Michael Keller, Virginia Commonwealth University; Gary Olson, University of South Florida; and Sally Barr Reagan, University of Missouri, St. Louis. Evelyn Ashton-Jones's prepublication review in *College Composition and Communication,* February 1993, was on time and on target.

The University of Connecticut, Storrs has provided support through the good offices of Sarah Aguiar, Nancy Andrix, Richard Fyffe, John Gatta, Kathy Heenan, Bill Rosen, and Ning Yu. Bill McLane and the staff of Harcourt, Brace made publication of the first edition a particularly happy experience from start to finish, a tradition continued with the second edition by Blair Press. Nancy Perry, legendary Publisher, is available for consultation round-the-clock, round the calendar. She reads, as she edits, with discernment, justice, and joy. LeeAnn Einert and Sue Brown of Blair Press have likewise paid meticulous and cheerful attention to the publication process from start to finish.

For thirty-five years Martin Bloom has enhanced the facts and artifacts of my life and work—with wit, good humor, unerring critical judgment, and homemade bread. No revision is necessary. None.

Lynn Z. Bloom
Storrs, Connecticut
July 1993

CONTENTS

CHAPTER 3
RE-VISION AND REVISION
51

CHAPTER 6
WRITING ABOUT PERFORMANCE
147

CHAPTER 7
WRITING HUMOR
175

CHAPTER 8
WRITING ABOUT PROCESSES
209

CHAPTER 9
WRITING ABOUT SCIENCE
241

CHAPTER 10
WRITING ABOUT CONTROVERSY
275

1

WRITING IN CONTEXT

If you wait for the perfect time to write, you'll never write. There is no time that isn't flawed somehow.

— Margaret Atwood

You never know what you will learn until you start writing. Then you discover truths you didn't know existed.

— Anita Brookner

I can't write without a reader. It's precisely like a kiss—you can't do it alone.

— John Cheever

Why Write? Assumptions About Writing and Writers

Most of us write, at times, because we have to—to fulfill an assignment, convey a message, record an event or other data, rebut an adversary, correct a misimpression. Maybe we also want to do this writing. Maybe not.

When we write because we want to, says George Orwell in "Why I Write," we do so from four main reasons:

1. **Sheer egoism.** We want to distinguish ourselves through words, to be known, admired, and respected during our lifetimes and perhaps, through our writings, for eternity.

2. **Aesthetic enthusiasm.** We write to share with readers what we perceive as beautiful in the world and beautiful in our language. We want to communicate our enjoyment of words and "their right arrangement"; to provide pleasure for our readers in the sounds of words, "in the firmness of good prose or the rhythm of a good story."

3. **Historical impulse.** We write to "see things as they are, to find out true facts and store them up for the use of posterity."

4. **Political purpose.** We write "to push the world in a certain direction, to alter other people's idea of the kind of society they should strive after."

Joan Didion in "Why I Write," inspired by Orwell, summarizes his message: "In many ways writing is the act of saying I, of imposing oneself upon other people, of saying, *listen to me, see it my way, change your mind* (italics added). Orwell and Didion assume that we write for an audience, whether in modes as utilitarian as letters, memos, and reports or as imaginative as fiction and poetry. We write for ourselves first, and then for everyone else, whether performing a solo, playing a duet, or jamming with a larger group. Writing, like music, drama, and dance, is a performing art and needs an audience to remain alive.

Fact and Artifact: Writing Nonfiction makes a fundamental assumption about writing. Whether it's a personal essay, an interview, a review, or a scientific report, nonfiction is expected to tell the truth. Nonfiction is assumed to be all writing that is not fiction, drama, or poetry. Although nonfiction writers usually tell the truth, as Emily Dickinson says, they often "tell it slant." Like telling a story, telling the truth or any portion of it implies selecting and interpreting facts or evidence; creating a structure and shaping it to fit the teller's purposes; emphasizing some parts while omitting others; using language, plain or fancy, to reinforce the mood or the point. To tell any truth is invariably to tell it slant; as human beings, we don't know any other way.

Fact and Artifact: Writing Nonfiction also makes the following assumptions about the writers reading this book.

1. You write for some if not all of the reasons described by Orwell: necessity; love of self, subject, beauty, language; desire to understand the truth as you have come to know it; and an intention to communicate your understanding to an audience.

2. You yourself are a reader. You love to immerse yourself in a sea of print—books, magazines, newspapers, the daily mail. Even if you only have time for a quick dip, you'd like to swim longer. Moreover, this book assumes that you are an active reader, not just a sponge passively soaking up other people's ideas. You bring to your reading a critical intelligence based not only on your previous reading, but also on your life experiences, values, and a host of other factors. So as you read, you make your own meaning. You never read the same book twice because each reading of a particular work informs every subsequent reading.

3. You're willing to expend some effort to transform your thinking and talking and reading into writing that other people will want to read.

4. You're an advanced writer. Whether or not you've taken a formal course in writing, you're usually comfortable with the conventions of standard English—grammar, punctuation, mechanics. You know how to write coherent sentences and paragraphs. You've probably already written a variety of nonfiction pieces—personal and business letters, explanations, arguments, term papers, lab reports, memos on or off the job, you name it. . . .

5. You're willing to experiment; to play with words and structures of sentences and paragraphs and whole essays, to put them together in new and different ways not once but many times. In other words, you're willing to take risks with your writing.

6. You have a favorite word processing program and know how much easier it is to draft, revise, and experiment with writing on a computer than by other means. There are exceptions, especially if you're making casual jottings away from your desk—lists, notebook or diary entries, short answers to profound questions ("Do you love me?" "Yes."), and perhaps, poetry.

7. You're hopeful that if you experiment, practice, write and rewrite, and rewrite again, you'll learn to say what you mean in ways that are distinctively yours, in ways that others will want to read. If you write from this belief, you are likely to accomplish what you intend.

What Influences Writing? Your Process, Your Milieus

Broadly conceived, your whole life is a writing process consisting of every moment of every activity experienced, awake or asleep, in actuality or imagination; every thought and feeling explored or repressed; every person and phenomenon known or observed; every bit of information learned and used or filed away; everything you've read. Indeed, the artist of any kind—painter, writer, dancer, musician, athlete, chef—if asked how long it takes to learn the craft or to perfect a particular aspect of it could truly answer, "All my life." From this perspective the writing process is continuous, without beginning, without end.

Composition specialists, using a more restricted definition, say that the writing process consists of whatever strategies, plans, and activities you use to proceed from the need or desire to write something to the completion of the finished product. Although this definition also implies that there are three broad stages—planning, drafting, and revising—for many writers the process is neither uniform nor linear. It could, for instance, be recursive, a series of loops, if you thought of an idea, wrote it down, and revised the sentence or paragraph in which it appeared before going on to the next idea. Or your writing process might be different not only for different types of writing (say, a report versus an interview), but also for different papers of the same type (for instance, an argument for and an argument against the same issue).

Yet all writing, like all reading, takes place in a variety of contexts. For instance, intellectual, social, and political developments of the past three decades have profoundly affected the ways we look at race, ethnicity, class, and gender. Scholars and teachers have dramatically changed their understanding of the ways people write and respond to writing—as writers, as readers, as participants in the general human conversation, or as members of more specialized "discourse communities," groups of people who share the same assumptions and values (see page 32). Let's examine some of the major influences, overt or subtle, on your writing process and on your writing itself.

The Cultural Context

As writers of nonfiction in Western culture, we're accustomed to linear thinking and writing. We've been taught that both should be logical and rational, that point A should lead to point B should lead to point C, and that we should offer reasons along with supporting evidence from authoritative sources. We've been taught to trust our heads over our hearts and to distrust intuition and emotion, our own and others'. We want facts, hard evidence. "Prove it," we say. We can't help but read nonfiction from this perspective that is so embedded in our culture, and we expect to write nonfiction this way as well. Like much of what we've been taught, this conventional wisdom is only partly true (see Belenky et al., Gilligan).

Moreover, we've been taught that the techniques writers use to communicate with readers of fiction, poetry, or drama are off limits to writers of nonfiction. Among these are the use of characters, the use of dialogue and dramatic scenes, the juxtaposition of seemingly unrelated phenomena, and the use of connotative language such as symbols, metaphors, and symbolic settings, events, and characters. But what we've been taught doesn't necessarily square with reality. Consider, for example, this brief scene from Maxine Hong Kingston's autobiography of her childhood, *The Woman Warrior,* created to characterize her mother, her Chinese-American culture, and the tensions between mother and children:

> "Eat! Eat!" my mother would shout at our heads bent over bowls, the blood pudding awobble in the middle of the table.
> She had one rule to keep us safe from toadstools and such: "If it tastes good, it's bad for you," she said. "If it tastes bad, it's good for you."
> We'd have to face four- and five-day-old leftovers until we ate it all. The squid eye would keep appearing at breakfast and dinner until eaten. Sometimes brown masses sat on every dish. I have seen revulsion on the faces of visitors who've caught us at meals.
> "Have you eaten yet?" the Chinese greet one another.
> "Yes, I have," they answer whether they have or not. "And you?"
> I would live on plastic.

Here Kingston uses characters (her mother in particular, herself and her siblings, and nameless Chinese who embody their culture by pretending to have eaten "whether they have or not"); dialogue ("Eat! Eat!"); a dinner scene featuring an item of food (the squid eye) that functions on both literal and symbolic levels; and a generic substance ("plastic") as a symbol of her intention to distance herself from her mother and the culture she represents. Such vigorous and vivid nonfiction writing is all around us—in newspapers, in magazines, in essays, and in some scholarly journals and books in a variety of disciplines—as a quick look at the examples throughout *Fact and Artifact* will reveal.

Our cultural frame of reference in America has changed dramatically in the past twenty years. Most writers that were studied in Western classrooms were reviewed in Western newspapers and magazines and published in mainstream Western presses. They were educated, white, middle- and upper-class men of European or American background. Although the grammatical "he" was presumed to include "she," the male-oriented grammar reflected the reality of the critical dialogue among editors, publishers, and professors—who were white men of similar backgrounds who believed it their sacred duty to reinforce "the best that has been known and thought in the world." Only recently, as a result of the civil, women's, and minority rights movements has the writing of women, people of color, and members of an underclass received much attention. The works of writers such as Frederick Douglass, Harriet Jacobs, Maya Angelou, Richard Rodriguez, and Maxine Hong Kingston both expand the familiar canon and contribute to a new one.

With the expansion of the canon has come a vigorous attention to the types of writing—often nonfiction—for which these writers have been known: diaries, journals, letters, autobiographies, and essays written in the first person (sometimes called "creative nonfiction" or "literary nonfiction") that make a political or social argument through literary devices such as those that Kingston uses. To understand nonfiction, critics and teachers are coming to realize, is to appreciate its infinite variety of forms and possibilities for expression. This Cinderella of genres has been rescued from the ashes and is on her way to the ball (see Anderson, Bloom, Elbow, Spellmeyer). One of the purposes of *Fact and Artifact* is to enable you to keep this engaging genre dancing.

Some people find the prospect of change, any change, threatening and unsettling. If the rules for writing—which were never very clear or fixed anyway—change, how can we know what to do or how to do it? *Fact and Artifact* is not a compendium of rigid rules, but rather an analysis of how real writers—students and professionals—actually write. Read it as a philosophy of ways to approach your reading, writing, and revising that is intended to make the writing process understandable, manageable, and enjoyable. Read it, too, as an encouragement to write, for yourself and an audience, in class and out, for personal pleasure and for publication.

Physical Context

Whatever you're writing, it helps to be comfortable. Maybe you're a person who can write anywhere—on menus in restaurants, on theater programs during intermission, in notebooks in bus or airline terminals, or with a computer on commuter trains. James Thurber says he wrote at parties, while Hemingway claims to have written at the front lines, under fire. You'll probably want a place that is both physically and psychologically satisfying, what Virginia Woolf called "a room of one's own," where you can think great thoughts, or trivial ones, where you can experiment and refine your ideas in your own time and on your own terms. The following suggestions can help you determine your most appropriate writing environment.

The Place. If you write at home or in an apartment or a dormitory, try to set aside a room or part of a room (preferably not in the middle of the kitchen or beside a blaring television set) exclusively for your writing. There you can assemble what you need to write: paper, favorite pens and pencils, computer or typewriter, dictionary, thesaurus, reference books and software, a stereo or compact disc player for background music. You can also add food, fine art, or favorite photographs—whatever you need to keep you happy as you work. There you can leave your materials out, ready for instant use. There you can maintain the environment you like best—neat or messy, sparse or cluttered, cozy or cool. You may have to train your family or friends to respect this space as "yours," especially if you've just created it. But it's worth the effort to stake out this territory. People who write uninterrupted in their own "space" accomplish about four times as much in a given time period than people who are continually interrupted by outside distractions.

The Time.   Even if you have to share your writing space, you can schedule your time to use it when others are out. If you haven't already discovered when you're most alert, when you have the best ideas and write the most easily, try writing at different times of the day or night to see whether there's a predictable pattern. Varying your writing time should also reveal whether you write best when you're hungry or full, tired or rested, slightly tense or more relaxed. With this self-knowledge, you can plan to write at the optimum time.

But what if your best writing time is in the morning, when your classes meet or you have to go to work? You can plan some writing time for weekend mornings or you can get up half an hour earlier and write during that extra time. (Save the revising and editing for another time; generating and writing ideas takes more effort than editing them.) If your best writing time is in the afternoon or evening, reserve segments of two or three afternoons or evenings for writing. Treat these periods as both appointments and commitments. If you keep such appointments with yourself, you'll come to expect them, as you would a jogging or swimming session, and if you diverge from your schedule, you'll regret not writing during those times. As Flannery O'Connor observed of her habit of sitting regularly at her writing desk each day from nine to noon, "Many times I just sit for three hours . . . but I know one thing, if an idea does come to me between 9 and 12, I am there ready for it."

Although it can be productive to reserve several hours at a stretch for writing, you can also learn to work in shorter segments of time—a half hour here and an hour there add up. Yet writing isn't an activity that shuts down when you're away from your desk. The ideas continue to percolate—while you're reading, driving, cooking, sleeping—as you recognize when a good night's sleep solves yesterday's problems. If you're writing against a deadline, you'll want to allow enough time to accommodate false starts, new thoughts, additional information gathering, and adequate rewriting, rather than sliding a skimpy first draft under the wire (see "A Writing Schedule"). You'll be treated seriously as a writer by your readers if they see that you treat your writing seriously.

A Writing Schedule.   Most writing, whether done in college, on the job, or for publication, is done against a deadline. So rather than aim for absolute and perhaps unattainable perfection, writers have to settle for doing the best they can in the time available. In explaining how she dovetails her writing schedule with her babysitter's schedule, Mary Gordon describes the way many professional writers work: "I try not to waste time. . . . Routine is a great grace. It's as if you don't have to invent your life. It's actually propelled by routine. You do what's expected of you."

One realistic way to meet a deadline is to decide how many hours you have available to work on a given piece, allowing some time for afterthoughts. Then, working backward from the due date, arrange your schedule. If a piece is due in a month and you have twenty-five hours to spend on it, you might spend the first two weeks, or twelve hours, in the planning stage doing the core background reading and other investigation, finding a focus, and perhaps constructing a working thesis. By the beginning of the third week, it's time to write a draft of the paper even if you haven't finished the preliminary reading; you can always leave gaps to fill in with focused information later. Allow six to eight hours to write the first draft. If you expect to revise extensively, allow the last week for revising, five to eight hours, saving alternative drafts in different computer files so you can use your best work in the final version. For minor revisions, three or four days should suffice. In any case, try to finish your paper at least two days before the due date so you can let the paper sit before looking at it again with an editor's acute eye for infelicities of spelling, grammar, and vocabulary. Then submit your paper and relax. Although writing well is the best reward, you also might give yourself something more tangible—dinner, an evening out, or even the purchase of something you've always wanted, but no trips to Tahiti for a ten-page paper!

Writers' Notebooks.   Keeping a writer's diary or notebook, whether you use a pencil, pen, typewriter, or word processor, can be a good way to get started or to keep going. If you write regularly, you'll have a lode of your own words to tap in to when you need them. Although you could record what you do every day, if your life is routine, your account might get monotonous. A provocative and potentially useful writer's notebook, what Maxine Kumin calls "an underground account of the state of my mind, the state of my letters," could contain any or all of the following types of writing, and more.

- *Reactions to your reading*: "I read that writer's block is 'reading old fat novels instead of new skinny ones.' My secret is out." (Richard Loftus, student)
- *Invented, read, or overheard provocative quotations; appealing figures of speech; dialogue, dialect, meanings and nuances of words*: "Gay politics is nothing if not rich in rhetoric. The differences between homosexual and gay? Homosexual is what the *New York Times* calls you; gay is what you earn the right to call yourself." (Richard Loftus)

- *Memorable details of clothing, objects, natural settings, processes*: "STANLEY—HE PLAYS HIS DRUMS, SOMETIMES, AND HE BANGS EM, HE BANGS EM AND HE BANGS EM, HE'LL ROLL EM, BACK AND FORTH AND BACK REAL QUICK WITH A BASE THUMP, AND HE'LL BANG EM AND HE'LL BANG EM AND HIS CYMBALS CRASH AND HISS WHILE HE BANGS EM AND THE BASE THUMPS." (Art Greenwood, student)
- *Personal aspirations, fears, joy, anger*: "I am afraid of getting older. I am afraid of getting married. Spare me . . . from the relentless cage of routine and rote. I want to be free." (Sylvia Plath)
- *Sketches of people who are either intrinsically interesting or engaged in novel or familiar activities*: "I want to get that look of intense concentration on judy's face as she plays cello bassoon duets with dan. . . . the two pairs of bare feet keeping a twitching time have a pathetic vulnerable look." (Maxine Kumin)
- *Analyses of friendships or family relationships*: "My parents are getting divorced. We did not put up a Christmas tree. This year [since dad was gone] mom said we could eat when we wanted. But we never did. I ate a beans n franks dinner by myself. My brother went to drink his gift certificate." (Tammy Weast, student)
- *Commentary on social, political, or cultural issues that are current or past, national or closer to home*: "In California thongs [sandals] are still Nipper Flippers or Jap Slaps. December seventh is the Ides of March. I'm asked how I can see, is my field of vision narrowed?" (Cheryl Watanabe, student)
- *Letting off steam*: "Today Dudley said he's 'tired of racial issues in class.' Well, if he's tired of them, how does he think I feel? For years I have been the only Black (or at most one of two or three) in class and I have had to deal with white negativism towards Blacks." (Rosalind Coles, student)
- *Humor such as jokes or anecdotes or humorous situations, characters, language, mannerisms, or settings*: "Stopped at Arkansas City April 24. This is a Hell of a place. One or two streets full of mud; 19 different stenches at the same time. A thriving place nevertheless." (Mark Twain)
- *Works in progress such as rough drafts, analyses of one's writing, ideas and plans for future writing*: "I think of the book not as narrative but as bulk, texture, color, weight, and size." (John Cheever)
- *Lists to identify the main points in any type of writing already mentioned*: itemizes many sights, sounds, scents in this "list of nothing in particular: 1. mockingbird . . . 6. two circling buzzards (not yet, boys) . . . 11. opossum skull . . . 28. earth 29. sky 30. wind (always)." (William Least Heat Moon)

You'll need to put enough explanatory information in the notebook to re-mind yourself three weeks—or three years—later what something meant when you wrote it down.

The Context of Audience

In a very important sense, every writer is a participant in the conversation among our cultural forebears that began long before every one of us was born and to which our writing will contribute (see Burke, Bruffee). Irrespective of your individual stamp as a writer, whatever you write—the literary form you adopt, the nature of your evidence, the frame of reference you use, the patterns of organization you select, your very language—inevitably reflect your relationship to the ongoing conversation. Whether or not a writer is consciously aware of this dynamic history, their influence is pervasive and inevitable.

"I write for myself and strangers," those others engaged in the ongoing conversation, said Gertrude Stein, making explicit the implicit principle that guides the writing of most skilled authors, professional or otherwise. In contrast, "I write for myself alone" or "I write for myself and intimates" appears to guide the composition of many less skilled writers unaware of or indifferent to what outside readers need to know to understand their writing. Writers who learn to accommodate an audience are on the road to professionalism.

Writers aware of an audience ask themselves nagging questions such as "Why would anyone want to read this?" "So what?" "Who cares?" They might even imagine the reader's dialogue in reply, such as, "I care a great deal, because. . . ." Although the questions may sound cynical, the answers are not. For once you move beyond writing grocery lists, notebook entries, or private poetry, you're writing to communicate something to someone else: an account of your latest exploits to a good friend, an essay exam to your teacher, a job application or a report to an employer, a resumé of your world views to an editor and someday, perhaps, to the Nobel Prize Committee. . . .

In theory, you can write on any subject for almost any audience: on death for very young children, on ballooning for people afraid of heights, on Communism for capitalists. Indeed, you can write more appropriately about your subject if you have a specific audience in mind. As the most immediate member of your audience, you'll have to satisfy yourself first. If you find your own writing tedious, boring, or incomprehensible, you'll want to either make what you're saying more interesting or switch to a more compelling subject; you can't expect your readers to tolerate what you yourself can't stand.

Once you're satisfied that the subject and your manner of handling it are compelling enough to keep you writing, you'll need to adapt your writing to your audience. Sometimes the audience is specific and predetermined—friends, teacher, boss, opponents of a controversial issue, readers of the student newspaper or another publication. Sometimes the audience consists of the "strangers" to whom Gertrude Stein referred—anyone who might want to read your writing—an imaginary readership of people like your friends or your instructor to keep in mind as you write.

For college writers there are no totally naive readers and few, if any, sponges of readers passively waiting to absorb every golden word. Every reader, like every writer, approaches any given subject and any given writing from a complex background of preferences, prejudices, and experiences, including a number of earlier encounters with writings on the same subject in the same literary mode. As an active thinker and writer, you can expect active readers to respond to your writing with critical intelligence determined not only by their level of knowledge about a subject but also by a variety of complicated and subtle influences. These influences can be described by a myriad of labels such as "feminist," "straight," "Afro-" or "Asian-American," "Southern," "environmentalist," "Democrat," "twentysomething," "middle class," "Roman Catholic," and a host of others. Although you can't anticipate all influences in everything you write, you'll need to address those most germane to your subject and presentation. We'll focus here on level of knowledge and on elements of a common heritage. Gender will be discussed in more detail in the next chapter.

General and specialized knowledge.   Knowledge is probably the most important single factor you'll need to consider in thinking of an audience. How much do my readers already know about the subject? What do they need to know in order to understand what I'm saying? What background information should I supply? What concepts or other terms must I define? What books have we all read, and what other sources of knowledge do we share? What perspectives and biases have affected these sources? Conversely, what do I know that my readers don't?

You expect your readers to have common sense and to share a fund of common knowledge. Do you also expect your readers to know as much as a fourth grader, an eighth grader, a high school graduate, or a college student? Do your readers have a hobbyist's interests or a professional education in a specialized field on which you're writing? Do you expect your readers to know more about the subject than you do (as would a sociology teacher reading your term paper), or less, or the same amount? Your expectations will determine whether you express your thoughts in a simple or complicated manner, what language to use, which terms to define, and how much background information and other explanations to include. However, even if you're explaining something elementary, you can avoid a condescending tone if you treat your readers as the collaborators they are in making the meaning of the text (see Bruffee, Lunsford and Ede) rather than as ignoramuses in need of a lecture.

For instance, Sue Hubbell, Ozark beekeeper and naturalist, wants her readers to share her appreciation of snakes, even poisonous ones. She can assume that many readers, even of her book *A Country Year,* fear snakes and that if they encountered a copperhead in the wild they would either flee or try to kill the snake. To disarm the suspicious, calm the fearful, and save the snakes, Hubbell opens her friendly commentary on copperheads with a humanizing explanation of their behavior. Once, she says, when she was smoking out bees,

> a copperhead came wriggling out from under the hive. He had been frightened from his protected spot by the smoke and the commotion I was making, and when he found himself in the open, he panicked and slithered for the nearest hole he could find which was the entrance to the next beehive. I don't know what went on inside, but he came out immediately, wearing a surprised look on his face. I hadn't known that a snake could look surprised, but this one did. Then, after pausing to study the matter more carefully, he glided off to the safety of the woods.

The single snake represents all snakes, peaceful and nonaggressive: "The surprising thing about copperheads are their mild manners, timidity and fearfulness. . . . Every time I come upon copperheads they simply try to get away from me and never offer to strike." Therefore, implies Hubbell without preaching, don't panic. Don't run away. And don't try to kill the snake.

Sometimes you can let the purpose of your writing determine the extent to which you spell out the fundamentals and what language you use. If you're writing on a matter of life and death, be absolutely clear, even at the risk of telling your readers what they already know. (See the analysis of the Red Cross first-aid manual's advice on heat stroke, pages 223–226.) Stuart Chase tells of the plumber who wrote the National Bureau of Standards

> that he had found hydrochloric acid fine for cleaning drains, and was it harmless? Washington replied: "The efficacy of hydrochloric acid is indisputable, but the chlorine residue is incompatible with metallic permanence."
>
> The plumber wrote back that he was mighty glad the Bureau agreed with him. The Bureau replied with a note of alarm: "We cannot assume responsibility for the production of toxic and noxious residues with hydrochloric acid, and suggest that you use an alternate procedure." The plumber was happy to learn that the Bureau still agreed with him.
>
> Whereupon Washington exploded: "Don't use hydrochloric acid; it eats hell out of the pipes!"

If, on the other hand, the matter isn't crucial, you might prefer to aim slightly above the average understanding of your readers, to make them stretch to pick the tantalizing peach of a phrase that hangs just overhead. Think of all the words in the Bible, *Gulliver's Travels,* or Shakespeare that readers eventually learn through context or sheer repetition; an explanation would be intrusive or condescending. You'll also want to consider, "What will my writing gain—or lose—if I ignore my audience entirely and write exclusively for myself?" If you're writing something highly creative, you may with good reason decide to disregard popular taste altogether, as did Emily Dickinson, James Joyce, and other writers who were ahead of their times. You may dramatically restrict the number of prospective readers, if you don't scare them off altogether. It's your choice, and exclusiveness—whether or not you achieve immortality—may be the price of experimentation.

If you really want to know whether your audience will understand what you're saying, let a typical member of that audience, perhaps a friend or colleague, read your manuscript. To encourage a candid response, you can ask your reader in advance to consider particular points about which you're doubtful or that gave you trouble as you wrote.

Common heritage.   If you're an American writing for other Americans, you can assume that you share some aspects of a common cultural heritage. You won't need to explain references to Batman or the Alamo. You can mention Washington as long as it's clear that you're talking about George, Booker T., Dinah, the District of Columbia, or the state. The more specific or limited the readers, the more limited or explanatory your writing may have to be. Or you may choose to direct your writing to a smaller cultural subgroup such as fellow students at your school (or only seniors or chemistry majors), employees at your company (or only secretaries or middle managers), or members of your church or neighborhood.

The smaller and more specialized the group, the more acceptable it is to generalize. If you're a fairly typical member of the group for which you're writing, you can probably assume that what you know and take for granted your audience will also understand. For instance, if you're an experienced cook writing for other knowledgeable cooks, you can presume that your readers have definite opinions on culinary matters such as truffles (both the fungus and the chocolate versions), microwave ovens, and Cajun cooking. In contrast, readers on a fast food diet probably would be innocent of or indifferent to such matters. Having common interests or common knowledge, however, does not necessarily mean that you have the same tastes as your readers, in food or anything else; much of what you write will be an argument, direct or implied, for your values.

Whatever writers mean when they conceive of "a general audience," they should not assume that all readers, even Americans, share a common set of values or experiences. For example, "The American Dream," which says that hard work will lead to success, is a symbol of hope for many immigrants, who indeed "make it" and enter the cultural and economic mainstream within two generations. But for the unemployed, whether chronic or newly laid off, that dream is a nightmare. White majority writers cannot assume that what is good for them is also good for blacks, Hispanics, Asians, or Native Americans; nor can men assume that women will always share their views or their experiences. Martin Luther King, Jr., wrote "Letter from Birmingham Jail" in 1963 while imprisoned for "parading without a permit" in a nonviolent civil right demonstration. In his letter he took issue with the white clergy who had written him urging that integration should proceed with deliberate slowness.

> For years now I have heard the word "Wait!" It rings in the ear of every Negro with piercing familiarity. This "Wait" has almost always meant "Never." We must come to see, with one of our distinguished jurists, that "justice too long delayed is justice denied." We have waited for more than 340 years for our constitutional and Godgiven rights.

Whites, King implies, have not had to wait for their "constitutional and Godgiven rights." Prolonging the wait for integration may benefit whites, but whites have not had the same experiences as blacks. All blacks under segregation have seen "vicious mobs lynch your mothers and fathers at will and drown your sisters and brothers at whim"; blacks have been "humiliated day in and day out by nagging signs reading 'white' and 'colored'"; and blacks have had their names erased, "your first name becomes 'nigger,' your middle name becomes 'boy' (however old you are) and your last name becomes 'John.'" If whites had had these experiences they would understand "why we find it difficult to wait."

The familiar advice to "write from what you know or can find out" and to "write what you believe" still prevails. Although it would be comfortable to assume that your readers share your understanding of the subject as well as your point of view, rarely will you be writing for clones of yourself, as King's powerful letter shows. It is more realistic to assume that among your audience, however sympathetic or antagonistic, there will be some whose religious, political, regional, racial, ethnic, class, sexual, or age perspective and values will be different from yours. To understand divergent views, try to imagine your subject as some disparate readers might see it. King asks his white readers to understand the perspective of a persecuted minority, knowing that his letter will be read not only by the eight clergy to whom he is replying, but also by the worldwide audience his civil rights activities commanded.

With each turn of the kaleidoscope, each aspect of the issue assumes a different perspective. Maybe you can't accommodate all possibilities and still be true to your vision of the subject. Maybe you won't want to. But at least, as you take your stand, because you've considered the alternatives you'll know why you've arrived at the views you now hold, and so will your readers.

The Collaborative Context

Although the image of the solitary writer scribbling in the silence of an isolated garret has a romantic appeal, it is as remote from contemporary reality as the quill is from the computer. Collaborative writing as a conscious, collective act is the norm for authors in the sciences and medicine, where research is done by teams rather than by individuals, and in many business settings, where projects almost always reflect team efforts. Even in humanistic fields, such as history or literary criticism, where collaboration is less common, many writers, students and professionals alike, share work in progress with their peers. Thus even a single author's completed work is likely to reflect the influence of a variety of commentators, in substance and in style.

Whatever the field, every collaboration is different, depending on the task at hand, the aim of the collaboration, the people involved, and the context. Although every team consequently works out its own style of collaboration and division of labor, there are three common patterns:

1. Every coauthor is concerned with every aspect of the work and makes an equal contribution to it.

2. Each coauthor is responsible for researching and writing a major section of the work or for making an equivalent contribution (for instance, a mathematician might generate or review all the calculations in a marine biology paper).

3. One author does most of the work under the nominal direction of another, as in a student-mentor relationship. The mentor, who usually directs the project, may be the senior researcher who has secured the funding to hire the research team or the boss in charge of the assistants who perform the actual work. In either case, the unequal distribution of work reflects the importance of the expert's authoritative vision and understanding of the field.

The main purpose of collaborative writing is to enable the coauthors to combine their efforts and expertise to do work they couldn't do easily—if at all—as individuals. Although collaboration may (or may not) mean half the work with twice the fun, the process by its nature involves the collaborators in discussion and debate at many stages.

- Generating good ideas that are exciting or fruitful to investigate.
- Asking critical questions about these ideas.
- Developing an appropriate methodology to pursue the investigation.
- Investigating, testing, and revising the ideas and the methodology.
- Recording and interpreting the results in light of the appropriate intellectual and disciplinary contexts.
- Writing and revising the text.
- Submitting the work to the teacher, the boss, or a publisher.

No matter who actually does what, the completed work really has only one author—the *team* who did the work. An ideal collaboration might work the way Belenky, Clinchy, Goldberger, and Tarule describe their work in *Women's Ways of Knowing*:

> In collaborating on writing this book we searched for a single voice—a way of submerging our individual perspectives for the sake of the collective "we." Not that we denied our individual convictions or squelched our objections to one another's points of view—we argued, tried to persuade, even cried at times when we reached an impasse of understanding—but we learned to listen to each other, build on each other's insights, and eventually to arrive at a way of communicating as a collective what we believe [sic]. Hence this book is not separated into parts that we wish to attribute to one or the other of us, even though each of us took the primary responsibility for different parts. There may be stylistic differences from one section to the next, but the book as a whole is the product of our joint efforts and interchange of ideas.

The authors' statement of how they worked reflects several principles of effective collaboration.

- The process should be cooperative, not competitive. ("Keep your own ego out of it," advises one confident collaborator, the author's son, Bard Bloom, a computer scientist who collaborated with his mother on this section.)
- Collaborators need to maintain the integrity of their own beliefs, understanding, and values.
- Collaborators need to compromise, but only after hearing and respecting each others' viewpoints. They need to develop a style of negotiation suitable to their personalities and to accomplishing the task at hand.
- Collaborators can act as immediate critics, commentators, and editors, intermittently or at every step, for each coauthor is also an audience. Although criticism given early in the writing process can be disconcerting, it can also anticipate problems and resolve difficulties before they get big and bothersome.

Having made an initial commitment, the members of a team of collaborators are roped together like mountaineers for the tough climb. An individual striking out alone endangers the success of the entire enterprise as well as that of her own independent path.

Collaboration, drawing on the strengths of the individual participants, should make the final work better than any single person could have produced. But what if it doesn't? Like marriages, not all collaborations are made in heaven. Any relationship that involves division of labor, subordination of individual ego, compromise, and acting for the common good can break down if the members don't play by the same rules.

Collaborators can get bogged down in too much talk and too little work, an unequal and galling division of labor, or unresolvable conflicts over ideas. When a collaboration generates more work, anxiety, or ill will than it saves, it's time to salvage what you can, change partners, or simply let the relationship stop.

Thus, whether you're writing as an individual or as a member of a team, whenever *Fact and Artifact* refers to *you,* feel free to decide whether that second person is singular or plural.

Checklist for Writing in Context

1. Under what conditions and in what place do I do my best writing? What can I do to create or maintain these?

2. Do I have a single, workable writing process or several, which I can adapt to various kinds of writing?

3. Are there particular enhancements or blocks to my writing process? In what ways can I overcome the problems to make my writing process more effective?

4. If I'm not keeping a writer's notebook or diary, should I try it?

5. Why am I writing the piece I'm working on right now? Will my customary writing process work well with this piece or should I try another?

6. How much time, effort, revision is this piece worth?

7. For what audience do I intend this particular writing? How must I accommodate their knowledge of the subject? their backgrounds and beliefs?

8. What do I need to learn in order to address this particular audience?

9. How would my writing differ if I were to write this essentially for myself, rather than for an audience?

10. Should I collaborate on this (or any other) paper? If so, with whom? What would be the advantages of such a collaboration? the disadvantages?

Selected Reference List of Writers on Writing

Anderson, Chris. "Hearsay Evidence and Second Class Citizenship." *College English* 50.3 (1988): 300–08.

Berg, Stephen, ed. *In Praise of What Persists.* New York: Harper, 1983.

Bloom, Lynn Z. "Why Don't We Write What We Teach? And Publish It?" *Journal of Advanced Composition* 10.1 (1990): 102–12.

Cheever, John. *The Journals of John Cheever.* New York: Knopf, 1991.

Elbow, Peter. "Reflections on Academic Discourse: How It Relates to Freshmen and Colleagues." *College English* 53.2 (1991): 135–55.

———. *Writing Without Teachers*. New York: Oxford, 1970.

Goldberg, Natalie. *Writing Down the Bones: Freeing the Writer Within*. Boston: Shambhala, 1986.

Murray, Donald M. *Shoptalk: Learning to Write with Writers*. Portsmouth, N.H.: Boynton/Cook-Heinemann, 1990.

———. *A Writer Teaches Writing*. 2nd ed. Boston: Houghton, 1985.

Spellmeyer, Kurt. *The Common Ground: Dialogue, Understanding, and the Teaching of Composition*. Prentice Hall, 1993.

Sternburg, Janet, ed. *The Writer on Her Work*. 2 vols. New York: Norton, 1980–91.

Tate, Claudia, ed. *Black Women Writers at Work*. New York: Continuum, 1983.

Woolf, Virginia. *A Writer's Diary*. Ed. Leonard Woolf. New York: Harcourt, 1954.

Writers at Work: The Paris Review Interviews. Ed. Malcolm Cowley, George Plimpton, and others. The *Paris Review* Interviews. Series 1–8. New York: Viking, 1958–1988.

Works Cited

Belenky, Mary Field, Blythe McVicker Clinchy, Nancy Rule Goldberger, and Jill Mattuck Tarule. *Women's Ways of Knowing: The Development of Self, Voice, and Mind*. New York: Basic, 1986.

Bruffee, Kenneth. "Collaborative Learning and the 'Conversation of Mankind'." *College English* 46 (1984): 635–52.

Burke, Kenneth. *The Philosophy of Literary Form*. Berkeley: U of California P, 1974.

Chase, Stewart, in collaboration with Marian Tyler Chase. "Gobbledygook." *The Power of Words*. New York: Harcourt, 1954. 253–59.

Didion, Joan. "Why I Write." *New York Times Book Review* 5 Dec. 1976: 4.

Gilligan, Carol. *In a Different Voice: Psychological Theory and Women's Development*. Cambridge: Harvard UP, 1982.

Hubbell, Sue. *A Country Year: Living the Questions*. 1986. New York: Harper, 1987.

King, Martin Luther, Jr. "Letter from Birmingham Jail." 1963. Rpt. in *The Essay Connection*. 3rd ed. Ed. Lynn Z. Bloom. Boston: Heath, 1991.

Kingston, Maxine Hong. *The Woman Warrior: Memoirs of a Girlhood Among Ghosts*. 1976. New York: Vintage, 1989.

Lunsford, Andrea, and Lisa Ede. *Singular Texts/Plural Authors: Perspectives on Collaborative Writing*. Carbondale, IL: Southern Illinois UP, 1990.

Orwell, George, "Why I Write." *An Age Like This*. Ed. Sonia Orwell and Ian Angus. Vol. 1 of *Collected Essays, Journalism, and Letters*. New York: Harcourt, 1968. 1–10.

2

STYLE

I never wrote a word that I didn't hear as I read.

— EUDORA WELTY

Style is organic to the person doing the writing, as much a part of him as his hair, or, if he is bald, his lack of it. Trying to add style is like adding a toupee.
— WILLIAM ZINSSER

The language must be careful and must appear effortless. It must not sweat. It must suggest and be provocative at the same time. It is the thing that black people love so much—the saying of words, holding them on the tongue, experimenting with them, playing with them.
— TONI MORRISON

Style and the Writer

"Style takes its final shape more from attitudes of mind than from principles of composition," observe William Strunk and E. B. White in their classic, *The Elements of Style*. "Style *is* the writer" implies that the kind of a person you are determines your style because there is no meaningful style independent of an author. Most writings, as reflections of their authors, have personalities that range from flippant and frivolous to deliberate and dignified. Even though your writing will vary in mood, mode, and subject, your style will be recognizably yours, as distinctive as your signature, as individual as your fingerprint.

As your style evolves and becomes as organic to your writing as your hand, you will want to consider how the presentation of your authorial self (persona) is established. There are a variety of ways in which your characteristic style can be expressed, including vocabulary and sentence structures that help to establish your voice, tone, and authority, as the following excerpts from student essays reveal.

In "Free Spirit, Narrow Circuit," Wanda Crawford defends hitchhiking in spite of having been raped by a man who picked her up near Jackson, Mississippi. Here's the end of the first section of her essay:

> After the man [who raped me] drives away, all I can do is shake and wonder if he will come back. I do not even glance at his license plate. Everything around me has turned blindingly bright. I feel caught in the glare of a searchlight, visible and accessible to all the evil that may come hurtling down the highway. My clothes—sensible jeans and shirt—are an illusion. I am naked and more assuredly alone than I have ever been. When I hear a car coming, I think of running, but then I see that it is a sheriff's patrol car and I break into tears and begin waving my arms to flag it down.
>
> The deputy who stops for me is supposed to be cavalry that has come over the hill, but he is not. He does not believe my story, at first, but after a few minutes of my hysteria he is convinced that I am in trouble of some kind. Despite the crackle and sudden blurts of voices from his radio, he makes no move to call in a report. When I ask him to take me to the hospital, he gets a canny look and asks, "How do I know you won't go blamin' all this on me?" Looking at my breasts he sneers, "I think you was just tryin out some of the local stuff and got exactly what you had comin to you."

The following excerpt is from the beginning of Bob Myhal's "Automatic Suspension," an account of his automobile accident on a snowy night in Boston:

> Growing up in northern New England, I quickly learned to appreciate the benefits of dressing in layers, to take some of the bite out of those mongrel winter days. The real advantage to layering doesn't have to do with keeping things out—in this case the bitter cold—but rather with preserving what is already

within, the precious warmth. Despite the advantages, this particular winter fashion statement causes considerable difficulty for the young man—he could be a nurse or intern, maybe even a doctor, no way to tell—with nine o'clock shadow and heavy knockwurst breath whose job it is to cut through the layers of clothing, the inner ones soaked with half-frozen blood and cemented to my skin, and expose me. . . .

I watch him cutting through the layers: wool sweater, oxford shirt, white turtleneck, Hanes T-shirt, sleeveless T-shirt. His large hands are steady and slow; his eyes are calm like summer lakes. I can hear the sharpness of the scissors as he cuts up the middle of my body: first the sweater, then another layer or two, finally the thin layers near the skin. He starts each cut at the waist by pulling downward on my clothing to create the necessary tension. The going is smooth for the first few inches, but as he cuts upwards towards the chest, the neck, he slows down, as if the instrument itself is conscious of the thick red boundary it now has to traverse. . . .

The following is an excerpt from Julia Dixon's introduction to "How to Survive Your Parents' Divorce."

My parents were so defensive with each other that once when my mother was driving our family down the parkway they got into an argument over changing lanes. My father told my mother, "You should move over now." She retorted, "I drive this way every day from work. I *know* when to change lanes." It escalated into shouts of, "I'll never drive in that lane again!" and "I'll never offer you any more advice!" Trapped with them as I was for the summer, I knew that [my] going back to college wouldn't release them from their emotional headlock and it wouldn't release me, either.

"Goin' Up Cripple Creek: Paul Jenkins at War," W. Dudley Bass's portrait of an Appalachian "mountain boy with a reputation as a hot-tempered drunkard and a damn good worker,"

> Goin' up Cripple Creek,
> Goin' mighty fast;
> Goin' up Cripple Creek,
> Gonna bust my ass!

Paul Jenkins sang that song, with special loudness when he was driving. He never could remember the words to the original bluegrass version; he just kept making them up. Humorous obscene little ditties which poked fun at himself. Anything would do so long as it rhymed. Well, sort of rhymed.

> Goin' up Cripple Creek,
> Goin' fast as shit;
> Goin' up Cripple Creek,
> I ain't nuthin' but a hick!

Paul sang through his gums. He had no front teeth. Had 'em all knocked out in a jailhouse fight. A fellow inmate who was sober and stronger than he was smashed him in the face with a lead pipe. It crushed his nose and beat his teeth out. When Paul did sing, it was a happy drunken monotone ragged with an edge of darkness.

In "Contrary Emotions," Patricia Vincent reflects on her birthday. The beginning includes these two paragraphs:

> "Unseasonably beautiful weather just about everywhere today," the weatherman reported during his pre-dawn forecast, casually and a little too jovially she suspected (in view of his emphasis on the "just about"), a suspicion the truth of which was soon to become reality. "With the exception of the Northeast section of the country," he continued, "where early morning fog (she thought about how she disliked driving in fog) will give way to some blue skies and glimpses of sunshine here and there, but clouds rolling in from the west will bring showers to the region by mid-day."
>
> What has happened, what is it that has gone wrong? she wondered . . . thinking today, October 11th, is my birthday, as she braked for a light. How can it possibly rain? Could it be that it was only in her imagination that the day, October 11th (the peak time for the blazing fall foliage), had always, in her childhood and even beyond (perhaps until only recently), dawned brightly (what golden sunshine, reminiscent of the warmth of summer, yet even more brilliant than that of the most beautiful summer day). . . .

Each of these writings uses some aspect of driving: as the vehicle for, and escape from, rape; as the cause of an accident; as the context for an impending divorce; as an incidental feature in the portrait of a drunk; and as the setting which introduces reflections on a birthday. Yet the styles and personae of the writers are as varied as their uses of this theme; there is no way we would confuse Crawford with Dixon or Vincent, Myhal with Bass. So distinctive are these writers, even in these short excerpts, that it's easy to imagine we'd recognize their other writings. Let's see why this is so and why we trust what they say and want to read more of their work, including the rest of these essays.

Yourself as a Writer

All writing has some sort of style, even if that style is dull and boring. You'll be happier as a writer if you cultivate a style that comes naturally to you rather than writing anything that comes to mind, without revising or editing it in hope that elegant expression will emerge spontaneously. Good writing arises out of the confidence that you have something to say and that you can control how you say it. In any given piece, you will want to write in a way that is appropriate to the material and your writing style, as Crawford, Myhal, Dixon, Bass, and Vincent have written.

Creating Your Authorial Persona

But who are these people as writers? As a writer, who are you? Very likely, a person who on paper plays a number of complex roles, just as you do in real life, though you may be more selective of your roles as writer. As a writer, you'll present yourself in one or, more likely, a cluster of roles, sometimes called *authorial personae*. In each of the five previous excerpts, for instance, the writer is a narrator and consequently an interpreter or commentator on the experience on which the essay focuses. In Crawford's, Myhal's, and Vincent's essays, the narrator is a major participant, while in Dixon's and Bass's essays, the narrator is more peripheral to the central characters or the action. The writers play a number of additional roles, which are apparent in the excerpts: advocate (Crawford goes on to argue that women should have freedom of the open road, no matter what the consequences); traveler (Crawford); victim (Myhal has no choice, Crawford resists the label); conscious experimenter with style (Bass, Vincent); humorist (Bass's readers laugh at Paul's "humorous obscene little ditties," no matter how they ultimately judge Paul). That the writers are also students, rather than researchers or critics (other common authorial roles) is clear from their commentary elsewhere in their writing. Crawford says, for example,

> All my fear and outrage came to a head that summer, when not only was I faced with moving to a brand-new city to study, but I actually made friends with a defense lawyer . . . who might have characterized me "Wanda the Hitch-Hooker," as the defense has characterized many other rape victims.

For most purposes, you'll want to present yourself as a person who knows and cares sufficiently about your subject, as these writers do, to write on it honestly and well, whether somberly or more light heartedly. Indeed, you can write successfully about a subject in which you've failed miserably or otherwise come to grief, as in the case of Wanda's rape and Bob's automobile accident. You'll decide, too, how personal or impersonal you want your relationship with your readers to be—whether you want to meet them as an intimate friend, a professional colleague, or an impersonal authority.

Though your approach to the subject may vary considerably from one mode and topic to another, the fundamental qualities of your mind and personality will be apparent to your readers. This is true even though your authorial persona will be a created version of yourself with certain features emphasized or diminished to better illustrate your subject. If your readers know you personally, they should be able to recognize your writing. If they know you only as a writer, they should soon be able to identify your style, as a writer and as a person, by your characteristic way of looking at life and at your subject as expressed in your choice and arrangement of words. However, nothing is static. As you change over time, so will your writing style—perhaps becoming wiser and more self-assured, less cynical and more tolerant, or the reverse.

Voice.   A voice will emerge in your writing whether you intend it to or not, simply through your attitude toward the subject and your choice of vocabulary, sentence structure, arrangement and selection of details. In short, everything that you say, every way that you say it, reveals your mind and personality. So you might as well control the stylistic elements of your writing in order to determine the voice in which your writing speaks.

Voice has two senses. The first, the grammatical sense, is less significant for our purposes, meaning the pronouns you as a writer use in acknowledging yourself and your readers. In the *personal voice,* you are likely to refer to yourself as *I* and your readers as *you.* This is the case whether or not you're writing on personal subjects, and intend to imply an intimacy with your readers, or you're simply using these pronouns to signal informality. However, just because a writing sounds personal doesn't necessarily mean that it is either intimate or revealing. The *impersonal voice* is more likely to use *one* or *we;* it sounds more formal. "One must do as one's conscience dictates" establishes a greater distance between writer and reader than "Let your conscience be your guide," though the message is the same. It's awkward to use *one* throughout a long piece of writing.

If you use the *third person—he, she,* and *they*—you establish distance between yourself and your subject, your subject and your readers. Wanda Crawford first wrote "Free Spirit, Narrow Circuit," in the third person:

> The deputy who stops for her is supposed to be the cavalry that has come over the hill, but after a few minutes of her hysteria, which he spends in staring at the treeline and pulling at his earlobes, he is convinced that she is in trouble of some kind. Despite the crackle and sudden blurts of voices from his radio, he makes no move to call in a report. When she asks him to take her to the hospital, he gets a canny look on his face and tells her that he doesn't trust her not to blame whatever happened on him, which jolts her out of her tears in astonishment. He sneers at her breasts and says he believes she has gotten exactly what she had coming to her.

Crawford's revision (20) changes third person to first and indirect discourse to dialogue. Both changes give her experience greater immediacy and horror than her original account has. They also make it easier for readers to identify with the author.

The second sense of *voice* is defined by William Safire, editorial writer and author of the *New York Times* column "On Language," as "the distinctive mode of expression, the expected quirks and trademark tone, the characteristic attitude of writer toward reader and subject. . . . Hemingway had a voice: spare, selective, easily parodied because readily identifiable." Although such a definition is hard to pin down, *voice* refers to the essential spirit of the author, as manifested in the writing. As we have seen in the students' writing quoted earlier, voice emerges, clear and true, when the ways of seeing are fresh and individual, not suppressed by clichés or subdued by formulaic thinking or rigid writing patterns.

Voiceless prose is often characteristic of bureaucratic, legal, and other types of "official" writing, parodied here in Susan Russ's "A Bureaucrat's Guide to Chocolate Chip Cookies":

Total Lead Time: 35 minutes.
Inputs:
    1 cup packed brown sugar
    1/2 cup granulated sugar
    1/2 cup shortening. . . .
Guidance:
    After procurement actions, decontainerize inputs. Perform measurement tasks on a case-by-case basis. In a mixing type bowl, impact heavily on brown sugar, granulated sugar, softened butter and shortening. Coordinate the interface of eggs and vanilla, avoiding an overrun scenario to the best of your skills and abilities.
    At this point in time, leverage flour, baking soda and salt into a bowl and aggregate. Equalize with prior mixture and develop intense and continuous liaison among inputs until well-coordinated. Associate key chocolate and nut subsystems and execute stirring operations. . . .
    Output: Six dozen official government chocolate-chip cookie units.

Such jargon-laden writing is deadly to decipher, difficult to follow, and disastrous to imitate.

Tone.   How lightly or seriously you want to treat your subject will influence your tone. Depending on your purpose, you could attack the social problem of drunken driving with somber analysis: "Half of all automobile accidents—including fatalities—are alcohol related." You could approach the subject with a reformer's indignation: "Auto accident fatalities automatically revoke the victim's life—with no postponement, no reprieve. Can we do less with the licenses of drunken drivers?" You could treat the subject with sardonic irony: "The last words he remembered before falling asleep at the wheel were, 'Sure, I'll have just one more, for the road. It'll pep me up.'" Or you could use understatement, also ironic: "Auto accidents? No problem—especially if you're dead."

The tone of your writing, like the tone of your spoken voice, conveys mood or emotional temper, which can vary, as your moods do, within a single writing or from one work to another. A given piece of writing might have one dominant tone—objective, pleading, argumentative, or playful, for instance—or a combination of compatible tones, such as serious and sad, or optimistic and cheerful. Bob Myhal describes the accident that could have been fatal:

> There's no pain, just a strange sensation . . . [of] sitting in one of those rocking infant swings, the kind where timed clicks mark the movement back and forth, when the motion runs out . . . the baby hangs there still, suspended twelve inches from the ground, tranquil and out of contact in space.
>
> As the aide slowly peels back the layers of my swaddling clothes, strangely he still seems in no rush, I realize that I can't move. But everyone else in that small room, two or three nurses and an equal number of doctors, compensates for my lack of activity by remaining in perpetual motion.

Myhal's calm objectivity re-creates the state of shock he must have been in at the time rather than suggesting a genuine absence of fear or self-pity. His stylistic control, like Crawford's, mirrors the self-control our culture expects of accident and rape victims, and of our writers, as well.

Although our culture generally prefers understatement rather than gushing emotion, the exuberant copiousness of writers such as William Faulkner, Flannery O'Connor, and Dudley Bass are welcome, too. When Bass writes about his anger at his father for hiring "the weirdest collection of social misfits," he carefully controls the tone in which he demonstrates that "I was angry":

> I told my father it was a poor way to run a business and Daddy yelled back something about helping people out. I said to Hell with that and stormed down to Paul's house to get him out of bed and up to work.
>
> After I pounded on the door, I heard a lot of shuffling and bumbling into furniture. Paul staggered out and plopped down on his little plank porch and swung his head back and forth between his knees. He screwed his ugly eyes up at me and grinned his toothless grin.
>
> "I can't milk no cows this morning," he said. "I'm sick."
>
> "Sick!" I bellowed, exasperated. All these trifling people were constantly sick, sick, sick.

Sometimes the tone lies in the mood of the situation you're depicting, the atmosphere in which events occur and characters act, as it does here. As do all the writers quoted in this chapter, you can use the atmosphere of the situation to reinforce the tone of your attitude toward what's going on. Bass creates the tone of a man ready to explode with anger through strong verbs, (*stormed, pounded, shuffling and bumbling, staggered out, plopped down, screwed, bellowed*); graphic adjectives (*ugly eyes, toothless grin, trifling people*); and vivid dialogue or indirect discourse ("I said to Hell with that"; "Sick!" I bellowed, exasperated).

Gender.   Do women and men write differently from one another? Do they read differently? If so, is each of us—through the accident of biology or the way our culture has treated our gender—locked into certain features of style that are beyond our control? There is considerable debate about this (see works by Flynn and Schweickhart, Spender, Tannen), but the argument, to date, is inconclusive.

Establishing Firsthand Authority

As a writer, you are what you know, and that shows in your work. If you're writing for an audience that knows you, either personally (such as classmates or coworkers) or by reputation (such as from your work or other writings), they've probably already determined whether or not you have sufficient authority to discuss the topic. If they choose to read your writing, presumably they believe you'll say something worth paying attention to—even if they agree to disagree.

Even though you want to validate your authority, for most audiences a recitation of your credentials would be distracting, if not boring. You can establish your authority in a variety of ways without actually inserting your press notices. We trust the authority of Myhal, Crawford, Vincent, Bass, and Dixon to explain and interpret their subjects. They were there and everything they say lets us know that they understand the meaning of the experiences they recount and the characters they present.

Show some originality.   The quickest way to establish authority is to be original. It's hard to be original when you've just begun exploring a field unless you've discovered some new material. Nevertheless, you can offer a novel interpretation of existing material or take issue with the prevailing views on a subject. You can always express your own opinion: "But is the Emperor really wearing new clothes—or clothes at all?" One teacher tells his students that when they're stuck for something to say, they "should use the following as a 'machine' for producing a paper: 'While most readers of _____ have said _____ , a close and careful reading shows that _____ '" (Bartholomae).

However simple or complicated your views are, you'll need to speak with some independence of mind to convince readers to accept your authority. The emphasis of *Fact and Artifact* is to enable you to make your writing your own original work, without depending too much on others. The more you know, the more liberties and risks you can take. If you decide to be truly outrageous, as critic Camille Paglia does in calling Emily Dickinson "Amherst's Madame de Sade" and in claiming Dickinson's poems "are the prison dreams of a self-incarcerated, sadomasochistic imaginist [sic]," you'll need extra expertise to defend your provocative views.

Use a confident tone that reflects your subject.   If you write in a tone that suits your subject and is under your careful control, your readers are likely to believe you. As we've seen in the student writers' examples, truthful presentation well supported with appropriate evidence, inspires confidence in writer and reader alike. Although to be accurate you'll want to qualify blanket generalizations ("Everyone should vote—unless they're uninformed"), you'll also want to avoid weasel words that diminish the force or commitment of your assertions, such as *perhaps* or *possibly*.

Likewise, don't undermine your authority with such caveats as, "I'm only twenty, but I think . . ." or "In my opinion . . ." Readers will assume that you're expressing your opinion unless you identify it as another's. If you genuinely don't know enough about a subject to write on it with confident authority, either learn more about it or switch to a subject you know better. Getting stuck as you try to write or having trouble organizing your ideas may be clues that you don't have enough to say.

Write about a compelling subject.   A subject that engages the writer will engage the reader. Often, the interest lies in the telling of the tale, the presentation of material, the voice and style that intrigue readers and reveal the author's personality and point of view, however feisty, witty, bitter, or sweet that might be. At the outset, readers might not have wanted to hear about Myhal's accident, Crawford's rape, Dixon's parents' divorce, Bass's account of the decline and fall of Paul Jenkins, or Vincent's birthday. But a few paragraphs told from a distinctive point of view and in compelling language arouse our interest. If you care about your subject, your writing will display competence and inspire confidence. If a potential subject bores you, don't write on it because you'll bore your readers.

Set the scene.   You can establish firsthand authority by using specific details to describe action, interaction, behavior, and costume. The student writers use a great many sensory details such as cutting through Myhal's numerous layers of clothing; Vincent's detailed weather report of "clouds rolling in from the west"; the "heavy knockwurst breath" of the medic administering aid to Myhal; and Bass's description of Paul Jenkins's "happy drunken monotone" sung "through his gums."

You can also use specific details to establish the context, whether it's physical, intellectual, spiritual, or political. All the student writers do this as we saw in the passages quoted at the beginning of the chapter. In this excerpt from "Goin' Up Cripple Creek," W. Dudley Bass illustrates Paul Jenkins's worsening alcoholism by showing how Jenkins worked on the Bass's Virginia farm:

> Paul was useless on the job, but my father kept him on, hoping to reform him. But he stopped going to AA meetings and drank harder. We were painting all the cowbarns and stables that summer, and he would just stand and stare with a dripping brush in his hand or sit on top of the ladder and crack jokes. He

was a belligerent bastard who enjoyed getting a rise out of people and seeing how far he could push them.

He picked on Ricky because he was fat. He picked on Raffie because he was old and black and angry but too scared to fight back. Paul fought with Joe, my brother, and leered at my mother and said nasty things about my wife. But Dad refused to fire him and kept trying to reform him, while the rest of us wished he would quit. Then one day Paul's second wife left him and she never came back and Paul cracked all to pieces.

Goin' up Cripple Creek,
Travelin' mighty fast;
Goin' up Cripple Creek,
I'm gonna whup her ass!

Here Bass shows the characters in action and in interaction, working, loafing, being picked on, arguing, and fighting as the tension Jenkins creates escalates. Readers infer from the single mention of drinking that Jenkins is continually drunk and that everyone else is sober.

Setting the scene with realistic dialogue also brings the action to life and further enhances the writers' credibility. Jenkins's drunken ditty, "Goin' up Cripple Creek," serves as a motif for the character and integrates the entire essay. We trust Dixon's interpretation of her parents' arguments that culminate in divorce ("I'll never drive in that lane again!") and Crawford's rendition of the suspicious and bullying state trooper ("I think you was just tryin out some of the local stuff. . . .") even though each writer is writing several years after the events took place. The dialogue sounds as if it was spoken by real people in real situations. Whether or not the written text incorporates the speakers' exact words, the dialogue suits the characters and their situations and reinforces the authors' points. If you use dialogue, read it out loud to hear whether it rings true. Better yet, have someone else—a writing partner, perhaps—read it to you.

Integrating Firsthand and Secondhand Authority

How hard you have to work to prove your competence may depend on how well versed you are in the field. If you are just entering a specialized field and discussing a topic that requires expertise, you'll have to work harder to prove your credibility. You cannot simply assert or imply, "I was there," as you can with a firsthand experience. As a newcomer writing a research paper in a particular field, you will have to cite sources and other established authorities in the field. That's why so many research reports and theses begin with a "Review of the Literature": when readers are confident that you know where you're coming from, they'll be more receptive to where you're going. A known authority can travel with less baggage; readers take for granted an expert's knowledge of a field.

Be scrupulously accurate.   Check your facts and figures, keeping in mind what is considered common knowledge in your field. When in doubt, double-check. (How many bytes are in a kilobyte, anyway?) Don't make up what you can't find out. Try some creative investigation; computer searches, for instance, have infinite possibilities. Make sure your facts and figures are up to date by checking, for example, current volumes of *World Almanac* and *Statistical Abstract.* One bit of imprecision in an otherwise authoritative presentation can cause the reader who detects it to question the accuracy of the entire work. This extends even to simple matters such as spelling and word usage (Do you know the difference between *flaunt* and *flout, ensure* and *insure?*) and correct names for individuals, places, and organizations (Is it *Woman Studies, Women Studies,* or *Women's Studies?* the *Seventh Day Adventist* Church or, as proclaimed by one innocent, the *Seventh Day at Venice?*).

Provide adequate support for your assertions.   What is self-evident to you may not be so obvious to your readers, for whom you'll need to supply representative evidence pertinent to your subject. For instance, if your topic is "solutions to the energy crisis," you might want to discuss several alternative sources of energy—coal, oil, wood, sun, nuclear power—as well as ways of conserving energy.

If you're using partisan sources, try to balance the relevant factors—the historical with the contemporary, the scientific with the humanitarian. You can still emphasize your own point of view and demonstrate that you are fair as well as knowledgeable. You may also wish to acknowledge the exception that tests the generality but raises an important issue. For instance, instead of saying, "Immigrants to the United States assimilate into the mainstream culture in a single generation," it would be more accurate to qualify the generalization with "usually assimilate" and to add, "except for members of closely knit cultural groups, such as Hasidic Jews, who associate primarily with each other."

You can use various types of evidence, primary (from the original source) or secondary (from reference books or periodicals). Among the most common forms of evidence are the following.

Personal experience.   Even for a topic on which you have to rely on other authorities, you can cite your own experience. "Trust yourself," reassures Dr. Benjamin Spock in *Baby and Child Care,* "You know more than you think you do." Indeed, just by being alive in a particular place during a certain period in history, you have learned a great deal about education (how long, by this time, have you been in school?), your gender and race, your family and/or dorm life, the American culture, some subcultures such as surfers or fast food workers, and a host of other subjects. If you're an expert on the subject of your paper, so much the better, but because you can call on a variety of authorities, you don't have to be an expert to write a convincing paper.

Scientific evidence from reliable sources, including firsthand investigations of your own or of others.   "In *The Voyage of the Beagle,* Charles Darwin reports that Galapagos tortoises. . . ." Your librarian can help you find general and specialized bibliographies in both printed form and on computer discs (CD-ROMs). It's easy to do a computer search using key words—*Darwin, Charles; tortoise, Galapagos; voyage, Beagle*—to get a printout of sources, sometimes annotated or cross-indexed by other key words, which makes your search even easier.

Facts and figures, accurately interpreted in context.   Figures in isolation are not intrinsically meaningful; you will need to interpret them to demonstrate their relevance to your purpose. For instance, in "Women and HIV/AIDS: The Silent Epidemic?," June E. Osborn, M.D., Chairwoman of the National Commission on AIDS, interprets statistics to contradict the common misconception that women are not at risk for AIDS: "We, in the United States, now have recorded more than 150,000 cases of AIDS in less than a decade, and there are almost sure to be more than 1,000,000 HIV-infected Americans who do not yet have clinical signs or symptoms to alert them to their infectious status." Although "the substantial majority of AIDS cases are in gay and bisexual men," women now total 10 percent of AIDS cases, up 3 percent from four years ago, and "since they are of childbearing age, children follow quickly behind." The date of Osborn's report is critical; readers would need to know that it reflects end-of-the-year figures for 1990; for contemporary relevance, it would have to be updated.

The opinions of reasonable, reliable, up-to-date authorities.   Neither writers nor readers are objective; they can't be, for to be human is to have opinions. Even if a piece sounds objective, the writer's opinions have inevitably shaped the presentation of facts and other information, just as the readers' prior experience and opinions color their reaction to the material. Thus Osborn's figures on AIDS suggest a warning to medical researchers, public health officials, and women in general that is reinforced later in the article by her explicit message:

> Whatever else we do, we must WARN. The misleading message, which suggests that women (or at least majority, nondrug-using women) need not worry, is a horrid postponement of our obligation to our children's children. After all, *education is going to be the vaccine for AIDS, for at least a decade to come,* but just as a vaccine is of no use in its bottle, so education will not help unless it is delivered, reiteratively and convincingly, in the language of our intended listeners.

All authorities aren't in books; you can learn a lot by talking to people who have experience or expertise in your subject (see Chapters 4, 9, and 10).

Discourse Communities

By now it should be clear that style is not only a matter of individual personality and preference. Your style is inevitably influenced by the times you live in, contemporary taste, and the language practices and preferences of your associates and your audience—your discourse community.

A discourse community is a group of people, large or small, with similar assumptions and values who converse in the same language and have the same general understanding of that language, its words as well as its nuances. As we saw in Chapter 1, this understanding is determined, in part, by factors such as nationality, race, class, gender, and sexual or political orientation. Because you fill many roles in life, you belong to a variety of discourse communities, some determined by your roles as a member of a particular family and as a resident of a particular city, state, and country and some determined by your own choices and preferences. You can be a music buff, a sports fan, and a good cook and use language that is appropriate for each of your interests.

Imagine each discourse community as a circle; the areas that overlap represent the knowledge, values, and consequently the language that the communities share. Every academic and professional discipline constitutes a discourse community and has a variety of subcommunities, which overlap somewhat. English studies, for instance, could be subdivided into theory, rhetoric and composition, creative writing (with its subdivisions of poetry, fiction, drama, film, and creative nonfiction), and literature (with its subdivisions of British, American, Canadian, Francophone and so forth).

When as a student you join a discourse community, you begin not only to learn what the members know, to act the way the members act, and to share the members' values, but also to speak the way the members speak. In *A Not Entirely Benign Procedure,* a narrative of her medical education, Perri Klass offers this clearheaded analysis of her initiation into the discourse community of doctors:

> If I learned nothing else during my first three months of working in the hospital as a medical student, I learned endless jargon and abbreviations. I started out in a state of primeval innocence, in which I didn't even know that "s CP, SOB, N/V" meant "without chest pain, shortness of breath, or nausea and vomiting." By the end I took the abbreviations so much for granted that I would complain to my mother the English professor, "And can you believe I had to put down *three* NG tubes last night?"
>
> "You'll have to tell me what an NG tube is if you want me to sympathize properly," my mother said. NG, nasogastric—isn't it obvious?

> I picked up not only the specific expressions but also the patterns of speech and the grammatical conventions; for example, you never say that a patient's blood pressure fell or that his cardiac enzymes rose. Instead, the patient is always the subject of the verb: "He dropped his pressure." "He bumped his enzymes." . . . When chemotherapy fails to cure Mrs. Bacon's cancer, what we say is, "Mrs. Bacon failed chemotherapy."

Medical jargon, the specialized or technical language of the medical profession (with no negative connotations unless it's used in the wrong context), says Klass, makes insiders of doctors and medical students, who use it to talk to one another, and makes outsiders of patients, who don't understand the language. The newness of the language leaves the initiate acutely sensitive to shades of meanings and embedded values that go unnoticed once the novelty wears off. For example, says Klass, medical students soon learn to take for granted such coded language as "CTD," an abbreviation for "circling the drain," medical jargon for an impending death.

There are no general rules for learning the specific vocabulary, attitudes, or ways of reasoning of a particular discourse community. Student initiates learn gradually from teachers, mentors, and fellow students. "At first," says Klass, "you may notice these new and alien assumptions every time you put together a sentence, but with time and increased fluency you stop being aware of them at all." As you lose that awareness, you move closer and closer to being a doctor instead of "just talking like one."

Nevertheless, your writing, in whatever discourse communities you belong to, will inevitably be influenced by contemporary taste, and to that extent your style will be a reflection of the times as well as of your personal preference. Historically, styles have been labeled "plain," "baroque," "rococo," among others. In Victorian times, writers and readers liked amplitude and some formality in writing, as in architecture and in dress. Novels and biographies ran to three overstuffed volumes; poems ran to thousands of lines; the sentences in literary reviews of the time averaged fifty-seven words, in contrast to the twenty-five word average of contemporary academic writing.

At present, lean, muscular prose is in many discourse communities considered the essence of good writing. The style commentators are the leaders of Word Watchers, exhorting writers to take off flabby phrases to maintain a taut, well-shaped body of prose. A spare style has ethical dimensions by promoting a better understanding between writer and reader, rather than creating mystery and obfuscation. Nevertheless, if your academic discipline or professional field characteristically uses technical language and long sentences you'll need to follow suit, at least in writing for your courses or on the job. In most other contexts, you'll do yourself and your readers a favor if you write with clarity and conciseness. Even a svelte style, however, allows for considerable variation according to your taste and your subject.

Levels of Language

You can and probably do alter your language, often unconsciously, as you address one discourse community in its "code" (a shared language that reflects the group members' behavior, values, and orientation to the world) rather than in another "code." You're experienced at switching codes; you write somewhat differently in English class than you do in sociology or microbiology; still differently to friends outside of class; and still differently in

LEVELS OF LANGUAGE

Characteristic	Informal Level	Middle Level	Formal Level
voice	personal—pronouns are *I, you*; author's personality and personal reactions prominent	somewhat less personal, may or may not use personal pronouns *I, you*, author's personality and personal reactions more subdued	impersonal—pronouns are *one, we, he,* or may be absent if passive voice is used; little or no direct representation of the author's personality
tone	wide range of tones possible, usually expressed conspicuously, sometimes without restraint	wide range of tones possible, expression more subdued	in theory, a wide range of tones is possible, but the expression is highly controlled
vocabulary	informal, conversational; may include slang, profanity, dialects; fairly simple vocabulary	ranges from conversational to more formal standard English; vocabulary varies from common to unusual; some figurative language	formal standard English, much more likely to be written than spoken except in oratory, speeches; more foreign and archaic words
sentences	short, simple with less variation than in middle or formal levels	wide range of lengths; average length in middle range; some variation in patterns and construction	wide variation in lengths; longest average number of words; most complex construction

letters to the newspaper, your landlord, and your boss. If you want to learn the style of the discipline that you're majoring in, find an article or book in the field that is written in a way that you and your professor or employer like. First, you'll have to study the material to figure out what makes it so good and try to understand its substance and spirit, which inform its style. Then try to imitate it.

To express themselves, in whatever voices and for whatever discourse communities, writers have a world of words to choose from, spanning a continuum from informal to middle level to highly formal. Likewise, as a writer you have a choice of sentence structures—simple, compound, and complex; loose and periodic; parallel, with repeated words and phrases. You can vary and repeat sentence patterns and lengths—short, medium, long. There is not necessarily a connection between formality of vocabulary and sentence complexity or length, although informal writing seems simpler than formal writing in both vocabulary and sentence construction. The rest of this chapter will focus on words, and to a lesser extent, on sentences (see also Chapter 11). Much of the next chapter, Re-vision and Revision, will emphasize larger units—sentences, paragraphs, and whole essays as well.

Informal Level

Informal English sounds relatively casual and conversational even when it is used in thoughtful, carefully crafted descriptions, commentaries, analyses, arguments, or other writings of the kinds discussed in Chapters 4 through 10. Indeed, you'll probably use a combination of informal and middle-level English when you write for any audience of nonspecialists, as do the student writers we saw at the beginning of this chapter. In informal writing, you select a more common vocabulary than when you write in the formal language of speeches and sermons or in the technical language of legal and business documents, scientific papers and some textbooks (this book ranges most of the time between informal and middle level). When you try to write informally, imagine yourself writing a letter to a friend who cares about both you and your language. The authorial personality, tone, conversational vocabulary, and sentence structure that come naturally will probably be just the level you want.

Informally you'd use *write* rather than *correspond, lover* rather than *paramour, giant panda* rather than *Ailuropoda melanoleuca*. Overall, a higher proportion of informal English words are native rather than borrowed; many words are shorter than their counterparts from Latinate or other foreign language origins: *house* vs *domicile, fishing* vs *piscatory*. The sentences in informal writing are often shorter and more simply constructed than the longer, more complicated structures with more grammatical subordination that are found in formal English.[1] You could write informally, "Researchers suspect a connection between love and chocolate. People in love produce the same chemical that chocolate contains" (18 words, 31 syllables). More formally, you could combine the sentences, subordinating the meaning and grammar of one component to the other and using more technical or elevated language: "Researchers, surmising a correlation between the chemical composition of chocolate and the biochemistry of the amorous, have discovered that lovers secrete the same chemical, phenylethylamine, that is an active constituent of chocolate" (32 words, 68 syllables).

Formal Level

Formal writing is at the other end of the continuum. It often sounds impersonal because the writer's personality is subordinate to the material at hand, as in much scientific and technical writing. The authorial voice that emerges through formal speeches and sermons often appears stylized for the occasion, using a vocabulary of words that are native and borrowed, simple and elevated, contemporary and older (even archaic), and that are arranged in sentences with a span of possibilities, from short and simple to highly subordinated and complex.

When you're trying to write formally, imagine yourself preparing a committee report, writing a paper for a professional journal whose audience is your academic discourse community, or delivering a speech like the *Gettysburg Address,* which begins "Fourscore and seven years ago our fathers brought forth on this continent a new nation conceived in liberty and dedicated to the proposition that all men are created equal." Instead of saying informally, "Eighty-seven years ago our country was founded on the principles of liberty and equality," Lincoln chose the archaic and Biblical "fourscore and seven." He used metaphors of conception and birth ("conceived" and "brought forth") and subordinated syntax in the second half of the sentence. Although the entire speech is only 255 words, it ends with a repetition of the birth metaphor, "this nation, under God, shall have a new birth of freedom," and an uncommon parallel construction of three phrases of three words each (triplets), "and that government of the people, by the people, for the people, shall not perish from the earth." This repetition enhances not only the meaning but also the sound and provides the momentum for the final thrust, "shall not perish from the earth," which is more resonant and emphatic than the more contemporary, less majestic "will not die."

Middle Level

Middle-level language spans a somewhat undefined range on the continuum between informal and formal; it is less casual and often less personal than most conversation and is less elevated, using somewhat shorter sentences and simpler vocabulary than formal speeches or documents. Editorials in the *New York Times* or the *Washington Post,* or articles in the *Atlantic* or the *New Yorker* are likely to be written in middle-level language, as are many essays, term papers, reports, analyses, articles, and books for an audience of thoughtful, general readers.

In "The Human Cost of an Illiterate Society," a chapter of *Illiterate America,* Jonathan Kozol, critic of society and education, writes in middle style:

> Illiterates live, in more than literal ways, an uninsured existence. They cannot understand the written details on a health insurance form. They cannot read the waivers that they sign preceding surgical procedures. Several women I have known in Boston have entered a slum hospital with the intention of obtaining a tubal ligation and have emerged a few days later after having been subjected to a hysterectomy. Unaware of their rights, incognizant of jargon, intimidated by the unfamiliar air of fear and atmosphere of ether that so many of us find oppressive in the confines even of the most attractive and expensive medical facilities, they have signed their names to documents they could not read and which nobody, in the hectic situation that prevails so often in those overcrowded hospitals that serve the urban poor, had even bothered to explain.

Although Kozol does not appear as a character in the book, his moral presence in his writing testifies his concern for his subject—illiteracy and its victims, for whom the devastating consequences may be irreversible (such as a hysterectomy). He knows these women and because his evidence is specific and his attitude serious, we believe him. That he cares deeply about what he says is apparent from his tone, somber, deliberate, indignant. His evidence and somber tone could be reflected in any style. However, the absence of contractions and the vocabulary that is not too simple, not slangy or profane, and not erudite (except for *incognizant*) signal middle-level style. So do the first four sentences, which have ten, eleven, eleven, and thirty-four words; the first three begin with subject-verb. The middle level dominates in spite of the seventy-four-word final sentence that has a complicated syntax meant to be read, not spoken, its subject buried in the middle after a thirty-seven-word preamble. Kozol's average of twenty-eight words per sentence masks great variation in actual sentence length.

The chart on page 34 graphically illustrates some of the principal features of the levels of language discussed here; you can use it to analyze your own writings or those of others. Each horizontal row represents a continuum that flows in either direction; there are no arbitrary demarcations from one level to another. You may, of course, choose to write different works in different levels of language or even to mix them for humorous, shocking, folksy, or other effects.

Nonsexist Writing

The conventions of English grammar reflect a dominant male orientation. Custom has for centuries dictated using the masculine gender (*he*) to refer to either an indefinite person (*he* or *she*) or a group composed of both men and women (All *men* are created equal). Critics contend that this language is sexist and that it reinforces the assumption that "unless otherwise identified, people in general are men," including "the hypothetical person (If a *man* can walk ten miles in two hours . . .), the average person (the *man* in the street), and the active person (the *man* on the move)" (Miller and Swift). Research supports the critics' view, finding that schoolchildren usually think that the generic *he* or *man* refers to men exclusively.

Over the past twenty years, usage has changed to give women linguistic equality. Some of the wordier alternatives, such as substituting *he or she* or *men and women* for the general *one* or *he,* have been generally supplanted by the more unobtrusive usages that follow. Collectively they imply that you treat men and women equally in your writing—and presumably, in your thinking.

- Use the plural instead of the singular when possible. Instead of writing, "The exhausted traveler will find himself welcomed in the bed-and-breakfast accommodations that dot the British countryside," say "Exhausted travelers will find themselves welcomed . . ." or eliminate the pronoun reference altogether: "The exhausted traveler will find a ready welcome . . ."
- Use all *she*s or *he*s in alternate sections of a work. (Don't change the gender in alternate sentences or short paragraphs, it's very confusing.)
- Use neutral substitutes for words that incorporate the generic *man: chair* or *head* for *chairman, mail carrier* for *mailman, humanity* for *mankind.*
- Use equivalent terms for equivalent categories. If you say *men* you should say *women,* not *ladies* or *girls.* If you say *Truman,* say *Hepburn,* not *Miss Hepburn* or *Kate.* Or say *President Truman* and *Ms. Hepburn.*
- Don't say anything about women that you wouldn't say about men, unless the context warrants attention to the differences. For instance, today many newspapers avoid references to women's clothes (*classy*), physical appearance (*a redhead*), marital status (*divorced*), and maternity (*grandmother of two*) if they wouldn't make comparable references for men. Or they refer similarly to men ("The groom wore . . ."). The effect is to avoid emphasizing women's sexuality and traditional stereotypes. There are instances, however, when stereotypes are

essential to the discussion, as in the opening of this *New York Times* story:

> Like Jean S. Harris, Arlene Caris, a 64-year-old grandmother with white hair and pink cheeks, is a cooperative prisoner at the Bedford Hills Correctional Facility. And like Ms. Harris, she was a hard worker with no criminal record until she shot and killed the man whose abuse she said she had endured for 14 years.
>
> Unlike Ms. Harris, 69, however, Mrs. Caris did not receive clemency from Gov. Mario M. Cuomo this week. She did not even get a hearing. (Sontag)

You'll need to judge the appropriateness of including such information on a case-by-case basis.

- Use written and visual illustrations that give equal emphasis to both sexes, where appropriate; and when possible use illustrations that reflect diversity among race, culture, age, and social class.

Some Other Aspects of Style

As you would for the rest of this book, feel free to modify these recommendations to suit yourself as a writer and the specific paper you're working on. For instance, in papers where freedom of form and stylistic latitude are possible, you may want to play more with language and sentence structure than you would in more restrained contexts; you might even come to know "the joys of excess" (see pages 46–48).

Conciseness and Amplitude

When teachers or editors urge, "Get to the point," and style experts say, "Be concise," they mean, "Make your writing full (or succinct) enough, long (or short) enough to suit your subject, purpose, and audience." They don't necessarily mean bare-bones skinny. There are various ways to achieve clear, uncluttered writing and you can do so without sounding like a Dick and Jane reader ("Run, Spot, run. See Spot run!"). You may find it easiest to write a long first draft, putting in anything that comes to mind, including redundancies, repetitions, and extra words for comfort or security.

As you write, trust yourself and your readers. Listen to the music and the movement of your writing and use your sense of the flow as a guide to avoid clutter and stylistic bric-a-brac (Why say *at this point in time* when *now* will do, *refer back* instead of *refer?*). You can count on your readers to get the point without verbal nudges supplied by extra modifiers—adjectives, adverbs, or phrases. Let nouns and verbs carry the weight. In general, you'll want to use single words or short phrases instead of longer phrases or sentences, as long as you can express your meaning and the resulting style is pleasing.

Repetition.   Nevertheless, don't be afraid of repetition that enhances your meaning or mood or gives emphasis. Whether a given repetition is necessary or stylistically pleasing is partly a matter of your preference as a writer. Some prose, like some poetry, contains repeated words, phrases, and refrains that do not alter the meaning but instead reinforce or intensify the meaning, integrate ideas, establish mood, or provide stylistic continuity. For instance, Nancy Mairs begins her essay, "On Being a Cripple," with five repetitions of the word *cripple,* the title's key word. All are shocking. The opening sentence startles: "The other day I was thinking of writing an essay on being a cripple." The repetitions of *cripple* are meant to shock, as are the subsequent repetitions of *handicapped, disabled,* and *wince.* Indeed, Mairs wants her readers to wince as they encounter her subject and her authorial persona.

> First, the matter of semantics. I am *a cripple.* I choose this word to name me. I choose from among several possibilities, the most common of which are *"handicapped" and "disabled."* I made the choice a number of years ago, without thinking, unaware of my motives for doing so. Even now, I'm not sure what those motives are, but I recognize that they are complex and not entirely flattering. People—*crippled* or not—wince at the word *"cripple,"* as they do not at *"handicapped" or "disabled."* Perhaps I want them to *wince.* I want them to see me as a tough customer, one to whom the fates/gods/viruses have not been kind, but who can face the brutal truth of her existence squarely. As *a cripple,* I swagger. (Italics added.)

In addition to the key words, italicized, there are other repeated words and phrases (*motives, I choose, I want them to*) that more subtly reinforce Mairs's self-assertive stance; as an author, she swaggers.

How can you, as a writer, distinguish between repetition that enhances your writing and repetition that clogs it up, slows it down, or dulls its edge? Try listening to how your writing sounds; have a friend read it to you, or record it and play it back. If the repetition drones on and bores you, omit it and listen again. Is your point sharper with or without the repetition? Is the writing more focused? Does the writing flow more rapidly or more smoothly? Is it more appealing or more moving?

Meaningless qualifiers.   Extra words and phrases such as *quite, rather, really, very, definitely, absolutely, fundamentally, honestly, of course,* and *you know what I mean* are meaningless qualifiers. I'll be honest with you, these fill up spaces in conversation, and sometimes in writing, when you're searching for something to say. They have the effect of, er, uh, a verbal tic, recurring at intervals as meaningless punctuation to slow down the flow of the discourse. They're so common in conversation that listeners skip over them. But actually, they're much less acceptable in writing, you know, because they basically occupy space without contributing either to the meaning or the music, don't you see? Delete them.

Yet, not all qualifiers are meaningless. When you make general, unqualified observations ("Everybody likes children"), you invite readers who can think of exceptions to mistrust what you say. ("In the immortal words of W. C. Fields, 'Anyone who hates children and dogs can't be all bad'"). Unless you're writing about a universal law or invariable truth, your generalizations are likely (note the qualifier) to be more accurate if they are qualified with terms such as *many, most, usually, often, some* ("*Nearly* everyone likes *some* children"). If you use qualifiers, you're not being wishy-washy—in most instances. To decide whether or not to qualify your generalizations, see if you can think of likely exceptions. If you can, you need to acknowledge them.

Specificity and Generality

How specific or general should your writing be? What details should you include, elaborate on, or omit? The answers depend on the kind of writing you're doing and on the nature of your audience. Some writing, such as a statement of public policy, philosophy, or scientific principles, has to be general in order to be broadly applicable. Thus the Ten Commandments ("Thou shalt not kill"), the Bill of Rights ("Congress shall make no law . . . abridging the freedom of speech or of the press"), and Newton's third law ("For every action there is an equal and opposite reaction") are intentionally general. This makes them both versatile and ambiguous, as attested to by the generations of subsequent interpretive commentary in and out of the churches, the courts, and scientific journals.

Other writing, such as a campaign speech, a sermon, or an analysis of a political or social phenomenon, may require a combination of the theoretical and the practical, general principles and specific applications. You might discuss from a general theoretical perspective the hypothesis that schizophrenia has a biochemical basis and then examine specific evidence from recent research on disorientation in fetal brain cells that control emotion. At the beginning of *Anna Karenina,* Tolstoy used the generalization, "Happy families are all alike. Every unhappy family is unhappy in its own way," as a springboard for seven hundred pages of a highly specific anatomization of one particular unhappy family.

Still other writing, such as a travel article on the pleasures of Papeete or a set of directions on how to build a kayak will necessarily be highly specific and may not require much if any general discussion. Even an argument intended to make a general point, such as Orwell's contention in "Marrakech" that colonial empires are founded on the dehumanization of the poor, can be made through specific examples. Orwell uses vivid illustrations of a burial ground of anonymous boneheaps, a zookeeper begging for animal food that he himself can eat, and old women bearing heavier burdens than donkeys to drive his message home. He uses generalizations to connect the particulars: "All people who work with their hands are partly invisible, and the more important the work they do, the less visible they are."

Figurative Language

Writing, a mirror of life, abounds in imagery, whether the child of Mother Nature or of the artist's passion. (How many images can you find in the preceding sentence?) Some imagery, familiar symbols (a cross) and metaphors, has such well-known symbolic meanings that we scarcely regard it literally. But the meanings of images are nevertheless in the minds of the beholders and not inherent in the images themselves, no matter how closely the image is physically related to the sensation, emotion, experience, or concept it is intended to represent. Sometimes to accurately interpret the meaning of a symbol, we need to examine its physical characteristics. A cross with an elongated vertical axis connotes Christianity, but only to people who already are familiar with that religious symbol. Moreover, the Christian cross may be modified to connote a specific denomination; the addition of an extra horizontal bar makes it a Greek cross. The context in which the symbol appears often dictates its meaning. If the cross has vertical and horizontal axes of equal length, its context will signal its meaning: mathematical (as in an addition sign, or an A-plus); cartographical (a crossroads on a map or road sign); electrical (a positive charge or magnetic pole). These are only some of the generally understood meanings of this versatile symbol; and to each of the common symbolic meanings we add our own private connotations, depending on what the symbol in its context means to us.

As a writer you'll continually decide what figurative language to use, how much, and in what contexts. In all cases, you'll want your figurative language to be functional and organic to your subject and your purpose, not just stuck on for decoration, like a bow on a baby's bald head. You'll want your figurative language to clarify, or explain your ideas, or to entertain with freshness, vigor, and wit. So you'll try to avoid clichés (often the first figurative language that comes to mind), stale language that clogs your writing as tea leaves plug up a sink drain. You'll want it to hint at your message rather than to send it in neon lights, like using cologne by the drop rather than by the bottleful.

Figurative language that works well must be appropriate to the subject without pushing either the literal or figurative meanings to extremes. You probably use many kinds of figurative expressions without knowing their names. A *simile* is an overt comparison of two things, usually signalled by "like" or "as". Anatole Broyard opens "Being There," an essay on the nature of travel, with the observation, "Travel is like adultery: one is always tempted to be unfaithful to one's own country." He continues with a *metaphor,* an implied comparison of two things that are literally unlike but figuratively similar: "In our wanderlust, we are lovers looking for consummation." *Personification* gives human attributes to natural phenomena, inanimate objects, or abstractions: the ocean murmurs and soothes; the car's engine grumbles and protests on cold mornings. *Synecdoche* is a form of metaphor in which a part, usually a significant one, represents the whole (*sail* for *ship, hands* for *helpers, bread* for *food*). *Metonomy* substitutes some attribute or suggestive word for what is actually meant: *brass* for *military officers, lip* for *backtalk.* Sir Winston Churchill's "I have nothing to offer but *blood, toil, tears, and sweat*" is a notable example. It doesn't matter whether you can label figurative expressions as a rhetorician would; the important thing is to be able to use them wisely (see Corbett).

If you enjoy playing with language, as many writers do, you probably won't want to restrict your writing to a single figure of speech. Feel free to use whatever figurative language is fruitful, but nip it in the bud if it becomes cloying. Broyard's "Being There" effectively uses many forms of figurative language, as the italicized portions indicate:

> When we travel, we put aside our defenses, our anxiety, and invite regression. *We go backward instead of forward.* . . . *It is our best selves that travel, just as we dress in our best clothes.* Only our passport reminds us how ordinary we actually are. We go abroad to meet our foreign persona, *that thrilling stranger born on the plane.* . . . *Something of the Crusades survive in the modern traveler—only his is a personal crusade, an impulse to go off and fight certain obscure battles of his own spirit.* . . .
>
> We travel in summer, when life comes out of doors, and so *we see only summery people, nothing of their sad falls, their long dark winters and cruel springs. The places we visit are gold-plated by the sun. The flowers and trees are like bouquets thrown to history.*
>
> And language—*what a pleasure to leave our own language, with its clichés stuck in our teeth.* How much better things sound in another tongue! *It's like having our ears cleaned out. So long as we don't understand it too well, every other language is poetry.* (Italics added.)

Whether such writing satisfies or satiates is a matter of taste, both the reader's and writer's. A jumble of figures of speech or comparisons pushed too far call attention to themselves whether or not, like W. Dudley Bass and Patricia Vincent or William H. Gass (page 46), you pile them on for sheer fun. In places where you believe that stylistic excesses, like the overgrown antlers of the Irish elk, will eventually cause the supporting structure to collapse, you'll need to prune your garden of earthly delights and to let the individual figures of speech flourish in the sun rather than be crowded out by other equally worthy specimens. (How much of the preceding sentence would you weed out, for instance, to make the figurative language tolerable? Or would you let everything struggle for survival?)

The extent to which you use figurative language may also depend on convention. Look at other writing of the kind that you're doing (articles in popular magazines or professional journals, interoffice memos, corporation reports) to learn what the norms, variations, and limits are. For instance, some scientific writing is strictly technical and seldom leavened by the yeast of metaphor. Yet other scientific writing is highly figurative as the writers try to explain abstractions for scientists and particularly for nonscientists by making them concrete, through analogies with familiar phenomena. In *The Dragons of Eden*, Carl Sagan invents a "Cosmic Calendar" and uses an extended analogy to explain

> the fifteen-billion-year lifetime of the universe . . . compressed into the span of a single year. Then every billion years of Earth history would correspond to about twenty-four days of our cosmic year, and one second of that year to 475 real revolutions of the earth about the sun. . . . dinosaurs emerge on Christmas Eve . . . men and women originate at 10:30 P.M. on New Year's Eve . . . and the time from the waning of the Middle Ages to the present occupies little more than one second.

Every kind of writing is full of dead metaphors, figurative language so familiar that we take it for granted and treat the meanings as literal (such as the arm and leg of a chair, the head and foot of a table). Don't worry about these metaphors that will appear naturally in your writing.

Clichés, on the other hand, although they may involve figurative expressions *as comfortable as an old shoe,* are more conspicuous and should be *avoided like the plague* to prevent the writing from being cluttered with overly familiar imagery that, like a dull party, deadens the readers' responses. More insidious are mixed metaphors, different images that pertain to the same thing. These slither into your writing like snakes through a letter slot, and lie there in the sunshine waiting to infect those shining apples of style in your carefully cultivated Garden of Eden. By confusing the logic that underlies the comparisons, that are the essence of figurative language, mixed metaphors dissipate the point and cause confusion. Avoid them.

Literal Language Used Figuratively

Some of the most memorable writing is simple and unadorned, free of metaphors or other figurative language. Each sentence makes sense on a literal level, as does the entire work. But if the reader understands its entire context, a particular passage—perhaps every character, conversation, setting, and action—takes on symbolic richness that illuminates the whole work. Student Ted Sherbahn's essay, "When the Winds Move," is an analysis of his complicated, often painful relationship with his father, a relationship still in flux as he prepares for a career as an English teacher and coach, rather than for the medical career his father had encouraged. Sherbahn renders key scenes literally and implies a great deal that, as a consequence, he doesn't need to spell out.

Sherbahn uses his early attempts at learning to play basketball to illustrate the pressure that his father, "a wrestling champ at college," and now a highly successful insurance salesman, exerted on him in a variety of overt and covert ways.

> In the sixth grade I played for my first basketball team, at the James Buchanan Elementary School. We were a part of the city school league, and for the most part we lost to the tough city kids. Several times my father left work early and went to these games. Inevitably, I would suffer tunnel vision after I noticed he was there, sitting in the bleachers with his big heavy coat and grey felt hat, and I usually had the ball thrown off my chest or on the side of my head before being taken out. On our way home in the car, both of us bundled against the cold and peering out through the frosted windshield, my father would say, "You've got to be more aggressive, Ted. You weren't fouled enough—a good player goes right at them." To toughen me some he signed me up to play at the YMCA downtown. On my first day there was a fight in the locker room concerning someone's "pansy" bathing suit, and within a week I could shoot a real jump shot from underneath the basket.
>
> At home I spent hours at the hoop in the driveway, trying to put more strength into my skinny arms and trying to dribble over all the cracks in the driveway without looking. Even in the dark after dinner, I wouldn't let myself go inside until I had hit every shot "around the world" in a row and then had made a long one from the porch steps. One cold night in the middle of winter my father switched on the floodlight and took me outside to practice. Snow began to fall, shimmering softly through the arc of the light and powdering our coats and hats. He covered me loosely, his dark form high over mine, both our breaths fogging in the night air. He gave me just enough room to stretch and run and said "That's the way" each time I managed to get one in the basket high above us. We played on into the dark until the snow piled around our ankles and the ball would bounce no more.

In Sherbahn's simple narrative everything works to demonstrate the multiple stresses of the relationship between the large, looming father and his small son, who is eager to please yet cries out in his sleep the night before spring baseball tryouts were to begin, "I don't want to play baseball . . . I don't want to play baseball." These scenes lead into the next scene that takes place when Sherbahn is twelve: the night before his father leaves home "to begin my parents' separation and divorce that would blind me for months with a different kind of tunnel vision."

> I woke when I heard someone open my door. I rolled over and saw the frame of my father silhouetted by the hall light. He came quietly to the bed and sat at my side. . . . I was aware only of the weight of his body next to me, the deep, sad look in his eyes and his calm hand on the side of my face. He then

leaned over and picked me up with both his arms around my back and, for the first time I can remember, told me he loved me. With my arms around him I could feel his hard, dry crying. We held each other, both crying, but I not fully knowing why, and then he let me down on my back again. Soon his figure blocked the hall light and the door shut. Darkness enveloped me as my arms and chest continued to shake and my father's footsteps moved down the hall and away.

Every action, word, image illustrates on both literal and figurative levels the relationship that Ted continued to find problematic and painful even as he wrote about it.

The Joys of Excess

To conclude this chapter, let's examine some exceptions to the conventional advice concerning clarity and brevity. When you're writing to play with language, for the sake of the sound as much as the literal meaning, you should feel free to take risks. If you want your readers to look at your writing with awe and wonderment, you can ride a galloping syntax across the page with a flamboyant flourish, spurring on those metaphors for all they're worth. But ride goeth before fall; you may want to try a few practice turns in front of the mirror before going out in public in full rodeo regalia. Above all, writing should be fun for you to experiment with. But, as with trick riding, writing is harder to do than it looks; you can learn to do it only through trial and error and it's potentially dangerous because if you fall, you fall hard. But once you get the hang of it you can make it look easy and your readers will admire your bravery as well as your bravura.

William H. Gass makes an exception to conventional advice about brevity in a twenty-five-page essay on the word *and*. Gass, who writes dazzlingly on everything, has this—among a lot of other things—to say about that lowly word, humble but necessary.

> The anonymity of "and," its very invisibility, recommends the word to the student of language, for when we really look at it, study it, listen to it, "and" no longer appears to be "and" at all, because "and" is, as we said, invisible, one of the threads that holds our clothes together: what business has it being a pants leg or the frilly panel of a blouse? The unwatched word is meaningless—a noise in the nose—it falls on the page as it pleases, while the writer is worrying about nouns and verbs, welfare checks or a love affair; whereas the watched word has many meanings, some of them profound; it has a wide range of functions, some of them essential; it has many lessons to teach us about language, some of them surprising; and it has metaphysical significance of an even salutary sort.

Here Gass writes two long sentences of 68 and 78 words. A minimalist paraphrase might read, "'And' is an anonymous, nearly invisible connective word, but when we look closely at "and" (or any other seemingly insignificant word), it becomes deeply rich in meanings and functions." This paraphrase takes 29 words instead of 126. The condensation misses the elasticity of language, the yo-yo-like play that sends the thought flying out into space and then snaps it back; the repetition ("look at it, study it, listen to it"); the metaphor ("one of the threads"); the first sentence that starts out as a series of assertions but ends as a rhetorical question, which must be read metaphorically because literally it doesn't make any sense ("what business has it being a pants leg or the frilly panel of a blouse?"); the rhythm and alliteration ("a noise in the nose," "on the page as it pleases," "the writer is worrying"); the punning repetition of syllables ("wel*fare* checks or a love af*fair*"); and the balance and antithesis ("The unwatched word is meaningless. . . whereas the watched word has many meanings"). These are just for starters. If you read this kind of writing in a rush, you will need to reread it at leisure.

A different but equally outrageous vein is Samuel Pickering's eulogy on the death of his father in "Let It Ride." Part of a typical paragraph halfway through the essay reads:

> Vicki and the children went to Tennessee with me for the funeral, and in order to catch a seven o'clock flight from Hartford, we got up at four-thirty the next morning. Father was on the same flight and was waiting for us on a baggage truck beside the plane. He was in a light gray box, and if I had not known better, I might have thought him a batch of gladiolas or long-stemmed roses. At two hundred and fifty-two dollars, his ticket cost less than ours. But then, his was not a round-trip. Neither did he get orange juice or read *USAir Magazine*. . . .

Here Pickering, like many humorists, violates his readers' conventional expectations of somberness, sentimentality, filial piety, and respect for the dead. Instead, readers get jokes, delivered deadpan so that they can't quite be sure whether the writer means what he says. Why isn't Pickering decorating his father's box with flowers, instead of imagining his father as "a batch of gladiolas or long-stemmed roses"? How can he be concerned with the price of an airline ticket at a time when he should be overcome with grief? How can he joke about the corpse not being able to perform the functions of the living, such as drinking orange juice or reading *USAir Magazine*?

The success or failure of writing such as Pickering's depends on the writer's tone and the reader's trust. If we are to believe that the author is not at worst an ungrateful son or at best a foolish boor, then we have to trust his benign motives toward both his pater and his matter. Throughout the first half of the essay Pickering had established the character of his relationship to his aged parent: he had been planning to build a room onto the house to accommodate his critically ill father; he and his family visit his father almost daily in a nearby nursing home; he shared with his father a lifetime of love and admiration: "When I said I loved him, saying he had always made me proud and happy, he said simply, 'No more accolades.' For the children he had one piece of advice. 'Tell them,' he said, 'to be on the facetious side,'" a trait Pickering amply demonstrates.

Because writing like Gass's and Pickering's is so conspicuous and mannered, it is not intended for readers in a hurry, readers who value efficiency over style, or readers who are looking primarily for information. It is included here, in this conspicuous spot, the end of the chapter on style, to encourage you to experiment, to play, to grow comfortable with, and to love this elusive quality called "style."

Checklist for Style

1. What is my approach to the subject? theoretical and abstract? concrete and specific? or some mixture? Do the conventions of the context or discourse community for which my writing is intended (a school newspaper, a business memo, a college course, a literary magazine, or other) determine the style? the format? the degree of specificity or generality? the number and nature of examples? the amount of interpretation?

2. What kind of authorial persona am I presenting? Do I consciously play or create a role (expert, advocate, humorist, or other)? through what means? Have any other characteristics of an authorial persona crept in unintentionally that might indicate an author uncontrolled, incompetent, rambling, self-centered, or insensitive to the audience? How can I avoid letting these characteristics influence my writing?

3. What is my prevailing tone and voice? Is each consistent? Should they be? If they vary what is the purpose of the variations and how have I accomplished them?

4. What level(s) of language have I used throughout this writing? formal? middle-level? informal? or some combination? Does this level suit my subject and perspective especially well? Does it suit me as a writer? Will my readers understand my words? If not, do I define unfamiliar words or illustrate them in context? Should I?

5. Have I obtained the particular level(s) of language largely through voice, tone, vocabulary, sentence and paragraph structure, and length? or through some combination of these? Do these elements reinforce each other?

6. Do I intend this writing to be concise or more ample? How much development of points and amount of detail should I include to make the subject clear and convincing to my readers?

7. If asked, could I give a good reason for my use of any word, phrase, il-

lustration, or sentence structure in the whole essay? (By the way, "It sounds better that way" is a very good reason.) Do I like what I've written? If the answer is "No," what am I willing to do to make the writing more acceptable to me?

8. Am I using much figurative language? If so, why? to clarify or explain? to make the writing interesting? because I enjoy playing with the language and want my readers to share in the fun? Is my figurative language related to the subject in a reasonable, natural way? Does it enhance what I'm saying? Have I avoided clichés, mixed metaphors, and excessive embellishment?

9. Have I tried this writing out on a critic/reader and taken that person's reactions and advice under consideration (even if I reject them)?

Note

[1]Susan Peck MacDonald, in "The Literary Argument and Its Discursive Conventions," is very critical of the fact that the writing of "vanguard literary critics [i.e., critics at elitist universities, who write primarily for one another] contravenes the best advice about readability and coherence." This writing is extremely difficult for outsiders, even other English professors, to understand because of its extremely long and convoluted sentences characterized by elaboration (some are 200 words); many nouns (instead of verbs); lots of self-conscious commentary about what the writer is doing; and many esoteric, nonstandard terms used in vague ways. MacDonald concludes that this professional prose is so specialized that it excludes too many readers, novices and professionals; its readership is confined to "too small a circle of insiders." English teachers, she says, have a professional and ethical obligation to write clearly so their audience can be *inclusive,* rather than *exclusive* (38–59).

Selected Reference List on Style

CBE Style Manual: A Guide for Authors, Editors, and Publishers in the Biological Sciences. 6th ed. Chicago: Council of Biology Editors Style Manual Committee, 1992.

Chicago Manual of Style. 13th ed. Chicago: U of Chicago P, 1982.

Gibaldi, Joseph, and Walter S. Achtert. *MLA Handbook for Writers of Research Papers.* 3rd ed. New York: Modern Language Association, 1988.

Lanham, Richard A. *Analyzing Prose.* New York: Scribner's, 1983.

———. *Style: An Anti-Textbook.* New Haven: Yale UP, 1974.

———. *Revising Prose.* 3rd ed. New York: Macmillan, 1992.

Murray, Donald M. *Shoptalk: Learning to Write with Writers.* Portsmouth, NH: Heinemann, 1990.

Publication Manual of the American Psychological Association. 3rd ed. Washington, DC: American Psychological Association, 1983.

Strunk, William, Jr., and E. B. White. *The Elements of Style.* 3rd ed. New York: Macmillan, 1979.

Williams, Joseph M. *Style: Toward Clarity and Grace.* Chicago: Scott, 1990.
Zinsser, William. *On Writing Well.* 4th ed. New York: Harper, 1990.

Works Cited

Bartholomae, David. "Inventing the University." *When a Writer Can't Write.* Ed. Mike Rose. New York: Guilford, 1985. 134–65.

Broyard, Anatole. "Being There." *The Bread Loaf Anthology of Contemporary American Essays.* Ed. Robert Pack and Jay Parini. Hanover, NH: UP of New England. 52–58.

Corbett, Edward P. J. *Classical Rhetoric for the Modern Student.* 3rd ed. New York: Oxford UP, 1989.

Flynn, Elizabeth and Patrocinio B. Schweickart, eds. Gender and Reading: Essays on Readers, Texts, and Contexts. Baltimore: Hopkins UP, 1986.

Gass, William H. "'And.'" *Habitations of the Word: Essays.* New York: Simon, 1985. 160–84.

Klass, Perri. *A Not Entirely Benign Procedure: Four Years as a Medical Student.* 1987. New York: Signet, 1988.

Kozol, Jonathan. "The Human Cost of an Illiterate Society." *Illiterate America.* Garden City, NY: Doubleday, 1985.

MacDonald, Susan Peck. "The Literary Argument and Its Discursive Conventions." *The Writing Scholar: Studies in Academic Discourse.* Ed. Walter Nash. *Written Communication Annual* 3 (1990): 31–62.

Mairs, Nancy. "On Being a Cripple." *Plaintext: Deciphering a Woman's Life.* Tucson: U of Arizona P, 1986. 9–20.

Miller, Casey, and Kate Swift. *The Handbook of Nonsexist Writing.* 1980. New York: Barnes and Noble, 1981.

Orwell, George. "Marrakech." *An Age Like This 1920–1940.* New York: Harcourt, 1968. 187–93. Vol. 1 of *The Collected Essays, Journalism and Letters of George Orwell.* Ed. Sonia Orwell and Ian Angus. 4 vols.

Osborne, June. "Women and HIV/AIDS: The Silent Epidemic?" SIECUS Report 19.2 (Dec. 90/ Jan. 91): 1–4.

Paglia, Camille. *Sexual Personae: Act and Decadence from Nefertiti to Emily Dickinson.* 1990. New York: Vintage, 1991.

Pickering, Samuel F. "Let It Ride." *Let It Ride.* Columbia, MO: U of Missouri P, 1991. 85–96.

Russ, Susan E. "A Bureaucrat's Guide to Chocolate Chip Cookies." *Washington Post* 4 Mar. 1982: C4.

Safire, William. "The Take on Voice." *New York Times Magazine* 5 July 1992: 14.

Sagan, Carl. *The Dragons of Eden: Speculations on the Evolution of Human Intelligence.* New York: Random, 1977.

Sontag, Deborah. "Clemency Given Jean Harris Leaves 3 Others Wondering." *New York Times* 1 Jan. 1993: A1, B4.

Spender, Dale. *The Writing or the Sex?* New York: Pergamon, 1989.

3

RE-VISION AND REVISION

I can't write five words but that I change seven.

—Dorothy Parker

Rewriting is when writing really gets to be fun. . . . In baseball you only get three swings and you're out. In rewriting, you get almost as many swings as you want and you know, sooner or later, you'll hit the ball.

—Neil Simon

The best part of all, the absolutely most delicious part, is finishing it and then doing it over. . . . I rewrite a lot, over and over again, so that it looks like I never did. I try to make it look like I never touched it, and that takes a lot of time and a lot of sweat.

—Toni Morrison

If it ain't broke, don't fix it.

—Ubiquitous

Re-vision

The hyphen in *re-vision* is intentional. *Re-vision* and *revision* both mean, literally, *to see again.* In a writing context, *re-vision* means coming to know yourself or some major aspect of your subject or your world differently than you used to—in a way that will give you a new vision to use in your writing.

In some cases this new understanding comes quickly, through an immediately available, external stimulus or activity: you're trying to answer a recurring question or solve an ongoing problem; you read an article or a book or simply sleep on the puzzle, and before you know it, voilà! A perfect solution comes to mind. Or, a friend asks, "What do you mean by that? What are you trying to say?" and the central idea crystallizes. Or, as Samuel Johnson observed of an impending hanging, the necessity of meeting a deadline "wonderfully focuses the mind."

In other cases, understanding comes slowly. You may write around a subject for awhile, as student Mary Ruffin does (page 56) in response to the general assignment to "write about people." Ruffin freewrites: "The page is glaring . . . ominous. . . . The poetry won't come. . . . The prose won't come. . . ." Time passes. "There must be a starting point somewhere, a thread to grasp." Finally she writes the crucial, resonant word "*Mama.*"

Sometimes you have to mature in order to understand your subject clearly enough to write about it. Ruffin's one word, *Mama,* looks like a starting point on paper and is in fact the first of ten drafts written over a period of two months. That word actually signals Ruffin's ability, at age twenty, to come to terms with her mother's death from lung cancer seven years earlier. During that time, she'd been trying to interpret the meaning of her mother's life and death and to write about it. But not until she felt peace within herself could she begin to address the subject; *Mama* was the first word of Ruffin's newfound maturity, her rebirth.

Sometimes the context—social, political, aesthetic, or other—has to change to make re-vision possible. The women's movement, the civil rights movement, a new aesthetic in poetry, and a new critical appreciation of feminist and minority writers coalesced in the 1970s and 1980s to enable numerous writers, such as Maxine Hong Kingston (page 103) and Richard Rodriguez, to find their identities and consequently their individual voices. In "When We Dead Awaken: Writing as Re-Vision," Adrienne Rich—looking anew at her life and her work—explains her own metamorphosis (page 281). Ning Yu needed a new country with an open political and intellectual climate to give him the voice and the language to utter his re-vision of Communist China. Only after he had been in the United States for five years did he gain the distance, literal and metaphorical, to be able to write "Red and Black, or One English Major's Beginning" (pages 312–19).

You can't rush these slowly evolving re-visions, but you know them when you experience them in, as Yeats says, "the deep heart's core." These are the truths that make you free; these are the cause of great joy. These re-visions also lead to multiple drafts of revised texts, some of which we will look at here.

What Revision Is—and Isn't

After re-vision has given you new insight, revision allows you to look again at the actual text of your writing. When you revise, you dare to make changes, some dramatic, some more subtle. In fact, an easy way to think of these changes is to use the acronym DARE:

Delete
Add
Reorganize
Edit

These operations are the means by which you can change focus, structure, emphasis, organization, development, and style to bring the written work closer to your ideal. You can dare to use these operations to change any unit of your writing: whole papers or book chapters, major sections of long papers, paragraphs, sentences, or individual words or phrases. If, for instance, you rethink your subject and change your mind about some major points, you can change your thesis and your supporting arguments. It helps to think of revising as macro-level changes—adding, deleting, reorganizing whole sentences, paragraphs, sections, even chapters of a book-length work. You may make such revisions at any time when you're writing, even while you're in the process of developing an essay or longer work.

Editing may involve some of the same changes—addition, deletion, or reorganization—but on a micro-level, focusing on individual words, sentences or parts of sentences, and punctuation (see Checklist in Chapter 11). It's more efficient to save these changes until you've finished the entire work, before you hand it in to a teacher or an editor. That way you won't waste your time fretting over word choice or sentence structure of material that will be deleted in a later version.

Taking a second, or third, or fourth look at your manuscript can help you see your work as a reader or an editor might. These new views can bring your sight and insight closer to 20/20 vision, dispelling the myopia that often plagues writers who have just finished a first draft and are too close to see it clearly. As John Ciardi says, writing "is a schizophrenic process. To begin passionately and end critically, to begin hot and to end cold; and, more important, to try to be passion-hot and critic-cold at the same time" aptly describes the ideal relation of writing to revising.

Occasionally professional writers, who know better, try to perpetuate the myth that they never revise, that "the best words in the best order" simply flow spontaneously from their brains to perfect response on the waiting page. This sets these divinely inspired Effortless Writers apart from mere mortals who labor hard even over a note to the newspaper deliverer, let alone over a letter to the editor. The image of an Effortless Writer is a pose, calculated to impress interviewers or a television audience, but an inaccurate representation of the way most thoughtful writers work, whether students or professionals.

Most early drafts can benefit from revising, whether they were produced easily or with difficulty. Newspaper columnist Ellen Goodman's process of revising works well for most nonfiction. She starts with an overall draft: "In the first draft you get your ideas and your theme clear, if you are using some kind of metaphor you get that established, and certainly you have to know where you're coming out." Then, like many professional writers, she refines the earlier version(s): "But the next time through it's like cleaning house, getting rid of all the junk, getting things in the right order, tightening things up. I like the process of making writing neat." Other writers work differently and build the final work by refining smaller units until they can integrate them in a larger whole. William Gass's elaborate sentences (page 46) are the result of extensive rewriting: "Each sentence has many drafts. Eventually there is a paragraph. This gets many drafts. Eventually there is a page. This gets many drafts."

How many drafts are necessary? The ideal would be to write as many as you need to make the final work the way you want, whether it's one or two or twenty. Hemingway says he rewrote the last page of *A Farewell to Arms* 39 times, "just getting the words right." Roald Dahl says that he revises his stories "at least 150 times" and that "good writing is essentially rewriting." This meticulous concern for what appears on the page distinguishes professional writers from novices, often students whose main concern is to get the paper out of the computer, off to the teacher, and out of their hair. Many beginning students see revising as "cleaning up the paper and crossing out," eliminating repeated words and finding substitute vocabulary. A good paper, to such students, is one that comes from a fairly clean first draft requiring at most simple changes in wording, spelling, or mechanics—editing changes—but not a thorough rewriting.

Advanced writers, such as more experienced students and people whose jobs entail considerable writing or editing, usually fall somewhere between the extremes of meticulous rewriters and casual editors. By now you're probably sophisticated enough as a writer to realize that editing is a relatively minor aspect of revising. Don't forget, however, that accurate spelling and mechanics are necessary to convince readers of your competence. (Just try writting, without paying attension to these nicetys and see what kind of an impresshun, you make.) Busy people with many responsibilities don't have the time to revise drafts 150 times, let alone 20, and in most instances the stakes aren't high enough to demand such perfection.

With most writing, however, even an informal memo, you will want to make the most of your message in the time you have to spend on it. Although it's usually safe to say, "Never be content with a first draft," there is no arbitrary number of revisions that can guarantee good writing. Maybe your school or work schedule allows you enough time for only one or two rewrites of the whole piece, or of selected portions. Even if you have more time, you'll eventually reach the point at which you lose perspective and make changes that are too minuscule to justify the time you spend staring at the screen, or paper. Or, worse, your tinkering doesn't seem to make any difference or it appears to make the writing worse instead of better. That's the time to stop. This chapter is designed to help you make your revising specific, effective, and manageable.

Revision and Your Writing Process

Revision is central to the writing process. That's why this chapter is near the beginning of this book rather than at the end. This placement reinforces the fact that revision doesn't always occur at the end of the writing process; you can revise continually as you compose to make what comes out on paper more closely match what's in your head.

Whether you do most of your composition in your mind, on paper, or on a computer screen, a lot of your thinking—and consequently, unobtrusive revising—goes on away from your desk, while you perform activities—running, swimming, cooking—seemingly unrelated to writing. As you mull over the subject, you're making many changes that go unrecorded until you finally write them down. Perhaps you've had the experience, common to many computer users, of writing something—a paragraph perhaps, several pages, or maybe an entire essay—and then losing it. No backup disk, no hard copy, only whatever you can remember. The sheer terror of it is enough to make you yearn for the days of quill and inkwell. After you calm down, you have no choice but to rewrite your work from memory. So you do. Then, sometime later, you find a copy of the earlier draft. You compare the two and, no surprise, the revision is better. It always is. Test the truth of this, if you wish, by rewriting a draft without looking at the preceding drafts; the act of remembering seems to penetrate to the core of your subject and help it emerge, sharper and clearer than before.

Between drafts, too, the work simmers on the back burner of your brain, and when you go back to it you're ready to make changes. The nature of these changes depends on what the preceding draft was like and the problems it raised. If you use a first draft to generate ideas, in revising you will want to prune and shape to achieve a precise subject and focus, and an organization that reinforces your emphasis. If your customary first draft is just a sketch of the basic ideas, little more than an outline in paragraph form, in revising you'd aim to elaborate on the essential points, supplying illustrations or consulting references that you didn't want to look up the first time around. On the other hand, you may typically write a great deal more than you need in your first draft just to be sure of capturing any ideas that may prove useful. Your revision would need to delete irrelevant ideas and redundant illustrations. Save the leftovers, however, perhaps in a writer's notebook, for possible recycling in other writing. If you have worked out the entire paper mentally, your first written version may be your satisfying last draft, except for editorial attention to spelling, mechanics, and some minor word changes.

The Evolution of "Mama's Smoke"

Before we examine revising that concentrates on specific issues, let's look at the genesis and evolution of one piece of writing from start to finish, Mary Ruffin's paper on her mother, an artist and aspiring writer. Ruffin was enrolled in a poetry class during her senior year, in the same semester that she took advanced composition. She wrote ten versions of her paper, using different modes of writing—poetry, free association, and prose—in the process of discovering the version that best suited her and her subject. Each of the first nine versions that preceded the tenth and final prose version is a revision, a new way in which Ruffin looked at her mother and at her own life. Each subsequent prose draft either expands or revises the earlier prose drafts and incorporates elements of the intervening poetic versions—key words, images, concepts, and bits of the mosaic that ultimately form a picture of Ruffin's relationship with her mother. In the tenth and final prose version, the language and concepts of all but one version, an unfruitful diversion, emerge in a controlled, refined, tightly integrated, and memorable picture.

Version One: 2/23 Freewriting in a Writer's Notebook

The prose won't come because it can't break out of the stillborn poetry. The academics won't come because they're forced into the name-dropping realm of pretension. . . . Plus, I hate traditional white male southern writers. With those accents that sound like my mother but aren't my mother at all. . . . There must be a starting point somewhere—a thread to grasp. Can't do it all. Must at least reach out to the part that reaches back.

Mama.

After writing around for awhile, commenting on the act and difficulty of writing and not writing, Ruffin could finally allow herself to get close enough finally to touch *Mama*. When she could put this word, with its lifetime of meaning, on paper, she could stop. She had just taken the biggest risk of her writing life, and she knew that she now would have to deal with the most compelling and most difficult subject of her life.

Version Two: 2/24 First Poetic Draft, No Title

Mama had fierce green eyes and black hair
I know from the black and white pictures
forty years old and more
and the salt and pepper I remember
and the tired hazel that I inherited
for she could have been my grandma.

Jet black hair so thick the sheen
Matched the fierceness of green eyes
That were my Mama I know cause I've
heard tell and seen the faded black and
white pictures stuffed in the cookie tin
she had for twenty some odd years
and I've kept for ten and the memory
of the permed salt and pepper I played
in dangling my feet in mid air hung
over the chair back and the tired
hazel nestled in the hooded lids,
I inherited her eyes but without
the green snap.

Once Ruffin decided on her subject, "mama," she started playing with what would become key words in her imagery in both the poetic and prose versions. This imagery contained what would become key concepts in her depiction of the relation between mother and daughter: *fierce green eyes, black hair, salt and pepper, faded black and white pictures, cookie tin, tired hazel* [eyes], *inherited.*

However you do it, it can be useful to extract key words—nuggets of gold—from the draft you're working on. You can highlight the words in the original text or break them out in lists, an outline, or a free-form poem to see what you're really talking about. Seeing the words in a more skeletal form makes it easy to rearrange them until their order, and hence their logic, makes sense.

Version Three: 2/25 Second Poetic Draft, "Rites"

Back when it was *cool* to *smoke*, she did, and was
I imagine, of course not able to remember,
the picture of *glamorousness.* It was
In the days before that surgeon general

Determined the *hazardousness*
That is now as immediate as
"*Once Upon a Time*," possessing the familiarity
Of that with which
we were reared.
An *ivory holder* I've heard tell
and seen the *legendary*
flash of her fierce green eyes
yellowing and wrinkled in the *cookie tin* of black and
white *snapshots* she hung onto for
twenty-some odd years, and I now
for ten.
The lid is difficult to pry open.
The spark miraculously passed on,
barely discernable in my hazel
mediated by chromosomes and the *bloodshot*
of *Menthol Virginia Slim Ultra Lights*
itches *incessant*.

In version three, Ruffin gives the poem a title, *Rites,* and provides a focus that her first poetic draft did not even allude to, her mother's smoking, which dominates this version. The words *glamorousness, spark,* and *miraculously passed on* unite smoking and the *flash* in the mother's *fierce green eyes* that is *barely discernable* in her daughter's *hazel* [eyes]. Ruffin acknowledges her own smoking and in the ritual of lighting up signals the relationship with her mother, *the spark* in her eyes and in the cigarette, *miraculously passed on.*

This poem gives her some concepts and language to use in the first prose version. Having waited so many years to write about her mother, the urge to explore as many alternative ways as possible of retrieving her lost parent was overwhelming. Taking concurrent courses in poetry writing and advanced composition gave Ruffin the opportunity she needed.

Version Four: 2/27 First Prose Draft, First Installment, no Title

She was a smoker, but that began in the days when it was cool to smoke. Long before that surgeon general determined the hazardousness of the habit, and the behaviorists blasted it as an infantile fixation, she was glamorous. It was unfiltered Camels in the beginning, though by the time I was around she had gone to Merits, clunky with thick filters wrapped in blotchy brown.

My mother was an artist. She used to paint, in a turquoise studio smock, portraits of everyone she knew. Though I don't remember her ever painting herself—that is except for the red polish on her toenails. Her fingernails stayed natural yellow, she said because of the turpentine, but I think nicotine contributed to the hue. I've heard that when she was young she was never without her ivory cigarette holder. She readily admitted to her vanity.

In this two-paragraph prose version, Ruffin reiterates the glamorousness of her mother's smoking but immediately contradicts it with the new and distinctly unglamorous image of "Merits, clunky with thick filters wrapped in blotchy brown." In the second paragraph, Ruffin adds more new material, about her mother as an artist—the *natural yellow* of her fingernails is the result of *turpentine* and *nicotine*—and she interprets the *ivory holder* as a symbol of vanity.

Version Four: 2/27 First Prose Draft, Second Installment, no Title

This version is an excerpt of one written the same day as the preceding one, after an interruption.

> She comes to me in the middle of the night, or rather I come to her, chase her even, through strange landscapes and insidescapes. Sometimes she is an old crone, witch-like, her black hair full of salt and her green eyes bloodshot knife-slits. . . .

The mother-daughter relationship gets more complicated with the addition of the middle-of-the-night visitations and the inclusion of the *black hair full of salt* and *green eyes* from the two poetry versions.

Version Five: 3/3 Second Prose Draft, no Title

> She can surface without warning, anytime, anyplace. Sometimes she comes and goes so quickly that I hardly notice her presence. The other day, for instance, I stood in the kitchen staring at the can of Crisco and a tattered, encrusted cookbook page. Spoon in hand, I wondered blankly for a moment how to measure solid shortening. When the idea of displacement struck me and I filled the cup half full with water, I thought it was the ghost of a physics text. By the time I realized that it had been her, she was long gone and I had to shake my head. That's the way it happens frequently.
>
> She never answers to her name—she almost seems to run away when she comes to mind. She is called Peggy, the only nickname for Margaret she ever could tolerate. She told me once that was why I had such a simple name, something virtually unalterable, to have forever. I resemble Peggy slightly, but just like the futility of calling her, when I look for the resemblance in the mirror it isn't there—It's those other times, catching an unexpected glimpse of my reflection out of the corner of my eye.

Ruffin begins this new material where the previous version left off, with the notion of her ghostly mother surfacing, related to the concept of displacement, literally in connection with cooking and metaphorically in connection with her mother's appearance and disappearance. From here Ruffin segues into names—*Peggy, Margaret,* and her own *simple name*—further resemblances captured fleetingly.

Ruffin's poetry teacher had seen the second poetic draft, "Rites," and suggested that Ruffin play around with the connections between medieval dragons emitting smoke and her mother's smoking. She tried and produced version six.

Version Six: 3/10 Free Association, "Dragons"

Cookie tin—shining armor—rusty knight
Desert—fire—camels—dragons
Green dragons
Slain dragons & fair maidens
Dark fair maidens—unfair damsels
Once upon a time hazardousness—dragon
Dragon—take a "drag on" a cigarette
Smoke—cool smoke—hot smoke—smoke breath
Dragon's lair—womb—cave
cookies & stories—yellowing green
eyes & hazel bloodshot
Grendel's mother
Damsel in distress
Legend—spark of the divine
Glamorousness—amorousness—clamorousness
Reptiles—evolution—snake—fake—fang
Red nails—red lips—glamour is dark—beauty light
Medieval—Middle Ages—
Middle age—
The Tale—the monomyth—hero's journey
Separation—Initiation—Return
Smoke—illusion
Birthrite—legacy—heir—air—smoke
Glamour as aloof passion—cool hotness—
artifice—surface image—imagination—
hard—glamour=armor—defense mechanism
Smoking as oral fixation
Smoking as magic
Fairy tales—scales—fear in fairy tails—wicked
stepmother—poison

Although Ruffin retains some of the imagery of the earlier poetry and prose versions, the medieval orientation leads her to summon a host of clichés— *fair maidens, Dragon's lair, Grendel's mother, Damsel in distress, wicked stepmother,* and others—that simply don't fit in with the other versions. Ruffin wisely abandoned this attempt, deleting the entire version from subsequent revisions. If a teacher's or another commentator's advice leads you down dead ends or gets you off the track, ignore it and trust your own instincts.

Version Seven: 3/17 Third Poetic Draft, Excerpt from "Rites"

Back when it was cool to smoke, she did, and was
I imagine, of course not able to remember, the picture
of glamorousness. It was in the days before the surgeon
general determined the dreadful gnawing
hazardousness that is now as immediate as
once-upon-a-time, possessing the familiarity
of that with which we were reared. . . .

This is tidier than version three, even with the addition of "*dreadful gnawing* hazardousness. . . ."

Version Eight: 3/28 Final Poetic Version, "Once Upon a Time"

Back when it was cool to smoke, she did, and was
I imagine, of course not able to remember, the picture
of glamorousness.
Chains of unfiltered Camels, never without the ivory
holder between blood-red nails, I've heard tell
and seen the legendary flash of her fierce green
eyes yellowing and wrinkled in the rusted
cookie tin filled to brimming with brittle
undated black and white snapshots she hung onto
for twenty-odd years, and I still keep.

It is difficult to pry open the lid.

Once I caught her in the mirror, her tears
a simple bewilderment to me then,
turning more complex. Now
I catch her only on the edges
of my own reflection. Her spark in my hazel,
barely discernable, bloodshot
itches, runs, waters, burns
incessant.

Ruffin makes some conspicuous improvements. One is to delete the
overwritten second sentence, "It was in the days before the surgeon general. . . ." Another is reorganize two sentences to put a short, emphatic
word at the end of each. The second half of version three's "Snapshots she
hung onto for twenty-some-odd years, and I now for ten" becomes "and I
still keep" in version eight. The most memorable sentence of version eight is
the single freestanding line in the middle, "It is difficult to pry open the lid"
(changed from version three's "The lid is difficult to pry open"). Listen to
this and you will hear why. The meter is now more regular and the stronger
words (*difficult, lid*) have more emphasis at the beginning and end. The third

improvement is to add the image of mother's mirrored reflection, refracted now "only on the edges" of Ruffin's "own reflection."

Some problems remain. Ruffin commented in her writer's notebook that she was "never happy" with this poem. She said she found the poem's first draft "far better than the final draft . . . because the VOICE IS REAL! I killed it." She's right. The fairy-tale title, of version eight, "Once Upon a Time," has irrelevant, inappropriate connotations as does much of the free association list in version six. The last sentence is overdone: barely discernable, bloodshot/itches, runs, waters, burns/incessant." The emotional excess may be a signal that Ruffin still can't control her feelings in a way that satisfies either herself or the reader. She needs to make more deletions but can't do so.

Version Nine: 4/2 Third Prose Draft, "Mama's Smoke"

"Not 'plain'! Pure and ageless, incorruptible! That's what your name is. I always hated mine with a passion! When people called me 'Margaret' I felt squeamish. And 'Maggie'—ugh—a literal punch in the stomach! But it's awkward to go through life with a nickname. It makes you feel always like you're not quite ever really yourself. I didn't want that for you."

Peggy wanted only the best for me, the best being an abstraction she pondered incessantly. When I was little, I would sit on the ancient wobbly wooden stool in the corner of the kitchen, rocking and squeaking, listening to her. I liked that spot because it was right over the heat duct in the winter, and caught the breeze from the screen door in the utility room in the summer. Evenings, I asked her all kinds of questions—never afraid to broach any subject—and her answers usually took off miraculously, soaring.

Sometimes I just listened to the rhythm of her plastic-soled slippers. . . .

This eighteen-paragraph draft expands the five-paragraph total of the preceding two prose drafts (versions four and five) and also incorporates a number of key words from the poems.

Version Ten: 4/28 Final Prose Version, "Mama's Smoke"

I never thought I would smoke. With her it was different—she started way 1
back when it was cool to smoke—had been the very picture of glamour. But that was before the surgeon general determined the hazardousness that is as immediate in the origins of my consciousness as once-upon-a-time.

Myths are absorbing. I've been told of the chains of unfiltered Camels she 2
used to smoke, never without the legendary ivory holder between fingers with blood-red nails. By the time I was around she had switched to Merits.

Peggy thrived on craving. She wanted only the best for me, the best being 3
an abstraction she pondered incessantly. When I was little I would sit on the ancient wobbly wooden stool in the corner of the kitchen, rocking and squeaking, listening to her. I liked that spot because it was right over the heat duct in

the winter, and caught the breeze through the screen door in the utility room in the summer. Evenings, I asked her all kinds of questions—never afraid to broach any subject—and her answers usually took off miraculously, soaring.

"Not 'plain'! Pure and ageless, incorruptible! That's what your name is. 4 That's why I gave it to you. I always hated mine with a passion! When people called me 'Margaret' I felt squeamish. And 'Maggie'—ugh—a literal punch in the stomach! But it's awkward to go through life with a nickname. It makes you feel always like you're not quite ever really yourself. I didn't want that for you."

If I didn't understand the songs she sang, I knew the syllables by heart. 5 Sometimes I would just listen to the rhythm of her plastic-soled slippers. I creaked my stool in time as her slippers slid on the red and white tiles, moving from one end of the long counter to the other and back, to the sink, ice box, sink again, stove, counter. There was a regularity to the irregularity that soothed me.

As I draw deeply on my menthol Virginia Slims Light, looking through the 6 yellowing black and white snapshots in the rusty old cookie tin she held onto for twenty-some-odd years, I wonder what happened to make me start smoking. The lid is difficult to open. Inside there are faces, one face altered over and over, with fierce green eyes flashing, despite the brittle fadedness of the images. My hazel eyes have the spark, but only enough of a spark to torment me, to always make me seem not quite all me. Peggy stays away when I look at the pictures of her—maybe she doesn't identify with them anymore herself. She certainly used to.

But she also used to answer me when I called, and she no longer does that 7 either. Often deep in my sleep I glimpse her and chase her through strange insidescapes, but she always refuses to recognize me. Once recently she consented to meet me in an abandoned ice rink. When I skated in late, she simply stared down my apologies. Suddenly busying herself with an old movie projector, her back to me, she became a flailing chaos of limbs in the darkness of the rink. I gave in to the oppression of futility and seated myself behind her. At first the picture jumped and lurched on the screen, out of focus, broke once, and then smoothed out. Peggy danced a vaudeville set in our old kitchen, twirling whisks and spatulas to the soundtrack of "Clementine." When the lights came on she had disappeared, and I was alone shivering, with the distorted tune ringing in my ears.

Usually she surfaces so briefly and unobtrusively that I'm not sure she has 8 been there until after she's gone. Sometimes she appears an old haggard crone, the salt in her hair so thick that the pepper looks like dirt streaks washing away. Other times she is vital, younger than I am, the sheen of her black hair almost blinding. In the buttered daylight of my kitchen, as I stand blankly staring at the can of Crisco and the Pyrex measuring cup, I guess it is the sudden memory of a physics lesson that makes me think of using water to measure the solid substance. Displacement. Only later, as I gently knead the biscuit dough, careful not to bruise it, I realize that she has been there. Her smirk of disgust at the soybean powder in the open cabinet gave her away—she couldn't resist a mild "eee-gad" under her breath.

Peggy is steeped in colloquialism, figures of speech that barely escape the   9
shallows of cliché. She wrote a novel once, some kind of sequel to *Gone With
The Wind* and now she comes to me at the typewriter sometimes, though rarely
at the notebook stage, and whispers more criticism than commentary. She
burned it, burned it in a fit of rage. Justified, for they wouldn't make her known.
One attempt, one refusal. The only grace is to make a clean break.

She is something like a sequel to herself, elliptical and confusing, out of con-   10
text. She speaks in fragments, interrupting in the middle of my own sentences,
giving to others the illusion that I have spoken her words. But that's not exactly accurate either. The others don't know her, don't know her words from
mine. The illusion is mine.

The hiss of the word "fixatif" on a spray can evokes a frustrated whimper   11
of reminiscence. The bite of turpentine and linseed oil draws her. She is a painter
of portraits and has rendered a likeness of almost everyone she is close to at
one time or another, I believe, with the exception of herself. When I pick up a
piece of charcoal she jumps in and jerks my hand, refusing to let me catch an
image clearly. I have forsaken our art and she will not let me be forgiven so
easily. But when I settle back and contemplate my own regrets, she relents. I
feel her take her dry brush in hand and trace my features, a delicious tickle I
revered as a child.

The legacy of paint stains on her pale turquoise smock, like the rhythm of   12
the shuffle of her slippers on the floor, is her highest art. She denies it, of course,
as obstinately as she refuses to appear when I look for her in the mirror. But
she proves it as she shows up at those moments when I catch my reflection un-
expectedly out of the corner of my eye.

The conversations we have now in black coffee cups and clouds of smoke   13
are the closest we come to shared sustenance. They are always late, the times
when it's most conspicuous to be awake. We plan the colors for the drapes and
throw pillows to furnish some future studio. The studio gradually takes shape,
perfect, and then shatters in a coughing fit. I hear her in another room, hack-
ing, fading, and then she's gone.

Just as she never stays, she never stays away for long. She was beautiful in   14
her day and she still preens, still believes underneath in the ultimate importance
of surfaces.

At parties, her old acquaintances appear as her friends. They ask me if I'm   15
in the art school and the flinching negative reply is overridden by their awe at
my study of "philosophy."

"So like her! Right down to the hair and eyes, though not quite so dark, not   16
quite so green. But underneath, Peggy *was* a philosopher, she was, so wise. . . ."

And Peggy surfaces and "eee-gads" so loudly in my ear that the friends' po-   17
litenesses go under and my own return politenesses are just-not-quite-right. I
sip my wine and kick Peggy in the shin. The acquaintances wander off whis-
pering, "Almost the spitting image, except not nearly so . . . *genuine*. . . . This
new generation. . . ."

Later, Peggy and I have pillow fights. The pillows are wet. The stains in the   18
morning are on my face in the angry mirror. My eyes are hazel, murky. Peggy's
eyes are clear, stinging green. When the lids began to droop, right before they

closed for good, she cried bitterly in the mirror. Then I felt simple bewilderment, turning more complex. She still will not understand that her spattered smock is finer than the portraits. We light up. We cough out our truce.

The major difference between versions nine and ten is the reorganization. Both versions discuss the same topics and include most of the same language. However, as a result of her classmates' suggestions during group discussion, Ruffin decided to revise the paper so that the opening paragraphs reinforced the theme of the title and the message of the essay. The new focus of version ten is, as the title signals, on the relation between mama and smoking and Ruffin, and smoking and life and death. Paragraphs 1 and 2 of version nine are now paragraphs 3 and 4 of the final version.

"Mama's Smoke," a combination of epitaph, eulogy, and portrait, is a tribute to the continuing and complex relationship between mother and daughter. Ruffin's characterization (in paragraph 10) of her mother now epitomizes her own complicated narrative technique and illustrates the poetic aspects of her prose: "She is something like a sequel to herself, elliptical and confusing, out of context. She speaks in fragments, interrupting . . . giving to others the illusion that I have spoken her words. . . . The others don't know her, don't know her words from mine. The illusion is mine." As the smoke through which Ruffin imagines her mother swirls and eddies, the image of her mother emerges with precision. The different aspects of her mother's activities—painting, singing, dancing, writing, talking, loving and nurturing her daughter—coalesce through the catalyst of love.

Revising for Focus

Focusing on a Thesis

If your writing process is epitomized by E. M. Forster's observation, "How do I know what I think until I see what I say?" your first draft may be a jumble of words in search of a controlling idea. Early in the revision of this kind of draft, written to produce ideas, you'll need to focus on a central topic ("the widespread use of computers") about which to frame a *thesis,* a statement of your attitude or opinion about the topic ("As computers take over the world they destroy individual freedom").

A quick way to find what Peter Elbow calls the "center of gravity" of your paper, the heart of your ideas (and perhaps your emotional investment, as well), is to highlight, to underline, or to write in bold key words wherever they appear in your draft. A cluster of key words indicates a focus, either of the whole paper or a smaller segment of it. If there are no clusters, move paragraphs around until they appear—easy to do if you draft on a computer.

You can also cut your paper draft up into paragraph-size pieces and rearrange these.

To help focus your thesis, the following questions will aid your revision.

1. Does this draft have a thesis, a focal point? If so, what is it?

2. Does the thesis cover the entire essay? That is, does it contain the major key words and, therefore, concepts?

3. Does the thesis convey my opinion of or attitude toward the topic?

Perhaps you'll be able to find an existing sentence that meets all of these criteria. But if you answer "no" to any of these questions, write a sample thesis statement and keep revising it until it accurately describes the scope of your topic and your attitude toward that topic. As you draft your paper, you can better stay on target if you keep your working thesis in sight at all times.

Not every paper, of course, will have an explicit thesis. As a rule, interviews, narrations, travel writings, and satires, among others, do not, particularly if the thesis can be easily inferred.

Focusing Paragraphs

Revising for focus inevitably requires revising individual paragraphs. This is a good time to decide either to eliminate what doesn't fit or to revise it to make it an integral part of the entire essay. As a *thesis* refers to an entire paper, a *topic sentence* refers to a paragraph. Indeed, the controlling idea of a paragraph, like the controlling idea of an essay, can be stated explicitly in a topic sentence or be spread out as key words throughout several contiguous paragraphs. Or it can be implied. In any case, to focus your paragraphs you can ask the following questions.

1. Does this paragraph focus on a particular or subtopic aspect of my topic?

2. Does every illustration, subpoint, example, and explanatory detail in the paragraph reflect that focus?

3. Is the paragraph's topic related to the essay's thesis?

(These questions do not apply to transition paragraphs, which are essentially bridges between one topic and another.)

Revising to Accommodate an Audience

Gertrude Stein's assertion "I write for myself and strangers" implies a major distinction between writer-oriented and reader-oriented authors. Writer-oriented authors write for themselves and egocentrically assume—if they think about it at all—that their readers are extensions of themselves.

Consequently, they expect their audience to share not only their interest in the subject at hand but also common values, perspectives, points of reference, and background information. Whatever they take for granted, they believe, will be equally apparent to their readers. So they seldom explain references, making no distinction between general and specialized knowledge or between public and private information. They would refer to Bugtussle as casually as they would refer to New York City, and they would supply no context for their allusions to a longstanding feud between Esmerelda and Uncle Willie. Even in ordinarily impersonal contexts, writer-oriented authors are likely to include a great many first-person pronouns and irrelevant personal information that shifts the focus from the intended subject to themselves.

On a first draft, it doesn't hurt to be writer-oriented because you begin to think about a topic by exploring what you know. But such egocentrism doesn't belong in second and later drafts that are directed toward an audience of strangers who cannot be expected to understand private allusions or to indulge the author's intimate point of view. So the major work of revising to accommodate an audience is to transform writer-oriented writing into reader-oriented writing. The following are key questions to ask in making this transformation.

1. Who are my readers?
2. What values, cultural and educational backgrounds, special knowledge or interests, do we share? Where do we differ, and how can I accommodate those differences?
3. What background information do I need to supply?
4. Why should my readers care about what I have to say? How can I make them care?
5. Are they likely to be receptive to my thesis? If not, what can I do to create a climate of consensus?

Janice Waymack, a senior at a southern state university, had spent an unhappy freshman year at Bryn Mawr, in Pennsylvania. In response to an assignment to "write an essay about a place" (see Chapter 5), she decided to write about her recent visit to her former school. Her thesis, she decided, would be: "Bryn Mawr fosters an atmosphere in which students are unable to distinguish illusion from reality." Her first, writer-oriented draft began:

> I got off the Silver Star at 30th Street Station in downtown Philadelphia and hurried up the ramp marked "Commuter Train Station B" to catch the Paoli Local. The handful of passengers already settled in glanced up and registered me—twentyish, jeans, suitcase. Tourist come north to visit her rich Mainline cousin. Or might they imagine I was returning to school after visiting my southern relatives? I smiled at my own foolishness.
>
> "Overbrook," announced the conductor. "Merion next." Yes, I thought,

and then Narberth, then Wynnewood. Old Maids Never Wed—Ardmore, Haverford, Bryn Mawr—and Have Babies."

I set to categorizing the people my own age in the car around me. Odd how, four years later, it was still so easy to label them. The Villanova jocks: frat sweatshirts, jeans, scraggly mustaches; the Shipley Preps: knee socks, fingertip-length kilts with knife-sharp pleats and scrubbed ponytails.

But contrast was unnecessary to pick out the Bryn Mawr Women (we proudly emphasized the capital letters among ourselves). . . .

Waymack's second version, revised a month later, eliminated the writer-oriented first paragraph almost entirely. Gone were her exit from the Silver Star, her rush to catch the Paoli Local, her self-sketch ("twentyish, jeans, suitcase"), her description of the other passengers' speculations on the purpose of her trip, her imagined "rich Mainline cousin" and "southern relatives," and her self-conscious smile "at my own foolishness." Although the essay was still a personal voyage of discovery showing that she had more in common with her Bryn Mawr counterparts than she realized, Waymack wisely recognized that the personal introductory paragraph was essentially a warmup. The original narrative was useful in getting her memories flowing, but irrelevant to her point and her emphasis. The revised introduction, now reader-oriented, combines essential material from the first three paragraphs of the original into one:

"Overbrook," announced the conductor as the train pulled out of the 30th Street Station in Philadelphia. Yes, I thought, then Merion, Narberth, then Wynnewood. Old Maids Never Wed—Ardmore, Haverford, Bryn Mawr—and Have Babies. I set to categorizing the people my age in the car around me. Four years later it was still easy to label them. The Villanova Jocks: scraggly mustaches, frat sweatshirts, jeans. The Shipley Preps: scrubbed ponytails, kilts with knife-sharp pleats, knee socks.

But contrast was unnecessary to pick out the Bryn Mawr Women (we proudly emphasized the capital letters among ourselves). . . .

Note, too, that the revised description of the *Jocks* and the *Preps* now proceeds from head to knee, a familiar way to survey people's bodies, rather than in the haphazard order of the original.

Revising for Structure, Emphasis, and Organization

Revising for Structure and Emphasis

Every work needs a structure that reinforces its meaning. Novelist Joyce Cary has observed, "Your form is your meaning and your meaning dictates form." The structure of some works, such as a scientific report, a sonnet, or a resumé, immediately enhances the meaning. Some forms and variations characteristic of particular genres will be discussed in the chapters that follow. Often, however, your essay's early draft will either be a narrative, whose casual chronology reflects the order in which the ideas occurred, or a string of loosely connected ideas in which one thought or nuance has led to another. When you revise such a draft you'll want to make sure the structure, and consequently, the emphasis, does justice to your meaning. Imagine your paper as a tower of building blocks, each block equivalent to a paragraph. Some blocks are thin and compact while others are bulky and chunky. You can move these blocks around at will, in search of an ultimate arrangement that will be pleasing to the eye as well as structurally sound. Some configurations will topple easily; others may be equally sturdy but will represent different conceptions of one idea.

As you search for the structure that best suits your view of a subject, bear in mind two basic principles concerning *placement* and *length* that determine emphasis in writing, whether the emphasis refers to a word, phrase, sentence, paragraph, section, chapter, or whole work.

Beginnings and endings are more emphatic than material in the middle. Your own experience will probably verify the observation that readers of essays, like listeners to speeches, tend to pay closer attention to the first and last parts of the entire work, of individual paragraphs, even of sentences. If their attention is going to wander, it will be most likely to do so in the middle—as the snores during Sunday morning sermons testify.

The greater the length, the greater the emphasis. This does not mean that you should strive for inflated, elephantine prose in hopes that its sheer bulk will overwhelm the reader with the force of your ideas. But it does mean that you should develop most fully those points you wish to emphasize, and give less space (and, consequently, less emphasis) to less important points of illustrations.

To revise an early draft, you first have to decide what your main points are. If you have highlighted the main ideas either in sentence form or, as described earlier, by key words, you can draw arrows to connect related terms. Or, to see the structure more clearly, you can make a topic sentence or key phrase outline of the draft. You may find that the existing pattern is just what you want and that you can leave well enough alone. If, however, the arrangement lacks a coherent pattern or does not reflect the emphasis you want, as Waymack's first draft did not (pages 67–68), you can rearrange the sentences or phrases.

It may be helpful to ask yourself the following questions about placement and length to find the most suitable structure for your view.

1. What comes first, last, and in the middle?

2. Why have I chosen this order? Will the reasons for using this order be apparent to my readers?

3. Which sections (sentences, paragraphs, or groups of paragraphs) are longest? are shortest? are of middle length? Which sections are of nearly equal length?

4. Do the respective lengths of the sentences, paragraphs, and sections reflect the emphasis I want to give to each? Am I expressing equivalent ideas in segments of approximately equal length?

Exploring Alternative Organizational Patterns

As the rest of *Fact and Artifact* reveals, for many types of writing you can choose from several basic organizational patterns and pick one that will best reinforce your meaning and intended emphasis. If your first choice doesn't work (and it may not, if your first draft has, for instance, a writer-oriented narrative structure), you can try others until you find one that provides the strongest possible structure. You won't necessarily know what organizational pattern works best until you've highlighted the key words in an early draft to see where the emphasis lies: where the words cluster and what segments are most (and least) fully developed. If you're writing on a computer, you can save alternative forms to different files and then compare the printouts. Better yet, trade papers with a fellow student grappling with the same assignment and see which version makes the most sense to an outside reader.

The following discussion describes some common patterns that determine the structure of paragraphs and of whole essays, and sometimes of sentences, as well. You can use these patterns either as the basis for the original structure or as alternative options for revision. This material on organization is presented in abbreviated form as a refresher to acknowledge the difficulty that even advanced writers, professionals included, often have in enabling a clear and logical pattern to emerge from a mass of material or a flutter of drafts.

Sequential or chronological organization.   In a sequential or chronological pattern, the main points are arranged in the order in which the process, event, or phenomenon they describe normally occurs. This format is particularly appropriate for narratives (including humorous stories and travel accounts), discussions of scientific processes and how-to procedures, biographical or historical sketches, plot summaries (what happened first, second, third) and play-by-play accounts of political and military occurrences (battle campaigns, invasions) and sporting events.

The sequential organization of a process usually starts with the beginning

("First, catch your hare") and proceeds step by step to the end ("Let it cool in the pan and voilà! the perfect rabbit pie"). Likewise, sequential organization can, like the progression of the calendar or Sherman's march through Georgia, move inexorably forward from beginning to end. Although a sequential organization is an easy pattern to arrange and makes a process admirably clear, if your readers can too easily guess what's coming next, it may make a narrative unbearably boring. If you have written a first draft using a basic sequential structure, you can use the following techniques, singly or in combination, to add variety.

Telescope events.   It isn't always necessary to give everything equal emphasis, as you might discover if you were writing a biographical portrait of an octogenarian and found that her thirty-fourth year was very much like her thirty-fifth and thirty-sixth years. You can treat similar matters as a unit to avoid redundancy.

Focus on the most significant or illuminating steps or events.   You can skip parts of a process familiar to your readers. Should a discussion of how to swim begin with an overview of possible sites (beaches versus pools, indoor pools or outdoor pools), with the selection of an appropriate swimsuit (designed for speed? for appearance?), or with an introduction to basic strokes or to underwater breathing?

Use a flashback.   You can begin by writing about what comes later in the sequence and then go back to earlier steps or events. It may help your readers if you describe the completed sauna before you tell them how to build it.

Alternate between the past and present.   Juxtapose past and present events or phenomena so that they illuminate each other. Biographer Plutarch did this in *Parallel Lives* by recounting equivalent events in the lives of his contemporary Roman leaders and notable Greeks of five centuries earlier.

Interpret the sequence through commentary that interrupts it.   A narrative without interpretation becomes a mere chronicle of events. What does it mean to specify the increasing numbers of U.S. troops sent to Vietnam in the 1960s, to Central America in the late 1970s, to Lebanon in the 1980s, and to Africa in the 1990s without interpreting the information? Authorial commentary may interrupt the chronology of troop buildup, but it helps readers to make sense of the facts and encourages them to see matters the way you do.

Topical organization.   In this pattern, major topics function like magnets, around which related ideas cluster. For example, each major topic—such as themes, plot, characterization, settings, symbols, style—serves as a heading under which to discuss ideas related to it: "The themes in *Romeo and Juliet* are . . ." This format is particularly effective in portraits, reviews or critical analyses, some writings about place, and even for some arguments. Once the related ideas have been grouped in clusters, however, each cluster and each idea within the cluster still has to be organized according to some overriding principle, and not just strung together like random beads on a necklace. For example, in a book review, you might discuss the themes, plot, etc. in order of their prominence in the book. You might write about how memorable each theme, plot, etc. is or with what originality the author handles each and arrange your discussion from most to least significant, or innovative.

The following discussion illustrates a number of organizational principles that you can use independently or further refine a topical discussion.

Cause and effect organization.   In this step-by-step pattern an inciting idea begins the sequence, is followed by an idea caused by the inciting idea, and so on. In other words, stimulus (idea 1) provokes response 1, response 1 in turn becomes idea 2, idea 2 provokes response 2, and so on. As illustrated in the following variations, this is a particularly effective pattern to use in an argument, an historical analysis, or in some explanations. This pattern is especially appropriate for historical analysis, for argumentation, and for explanation of a process.

Single cause, multiple effects.   This format, which emphasizes *effects,* first identifies a single cause and then looks at a series of effects arranged according to one of several patterns: the order in which they occur (cause 1 leads to effects 1a, 1b, 1c), from most to least important (or, occasionally, vice versa), or from the most to least compelling psychologically or emotionally. Note that a given effect, say 1b, could be the cause of the effect that follows, 1c, and on down the line.

Multiple causes, single or limited effect.   This pattern focuses on multiple *causes* before discussing their cumulative effect. Discussion of the causes can be arranged according to the same patterns used for the single cause, multiple effects format. If the causes are interrelated, you will need to arrange them in a way that demonstrates the nature of their relationship.

Organization by comparison and contrast.   This pattern is particularly useful for comparative analyses, for commentaries on performance (how one film or restaurant stacks up against others), and for relative estimates of persons, products, processes, policies, and places (Is Madrid, Paris, or London a better city to visit in October?).

Block design.   Using this pattern, you present all the material about the first item in a block of sentences or paragraphs, then all the material about the second item, then all the material about the third item, and so on for all the items involved in the comparison. Choose block organization if you want to emphasize the wholeness of each unit discussed or if there is no exact point-by-point correspondence between larger units. However, if there are corresponding points and you discuss them in the same order within each block, the essay will be easier to follow because the first block will have set the pattern for the rest. Using parallel organization within each block also helps to emphasize the comparison among the items discussed. Thus you could organize an analysis of which personal computer to buy with separate sections on the IBM, Macintosh, and Zenith. Each section would comment in sequence on the machine's capacity, monitor, keyboard, software, and consequent potential uses of the machine. However, unless you repeat in later blocks much of what you've said in earlier sections, the comparisons and contrasts remain implicit and may get lost. You can compensate for this by providing a conclusion that integrates the separate discussions.

Point-by-point design. This format emphasizes the various separate points of comparison. Using point-by-point design, you compare one feature of all the items discussed and then proceed to the next. It is a particularly efficient format for a complicated subject in which each part needs considerable explanation. You could, for instance, compare and contrast first the respective capacities of the IBM, Macintosh, and Zenith computers, then their monitors, then their keyboards, and finally their software. Point-by-point organization enables immediate comparison and contrast of each aspect of the subject. Because each major topic is treated in a separate unit, you won't need to repeat what you've already said about one item when you discuss its counterpart. However, this organizational pattern emphasizes the parts at the expense of the whole, the opposite from block design. Somewhere, perhaps at the end, you'll need to put Humpty Dumpty together again by integrating the separate segments of each whole unit.

Comparison first, followed by contrast (or vice versa). A comparison of the similarities of two or more entities establishes their common features; a discussion of their differences as a group makes it easy to discriminate among their divergent elements. A prospective computer purchaser might find it useful to know what features the IBM, Macintosh, and Zenith have in common before learning of their significant differences.

The following questions are useful in assessing a writing's structure and emphasis. You can use them as the basis for revising either an outline or a draft.

1. Is the central issue defined fairly early in the writing? If not, should it be?
2. Does every subordinate issue relate to the thesis?
3. What are the strongest points?
4. Is each major point developed sufficiently to give it appropriate emphasis?
5. Is there a pattern governing the arrangement of the points? of the subpoints? of the illustrations?
6. If so, does this pattern reflect my intended organization and emphasis?

7. If there is no discernible pattern or if the existing pattern is inappropriate, what alternative patterns of organization can I use?

8. Do the paragraph breaks reinforce my emphasis?

9. What proportion of the work does the introduction occupy? (If it occupies more than 20 percent, it's probably too long.) What proportion of the work does the conclusion occupy?

10. Do the relative lengths of the introduction, body, and conclusion reflect my desired emphasis?

Revising for Development

To some extent, adequate development of a work depends on the expectations of both writer and readers. Because there are so many possibilities, it's hard to decide whether a given work is developed appropriately. You could write a review of a movie in five hundred words, one thousand words, two thousand words, or more. Any one could be sufficiently developed for its purpose, such as to give readers enough information to decide whether or not to see the movie. Or any one could lack crucial information (Who are the main actors? What is the plot?) and therefore be underdeveloped. Or, any review could be overdeveloped, too long and stuffed with trivial, irrelevant, or redundant material that buries the point or distorts the focus. (Does it matter that the getaway car was a bright blue stickshift Camry with a custom sunroof that was open throughout the seventy-mile-an-hour gale? If so, what's the point? If not, why include these details?)

When you're reading over a draft of your writing to revise it, you'll be aiming for the golden mean in development—you'll want the work to be neither too short nor too long, but about right. Here "about right" means that you've focused on your subject and covered it adequately enough to satisfy yourself and your readers. By the time your paper ends, nothing crucial is missing and nothing needs to be deleted. Here are some questions to help you decide whether your work is appropriately developed.

1. What do I want this particular piece of writing to accomplish? Does my first draft succeed in doing this?

2. Is this writing self-contained? That is, does it contain enough information about the subject so that readers won't have to search outside the text for crucial evidence?

3. Is each major point developed sufficiently and given appropriate emphasis?

4. Do comparable points receive equal development and emphasis?

5. Do I slide over or ignore important points? Do I overemphasize minor ones?

6. Are there false generalities, missing steps in an argument, or interpretations or conclusions that don't follow logically from the evidence?

7. Do I include more information than I need? Is everything relevant to my thesis? Do I use multiple examples or other information unnecessarily?

8. Finally, is the development of this work "about right"?

Revising Underdeveloped Drafts

If your writing is too skeletal, you may be assuming that your readers know more about the subject than they actually do. As you read over your draft, you'll want to make sure to anticipate all the questions your readers might have. Ask yourself the following questions and see whether your writing answers them satisfactorily.

Who?   Do you identify references to unfamiliar people (or other living creatures) who are important to the writing at hand? Which Roosevelt: Teddy, Franklin D., Eleanor, or your dog Mozart?

What?   If circumstances are crucial to your account, do your readers know what's going on? Do you need to define or otherwise illustrate unfamiliar words (*quark*), concepts (*weltanschauung*), and principles (the second law of thermodynamics), or can you include a definition in the context?

When?   If it's relevant do you identify time, date, century, era, or people's ages?

Where?   Do you locate unfamiliar places or is there good reason for leaving them unspecific (Bora Bora, Main Street, that lake in the north woods)?

How?   If you're writing about a process (say, gene splicing) or a phenomenon (such as hypertext), do you explain how it works? Do your readers need this information?

Why?   If the causes of a condition or phenomenon are necessary to justify your views, do you explain them? (Should genetic engineering or nuclear disarmament or the death penalty be encouraged or abolished?)

If you decide that your writing needs more evidence or information, you'll need to choose the kind that best suits your purpose and mode. Possibilities include anecdotes or incidents from personal experience; characterizations of key people; case histories; examples from history; analogies; statistics, numbers, graphs, diagrams, tables; references to or evidence from outside authorities.

The first draft of Theresa Whitlock's humorous essay, "My 'Professional'

Hairstyle," tells a too-brief story of her first haircut at college. To be understood and to make the most of the subject's humorous potential, she needs to supply a great deal more information than her first version contains.

Version One: My "Professional" Hairstyle

Risks are a part of everyone's life. Since I'm usually a trusting person, I often get myself into situations that I later realize I could have avoided. After getting into one of these situations, I learned that a favor may not be a favor at all.   1

About two years ago just after I entered my freshman year, I decided I wanted a change. One Saturday before dinner I decided to wash my hair. Afterwards, I went to my friend's room to ask if I could use her hair dryer and mentioned that I wished I could get my hair cut into a carefree style. She said she'd do me a favor and that she'd be happy to cut my hair for me. Since her hair always looked good, I agreed to let her cut mine. Several other people were in the room also, talking and waiting around for dinner. As my friend cut my hair, I was thinking how nice it was to finally get my hair cut into a carefree style. After telling her what style I wanted, I relaxed.   2

After what seemed like an eternity, she finally said she was finished and let me look at the results. When I looked in the mirror, I thought I was looking at another person. My hair was so short that it stood up on my head like Woodstock's! I couldn't believe it! Gone were my long locks, replaced by short curly stubs of what was supposedly hair. Everyone in the room was laughing at my head and my friend who had committed this act kept saying, "Oh, I'm sorry, I didn't mean to cut it so short." Her apologies didn't calm me. I was still furious.   3

Finally everyone managed to control their laughter and someone suggested trying a curling iron to make the hair lie down a bit. Not knowing what else to do, I gave it a try, only to find that my hair was too short to fit around the curlers! By now I was really upset, but had to laugh at my predicament because it was somewhat funny. After trying everything we could think of to make my hair presentable, I finally came up with the perfect solution. A hat! Yes, I ended up wearing a hat to dinner and to classes for a few weeks until my hair started growing again. Lucky for me it was winter. Boy, did I learn a lesson!   4

Whitlock's first draft isn't as humorous as its material promises. The writer erroneously counts on her readers to know what her hair looks like before it is cut. Yet without this information they can't assess the ultimate damage. She also assumes that the readers will understand what went on during the cutting process; without this information the incident isn't nearly as funny. But the readers weren't there, so Whitlock needs to *show* them what happened rather than *tell* them about the incident. Moreover, the readers don't know Whitlock: is she foolish, vain, naive, too trusting, sadder but wiser, or a combination of the above? A more fully characterized authorial personality would make her story more interesting. Yet in spite of the lack of development, the language, especially in the first two paragraphs, is unnecessarily repetitive.

In her revision, Whitlock focuses on adding information about *who* is present; *what* they say and do; *what* her hair looks like, before, during, and after the massacre; *why* Chantay, with Whitlock's encouragement, continues to cut her hair shorter and shorter. In the process of adding this information, Whitlock characterizes herself more fully: she's a likeable person, the optimistic victim of her own flaws, and a person with whom most readers can fully sympathize. She enhances the humor by adding the satiric remarks from a chorus of onlookers (who, like the chorus in a Greek tragedy, know full well what's happening even though the main character does not), and the aftermath incident in which a tormentor snatches her concealing hat and calls her "Baldilocks." She has enough control over the language in the revision not only to eliminate repetitive wording, but also to make a few subtle puns and allusions; her wishes will be "executed" (paragraph 2) and "there is no free haircut" (paragraph 3, which revitalizes the meaning of the cliché, "there is no free lunch"). She also uses repetition effectively with each variation on "Chantay always knew what she was doing" at the ends of paragraphs 4, 5, and 6.

Revision: My "Professional" Hairstyle

I'm too trusting, and because I trust others too much I take unnecessary 1
risks. When people tell me they know how to do something, I believe them. When they offer to help me, in their supposed expertise, I let them—a risk indeed, as I too often learn that their aid does more harm than good.

Two years ago, in the fall of my freshman year, I decided to wash my shoul- 2
der-length hair before Saturday dinner. Afterwards, when borrowing my friend's hair dryer, I mentioned that I wanted to get my hair cut into a shorter style that would be easy to care for. I wanted to be able to wash it, blow it dry, and curl it just a little on the ends to make it look pretty. "I'll do you a favor," beamed Chantay. "I'll be happy to cut your hair." Since she cut and permed her own hair and it always looked good, I agreed, pleased that my wish could be executed so soon—and for free.

I should have realized that there is no free haircut. But instead, I trustingly 3
told her to cut two or three inches off the back, and to cut the front even shorter so it would hold the curl better. Then I relaxed and joined in the conversation with our other friends in the room who were waiting to go down to dinner.

Chantay began to cut my hair from the back first, so I couldn't see how 4
much she was cutting off. I could tell by the feel that she was working from the top down to create a layered look, which was fine with me as long as it curled. As the hair began to pile up on the floor, I was still pleased; after all, Chantay knew more about what she was doing than I did. Before she started to cut the

front, she stopped and asked me to look at the back to see whether it was short enough. I looked in the mirror, foolishly trusting what I saw in the dim light, and told her to cut another inch off. Which she did.

When Chantay began to cut the front, she repeated the procedure she'd used   5 on the back, starting at the top and working down. At first she cut only an inch off. But that made it even with the back, and I wanted the front shorter, so she obligingly cut off another inch in front. At this point I became aware of remarks from the others in the room; "You gonna cut off all her hair, or what?" "Good thing Halloween was last week!" And I began to get a little nervous, but Chantay always knew what she was doing.

So I said "O.K." when she told me she was going to cut off "just a little   6 more in the back to make it curl faster on the ends." After all, that was just what I'd wanted. The remarks continued, this time with sneers: "You getting scissor happy, ain'tcha?" "Girl, you should see the back of your head!" Whether or not Chantay always knew what she was doing, I decided to see for myself.

When I looked in the mirror, I thought I was seeing another person. My hair   7 was so short that it stood up on my head like Woodstock's! I couldn't believe it! Gone were my long locks, replaced by short curly stubs of what was supposedly hair. Everyone in the room was laughing at my head. "Pure punk!" "The New Wave—ain't never gonna wave again!" Chantay looked remorseful. "Oh, I'm so sorry, I didn't mean to cut it so short. I'm so sorry. And, besides, it looks kinda cute." Her apologies didn't calm me. I was so furious I couldn't speak.

Amidst the laughter—even Chantay was by this time beginning to smile—   8 someone suggested trying a curling iron to make the hair lie down a bit. Not knowing what else to do, I gave it a try, only to find that my hair was too short to fit around the curlers. Even though I was horrified by the mass of wiry wisps that sprouted from my scalp, I was beginning to laugh at my predicament. After all, everyone else was. But I wasn't going to dinner until I did something with my hair.

So I starved that night as I tried different solutions. As my friends cut out   9 for a good evening, Chantay gave me some tiny rollers that she had used to perm her hair. Fortunately, my hair fit around them, but they curled it so tight that it came out matted to my head. I thought I could solve the problem by washing my hair and using a brush to curl it while blowing it dry. That only made me look scared to death. My well-fed friends gave me some hairspray, but that was no better. And creams simply changed the wires to scraggles.

Before I missed yet another meal I came up with the perfect solution. A hat!   10 I wore a cream-colored knitted hat to meals and to classes, but when some wise-guy snatched off my hat and called me "Baldilocks," I bought a black beret to match my gloves. Chantay was the first to admit that it looked chic. After that, the smart comments ceased, and I trusted in the black beret until my hair grew long enough to look good. Lucky for me it was winter.

Neither version is very long. The original is slightly less than 400 words; the revision is more than twice as long, around 900 words. Both have a one-paragraph introduction but the revised introduction is more focused and begins with what Whitlock sees as her main problem, being "too trusting," rather than being "risk-taking" as the original leads readers to anticipate. Version one has two paragraphs of development and a one-paragraph conclusion discussing the aftermath of the ill-fated haircut. As we've seen, this version omits too much to tell the tale adequately. The revision, in contrast, develops the rising action of the haircut for five paragraphs (2–6) leading up to the recognition (in paragraph 7) of the damage. The conclusion winds down slowly in three paragraphs that explore the humor of Whitlock's attempts to rehabilitate her hairdo.

The first paragraph in the revision is somewhat misleading, as it was in the original. Whitlock is on the defensive in both versions without acknowledging her own responsibility for the unfortunate results. Perhaps she should not have trusted an amateur to do a professional job, though Chantay seems considerate and cautious enough until the reckless finale, when all has been lost anyway. After all, Whitlock made the primary error of judgment in telling her friend to cut off an extra inch when she couldn't see how short her hair already was (paragraph 4). Perhaps in yet another revision of the first paragraph, Whitlock might gain enough perspective to acknowledge her share of the responsibility.

The rest of the revised version accomplishes just what Whitlock intended it to do. The original is too skimpy to be very funny while the revision explains enough to be hilarious without including extraneous details (such as what the dorm room looked like, how many other people were in the room, or what their hair styles were like). By including enough information for outsiders to visualize the scene and hear the dialogue (especially the marvelous cacophony of commentators), the revision puts the readers right in the dorm room and lets them share the suspense and ultimately the joke along with the participants.

In the revision, Whitlock becomes a more fully realized character than she is in the first version—trusting, self-confident, complacent—until she suffers Samson's fate at the well-meaning hands of an invited Delilah. Yet she redeems herself by her humanness; she can make mistakes and can acknowledge them through the act of telling the tale. She is resilient enough to laugh off her mistake and resourceful enough to adapt her clothing to conceal the mishap. Moreover, she is controlled enough to exhibit that control in the shape, content, and tone of her writing.

Revising Overdeveloped Drafts

Within every walrus of an overdeveloped writing lurks a svelte seal waiting to get out. Overdeveloped drafts do not necessarily suffer from the converse of the problems that plague underdeveloped drafts, though they may. Although overdeveloped drafts may contain some, but probably not all, of the necessary information about who, what, when, where, how, and why, they may lack a clear focus, a clear sense of audience, a coherent structure, or a recognizable authorial voice. Excess occurs when the writer tries to supply one or another of these missing elements by throwing in not only the kitchen sink but all the dishes, pots, and cooking utensils. These extraneous materials only clog up the prose.

If your first drafts are freewritings in search of a subject, audience, structure, or point of view, you may say a great deal more than you need to and much of it will be irrelevant to the subject. As you examine your draft, consider the following:

1. What am I really trying to say?

2. What is the "heart" or the "center of gravity" of my material? Does my draft emphasize this?

3. What bores me in this draft? Where do I tune out? Could I sharpen the focus by deleting these segments, illustrations, repetitions of ideas, or irrelevancies? What, if anything, do I need to add?

4. Having pared the draft, are the supporting points or illustrations apparent? Do they occur in an order that reinforces the main point and reflects the emphasis I want? If they don't, how can I rearrange them?

5. Do the repetitions (if any) that remain appropriately emphasize or integrate the material? Can anything (such as warmup paragraphs or summaries) be eliminated from the introduction or conclusion?

As these questions suggest, in the process of deletion you may need to add information to clarify your newly sharpened point. As you revise, you might also refer to the questions on focus (pages 66 and 67), structure, emphasis, and organization (pages 70 and 73); and style (see Chapter 2, Chapter 5). When your paper's focus and structure emerge, after the underbrush is pruned away, you are likely to find other features—such as a more distinctive authorial persona or unifying, recurrent metaphors, symbols, or language patterns—taking their rightful place in the sun.

The power of revision is the power of re-vision. For revisions such as those illustrated in this chapter are the revisions that add power to your work.

Checklist for Revision

The Beginning

1. Is the title specific? accurate? provocative or otherwise appealing?

2. Is the lead (first paragraph or longer opening section) interesting, compelling? Does it provide clues to the paper's subject? focus? authorial attitude toward the subject?

3. Is it consistent in pace, tone, voice with the rest of the paper?

The Body

See the checklists throughout this chapter and at the ends of Chapters 4 through 10.

The Ending

1. Does the ending flow naturally from the events in the narrative, the steps in the process, the strongest points in the argument?
2. Does the writing really stop where it ends? Does it leave readers with a sense of completion ("that's all," *finis*)? Or is it meant to be continued . . . ?
3. What clues, in tone and content, do I provide to signal the end?

Word Choice, Sentences, and Spelling and Mechanics

See "A Checklist for Editing" on pages 320–21.

The Last Word

1. Have I said what I meant?
2. Have I felt free to take risks, break rules, and disregard suggestions that violate the spirit or sense of my writing?
3. How does my paper sound when I read it aloud? when someone else reads it aloud? What, if anything, do I need to do to give it the energy, pace, and emphasis I intended?
4. Is this version the best that I can produce at this time? If it isn't, am I willing to change it even now?

Selected Reference List of Readings on Revision

See also "A Selected List of Readings on Style," (pages 48–49).

Lanham, Richard A. *Revising Business Prose*. New York: Scribner's, 1981.
———. *Revising Prose*. 2nd ed. New York: Scribner's, 1987.
Murray, Donald M. *Write to Learn*. 3rd ed. Fort Worth: Holt, 1990.
———. *The Craft of Revision*. Fort Worth: Holt, 1991.

Work Cited

Rich, Adrienne. "When We Dead Awaken: Writing as Re-Vision." 1972. Rpt. in *On Lies, Secrets, and Silence: Selected Prose 1966–1978*. New York: Norton, 1979.

4

WRITING ABOUT PEOPLE

A biography is considered complete if it merely accounts for six or seven selves, whereas a person may have as many thousand.

—Virginia Woolf

You can't put together a memoir without cannibalizing your own life for parts. The work battens on your memories. And it replaces them.

—Annie Dillard

When I was younger I could remember anything, whether it had happened or not; but my faculties are decaying now, and soon I shall be so I cannot remember any but the things that never happened.

—Mark Twain

Why We Write About People

When critics asked H. L. Mencken why he continued to write about people if the human race, "the booboisie," as he called it, bothered him so, he replied, "Why do people go to zoos?" People write about people more than they write about any other subject. They write *portraits* or *character sketches, interviews, personal narratives* or *vignettes* contained in other types of writing, as well as full-scale *biographies* and *autobiographies.* We find our own species, in all its myriad aspects, a source of fascination, pleasure, excitement, envy, inspiration; many writers find themselves the most intriguing subject of all.

By writing about ourselves or others, we learn who we are and who we can be. We can discover our past—as a race, an ethnic group, a family, or an individual. We can explore what it's like to grow up, male or female, in a particular environment—on a farm, in a tenement, in a small town or a suburb, or a large city. We can explain the meaning of a watershed experience—an insight, discovery, or mastery of a skill, the pivotal moment (learning to read, gaining or losing a religious experience)—when life was one way before the watershed happened, and utterly changed thereafter.

Through personal writings we can share our witnessing of history whether remote or recent. We can explore an individual's role in or recollection of a memorable event such as the Vietnam war, the civil rights movement, or a presidential election—just name the year and the candidates. We discuss how people used to live in the days B.C. (before computers); with disease before the discovery of antibiotics; or with travel before the advent of freeways, cheap airline tickets, or racial integration. Written reminiscences help to make a permanent record of vanishing occupations (blacksmith, beekeeper) or ways of life (dating in more innocent times, family life before the advent of television).

Personal writings also help us understand our contemporaries and the world we live in. We can learn about the good times—parties and courtship, creation and recreation, worldly success and spirituality. We come to understand the bad times, as well—failure, loneliness, poverty, alcoholism, brutality. Personal writings show us the fascinating variety of ways to behave in a variety of roles: as fathers and mothers, sons and daughters, friends and lovers, spouses, grandparents, employers or employees, public and private citizens. Through personal writings we learn how people live and what they live for: whether they live on the land, on the fat of the land, or on the dole; whether their beliefs are the formal tenets of a particular church, union, or political party or are manifested in informal stands that become acts of cowardice, indifference, or courage. People can tell us about their way of life simply by recounting how they live. And so our lives can touch.

Guidelines for Writing About Yourself or Others

Know your subject.   Philosophers might argue that it is impossible to know yourself, let alone to know another person. Nevertheless, the act of writing about someone, whether yourself or another, is an attempt to know that person and to transmit your understanding to an audience. It is often easiest to learn about someone else in the same way that you learn about yourself, through firsthand experience. As Samuel Johnson, the great eighteenth-century biographer, has observed, "Nobody can write the life of a man, but those who have eat [sic] and drunk and lived in social intercourse with him." Consequently, it's natural to start writing about people whom you have lived with the longest and thought about the most: family members, close neighbors, best friends, lovers.

From an insider's point of view, you'll be explaining your subject to an audience of outsiders, people who don't know this stranger and who have to be introduced, not with a fancy pedigree but through illustrations of the dominant aspects of character or personality. Thus you might consider the implications of questions such as: In what ways is the subject like other people? In what ways is the subject unique or unusual? What makes this person seem interesting, colorful, bizarre? commonplace or dull? attractive or unattractive? What is the subject's characteristic temperament: constant or mercurial, optimistic or pessimistic, realistic or idealistic, theoretical or practical? Do others see this person as you do?

In her prize-winning essay, "Framing My Father," student Leslie Moore focuses on her father's caustic temperament, his character annealed in flame and honed on brimstone, which made him not only unusual and difficult to live with but, ultimately, worthy of love and respect. After describing her father's ten-day visit to her home "with his wife of only two months," during which he monopolized the living room and disrupted the routine, Moore devotes the paper's fourth section, "The Human Being," to character analysis. She begins by emphasizing the negatives:

> My father has made a name for himself as a son-of-a-bitch. He has spent a lifetime cultivating a fierceness that intimidates adults and terrorizes children. That's one reason he gave up pediatrics to go into public health. He honed his fierceness on his own children. When my brothers and I were growing up, his favorite phrase was "Stop crying or I'll spank you again." His favorite epithet was, "You dumb stupe!" We cringed at the sound of his explosive "God damn it all to hells!" and ducked out of reach of his backhands. Recently my father admitted to me that the way he treated us as children would be considered child abuse today.

Then she pulls back, anticipating the balance that her illustrations will ultimately provide: "The lessons our father taught us were stamped in fear and humiliation. Somehow we survived. Somehow the lessons stuck. Somehow

I am grateful for the things I learned." Moore demonstrates this with three examples, how he taught her to body surf, to pitch, and to write. Her first illustration begins:

> My father taught me to body surf at Laguna Beach in Southern California. One moment I would be patting wet sand onto a castle, the next I would be tucked under his arm like a football and carried full speed into the surf kicking and screaming and swallowing salt water. . . . I learned how to get out past the breakers, diving under the walls of thundering surf. I learned what to look for in a wave—the green swell on the horizon, the slow build, the fingers of foam tickling the top. I learned how to time my take-off, poised under the wave's foaming lip, arms cocked for their furious windmilling, feet set to kick. I learned how to let the wave take me, my body rigid and horizontal, head jutting out of the wave, one arm straight-fisted before me, the other clasped to my side. Finally I learned how to finish, tucking and rolling out of the breaker as it ground its way onto the shore.

What she learned from her father about body surfing is a metaphor for what she learned from him about life—a tough and complicated physical skill, body control, and, as a condition of surviving and enjoying the sport, how to work in harmony with violent and only partly predictable natural forces. His fierce insistence on quality dominated the writing lessons as well. In high school, says Moore,

> I slaved over my manuscripts in longhand, leaving margins where my father wrote my literary pretensions clean off the page. . . . He muttered my sentences out loud, his pencil poised over the page, ready to attack my excesses—"You don't need *this*. Get rid of *that*."—my obscurities—"What in the hell is *that* supposed to mean?"—my stumblings—"You dumb stupe!"—my misspellings—"Look it up!" He jabbed holes through the paper where I used big words to conceal incomplete thoughts. . . . And so we worked our way through my papers, paragraph by painful paragraph, page after painful page. By the end of an editing session with my father, my papers and my pretensions were returned to me, battered and bleeding, and I limped back to my room to start the rewrites.

The quality of Moore's writing—precise, concise, clear, vivid, elegant—validates her father's teaching. She continues,

> My father's fierceness has cut both ways. It has cut all of his children, leaving scars on each. It has also cut him off, isolated him from human kindness, left him lonely and needy. And so, like King Lear in his retirement, my father invites himself to his grown children's houses. He commandeers the best chairs. . . . He has spent much of his fierceness and now he needs friends.

Moore's next sentence foreshadows the rest of her essay: "Oscar Wilde says, 'Children begin by loving their parents; then they judge them; sometimes they forgive them.' As I trip over my father's feet in my livingroom, I wonder if I've forgiven him." As, indeed, she does. In the process of portraying her father, she characterizes herself, as well, and demonstrates that she is, indeed, her father's daughter.

React strongly to your subject.   Anyone on earth, from yourself to your neighborhood 7-Eleven clerk to Henry VIII to Mother Theresa, can be compelling—in a positive or negative way—because of personality, life experiences, job, hobby, or relationships with others. If your subject sustains your interest throughout the writing, you'll probably compel your readers' interest as well, as Moore does. Your attitude toward your subject will be apparent in your *choice of vocabulary* (is your subject "firm," "stubborn," or a "pig-headed fool"?), your *tone*, and your *selection of incidents and details*. These elements will convince your readers to find the subject either as fascinating or as repulsive as you do. Unless you want to portray someone as the essence of dullness, why write about a boring subject? You'll only bore yourself and any readers who stick it out.

Tell the truth.   This may mean, if you're writing about yourself, being scrupulously honest about the essential meaning of an event or another person's relationship with you (the "heart's truth" or the "felt truth"), whether or not you can remember all the facts. It doesn't matter if you can't recall the name of the person you went with on your first "real" date; but how you felt about the experience before, during, and afterward is indeed important. Mary McCarthy, like many writers, deliberately uses fictional techniques. In her autobiography, *Memories of a Catholic Girlhood*, she recreates the essence of her painful, orphaned childhood, explaining, "This account is highly fictionalized. . . . The story is true in substance, but the details have been invented or guessed at."

When you're writing about someone else, however, you don't have the liberty to fill in the gaps with invented "facts," as McCarthy does. Unless you can corroborate what you say about someone else, and from two (not one) reliable sources, you shouldn't say it. The reason for this double standard is simple. When you're writing about yourself, you're in a unique position to verify and interpret the meanings of all your experiences, including private thoughts and feelings that no one else would suspect. You can include everything in your own life that feels "true," without supplying objective evidence. When you write about someone else, however, you need to corroborate externally the truth of the life.

Whether or not student Carolina Broccardo precisely remembered every detail of her lifelong problem with chronic obesity, "Confessions of a Compulsive Overeater" is compelling because of its fidelity and honesty in relating a chronic overeater's typical experiences of sneaking food and typical reactions of guilt, denial, self-deception, and continued abuse of good nutrition. She begins her account of ten years of dieting and binge eating with three characteristic vignettes:

> Eleven A.M. The third day of semester break. I am home with nothing to do, so I decide to bake chocolate chip cookies. Two hours later I am still baking. I have snitched so much of the dough from the first batch that I have to bake a second batch or run the risk of having my mother ask me how it is that a full, twelve ounce bag of chocolate chips yielded so few cookies. But the dough is so tasty.
>
> Twelve midnight. The end of another uneventful party. A bowl, half-filled with peanut M&Ms beckons me. I sit by the bowl and begin downing the candy. Why not? The party's almost over. No one's said more than "hello" to me all night. I might as well save the hostess the chore of putting the M&Ms away.
>
> A family birthday party. I nonchalantly pass up the cake and ice cream. Three hours later, when no one is looking, I cut myself a "sliver" of cake. And another. And still another.
>
> The situations are endless.

That Broccardo understands very well her attempts to deceive herself and others is implicit in the candor of her account and explicit in her title, which includes her self-designation "compulsive overeater." She admits on paper the self-image she denied during her senior year: "My body was a part of me I seldom saw in the short dorm mirrors. I could easily hide it under flannel shirts and old jeans. My weight went up and up and up." She also admits, as the word "confessions" in title indicates, her discovery that "I could eat all that I wanted and then vomit and still lose weight." And she admits the detrimental consequences of "nights of being unable to study, of being unable to do anything but eat and vomit" that impelled her to seek help, successfully, from Overeaters Anonymous. Broccardo's subject, though hardly pleasant, is compelling and makes readers sympathetic because of the writer's unsentimental acknowledgement of her problem and her ultimate willingness to try to overcome it.

Select material to reinforce your focus.   Choose a focus—a particular angle of vision—and select details, examples, vignettes, conversations, or actions to reinforce it. Although you tell the truth, you can't tell the whole truth in a character sketch, interview, portrait, or other writing about a person; too many interpretations would bury both you and your subject under a mountain of trivia.

If you establish a *hierarchy of selectivity* for your subject you'll discuss the most important (and perhaps the second most important, third most important, and so on) aspect, or the most representative, the most unusual, or the most memorable aspect. And you'll leave out those that are low on the list. Consequently, even in a limited space, your choice of revealing information will convey the essence of what you want to emphasize about your subject.

Leslie Moore concentrates on her father's relationship with his children, particularly herself, incorporating a lifetime of complex personality traits and family dynamics in her father's lessons on body surfing, softball pitching, and writing. Although she alludes to other aspects of his life, such as his career change from pediatrics to public health, and his wife of two months who melts into the background, and that he "would read with a drink in one hand and a cigar in the other," she does not elaborate on these features, although they might be prominent in another's account.

Show, don't tell.   Showing rather than telling is good practice for many kinds of writing, particularly for writing about people. You'll want your readers to see the subject in action, to understand the subject's characteristic temperament, thought processes, emotions, or behavior. So treat your subject like a character in a drama. You can place *the subject in a dramatic situation,* acting or reacting in a typical way, just as Carolina Broccardo depicts herself systematically working her way through the cookie dough, the M&Ms, and the leftover cake. You can *convey an active state of mind* by recreating the subject's interior monologue, thought process—if you can do so, using interviews or other information—or by the subject's conversation with others—told as either dialogue or paraphrase. Through this means, your subject and companions (if any) do the acting and the talking and do not require lengthy explanations from you as the writer. Be careful to *let your subjects speak in their own voices*—their own language and dialect—so they won't all sound like you. "You dumb stupe!" is Moore's father's expression, not hers.

H. D. ("Red") Eubanks, construction supervisor, roars into action in student Steve O'Connor's account of the first day of his summer job as a laborer building oil storage tanks in the 110-degree Texas panhandle:

> Just then a huge, jacked-up green Chevy pick-up roared in through the mud tracks left by the derrick-tractor. I could see a Confederate flag decal on the back window and a fat, freckled hand grabbing the can of Skoal off the dashboard. . . .
>
> Red seemed glad to see me when I introduced myself, and he smothered my hand as I shook his beefy paw. My new boss was a short man, but built like a tank, with forearms as thick as telephone poles. With his fiery orange hair and sharp, inspecting eyes riveting on me over his barrel chest, I hoped that I would never be the object of this man's anger. I jumped at his heels when he motioned for me to follow him over to a large, white trailer-end of a semitruck, our daily meeting place. A dozen men of various ages were sitting on twin benches along the plywood walls. Opening a can of Skoal and, to my shock, shoving the entire contents into his fat cheek, Red called the attention of the crew.
>
> "Men, this here's Steve. He's a college boy from New Mexico State, the Aggies, and he's gonna be with us for the summer." Bits of the powdered tobacco were flying out of his mouth. "Now I want you all to go easy on this boy for the first couple days, so's we can show him we got nuthin' against Yankees."

I was glad to hear that, even though I wish he hadn't brought up my Northern heritage. The wall full of leather-skinned faces waited for my reaction when Red turned to speak to me.

"Steve, we're gonna follow the tradition of the Tankies by givin' you a full week to show that you can work as hard as the rest of us. You'll be doin' all the shit-work, and yore gonna git hollered at a lot, but we're goin' to give y'all a fair chance to prove yerself."

By "Tankies" I presumed that he was referring to the men who do the kind of work I was about to try, to build those huge, round natural gas and water storage tanks that appear along every highway and shipping canal in the country. This was a group of men who welded, pounded, hoisted, and cussed the tank together from the ground up. It was toilsome and hazardous work, and I was told that if anything was going to make a man out of me, this job would.

Red began to introduce me to the line of half-interested faces that were showing the effects of the previous night's heavy drinking: "Lessee, well you met Ed already. That's Dempsey next to him; he's the man that'll keep you busy. Over there on the flux bags is Gary and that long-hair, Tony"—his curly mop barely covered his ears—"and those two boys a-settin' there on them weldin' rods is Ron and his brother, Spyder. Now Steve, these fellers here are just a bunch of hard-workin', hard-drinkin' boys, and we know yore gonna fit in real good with us all. I don't think there's a man here who don't drink up at least a gallon of that ol' Coors every night, so if you're no alcoholic now, you will be right shortly."

O'Connor shows us how Red drives, looks, moves, chews tobacco, and has control over his work crew. Red's language, like his behavior, labels him as unassuming, down-to-earth, a mixture of strength and kindliness, competence and good humor. He is very powerful. O'Connor's language, with its correct grammar and standard pronunciation, emphasizes the gap between the college student and his less educated, more muscular colleagues. His writing illustrates not only the precept of "Show, don't tell," but its corollaries, "Don't preach" and "Keep your explanations to a minimum." When you show your main characters in action, your point will emerge from their thoughts and behavior, from the events narrated, and from the reactions of subordinate characters to the subjects or the situation.

Make your private references public.   Your life, like everyone else's, is full of private words, jokes, symbols, experiences that only you and perhaps a few intimates understand and fully appreciate. Don Marquis's cryptic dedication of *archy and mehitabel*, "to babs/with babs knows what/and babs knows why," tantalizes readers, but outsiders can only imagine what Marquis and Babs know. Part of your responsibility as a writer is to make private meanings public.

This doesn't mean you have to explain the obvious or belabor the nuances of familiar expressions and behavior—such as a come-hither look, a pout, or a frown—that have the same meanings in comparable contexts of many cultures. If you're in doubt about whether your readers will understand a private allusion, try it out on someone who is unfamiliar with the personal meaning. If that person comprehends it as is, enough said. If the person doesn't understand it, try to supply more context rather than resort to an overt explanation; as with a joke, if you have to explain the punch line, the wit evaporates.

O'Connor doesn't need to tell his readers that the "Tankies" live a hard, dangerous, and stressful life that demands enormous strength and teamwork. But by describing the supervisor's "forearms as thick as telephone poles," by specifying the Texas temperature as 110 degrees in the sun, by having Red express his concern that the new worker "fit in real good with us all," even by indicating—with or without exaggeration—the quantity of beer consumed, O'Connor conveys the ethos of the workers and the ambience of their life.

Use an appropriate pattern of organization.   Different patterns of organization—chronological, psychological dominance, or the juxtaposition of vignettes—work well for different kinds of writings about people.

Writers often employ a *chronological pattern* to narrate a particular experience or relationship, if not an entire life, from start to finish. Writers also use this pattern to emphasize the gaining of an insight, as they recount an experience whose significance gradually becomes apparent. Likewise, writers who focus on the process of emotional, psychological, physical, or professional maturation—such as growing up or coming of age—usually proceed from beginning to the end.

Thus student Aubergine Field characterizes her first love affair in the context of the first semester of her freshman year:

> i met up with a crazy violinist engineering student who was my partner in acting class who had a nice smile and was knowledgeable in the ways of st. louis. and it was someone named stu and pretty soon he said let's go to the ozark folk festival and we did and we didn't know how to dance the way the ozark people were doing but we pretended we did and there was lots of fun in dancing bluegrass like the ozark mountain people do.
>
> the crazy violinist became stu—a friend and a sweetheart and a lover all rolled into one. my days were taken up with eating apple pancakes and rich thick green pea soup and homemade whole wheat bread and other vegetarian goodies. we practiced our acting exercises and we read kurt vonnegut and richard brautigan and t. s. eliot aloud to each other and we walked around st. louis and gave dinner parties but mostly we just sat around and loved each other.

Such an intense relationship this early in one's college career is too hot not to cool down. Field implies its conclusion at the conclusion of her narrative, which she writes from the perspective of a sadder-but-wiser sophomore contrasting the then and now of her experience:

> there were so many firsts that fall: first semester of college, first long-lasting love affair, first time i was in the south, first time i was ever so unabashedly happy. i can't remember how i did it, if i was drugged by something in the air or it was the spice in stu's cooking or some magic combination of everything but the problems of existence didn't confront me.
>
> one day walking back from classes i looked at one of the flaming trees along the path. in a burst of glory i set up shop by the tree to offer a leaf to everyone who passed. this was glory for me to open up fully like a flower on the sunniest day of fall and simply offer myself up to the world. i could do it then and not worry about how it would look. but i am no longer in my first semester of college and i feel too battered to risk somebody knocking off a petal so i no longer offer leaves or petals to strangers. but the smell in the air is the same as ever this fall and i recall the story to offer to you.

That Field was a flower child of the early 1970s is implied in the details—folk dancing, vegetarianism, reading Vonnegut and Brautigan—which in combination make this a nostalgic period piece to readers of the 1990s.

Writers may also organize works about people according to a *pattern of psychological dominance,* proceeding either from the least compelling or least intense feature or phenomenon to the most attractive or most intense one, or the reverse. Leslie Moore's portrait of her father escalates in intensity. Moore begins the first section, "The Scene," by describing her father's "long frame" "folded into the low-slung chair" in her living room, "his white beard nestled into his chest." In the second section, "The Situation," she uses her father's capture and monopoly of the family's favorite chair, the heirloom "citadel that no one vacates willingly," to show his selfish domination of the other members of the household. In the third section, "The Implication," Moore elaborates on the impact of her father's selfishness on the household, which "forces us to move around him—around his feet, his books, his games—around a lifestyle that we don't share." So when Moore both expands and softens her gaze in the fourth (and last) section, "The Human Being" (pages 85–87), we are prepared for her father's harshness and pleased by its positive effects, which we hadn't seen before. Her father's severe insistence on perfection that led him to coach her endlessly is also his expression of love and it is mirrored in his daughter's acerbic, double-edged portrait. Writing with power and clarity, she shares his unsentimental vision that is the sure, steady gaze of love.

Writings about people may also be organized through a *pattern of juxtaposing vignettes,* telling brief stories that either symbolically or actually manifest the subject's character or an important aspect of the life. These may or may not have a connecting matrix. To demonstrate the difficulties of being a compulsive overeater, Broccardo selects three revealing incidents of gorging on sweets—cookie dough, M&Ms, and cake; these are related in theme but not necessarily in time.

Demonstrate why readers should share your attitude.   You want your readers to like the people you like (including, presumably yourself) and to dislike those you dislike. Readers don't necessarily have to admire everything about the subject in order to find it interesting, or even appealing. You may find Moore's ambiguous relationship with her crusty father problematic, because it departs so far from the sentimental (and perhaps unreal) ideal, but as compelling as King Lear's excoriating relationship with his daughters.

Likewise, readers may find weight a painful subject if you dislike being fat or thinking of people whose struggle to stay slender reminds you of your own battle of the bulge, you can sympathize with Broccardo's straightforward acknowledgement of her bulimia and rejoice in her successful attempts to overcome the daily difficulties:

> I cannot swear that I will not have a relapse. Indeed, the philosophy of Overeaters Anonymous, that members take one day at a time, makes me unwilling to prophesize anything. However, I can state that I no longer fear going grocery shopping (and somehow finding in the bag the Twinkies I really did not want to buy) or going to the movies (and somehow eating an entire box of miniature Heath bars), or just going for a walk (and ending up inside Baskin Robbins). I no longer add up the calories of every morsel of food I consume and then try to "burn" off that total. Instead, I follow a preplanned food guide. . . .

Such candid admissions of the faults, problems, difficulties, even failures of yourself or another person will attract readers, rather than alienate them, as long as they are not whining or self-serving. Readers who stay with writings about prickly or difficult personalities are somehow comforted to recognize that others besides themselves have problems but, as the Duc de La Rochefoucauld cynically observed, "We all have strength enough to bear the misfortunes of others." It is less easy for readers to bear another's unmitigated good fortune or to tolerate the world's Pollyannas, the people on whom rain never falls. Their constant happiness seems unreal and could consequently be repellent to readers who may be envious or simply unconvinced.

Characterization

Four approaches to writing about people—descriptive, dramatic, impressionistic, and historical or contextual—are particularly revealing of a character either in action or in a more analytic portrait. These approaches may be used separately or in combination to convey someone's essential self.

The Descriptive Approach

In this approach, you'll use a great many specific details to reveal the personality, temperament, and characteristic or atypical behavior of the central character and perhaps of others in the character's world. You will emphasize the private or the public selves of your subject in one or more roles. You'll show this person thinking specific thoughts and, from particular motives, performing (or refusing to perform) certain actions. You may or may not describe the subject's appearance. Although Homer tells us that Helen is the most beautiful woman in the world, even worth waging the Trojan War over, he never says what she looks like. Indeed, many verbal portraits are painted without reference to the subject's height, weight, degree of attractiveness, or customary clothing, although many portraits indicate the person's age range, if not the specific year. In using the descriptive approach, you'll consider the elements listed in the five paragraphs that follow.

What are the dominant features of the subject's character and temperament?   Where does the subject fit in on a continuum from aggressive to easygoing? from energetic to lethargic? from expressive to reserved? from organized to chaotic? from serious to fun-loving? from open to secretive? from ethical to unethical? How can I tell?

What kind of mind does the subject have?   Is the subject intellectual, anti-intellectual, or somewhere in between? theoretically oriented or practical? good with abstractions, with people, and or with machines?

How does the subject look?   Is the person attractive? If so, in what ways? What is the subject's body size, shape, and physical condition? What are the subject's characteristic facial expressions, postures, gestures? Is the person graceful or clumsy? Does the subject display any unusual behaviors? How well groomed is the subject? What sort of clothing does the person wear (style, quality, age, condition) and how suitable is it to the wearer or the occasion?

What kind of language does the subject use?   Formal, conversational, slangy, or profane language? What dialectal or regional pronunciations and vocabulary does the speaker use? How simple or complex are the sentences? How colorful or mundane are the expressions? (See "Suggestions for Writing Dialogue," pages 98–99.) What do the silences say? What does the body language mean?

What are the subject's activities?   What is (or were) the subject's job, hobby, or skill? What training or experience does the person have to qualify as a professional or to enhance an amateur status? Why choose this particular job or activity? What opportunities does it provide? What are its limitations? or the performer's? How good is the person at what he or she does? Does the subject have a reputation, international, national, or local?

As you describe relevant aspects of these characteristics through details of sight, sound, taste, touch, smell, and action, mental or physical, you will provide both a portrait of your subject and an interpretation of character. Your interpretation will be explicit if you offer specific reasons for why something is significant or trivial, benign or sinister. Or it may be implied by your choice and arrangement of details and by the tone of your words.

Student Max Baker's portrait of farmer Homer Alumbaugh begins with description:

> The hanging yellow teapot clock ticks away at five in the afternoon. The sun comes through the west window of the small kitchen of yellow walls and potted plants. The counters are cluttered with dishes, glasses, pots of jam, and two large cookie jars. On the aging refrigerator in the corner hang notes and crayon pictures (one saying in childish script, "To Grandpa"). The room is simple and comfortable; nothing seems strange or out of place here.
>
> In the middle, at a long, rectangular table, sits Homer Alumbaugh, a thin, wispy-haired man of 79. His skin is a proud outdoor tan, not a confined, delicate white. His whole body throbs with energy and eagerness, even though he is quiet now.
>
> By his hand sits a coffee cup, full and steaming. He knows that it is waiting, for he put it here, and his game with it is about to begin. Two weeks ago Homer Alumbaugh underwent surgery for cataracts, necessary if he wanted to see and to read. Although his movements are rough and uncertain, he is determined to shed the black-handled magnifying glass soon. This night he is missing a big event, his granddaughter's wedding, and he intends to miss no more.
>
> His hand creeps out like an animal, almost unnoticeably moving about, probing the slick white table top, wanting to feel the heat of the cup. Then, as the hand feels the warmth growing closer, then contact, it just as slowly withdraws.
>
> He sits for a moment, rubbing his hair back, running his fingers across his face. Again, on a direct course devoid of clumsiness, his hand returns to the cup. Without mishap he places his finger in the handle and starts to raise the cup (steady, Homer, he says to himself). The cup is half way to his lips (easy, wait, and stop that damn shaking) and continues on. He takes a grateful sip, and returns the cup to its saucer base.
>
> Homer Alumbaugh was born on a farm twelve or thirteen miles outside of Odessa, Missouri . . .

Baker describes a great deal and implies still more. The setting, a farm kitchen, is "simple and comfortable," complete with the teapot-shaped clock, the potted plants, and the cookie jars. Homer Alumbaugh's dignity is enhanced by the repetition of his full name each time he is referred to. He is a man of firm character and quiet strength despite his years and his recent surgery. Baker wisely shows this man in action, his body throbbing "with energy and eagerness." The game with the coffee cup reveals Alumbaugh's resourcefulness and determination to control himself and his environment; it satisfies him (he takes a "grateful sip" of coffee) and the readers that he wins.

The Dramatic Approach

Three major ways to portray characters dramatically are through their *actions, thoughts,* and *dialogue.* You can use these singly or, more likely, in combination.

How can actions be presented in dramatic scenes?   When you show characters in action, you often set scenes, as Baker did in presenting Homer Alumbaugh and as O'Connor did in introducing readers to supervisor Red Eubanks. Some actions such as Homer's approach, retreat, and approach to the coffee cup, are physical and apparent to the observer. Other scenes are like photographs, either single pictures or a series of snapshots flipped through to show the actors in motion. In "Mirror Dance" student Margaret Ervin frames a quartet, herself and three sisters, capturing in an economical image the essence of a complex family relationship, close and interwoven:

> We four sisters are standing barefoot and half dressed in Helen's room before the dressing table that used to be our grandmother's. Huge, refinished, mahogany, completely out of scale with the room, it takes up a whole wall. We weave in and out among each other in the clutter of a sixteen-year-old's bedroom, each of us intent upon our own reflection in the glass.
>
> One sister moves up close to put on her eyemakeup and now back a bit to fix her hair. Another, never taking her eyes off her reflection, as if moving through a choreographed sequence, replaces her face with the mirror's edge, to conceal a blemish on her chin. I borrow Helen's slip. Mary trades stockings with Miriam. Miriam puts hairspray in Mary's hair, one hand protectively masking her sister's face. One layer after another goes on. Underwear, makeup, hairspray.
>
> Framed in mahogany, bare arms and hair cascading, we dance a web of sisterhood, each sister an extension of the other. And I am half-wishing, half-believing that I can borrow Miriam's flair and style, Helen's innocence, Mary's fortitude and determination. . . .

How can thoughts be presented in dramatic monologues?   Another form of dramatic approach expresses actions that are mental or emotional by recreating the character's thoughts in direct or indirect quotations. Some of

Homer's thoughts are cited in parentheses ("easy, wait, and stop that damn shaking"); others are supplied by the author: "Tonight he is missing a big event . . . and he intends to miss no more." You can write an entire essay as an interior monologue or meditation, as E. B. White often does. In "Once More to the Lake," White explores the significance of the continuity of generations from grandfather to father to son. White does with his son the same things at the same Maine lake that he and his own father had done a generation before. Through understanding his own reactions, he comes to understand the identical reactions of his father and his son:

> . . . when [my boy and I] settled into a camp near a farmhouse and into the kind of summertime I had known, I could tell that it was going to be pretty much the same as it had been before—I knew it, lying in bed the first morning . . . and hearing the boy sneak quietly out and go off along the shore in a boat [as I had done when I was his age]. I began to sustain the illusion that he was I, and therefore by simple transposition, that I was my father. This sensation persisted, kept cropping up all the time we were there. It was not an entirely new feeling, but in this setting it grew much stronger. I seemed to be living a dual existence. I would be in the middle of some simple act, I would be picking up a bait box or laying down a table fork, or I would be saying something, and suddenly it would be not I but my father who was saying the words or making the gesture.

How can dialogue convey dramatic relationships?   As people talk to each other, or to an interviewer, they reveal their thoughts, moods, feelings, conflicts, and tensions; their hopes and fears; their intended actions and past history; their opinions and interpretations of relationships and events. Keep in mind, however, that in most portraits and in some interviews you will need to supplement the dialogue with an account of the characters' thoughts and actions, and perhaps with other description and analysis, to avoid turning the essay into a play.

Dialogues can be particularly useful in delineating significant relationships between the subject and another individual or group. Nuances of expression can convey uneasiness or comfort, distance or intimacy, tension or relaxation, and a host of other feelings that characterize the complexities of a relationship. Student Myrna Greenfield begins an essay about her ambivalent relationship with her family with the following dialogue that reveals her mother's aggressiveness, mild deception, and urge to nurture her grown-up child in opposition to Myrna's own determined resistance to her mother's well-intentioned efforts.

> "Tastes like ICE CREAM!" my mother exclaimed, as she dipped her spoon into a carton of plain yogurt. "Try some."
> "Ugh," I said, and made a face at her. "I bet it's like sour cream."

> "No, try some!" my mother protested. She thrust a spoonful of yogurt to-wards my mouth.
> "No!" I squealed, pushing her hand away.
> "You don't know what you're missing," my mother told me.
> After my mother left the room I tried half a spoonful of plain yogurt. It tasted like sour cream.

Having shown her typical Jewish mother in an act of typical Jewish moth-erhood, Greenfield follows the scene with some analytical statements that would be hard to convey through dialogue: "We were the typical Jewish fam-ily in the typical middle-class typical mostly Jewish Chicago suburb of Skokie. Only we weren't typical—no family is. . . ."

Another form of dialogue is the question and answer format of some in-terviews. Usually interviewers try to be inconspicuous and not to call atten-tion to their own language even when quoting their own questions, in order to allow readers to concentrate on the thoughts, character, and style of the interviewee. In other interviews, interviewers absent themselves entirely, deleting from the completed portrait all personal references and thereby al-lowing the subject to speak as if engaging in a monologue (see pages 107–112).

The following suggestions for writing dialogue can serve as guidelines for dramatic portraits.

Suggestions for Writing Dialogue

1. Listen for the speaker's characteristic sentence patterns, cadence, empha-sis, and rhythm. Pay attention to the "music" as well as to the words, and note the variations. If you can tape the speaker and listen as often as you need to, so much the better, as long as taping doesn't inhibit the speaker's natural discourse.

2. Determine the speaker's general level of vocabulary, whether it's formal, conversational, or full of slang; concrete or abstract; simple or complex. In your rendering of dialogue, be sure to include key words, such as jargon, technical language, foreign expressions, slang, clichés, dialect, and typical personal expressions. To keep the flavor, it helps to include a sprinkling of the speaker's characteristic allusions to people, places, and other personal references; it's not necessary to explain them.

3. If the speaker uses contractions (I'm, you're, can't), keep these in the di-alogue so it'll sound natural.

4. Aim for the essence of someone's speech rather than to literally recreate every word and stammer. Edit out the redundancies and the vague sentences that trail off without saying anything, and include only enough meaningless filler words (such as *like* and *you know*) to hint at their flavor.

5. Supply adverbs or other directions ("mother protested," "I squealed") when necessary to indicate the tone, pitch, speed, and other features of the

discourse. Avoid unnecessary adverbs and overly colorful verbs, such as Tom Swifties—named after the character Tom Swift in the series of novels of the same name), as in "Close the refrigerator door," she said, frostily, and "Whose lost dog is this?" he barked. When in doubt, it's preferable to understate with a simple "he said" or "she said."

6. Use dialect sparingly. An occasional "y'all" or "youse" is sufficient to convey an entire accent to a careful reader, whose mind's ear supplies the rest. If you write everything in dialect, the language will sound unreal and will be unreadable.

7. Read the finished dialogue out loud or have someone read it to you. Does it sound like the speaker you're trying to present? If not, tinker with it, changing a word here, a phrase or cadence there, until it sounds right and conveys the essence of a real person speaking.

The Impressionistic Approach

An impressionistic approach to writing a portrait is similar to an impressionistic approach to painting a picture. You assemble scraps of description such as appearances, actions, moods, details of setting or clothing. You provide bits of relevant historical information about the subject's ancestry, career, past life, typical milieus. You might intersperse snatches of dialogue among these to illustrate a relationship, activity, or state of mind. Each piece of information is connotative and evokes in the reader a reaction to the larger unit that it suggests, like thinking about the genius of Leonardo da Vinci by looking at a reproduction of Mona Lisa's smile.

In an impressionistic approach, you don't elaborate on any single element. But when the elements are assembled in juxtaposition, they reflect and refract on one another to provide a more comprehensive meaning; the whole becomes greater than the sum of its parts. You might juxtapose contrasting elements such as evidence of your subject's stinginess and generosity. You might arrange fragments in chronological or historical order, proceeding from earliest to most recent or the reverse or shifting back and forth in time. You could move from the items with the simplest or fewest emotional connotations to those fragments most complex or most highly charged; though to avoid anticlimax you would not want to reverse the order.

Sandy Richardson wrote "Bah, Humbug!" to demonstrate her attempt to free herself from an unwilling adherence to her mother's standards of behavior, housekeeping, and morality. She impressionistically identifies some of her deviations from these standards and in the process paints a portrait encompassing her childhood, teenage, and adult selves:

> My mother had been dead seven years when I first noticed that I apologized a lot—often to people I didn't know or didn't like and who didn't care anyway.

I think I had been apologizing or at least feeling amply and vaguely apologetic for most of my 27 years. In my family there was a lot that one could do wrong, and if few others recognized my many sins, I did, my mother had, her ghost continued to, and the rest of the world certainly would soon.

I had apologized for disliking my sister, trying to avoid watching Mother die, not seeing Dad enough, gaining 40 pounds, not staying physically fit, disliking *anybody* (it was O.K. to dislike whole races and nationalities), drinking beer, suffering multitudes of anxieties in graduate school, being too competent at building fires, tying knots, and pitching tents, refusing to sing "I Believe" or "Jerusalem, Jerusalem" at church any longer, not being married (until that day not one of Aunt Ella's 52 handmade quilts will be mine), being too conscientious and responsible (or too little), crying when Mother died, not crying enough when Mother died. Aways too much, too little, not right.

Further back, I knew the sinfulness of walking with toes pointed out, cutting the sandwiches horizontally, saying icebox instead of refrigerator, "you guys" instead of y'all and Louweesianna instead of Louisiana, hating the animal books mother believed in but getting in trouble for reading *Travels with Charley* (who was very much a dog, I did want to please, but who belonged to John Steinbeck who swore and believed in integrating Little Rock) and refusing to read the biographies of Queen Elizabeth and Mamie Eisenhower thoughtfully produced by Aunt Gustava. Furthermore, I more often than not forgot to dust the baseboards, the bottom rungs on chairs, and behind the books on the bookshelves.

Richardson juxtaposes and intermingles her violations of manners and morality; her refusal to accept the family's religion, code of behavior, or role stereotyping; the development of her own taste and style with rebellion against those of her family. Readers can infer from these details the pattern of Richardson's gradual maturation and moral coming of age, her acceptance of racial equality despite racist family pressures, and her ambivalence about her family. She emerges from her confession as candid, likeable, and still growing in character and moral stature—indeed, she used the writing of this self-portrait to enhance her growth.

The main danger of an impressionistic approach is that you'll include irrelevancies or details whose significance will escape the readers. If you can justify including something not only because it actually happened (a great deal will have happened that you won't have room for) but also because it provides or emphasizes a facet of meaning that would otherwise be lost, then leave it in. If it doesn't make sense to a trial reader, provide more context or slightly more elaboration, but stop short of belaboring even the allusive.

The Historical or Contextual Approach

When you focus on the life of a subject from a historical or contextual approach, you'll emphasize the relevant aspects of that person's background and contexts—familial, racial, national or regional, political, economic, religious, social, intellectual, aesthetic, and geographic. You will be particularly concerned with how and why the subject developed as she did, how she matured (or why she failed to do so), and how she relates to her present circumstances. You might, for example, want to explain how the subject developed a particular set of values, what impact she made on the times or on her profession, or how she was alike or different from other members of her family or social class—the focus of Richardson's self-portrait. If you emphasize the process your subject goes through, the success of an exemplary life becomes easier for readers to accept and to imitate (if they wish) than if they see only the perfect completed model. If the outcome is ambiguous or problematic, it, too, can be explored. What personal price, for instance, does an executive pay to achieve power—and to keep it?

Fully aware of his historical significance even as he wrote, Benjamin Franklin recounts his rise from rags to riches and worldly esteem in his quintessentially American *Autobiography,* told in the spirit that inspired the popular Horatio Alger novels and other manifestations of the American dream. Although he nominally writes to offer good advice to his son, Franklin clearly provides instructions on how to achieve success to a larger audience of fellow citizens:

> From the poverty and obscurity in which I was born and in which I passed my earliest years, I have raised myself to a state of affluence and some degree of celebrity in the world. As constant good fortune has accompanied me even to an advanced period of life, my posterity will perhaps be desirous of learning the means, which I employed, and which, thanks to Providence, so well succeeded with me. They may also deem them fit to be imitated. . . .

Here are some of the many considerations you might explore in a historical or contextual approach.

What is the subject's background and heritage?   What is the subject's family background? What heritage—racial, ethnic, and familial—has been transmitted? with what changes? Are there any notable ancestors, famous or infamous? Has the person been an integral member of a particular family, tribe, or clan? or has she been an outcast, or a rebel? what reasons?

In interpreting the effect of one event on the subject, remember not to consider it in isolation. Although Eudora Welty and Richard Wright were born a year apart and both grew up in Mississippi, residing for a time in Jackson, their autobiographies reveal that they lived in decidedly different worlds.

What is the subject's physical setting?   In what country, state, and setting (urban, suburban, rural) does the subject live? Where did he grow up and in what particular period of history? How did time and place affect his choice of companions, job, ways of spending time and money? Did he participate in memorable events or characteristic activities of that time or place, such as an exploration, a strike, a political protest, a cultural phenomenon—perhaps a dance marathon, a Thanksgiving celebration, a wedding, or a rock festival? How have residence and travel affected the subject's world view?

Is the subject a member of a group?   Is the subject a member of a particular economic or occupational group, say, a factory worker, farmer, doctor, or business executive? In what ways is the subject a typical or atypical member? How—and how well—has she performed the expected tasks of the job? with what attitudes and current and future expectations? Has she made innovations, other contributions, or been successful in other ways? according to what standards? Why does she consider the job enjoyable—or not much fun?

To what social class does the subject belong?   by heritage or by choice? How have the values and behaviors of this class influenced him? How does he function as a member of society? Is he a leader of a particular social organization, group, or movement? a member or a dropout? Who are his peers, friends, associates, antagonists or enemies, and what are they like?

What are the subject's values and way of life?   To what extent have they been influenced by her religious background or beliefs, religious affiliation, education, or a person (clergy or family member)? Has she rejected any religious tenets? If so, which ones, and why? You could ask similar questions about how the subject's political beliefs and actions have affected her values, especially if she is deeply involved in party politics or has escaped from the regime of another country. Or you could explore the growth and manifestations of any other belief or value system—aesthetic, feminist, or nationalist—that the subject holds.

What education has this person had?   in what particular intellectual field, trade, or skill (including athletics, cooking, farming)? Has the education been formal or informal? public or private? limited or ongoing? Did the subject have any notable teachers or mentors?

What kind of taste does the subject have?   How does this reflect his heritage? his economic status? the times in which he lives? How is his taste manifested in his choice of furniture, clothing, food, music, recreation, and other cultural phenomena? in his contributions to his culture?

Sources of historical and contextual information
Primary sources.   Any information learned firsthand is considered a *primary source*. Obviously, if you're writing about yourself, you'll be the ma-

jor source of your own information. Most autobiographical writers rarely consult other sources, except possibly photographs, their own correspondence, or commentary on their work, such as book reviews or citations accompanying awards. For the most part, autobiographers mine their memories and whether or not they remember what actually happened, what they remember—or invent—becomes the material of their personal writings. As Annie Dillard says, "After you've written, you can no longer remember anything but the writing. . . . After I've written about any experience, my memories . . . are gone; they've been replaced by the work."

If you write about someone else, the primary sources remain the same: whatever your subject said, did, wrote, created, wore, used, wherever he or she lived and worked and played. If you interview someone for a biographical portrait, you may depend mostly or entirely on that primary source for information.

Maxine Hong Kingston knows exactly what she needs to explain to American readers of *The Woman Warrior*. Her own experience growing up as a child of Chinese immigrant parents in twentieth-century California enables her to focus on striking differences between American culture and her family's heritage of history, beliefs, values, customs. Thus, Kingston studs her narrative with explanations of what it's like to work in a Chinese laundry (which her parents ran), what it's like to attend Chinese school (as she did every day after American school), what it means for a Chinese-American teenager to contend with the "fresh-off-the-boat" immigrants her parents promote as suitors. She counts on her readers to compare this information with what they know about their own culture. Thus when she explains her mother's traditional cooking, she does not need to point out its obvious departures from a conventional American diet:

> My mother cooked for us: racoons, skunks, hawks, city pigeons, wild ducks, wild geese, black-skinned bantams, snakes, garden snails, turtles that crawled about the pantry floor and sometimes escaped under the refrigerator or stove, catfish that swam in the bathtub. . . . When I was as tall as the washing machine, I stepped out on the back porch one night, and some heavy, ruffling, windy, clawed thing dived at me. Even after getting chanted back to sensibility, I shook when I recalled that perched everywhere there were owls with great hunched shoulders and yellow scowls. They were a surprise for my mother from my father. We children used to hide under the beds with our fingers in our ears to shut out the bird screams and the thud, thud of the turtles swimming in the boiling water, their shells hitting the sides of the pot. Once the third aunt who worked at the laundry ran out and bought us bags of candy to hold over our noses; my mother was dismembering a skunk on the chopping block. I could smell the rubbery odor through the candy.

Kingston lets these details do the work; she doesn't need to spell out the repellent aspects of her mother's preferred diet. Her only explicit interpretive comment wraps up this analysis, "I would live on plastic."

Secondary sources.   All information other than that learned firsthand is a *secondary source.* For an interview or a more extensive biographical portrait, you may need to consult secondary sources as well. You can interview one or more of the subject's relatives, friends, associates, and enemies. If the person participated in events of historical or local significance, you can examine appropriate reference materials such as encyclopedias, newspaper and magazine articles, or historical accounts. You can learn about the subject's work from others in the same field, from specialized publications, or a visit to the work place. If the subject is famous, you can see what biographers and historians have had to say and check their references for additional sources—photographs, films, videotapes, wills and other legal documents, canceled checks and income tax records—but beware of publicists' hype. Potential sources may be endless if the subject is well known. You'll be limited only by the amount of effort you wish to spend to find and examine them, or by their own redundancy. If your subject is not well known, secondary sources about the person himself may be regrettably sparse and you may need to flesh out your interpretation with information about relevant aspects of the culture—political, social, economic, literary, and so on—and the place(s) in which he lived.

This single example of how a careful biographer uses secondary sources to verify or take issue with primary sources is representative of the technique. In *By Force of Will: The Life and Art of Ernest Hemingway,* Scott Donaldson, a literary scholar, examines the evidence of Hemingway's athletic prowess and concludes that after Hemingway became a famous writer he took pains to "construct a myth about the athletic feats of his youth that hardly squares with the facts":

> Thus [Hemingway] wrote Harvey Breit, a writer and assistant editor of *The New York Times Book Review,* that he had been a football star at Oak Park High School, as well as an outstanding pitcher and hitter on the baseball team. Somewhere, he told Breit, there was a picture of his hitting the ball over the left-field fence, but he could not locate it. In point of fact, however, Hemingway never played high-school baseball, though he used to throw the ball around with Bill Smith in summer vacation pick-up games. As Smith recalls, Ernest would usually catch and Smith would pitch. "He wasn't so hot actually," Smith remembers, "but the picture he had of himself was pitching, not catching. He insisted on pitching in one game but I had to relieve him with three runs in and only one out in the first inning." As a ball player, his brother Leicester writes, Ernest was a pretty studious reader. His mother used to find him poring over a book, and propose that he go out and play some baseball. "Aw, Mother," Ernest would answer, "I pitch like a hen," and go on reading. . . .
>
> In sports as in other areas, the Hemingway image did not fit reality. Actually he had been a sensitive boy, something of a loner, given to shying away from head-on blocks and tackles on the football field. But while still in his early twenties, Hemingway set about altering the facts. Though he never really cottoned

to team sports, he wanted, like Walt Whitman, to be regarded as "one of the roughs." So he spun apocryphal yarns about running away from home, about brawls in and out of the ring, about the tough neighborhoods he had frequented.

Donaldson's sources include a letter from Hemingway to Breit; an interview ("Interview with Hemingway's 'Bill Gorton'" by Donald St. John, published in *Hemingway and the Sun Set*); a recollection by Hemingway's brother, Leicester, published in biography, *My Brother, Ernest Hemingway*; and Hemingway's high school newspaper, the Oak Park *Trapeze*. On these sources Donaldson imposes his own interpretation of Hemingway's character.

Interviews

How to Conduct an Interview

Talking with people about themselves is a pleasant and fairly simple way to do original writing without elaborate research. Nearly anyone can be a successful interviewer. You don't have to be particularly sophisticated, a fluent talker, or trained as a scholar or investigative journalist to do a good job. But you do need a lively curiosity and a sympathetic ear. The interview should go smoothly if you use the following procedure.

Keep the purpose clearly in mind.   Do you want to present a portrait of the subject's life or personality? to obtain information about something the subject knows (blizzards, Bach, the Bible)? or has experienced, such as a historical period (the 60s) a significant event (the Vietnam War), or an unusual opportunity (to serve with the Peace Corps in Chad). Let your purpose dictate your questions.

Set up the interview in advance.   Write or call the person you want to interview, identifying yourself and your purpose. Someone who is not used to being interviewed may shy away at first. But your implicit judgment in requesting an interview, that this person is worth paying attention to, is bound to be flattering. You can set your subject at ease by beginning with non-threatening questions: "Have you always lived in this town?" or "I've admired your success in sailing/school/business and would like to find out more about it. How did you get started?"

Do your homework.   Learn enough about your topic before the interview so you won't waste your time or your subject's on the trivial or the obvious. You'll get more interesting information if your subject believes that you're moderately well-informed and doesn't have to start at ground zero.

To find out what it's like to be a cocktail waitress, skim a book on the subject before the interview, to get a sense of a bartender's job.

Make a list of specific questions about the main issues and subtopics. Try to keep values and judgments out of the questions. Say "What do you think about bartending as a job?" rather than "Don't you hate the way your customers flirt with you?" Avoid questions that can be answered with a simple "yes" or "no" or you'll miss the colorful details that come with explanations. Although you'll compile your questions in advance, don't submit them to your subject; people talk more candidly if they haven't rehearsed their answers.

Practice. If you've never conducted an interview before, try a practice interview first with someone other than your subject. Ask the person you practice with to tell you whether the questions are clear, whether you appear to be rushing or probing too hard, and whether you came across as a sympathetic listener.

Talk as little as possible during the interview. You'll want to express your interest, but with a minimum of words, except to ask for occasional clarification or to encourage the subject to say more. Use nonverbal gestures— smiles, nods, leaning slightly toward the speaker—to indicate your attention and appreciation.

If in response to a question the speaker pauses . . . and the pause gets longer . . . and longer . . . . and longer . . . . wait! North Americans, afraid of conversational vacuums, rush to fill up the empty spaces with words. Fight this impulse during an interview, or you'll talk too much. You may be able to restrain yourself if you remember to focus on the person you're interviewing. You're not there to participate in a dialogue but to hear the subject's story. If you're patient, even after a very long pause the speaker will usually start in again. . . . . . . Try it.

You will want to steer the interview clear of evasions or ramblings too far afield from your topic—unless the digressions turn out to be interesting. Sometimes the unexpected, chance observation or the unguarded comment opens up new worlds, fascinating to explore.

Be aware of your subject's self-serving remarks and biases. What does the subject strongly favor or oppose? Who are her heroes and villains and particular friends? Is she—as far as you can tell—withholding any crucial information or changing the facts to put herself in a better light? Is she telling you the whole truth? Although you'll want to give the speaker the benefit of the doubt, sometimes a partial truth is intended to mislead. As Lawrence Durrell has observed, "Our lives are made up of selected fictions." When in doubt, check it out through another source.

Take notes and simultaneously tape the interview.   Do this to ensure accuracy, but only if your subject agrees to it. If he won't talk with the tape running, you might warm up for a while without it and then ask again. If he still says "no," you'll have to be content with note taking. When the interview is over, you can ask your subject to verify the spellings of unfamiliar names of people and places.

If your subject talks rapidly, you'll be lucky to be able to write down key words and some short, quotable phrases. The tape recorder can help you fill in the gaps in your notes. Most writers can't work directly from tapes, however, because they are too time-consuming to move around in. Transcription of every word isn't feasible for the purposes of most interviews (an hour's tape takes ten to twelve hours to transcribe verbatim). However, if you're writing a book it might be worth the effort. So for a shorter piece, don't try to transcribe the whole tape; just concentrate on the memorable and useful quotations. You'll find that a written text is easier to visualize and to edit.

Prepare for the possibility of a return visit.   As you wrap up the interview, ask your subject if you can check the facts with her later, if necessary, and thank her. A written note of appreciation is not only thoughtful, but a reminder that you might be back.

Editing an Interview

Most interviews are initially repetitive and disorganized, however articulate the subject. Like a fox's trail through the forest, interviews-in-process circle around a given topic, double back on themselves, head off along diverse paths, and may or may not end up in the direction toward which they started. Even educated speakers are likely to use sloppy grammar and clichés and to let their sentences wander and trail off. . . . If you quote whole blocks of discourse, chances are that the speaker will appear to be far more rambling and out of control in cold print than in warm conversation.

To write an interesting portrait of your subject or a coherent account of the topics discussed, you'll have to edit the information you've collected, so you can organize and use the salvageable and quotable ten percent (or thereabouts) of your interview's "pure gold," as Studs Terkel called it. You'll want to limit your topic to a particular focus, the most significant or the most typical aspect of your subject's life or work, or the most revealing of new information. You will need to organize your material—chronologically, topically, logically, or psychologically—even if you have to regroup portions of the interview in a sequence different from the way the subject initially discussed them. In the process, you'll condense material and edit out the excess. Just because your subject said it doesn't mean you have to quote it. Indeed, you'll want to eliminate unnecessary repetition, circumlocution, boring passages, and meaningless or irrelevant details. It is a convention of interviews not to supply ellipses each time words are omitted or passages are shifted around. To do so would make it look . . . as if . . . the subject . . . were stuttering. You're aiming for writing that reads smoothly, with a naturalness supplied as much by the interviewer's subtle editing as by the subject's uninhibited speech, however salty, peppery, or vinegary.

Because you want your readers to hear and see the subject as a credible, interesting, vital person, you'll need to re-create typical speech and supply enough information to make the interview self-contained, such as revealing, specific details about manner and mannerisms, clothing, setting, and typical milieus. You can include such supplementary material in an introduction or insert it throughout the interview. Be sure to identify any references to people, places, or practices that are unfamiliar to your readers.

The process of editing an interview becomes the process of interpreting the subject, either directly or indirectly. Even if you say nothing in your authorial voice, your interpretation will be apparent through your selection and arrangement of the subject's words. If you approve of the subject, you'll choose quotations that show the person in the best light. If you are neutral toward the subject, you'll use a balanced selection of quotations. If you want to convey disapproval, you can choose damning quotations ("I am not a crook") or ironically juxtapose the subject's words or paraphrases of them with contradictory aspects of her behavior. Thus in the opening sentence of "Pretty Far Out Little Dude," columnist Henry Allen makes clear his distaste for what he sees as the hypocrisy of his subject, Balyogeshwar Shri Sant Ji Maharaj, "a 13-year-old Indian guru-saint with 3 million disciples, a dime-store Frankenstein mask, the certainty that he can put you face to face with God, a fondness for zapping people with a water pistol, [and] a boundless love for all mankind and automobiles. . . ."

From Interview to Essay

The interview.   The following material is a portion of the unedited transcript of an interview that student Mary Langenberg conducted with Alfred Everett, a respectable St. Louis banker who grew up in East St. Louis, Illinois. She interviewed him to find out what life there was like in the 1920s. She indicates Everett's actions in brackets: [ ].

M: Mr. Everett, the era of the 1920s has been called the Jazz Age and you were in college about that time, weren't you?

A: Yes. The Jazz Age or the Roaring Twenties, which was, of course, a very unique time, and as time passes, seems to become more unique. I was 14 years old in 1920 and I went to college in 1922 at 16, which I do not recommend. Nevertheless, I was in college—two different schools—with an interval between, from '22 to '27. I came out to begin my business. I think it was an interesting time, as far as I am concerned, to have been in the '20s from age 14 to 24 in age.

M: It was an impressionable age, right?

A: Very. [smiles and then begins to guffaw]

M: Tell me about the young people of that period, your peer groups at that time. How did they dress, for instance?

A: [eyes glowing] Well, that was the age of the Flappers. The girls all had short dresses and there was lots of swinging around. Dancing the Charleston and the Black Bottom were the big deals. We danced on the excursion boats, the *J. S.* and *St. Paul* and they were the greatest places ever for dancing. Big floors, fine bands. Our proms at the East St. Louis High School were twelve to twelve deals. We had twelve hours of dancing. You always took a girl who was a good dancer cause you danced [snaps his fingers] about 43 or 44 dances—and you wanted somebody you could trade!

Everett then discusses his physical appearance in high school (bell-bottom trousers and slicked-down hair like Rudolph Valentino) and college (four-button suits, button-down shirts) and moves on to talk about his being expelled from college and his attendance at Southern Illinois Normal School—a one-year course. His talk then shifts to sports, Babe Ruth and baseball, Jack Dempsey and boxing, Red Grange and football, Bill Tilden and tennis, although none of these topics appears in the final essay. Then Langenberg asks him about Prohibition:

M: Midnight, January 16, 1920, was the beginning of Prohibition, when the 18th Amendment went into effect. Did you ever visit a speakeasy?

A: [laughing] I guess I visited about two hundred speakeasies!!

M: Would you describe a typical speakeasy?

A: Well, East St. Louis and Toledo, Ohio, were known as the two most wide open towns in the United States, in the speakeasy era. The speakeasy was a saloon, or a flat, first floor, second floor, third floor. They always had a peep-hole in the door, so they could check you out, so that they'd know you. [pauses to think] We had a little trouble with one speakeasy in East St. Louis because the proprietor had a glass eye. He'd get drunk with the customers. That was [thinks hard] old Duke Davis. And we'd rap on his door and then we'd wait and wait. Finally we'd yell to him, "Get your good eye on the peep-hole," because he'd be looking out with his glass eye and couldn't see anybody! [laughs hard]

M: How did you know where these speakeasies were?

A: Oh, we just knew 'em. The Stevenson Brothers were a famous pair in East St. Louis. They originated with the booze in Cuba and they'd bring it to New Orleans. They had a fleet of trucks with license plates for every state between New Orleans and there. . . .

They had a "Valley" there that was unpaved. And left unpaved cause there were so many ruts that you couldn't rush through and had to slow down. You had to pay attention to the people who were advertising their wares. This was an area of two streets, about four blocks long. Flood lights for the different houses were provided by the city! They had a wide-open valley . . . colored and white . . . and all sorts of horse parlors, or bookie joints.

The interview continues at considerable length and includes the following topics (those italicized are included in the final essay): boxer Jack Dempsey visiting East St. Louis, how to make bathtub gin, women's suffrage, Warren Harding's presidential election, Everett's father's political activities, driving automobiles, Charles Lindbergh's flight to Paris, Everett's fellow student, Al Jolson's talking movies, movie serials, the Stock Market crash, making bathtub gin (again), *crime and bootlegging, the Al Smith-Herbert Hoover presidential campaign,* Schumacher's restaurant, free lunches, *shirts to wear for dancing, a drunk-driving accident,* drinking in Tennessee with college friends, working as a shoe salesman, Everett's decision to become a banker, Saturday-night dates.

This interesting interview is typical in that it covers a large number of topics, all more or less related to the subject. Several topics are discussed in considerably greater detail than others. Some of the details can be used in the final essay, although many will prove to be expendable.

The essay.   Typically, also, this interview is incomplete for the writer's purpose. Everett saw the 1920s exclusively from his point of view, one among many possible perspectives. To supplement what she learned from the interview, Langenberg consulted newspaper files, histories, and magazines of the 1920s. She looked at photographs and visited the territory Everett had described to see for herself whether any traces of life in the 1920s remained. She thought about what she knew of the period from histories of the time. During her investigation the focus for her essay became clear. She decided to emphasize the period and the place in which Everett had lived rather than to concentrate on him exclusively. She marked portions of the transcribed interview that looked both relevant and interesting for this purpose.

Then she was ready to write her lively essay, "East St. Louis, from Jazz to Dirge." The sections of the final draft (below) incorporate material from the transcript quoted earlier; the italicized portions are derived from the interview. The essay begins with song lyrics:

> "I want to be happy,
> But I won't be happy,
> 'Til I make you happy, too. . . ."
> —*No, No, Nanette,* 1924

The War was over. The Great Depression had not yet begun. Everybody wanted to be happy!

In the decade of the twenties, happiness wore many faces. It was the new freedom of short skirts, bobbed hair, and the demise of the chaperone. It was the stimulation of jazz bands and the Dance Cult. It was found in the forbidden Casbah of the speakeasy and the titillation of bathtub gin.

As this social revolution swept the country, every city, town and hamlet was affected in some way, including the community of East St. Louis, Illinois. Just three hundred miles south of Chicago and separated from St. Louis, Missouri, by the waters of the Mississippi River, *East Saint Louis, in the twenties, became one of the most "wide-open" towns in the United States. Bootlegging and gambling operations took place in the shadow of City Hall. The red-light district known as the "Valley" was located within easy walking distance of the Court House. . . .*

Langenberg then discusses the character of East St. Louis citizens in the 1920s, introduces Everett, and begins his reminiscences:

Among the highlights of his youth were trips on the excursion boats. Because of their proximity to the Mississippi River, *East St. Louisans* had easy access to the two river steamers, the *J. S.* and *St. Paul,* both owned and operated by Streckfus Steamers, Inc. . . .

The riverboat's ballroom was a place of special enchantment. Two large mirrored globes hung from the ceiling. As they rotated slowly in the intense beam of the spotlights, thousands of tiny diamond-like reflections spun around the ceiling, creating a shower of starlight in the darkened hall. *It was heady stuff for those young dancers as they swayed and shimmied to the intoxicating syncopation of Jazz! The Charleston, the Black Bottom,* Balling the Jack. Everybody knew those dance steps and vied with each other to display their expertise.

Alfred recalls an East St. Louis High School prom on board one of the excursion boats. *"It was a twelve-to-twelve deal,"* he said, *"We had twelve hours of dancing. You always took a girl who was a good dancer, 'cause you danced every dance . . . and you wanted somebody you could trade."*

Several pages later, Langenberg writes about speakeasies and prostitution:

With the passage of the Volstead Act, saloon keepers were supposed to close their doors, or change their bars into soda fountains, but many continued to sell alcohol illegally. The speakeasy was born.

Alfred remembers many speakeasies on the East Side. *Some were saloons and some operated in flats or apartment buildings. They always had a peephole in the front door for identification of the caller.* "We had a little trouble with one speakeasy in East St. Louis," Alfred said, "because the proprietor had a glass eye . . . that was old 'Duke' Davis. He'd get drunk with the customers. We'd rap on his door and then we'd wait and wait. Finally, we'd yell at him, 'Get your good eye on the peephole, Duke!'"

Even before speakeasies became so abundant on the East Side, prostitution was a well-established fact of life there. *The activity was confined to one section of town known as the "Valley,"* an area bounded by Missouri, Ohio, and Collinsville Avenues, and Second Street. Alfred remembers that the streets were unpaved, by design, "It *was left unpaved because there were so many ruts, you couldn't rush through in your automobile. You had to slow down. You had to pay attention to the people who were advertising their wares."*

Note that throughout Langenberg follows standard interviewing practice by mingling direct and indirect quotations and by eliminating excessive words. She also provides information that Everett implied but didn't state overtly, such as the fact that the rutted roads in the "Valley" were intended to slow down automobile traffic. Mary wisely does not tamper with Everett's natural vocabulary. Although his use of "colored" may sound dated, prejudiced, or insensitive, it reflects his times and his values, which are not necessarily those of Langenberg as an author. To change his language would falsify the speech and the personality of the speaker by making both too bland.

Checklist for Writing About People

1. Do I know my subject (myself or someone else) well enough to write about this person? Do I have a sense of the subject's inner and outer selves? Am I aware of the immediate and longer term significance of the person's life or of the portion of it or incidents that I'm writing about?

2. Is my reaction to my subject positive or negative? Is my reaction strong enough to sustain my interest and that of my readers? Are my readers likely, at the outset, to share my opinion of the subject, or will I have to work with special care to convince them of the validity of my interpretation?

3. What is my emphasis? on character or personality, unusual or commonplace? on activities, skills, or lack of either? on roles, relationships? on growth and maturation (intellectual, social, psychological, or other)? on representativeness as a group member? on a particular time or place?

4. How selective or comprehensive am I in conveying this emphasis? Do I say enough to make my subject understandable? Do I restrict my portrait to the relevant events, actions, topics, conflicts, and characters?

5. Do I use an approach or combination of approaches that reflects my emphasis: descriptive, dramatic, impressionistic, or historical or contextual?

6. Do I have enough information from primary sources? from secondary sources? Are the sources reliable? Is the information accurate? up-to-date? If there are gaps, how can I fill them in?

7. If the subject has been written about before, what new information or perspective does my portrait contribute?

8. Do I try to recreate my subject's manner of speaking, gesturing, or other forms of verbal and nonverbal communication? through what means? Do I succeed?

9. Do I say or imply only what I can corroborate?

10. Through what means, direct (such as commentary) or indirect (such as selection of the subject's words and use of revealing details), do I interpret the subject? Is my representation fair? Should it be?

Selected Reference List of Writings About People

Collections of Interviews

See also Chapter 1.

Terkel, Studs. *American Dreams: Lost and Found*. 1980. New York: Ballantine, 1981.
———. *The Good War: An Oral History of World War Two*. New York: Pantheon, 1984.
———. *Working*. 1974, New York: Avon, 1975.

Autobiographies and Autobiographical Essays

Angelou, Maya. *I Know Why the Caged Bird Sings*. New York: Random, 1970.
Baker, Russell. *Growing Up*. New York: Congdon, 1982.
Conroy, Jill Ker. *The Road from Coorain*. New York: Knopf, 1989.
Douglass, Frederick. *Narrative of the Life,* 1845; *Life and Times,* 1892. Many reprints.
Hampl, Patricia. *A Romantic Education*. 1981. Boston: Houghton, 1983.
Monette, Paul. *Becoming a Man: Half a Life Story*. New York: Harcourt, 1992.
Neihardt, John G. *Black Elk Speaks*. 1932. New York: Washington Square, 1959.
Wright, Richard. *Black Boy*. 1937. New York: Harper, 1966.

Collections of Portraits

Brown, Wesley, and Amy Ling, eds. *Victims of America: Personal Narratives from the Promised Land*. New York: Persea, 1993.
Didion, Joan. *After Henry*. New York: Simon, 1992.
Hellman, Lillian. *Pentimento: A Book of Portraits*. Boston: Little, 1973.
Murray, Pauli. *Proud Shoes*. 1956. New York: Harper, 1984.

Biographies

Bair, Deirdre. *Simone de Beauvoir*. New York: Summit, 1990.
McCullough, David. *Truman*. New York: Simon, 1992.
McFeeley, William S. *Frederick Douglass*. New York: Norton, 1991.
Ulrich, Laurel Thatcher. *A Midwife's Tale: The Life of Martha Ballard, Based on Her Diary, 1785–1812*. New York: Knopf, 1990.

Works Cited

Allen, Henry. "Pretty Far Out Little Dude." *Writing in Style*. Ed. Laura Babb. Boston: Washington Post Writers Group, 1975. 106–11.
Dillard, Annie. "To Fashion a Text." *Inventing the Truth: The Art and Craft of Memoir*. Ed. William Zinsser. Boston: Houghton, 1987. 55–76.

Donaldson, Scott. *By Force of Will: The Life and Art of Ernest Hemingway.* New York: Viking, 1977. 60–62.

Franklin, Benjamin. *The Autobiography of Benjamin Franklin: A Restoration of a Fair Copy.* Ed. Max Ferrand. Berkeley: U of California P, 1949. 2.

Kingston, Maxine Hong. *The Woman Warrior: Memoirs of a Girlhood Among Ghosts.* 1976. New York: Vintage, 1989.

McCarthy, Mary. *Memories of a Catholic Girlhood.* New York: Harcourt, 1957. 96.

White, E. B. "Once More to the Lake." *Essays of E. B. White.* New York: Harper, 1977. 197–202.

5

WRITING ABOUT PLACES

The landscape came before the words.

—Terry Tempest Williams

In wildness is the preservation of the world.

—Henry David Thoreau

Natural history writing is not just about polar bears . . . or plants, or birds. It's about the fundamental issues of life.

—Barry Lopez

"Glorious, stirring sight!" murmured Toad. "The poetry of motion! . . . The only way to travel! Here today, in—next week, tomorrow! Villages skipped, towns and cities jumped—always somebody else's horizons! O Bliss! O poop-poop! O my! O my!"

—Kenneth Grahame

Perspectives for Looking at Places

Places don't proclaim their own significance, people do. Each place is in some ways unique, yet each can be understood, even by strangers because of the features the place has in common with other places. When you write about a place, you have a surprising number of options. Indeed, there are almost as many ways to write about a place as there are places and people's perspectives of them.

Suppose that you want to write about Washington, D.C., from a personal perspective. If you live in or near the nation's capital, you could write about its unique features as a hometown, discussing the pressures and the pleasures of growing up in proximity to politicians and public institutions or of living among them as an adult. If, on the other hand, you've only visited the city, you could offer an impressionistic tale of your encounters with it, for better or for worse. Or you could use this city as a context for your philosophy of what it means to be an American citizen.

You could also look at the capital from an historic perspective. You could provide an overview of significant events that occurred there since its creation in 1791, including its role in the Civil War and the revitalization of its residential areas in the 1970s. Or you could pick a particular time period, such as the Depression, and interpret Washington during that time.

It would be particularly appropriate to discuss how Washington, D.C., works as a political and bureaucratic city, or to examine its political climate during a given presidential administration. You might consider the interrelation of its social and political life and provide vignettes of typical participants in action. Or you could look at its meaning—as the symbol of our country from the perspective of foreign visitors, immigrants, or yourself as an individual or as a representative citizen. You could discuss Washington as an international city, or compare it with the capitals of other nations.

You could write about Washington, D.C., as a model of city planning, perhaps perverted by twentieth-century additions. You could concentrate on its architecture or on its function as a repository of national treasures from art to archives. You could explore its other special features from either a resident's or a tourist's perspective, looking at its museums, monuments, theaters, zoo and arboretum, restaurants, night life, transportation (by Metro, bus, or foot). Or you could emphasize the shopping in the city or its suburbs, focusing on the elegant clothes, the bargains, or the unusual or specialty items to be found in shopping malls, particular stores, or open-air markets.

This chapter discusses in detail how to write about a place from many vistas, many views.

Guidelines for Writing About Places

When you write about places either intimately as an inhabitant or impressionistically as a visitor, you interpret them for your readers. Your view, a reflection of your interests and values, becomes their window on the segment of the world you present. You can be as individualistic, as idiosyncratic as you want; the best writings about places and travel bear the powerful imprint of the writer interacting with the place—sometimes in conflict, sometimes in harmony, always with a lively intelligence. You don't even have to try for balance in your description or fairness in your analysis; readers can look to others' views or their own experience for alternative opinions.

You'll write more memorably about places if you bear in mind the following guidelines.

Use your senses to interpret the character of the place.   To write well about a place, you'll need to be extraordinarily aware of and responsive to your surroundings, sensitive to the nuances as well as the overt features of the geography, the climate, the environment, the culture, and the people. You'll probably want to use a higher proportion of sensory details than you would in your other writing, as you recreate the sights, sounds, smells, tastes, and texture of a place. Janice Law Trecker, a student and novelist when she wrote the op-ed essay "Reaping Late Summer's Sweet Bounty," begins by inviting readers to her rural Connecticut home:

> In addition to a leaky roof, a burned-out furnace, and an assortment of broken windows, the couple who owned the house before us left us a tiny orchard: two pear trees with neither blossom nor pears, four nearly fruitless apple trees, and two peach trees. Not imposing as trees go, these last yearly sprout a myriad of young red branches, clothe them in dainty blossoms, and load them with small but delicious fruit. For whatever reason, last year was particularly good.
>
> From late summer on, the branches were literally bent under the weight of peaches, and the ground beneath hummed with the wasps attracted to the dropped fruit. We ate what we could, baked some into pies, froze more and began dispatching bags as gifts. Every morning there was more fruit—warm, thin-skinned, fragrant.

After taking readers past the ramshackle house, Trecker lets us *see* the "tiny orchard," with its red branches and "dainty blossoms," *hear* the humming wasps, *touch* the warm, "thin-skinned" peaches, *smell* their fragrance, and imagine the *taste* of the pies. Exactly as she intends, Trecker whets our appetite for more.

Be open-minded.   To write memorably about a place it helps to be open-minded about terrain, climate, people, and customs that may be very different from our own. Ask yourself: Why do the natives behave as they do? What do they like or dislike about where they live? And why? Why do they tolerate what people from another culture might find intolerable?

If you can see a place from the multiple perspectives of various types of inhabitants or visitors in various roles and circumstances, in addition to your own, you'll be able to understand it better and you can begin to answer such questions. With diverse points of view in mind, you are less likely to be chauvinistic or to judge the place and its culture according to the norms of your home point of reference. Nevertheless, as Clifford Geertz demonstrates in *Works and Lives*, his analysis of four extremely varied styles of writing anthropology, your writing ultimately reflects your own judgment. For you not only choose what to say, but also select from an entire universe of possibilities—the "imagery, metaphor, phraseology, voice," and details with which to say it.

Indeed, a favorite sport of supercilious nineteenth-century visitors to America was to jeer the natives and assault the countryside, a sport continued today by ugly Americans abroad, who are jeered in return by a less-than-grateful populace. Charles Dickens, in *American Notes,* appeals to the superiority of his English contemporaries with unsympathetic accounts of the boorish former colonists. He is repelled by the droves of pigs, "city scavengers, ugly brutes" roving the streets of New York; by the tobacco-chewing members of the U.S. Senate who "miss the spittoon at five paces"; and by the Mississippi River, "an enormous ditch, sometimes two or three miles wide, running liquid mud, six miles an hour; its strong and frothy current choked and obstructed everywhere by huge logs. . . . The banks low, the trees dwarfish, the marshes swarming with frogs [and] mosquitoes."

If you see your subject this negatively, that's how you'll want to describe it, but the focus of such writings is often the author's revulsion rather than the place that provokes such antipathy. But first, unless you intend to write satire, give the place and its inhabitants a chance. John McPhee's thoughtful, appreciative writings about places convey the impression that he's been soaking up the atmosphere, is acutely receptive to whatever a place has to offer, and is willing to accept it on its own terms. Thus his analysis of *The Pine Barrens* presents a compelling and sympathetic view of the one-thousand-square-mile New Jersey forest that, though visible from the Empire State Building, is "still so undeveloped that it can be called wilderness," a complex ecosystem of terrain, vegetation, and animal and human populations. McPhee describes his first glimpse of the house of Fred Brown, a resident of Hog Wallow (pop. 25):

> Fred Brown's house is on an unpaved road that curves along the edge of a wide cranberry bog. What attracted me to it was the pump that stands in his yard. It was something of a wonder that I noticed the pump because there were among other things, eight automobiles in the yard, two of them on their sides and one of them upside down, all ten years old or older. Around the cars were

old refrigerators, vacuum cleaners, partly dismantled radios, cathode-ray tubes, a short wooden ski, a large wooden mallet, dozens of cranberry pickers' boxes, many tires, an orange crate dated 1946, a cord or so of firewood, mandolins, engine heads, and maybe a thousand other things. The house itself, two stories high, was covered with tarpaper that was peeling away in some places, revealing its original shingles made of Atlantic white cedar from the stream courses of the surrounding forest. I called out to ask if anyone was home, and a voice called back, "Come in. Come in. Come on the hell in."

There is no hint of city sophisticate condescension here, no denigrating view that regards Brown's domain as either disreputable or a slum. Instead, McPhee is fascinated and, as he becomes acquainted with Brown, admiring of this lifelong native:

He had a raw onion in one hand, and while he talked he shaved slices from the onion and ate them. . . . He was a muscular and well-built man, with short, bristly white hair, and he had bright, fast-moving eyes in a wide-open face. His legs were trim and strong, with large muscles in the calves. I guessed that he was about sixty, and for a man of sixty he seemed to be in remarkably good shape. He was actually seventy-nine. "My rule is: Never eat except when you're hungry," he said, and he ate another slice of the onion.

In writing about the Pine Barrens, McPhee accepts the standards of Brown's community, including an appreciation of rusticity, miscellany, and raw onions. As we can see, the description of a place can extend beyond the physical details of the terrain to encompass the human dimension, as well. Without romanticizing what he finds, he makes this rare territory and its people comprehensible to an audience of outsiders.

React strongly to the place.   You'll write better if you write about places to which you react strongly, whether you passionately like or dislike them or have mixed but powerful feelings. Indifference is deadly, for if you're indifferent to a place, you can't expect your writing to engage your readers. Your preferences (such as McPhee's affection for the free-spirited Pine Barrens) and prejudices (such as Dickens's disgusted view of America) will surface in your selection of revealing details, descriptive adjectives and adverbs, similes, and sometimes even in your tantalizing title. Thus student Gail Montany provocatively titles a paper about her and her husband's impulsive purchase of 170 acres in remote Vermont "It's a Great Place to Visit, but My Husband's Moving There" (see pages 122–23).

Ray Hatcher, fullback on a college team ranked among the ten lowest in the country, approaches his subject—the post-game locker room—with no ambivalence whatsoever. He finds no solace in the desolate and depressing locker room, a reflection of the team's standing:

As John dresses he notices through the steel grated window that the parking lot is emptying fast; nobody sticks around after a loss. Air from the cheap

K-mart fan gives John goose pimples. With no one in the locker room except himself, he is struck by the emptiness. He hears the water drip from a leaky shower head, and the meow of an abandoned cat. A stale smell of body odor and moldy clothes fills his sinuses. On the filthy carpet his laundry bag resembles a dead animal run over by a truck, and in the dim light the shoulder pads piled on top of the lockers look like the carcasses of some prehistoric creatures. The locker room door echoes as he slams it. Nobody sticks around after a loss.

This interpretation of a common experience is Hatcher's own; no one else would think to combine details such as the "steel grated window," "cheap K-mart fan," dripping water, body odor, moldy clothes, and to throw in "an abandoned cat" for good measure. Yet when you show what a place means to you, as Hatcher does, readers who have had similar experiences—even if they occurred in places very different from those you describe—will be able to recognize the truth of your situation and to identify with it. You don't need to make an overt connection between your experience and that of your readers. Your readers have doubtless been unhappy losers some time, somewhere, whether as members of a defeated team or as victims of a severed friendship, a terminated job, or a broken marriage. Through the specific example of this specific forlorn locker room, readers will recognize that it represents all the other nowheres harboring a legion of losers.

Don't sanitize your subject.   When you write about places, unless you're employed by a chamber of commerce or an advertising firm, your view is not likely to be the glossy glimpse that appears on travel folders, but rather a more penetrating look beneath the surface, whether pleasant or problematic. Memorable writings about places exemplify the precept, "Identify what you see; interpret it as you understand it." Indeed, Don Aker, whose prize-winning publications have transformed him from a student to a professional writer, describes the winter of 1992 in his native Nova Scotia from a wry perspective that the Chamber of Commerce undoubtedly would suppress:

> February continues to snarl about the province with theatrical menace. Winter here has been so miserable that I often find myself gazing longingly at the picture of spring on the calendar that Lauren, in first grade, made us for Christmas. (She drew all the pictures herself, and it cannot be a coincidence that none of the people in her winter scenes are smiling. A few renditions of me actually sport grimaces.) While we've been enduring record snowfalls, I've shovelled out my driveway more times in the last week than in the last three years combined, the record low temperatures are more difficult to endure. Atmospheric conditions appear to be funneling frigid air directly from an Arctic glacier to my doorway, and −27 (Celsius) temperatures are a shock to the system for Nova Scotians accustomed to average winter lows of −5.

Readers are likely to read this for what it is, an account of one man's difficulties in coping with a specific feature of Nova Scotia—an unusually cold winter—rather than as an indictment of an entire culture, as was Dickens's warning to his British readers about the horrors of that upstart adolescent, the rebellious United States of America.

Choose an appropriate organizational pattern that reinforces your emphasis.

Chronological pattern.   You can organize your discussion of a place according to the order in which you experienced events there, as many visitors or travelers do. If you're writing an historical overview, you can discuss events in order, from earliest times to more recent or vice versa. If you're making comparisons such as between old and new, as James Michener does in *Iberia,* you can zigzag between past and present.

Writers concerned with natural history often let the natural rhythms or natural phenomena, such as the ebb and flow of the waters or the seasons, dictate the organization of their writing, as well as its pace and emphasis. Henry Beston's *The Outermost House: A Year of Life on the Great Beach of Cape Cod* flows with the seasons and is organized according to their progress, beginning with early autumn when Beston first went to Cape Cod, through winter, spring, and summer.

Geographical pattern.   You can organize your discussion according to a particular route: on a walking tour through a city, on a highway, on a cattle drivers' trail (such as the Santa Fe or the Chisholm), over a river or mountain range, or from country to country. In this fashion Jonathan Raban follows the Mississippi River in *Old Glory: An American Voyage* (pages 137–38).

In your discussion, you can juxtapose noncontiguous spots, as you might when island-, city-, or country-hopping. To enhance a comparison and contrast or to reflect a travel route, you can arrange your discussion of these locations in order of increasing or decreasing interest or importance. Jan Morris uses a pattern of contrasts in *Journeys,* which she identifies as "a jumbled succession of journeys offered without benefit of itinerary" to Australia, Las Vegas, Wells (England), India, Santa Fe, and China—in that order.

You can provide a spatial organization arranged according to the perspective of what you or visitors see first, second, and later or by proceeding from outside to inside a country, rural area, city, or building. McPhee's *The Pine Barrens* begins with a wide vista that locates the Pine Barrens geographically—north, south, east, and west—and gradually narrows the focus to vegetation, then to Fred Brown's yard, then to his house, and finally to Fred Brown himself.

Topical pattern.   You can divide your discussion of the major aspects of a place into categories such as political, historical, military, economic, social, cultural, religious. Ved Mehta uses this pattern in a book-length study, *Portrait of India,* as do most travel guides, such as the Fodor and Michelin series. As a rule, the most important topics come first and in the most detail.

You can compare and contrast one place with another, either by dealing will all of one place before discussing the other, as George Orwell does in *Down and Out in Paris and London,* or by comparing the two places point by parallel point, or by examining similarities first, and then their differences.

Personal/psychological pattern. In writing about places using this approach, you usually start with what is emotionally low key and work up to what is the most demanding and emotionally involving. Most of E. B. White's essays on places, such as "Once More to the Lake" and "The Ring of Time" use this pattern, though they are generally understated even by the end. If you begin with the climax you have nowhere to go but down.

Control your style. The style in which you write affects the way readers see the place you describe.

Be original. Avoid stereotyped language and a selection of obvious or conventional details. You may have to stretch your vocabulary, or your imagination, to say something original about the briny ocean, the snowcapped Rockies, or the inscrutable Orient. But the result is worth the verbal exercise. Identifying what makes the place unique, special, or problematic to you may help you avoid clichés, obvious illustrations, or overly familiar descriptions.

In "It's a Great Place to Visit, but My Husband's Moving There," Gail Montany describes her initial view of the Vermont farm she and her husband snapped up like starving trout lunging for a fly:

> When I saw the imposing but shabby red barn with its incongruous milk-ing parlor jutting out one hundred feet on its east side, and the pile of rubble from the farmhouse which had burned down several years earlier and was barely concealed behind a run-down mobile home, I turned to Gene and said, "Go tell the real estate guy we're not interested before he gets out of his car . . . shit, too late, here he comes." As the kids wandered over to admire a tractor tire, painted white and planted with geraniums, I could hear the occasional unmistakable rumble of eighteen wheelers. Gene asked if part of the property bordered I-91; it did; we were standing only about three hundred yards from its southbound lane.

The crafty (or thoroughly professional, depending on one's point of view) agent quickly maneuvers the slippery couple "back into the car and down an impossibly steep dirt road, engulfed in a cloud of dust." Then come the counterdetails. They are predictable in their placement because they have to contrast with the opening but their specific nature is distinctive: "two freshly-mown fifteen acre hayfields, the first bordered on its west edge by an oxbow of the wide and murky Passumpsic River," the second "dotted with bales of hay that looked like Shredded Wheat bundles," a hawk soaring overhead, "circling the field, dipping and ascending effortlessly, her chick following directly above her in perfect unison." The couple walk, like Adam and Eve in Paradise, through a forested glen, where a stream "babbled past hemlock, beech, and pine groves, and pooled near the woods' entrance over two levels of flat granite slabs, forming a tiny waterfall before continuing on through the meadow and into the Passumpsic." And there the Montanys are hooked, despite the fact that "there was no house on the property, parts of the barn were near collapse, the meadows were in a twenty-five year flood plain (they have since flooded three times in four years), and I-91 bordered one edge."

Despite the familiar presence of the red barn, the hay meadows, and the woods, Montany chisels the scene with a precise specificity and an ambivalent tone that signal her independent, individual reaction to its charms, its drawbacks.

Avoid excess and sentimentality.   Being in love with a place, like being in love with a person, is a stimulus for excessive eloquence. Writers who love what they're discussing often describe every nuance, every facet in exquisite detail, laden with adjectives, adverbs, and modifying clauses, often clichés. Or fearful that their audience will miss the point, some writers overstate the case. In either circumstance, their writing is full of verbal winks and nudges and the piling on of adjectives, adverbs, and analyses as if they are constantly asking "Get it? See what I mean? Isn't that sweet?"

You can put as much as you want into a first draft to get the effusion out of your system, but when you rewrite, edit out cute, overwritten, sentimental material. Readers will appreciate your description of a place if you present intriguing details or vignettes that speak for themselves instead of verbal stage directions that tell your readers how to react. Less *is* more, as the illustrations throughout this chapter reveal. When you trust yourself as a writer, you'll be able to trust your readers to find their way—your way—without excessive direction.

Student Kate Bradley approaches her hometown of Howells, Nebraska, from the perspective of a passionate tourist. In her eagerness to make sure readers see the town her way, Bradley's initial version is unnecessarily repetitive and full of intrusive directions. As a result, it gets off to a slow start. The italicized passages indicate redundancy, unnecessary interpretation, sentimentality, or all three:

> *Howells is home.* New York *City,* Chicago, Houston, Los Angeles—while tens of millions may claim these renowned places as "home," there are only a select few hundred *in this world* who call Howells, Nebraska, "home." *I am one of those few. Though I've spent more than half my life in the city, the village of Howells will always be home.*
>
> *This tiny town of between five and six hundred souls is unremarkable in rural America, but* if I came upon *this town* in a foreign land, I'd *probably pull over to the side of the road and* get out my camera. I would jot down my impressions in my travel journal: community pride is evident everywhere—in tidy

properties, abundant *blooming* flower beds, patchwork quilt vegetable gardens—*this is a pretty place made so by obviously industrious people. I'd say something about wholesomeness, probably brought on by the heartwarming aroma of bread baking.* I might even conclude that *the world is not, after all, going to hell in a handbasket—because in this small corner of the world, good people are going about their business* of getting the laundry out on the line early in the morning and checking up on their elderly neighbors. I'd feel good at having discovered this *special little* community, and I'd vow to remember it. *I think any observant traveler would appreciate Howells as a very civilized place in the world.*

Only six blocks long and four or five blocks wide (depending on where you cut across town), *it's impossible not to call Howells quaint, but it is more than a relic of time gone by. . . .*

The rewrite (120 words compared to the original 260) eliminates the obvious and the overwritten but nevertheless conveys the author's appreciation and love for her hometown:

Howells, Nebraska (pop. 550), six blocks long and four or five blocks wide (depending on where you cut across), is unremarkable in rural America, but if I came upon it in a foreign land, I'd get out my camera. I would jot down impressions in my travel journal: the community pride manifested in its tidy properties, abundant flower beds, patchwork quilt vegetable gardens. I would conclude that something, after all, is right with a world where conscientious citizens get their laundry out on the line early in the morning, know all the children and cats and dogs by name, and check up on their elderly neighbors. I'd feel good at having discovered this community, and I'd vow to remember it.

In the revision Bradley deletes comments such as "quaint," "good people are going about their business," "special little community," and "I'd say something about wholesomeness, probably brought on by the heartwarming aroma of bread baking." Even if the interpretation is true, such overkill would turn away readers suspicious of uncritical exaggeration. Trust the details, told true, to make your point and in the process to allow your readers the delight of discovering for themselves what you've known all along.

Nevertheless, some cynical readers might suspect the honesty of the second version, noting the absence of negative details or gritty realism—what, no slobs? no grouches? no self-centered people who couldn't care less about their neighbors? Bradley is willing to take that risk at the outset because she quickly moves on to show the insider's intimate understanding of Howells, as opposed to the tourist's snapshot glance:

Stern taskmasters, Grandpa and Grandma Baumann instilled a sense of WORK-TO-BE-WORTHY in all of their five children, and four of them worked themselves right into psychiatric problems in the process. Dad was the first. . . .

Overstate when appropriate.   As Bradley's revised overview of Howells, Nebraska, illustrates, understatement is generally preferable to overstatement. There are two major exceptions. When you want to convey the impression of abundance, superabundance, crowdedness, or other excesses, as Mae West has observed, "Too much of a good thing is absolutely splendid." Or you may prefer to use overstatement as the basis of burlesque, satire, or other criticism that uses exaggeration to make its point. In an ironic, disapproving essay, "The Millionaires," student Kris King piles detail on detail in describing "a three-hundred-thousand-dollar house that looked," she says,

> like a sty. I remember walking into the living room once and seeing the abuse. On one wall was a dart board with no darts and the wall behind pocked with holes. The lining had been torn from the bottom of a yellow Chippendale sofa and stuffing poked through where the buttons had been ripped off. In front of the sofa was a cherry table with a half-finished model spread out and a tube of glue dripping. There were several high-backed chairs in the room, one Windsor without an arm, another with a torn velvet cover. On the carpet in front of the chair was a bowl of milk with Cheerios floating. . . . Someone had tossed a crumpled McDonald's bag on the ashes of last winter's fires. A Steinway stretched underneath a broad picture window. Water rings spoiled the finish and a tinker toy was wedged between two keys. . . . A china bureau, filled with Wedgewood and Lenox, stood in the corner next to the door. A lacrosse stick was propped against one of its broken panes. A black woman in a blue housecoat was attempting to compensate for the absence of a cat's litter box by pushing a vacuum back and forth over the stained carpet.

Except for the interpretive introductory observation, "They had a three-hundred-thousand-dollar house that looked like a sty," King provides little overt analysis or commentary except to note that water rings "spoiled" the Steinway's finish. She doesn't need to because the details graphically depict the neglected room and its abused furnishings, pockmarked, torn, broken, ruined. The specific names of quality designers and manufacturers (Chippendale, Steinway, Wedgewood) signify the potential for elegance, undermined by the presence of the out-of-place bowl of Cheerios, the McDonald's bag, the lacrosse stick, the dripping glue, and other evidence of mayhem.

Show, don't tell is a key precept of writing about places, as the illustrations in this chapter and throughout *Fact and Artifact* reveal in abundance.

Writing About the Natural World

Why We Write About the Natural World

You may want to write about the natural world for its own sake, or for yours. Whatever your motive, you'll be inspired, perhaps, by the Muse described by Annie Dillard in *Pilgrim at Tinker Creek,* who arrives with emphatic energy: "She doesn't tell you to write: She says get up for a minute, I've something to show you, stand here." You'll see what the natural world looks like from a distance and from close up, its terrain and topography, as your gaze ranges from earth to the heavens to the sea and home again. You'll observe the animals and plants that live where you are and how they interact with and without human interference. You'll move to the rhythm of the day and the night, the seasons, the life cycles of myriads of creatures—possibly even your own—as you try through understanding nature to understand yourself or to develop a philosophy of life as your understanding grows. This kind of writing about nature presents a good deal of scientific information but from the naturalist's conspicuously personal point of view, in an impressionistic and idiosyncratic manner.

When you respond to the natural world in this way, you're part of a long and important tradition of thinkers and writers. The Romantic poets used the microcosm as a reflection of the macrocosm, as they saw, in William Blake's words, "a World in a Grain of Sand/And a Heaven in a Wild Flower." Izaak Walton, in *The Compleat Angler,* found fishing—really his meditations in natural settings—"an employment for his idle time, which was then not idly spent . . . a rest to his mind, a cheerer of his spirits, a diverter of sadness, a calmer of unquiet thoughts, a moderator of passions, a procurer of contentedness." Thoreau went to the woods at Walden Pond for a purpose quite different from Walton's, "because I wished to live deliberately, to front only the essential facts of life, and see if I could not learn what it had to teach, and not, when I came to die, discover that I had not lived."

Annie Dillard is a writer in this tradition. Self-appointed *Pilgrim at Tinker Creek,* she explains the personal, natural, and spiritual reasons for her choice of habitat:

> It's a good place to live; there's a lot to think about. The creeks . . . are an active mystery, fresh every minute. Theirs is the mystery of the continuous creation and all that providence implies: . . . the dissolution of the present, the intricacy of beauty, the pressure of fecundity, the elusiveness of the free, and the flawed nature of perfection. The mountains . . . are the one simple mystery, the creation from nothing, of matter itself, anything at all, the given. Mountains are giant, restful, absorbent. You can heave your spirit into a mountain and the mountain will keep it, folded, and not throw it back as some creeks will. The creeks are the world with all its stimulus and beauty; I live there. But the mountains are home.

Key Characteristics of Nature Writers

Because nature writings such as Dillard's are highly individualistic as well as distinctively personal, there is no common format, formula, or pattern of thought to follow in writing an essay or longer work of reflections on the natural world. Yet Thoreau, Dillard, and other quintessential nature writers have some common characteristics shared by other writers, but seldom found elsewhere in as high or as conspicuous a concentration as they are in personal writing on natural subjects.

First person perspective.   The point of reference in such reflections on the natural world is almost always the first person perspective, the "I" of a distinctive personality that emerges clearly and emphatically even when focusing, as Dillard does, on the surroundings. Tinker Creek, Walden, and other places are invariably filtered through the very powerful lenses of the individual writer's personal vision.

Unassuming authorial persona.   When you write about nature you'll present yourself as unassuming and in touch with nature, both literally and figuratively. Although you will carefully control your language and the structure of your writing, you'll convey the impression of being unselfconscious. To explore the universe, you'll wear comfortable old clothes, symbolically unpretentious and suitable for tramping through the woods, chopping logs, or getting caught in the rain. "When I slide under a barbed-wire fence, cross a field, and run over a sycamore trunk felled across the water, I'm on a little island," explains Dillard in *Pilgrim at Tinker Creek,* whose cover picture shows the author sitting on that island in windbreaker, jeans, and sturdy hiking boots.

Self-reliance and resourcefulness.   Your authorial persona as a nature writer is likely to be resourceful and self-reliant, either fully realized or in the process of development. Thoreau makes these qualities primary virtues of his stay at Walden Pond, where he built his own cabin; raised, hunted, and fished his own food; and read and wrote on his own terms for two years. His authorial persona reveals an independent, adventuresome, toughminded but thoughtful soul, ready to take on provocateurs, whether the Concord tax collector or the universe.

From an unanticipated source, student Tim Payne learns self-reliance during a camping trip in Bar Harbor, Maine. He had expected

> beaches and vacations that played for you. And you would play up to them, and they would play some more, selling themselves. This beach [however], was unkempt and unpolished, colored by its stark boulders and the clumps of green and yellow sea plants, varnished so heavily with a lifeless brown as to look like vomit. It was indifferent . . . and this indifference whetted my combative spirit, my desire to overcome and take something.

When Payne, inspired by "Mr. Thoreau," learns to respect the strength, stability, and power of the environment, he becomes able to accept the sea on its own terms, rather than on the terms he had initially anticipated:

> The tide was coming in, and as it rose it reabsorbed and inspirited the vomited sea plants which, I could now see, were actually connected on to what *had* been the beach and was *now* the harbor floor. And then I also spotted a *real* shell-find—whole sand dollars. No too-small fish this time. I quickly collected several of the sand dollars, but then I got selective and threw back all but the few most perfect ones. As I got up from the rocks, however, to escape being overtaken by the tide, even these felt too heavy in my hand to carry home, and I threw them back in as well.

In the process of this discovery comes the self-reliance Payne needs to enhance his maturity; in his newfound respect for nature, he is unwilling to carry away from the beach even a perfect sand dollar.

Love of solitude.   When you write about nature, you may choose to assume a solitary posture to accompany your self-reliance. "I love to be alone," says Thoreau. This persona prefers to spend days and nights observing and communing with the natural and spiritual worlds rather than with other people. As Thoreau says,

> My nearest neighbor is a mile distant, and no house is visible from any place but the hill-tops within half a mile of my own. I have my horizon bounded by woods all to myself. . . . For the most part it is as solitary where I live as on the prairies. . . . I have, as it were, my own sun and moon and stars, and a little world all to myself. . . . I find it wholesome to be alone the greater part of the time. To be in company, even with the best, is soon wearisome and dissipating.

Sensitivity to the natural world.   As a nature writer you become a part of what you observe; the familiar becomes new under your probing and receptive gaze as you merge with the universe you describe or analyze. Dillard exclaims, "I don't want to miss spring this year. . . . I want to be there on the spot the moment the grass turns green."

Naturalist Henry Beston's *The Outermost House: A Year of Life on the Great Beach of Cape Cod,* first published in 1928 but still as fresh as Friday's footprint, is imbued with the same spirit. Here he immerses himself in a winter scene, noting the intensity and gradations of colors, textures, temperature, lights and shadows, and spatial relationships:

> There are patches of snow on the hay fields and the marshes, and on the dunes, nests of snow held up off the ground by wiry spears of beach grass bent over and tangled into a cup. Such little pictures as this last are often to be seen on the winter dunes; I pause to enjoy them, for they have the quality and delicacy of Japanese painting. There is a blueness in the air, a blue coldness on the

moors, and across the sky to the south, a pale streamer of cloud smoking from its upper edge. Every now and then, I see ahead of me a round, blackish spot in the thin snow; these are the cast-off shells of horseshoe crabs, from whose thin tegument the snow has melted.

Beston responds not only to the aesthetic aspects of the scene's pictorial qualities but to the natural significance of each phenomenon, which he interprets for his readers. He knows, for instance, what most readers would not know, that the "round, blackish spot in the thin snow" is a horseshoe crab's delicate shell.

Optimistic, yet realistic.   Nature writers have an optimism and a confidence that careful observation will be revealing and rewarding. "I wake expectant, hoping to see a new thing," says Dillard. "There are lots of things to see, unwrapped gifts and free surprises." Every day dawns on new facets of the nature writer's corner of the world. As Dillard puts it, "I walk out; I see something, some event that would otherwise have been utterly missed and lost; or something sees me, some enormous power brushes me with its clean wing and I resound like a beaten bell."

But nature writers are also realistic. Your enthusiasm won't blind you to the harsh or unpleasant features of the natural world and you won't censor such manifestations of "nature red in tooth and claw" in your writing. Beston, for instance, observes the annual April migration of alewives, or herrings:

> The fish were "in," moving up the brook as thickly massed as a battalion along a narrow road. . . . Through the brownish stream the eye looked down to numberless long backs of a subdued dark lavender-grey and to a fleet of dorsal fins breaking water. The brook smelt of fish. Here and there were dead ones, aground on the edges of the stream or held by the current against a rock; dead things lying on their sides, with opaque, slime-coated eyes, and rock bruises on their sides—raw spots of fish blood red in a side of brown and golden scales.

When you write the truth about nature, even if you like the subject, it isn't always pretty. Authentic details, even when they're fierce, raw, malodorous— "dead things lying on their sides, with opaque, slime-coated eyes"—compel far greater attention and interest than does a retouched view of a predictable scene, glossy and sentimental. For balance and truth, include representative glimpses of the total scene, the hurricanes as well as the blue skies.

Concern for the microcosm as well as the macrocosm.   In addition to their affinity for skies, mountains, and seas, nature writers also are attracted to small things that require patience and perseverance to scrutinize. In *A Country Year*, Sue Hubbell interprets the relationships among honeybees, bald-faced hornets, and "hordes of caterpillars" that frequent orchards. The adult bald-faced hornets "kill enormous quantities of caterpillars" to feed their developing larvae. They butcher their prey alive, cut it up with their mouths, chew the solid parts into pellets, and carry these back to the nest where "nurse hornets take over the bits of flesh to break into still smaller morsels with which to feed the developing brood."

Although it is possible, of course, for nature writers to get such detailed information from books, much of what they know comes from firsthand observation, conducted over a very long time. Hubbell, for instance, tells us that she often sees these hornets "in the summer when their brood-rearing is at its peak, flying low over the ground . . . looking for prey." Precise observation leads to precise interpretation. From the perspective of human ecology—a naturalist's common stance—Hubbell interprets the significance of what she has seen: "Considering that there may be 10,000 hornets in one of the big nests, the requirements of a single colony may serve as a considerable check on destructive caterpillars in an orchard." Often the nature writer's commentary has an ecological or legislative imperative. Says Hubbell, "A number of nests should cheer an orchardist."

Keen imagination.   All writers need imagination; natural scientists use their imagination to draw analogies between known phenomena and the unknown and to provide elegant interpretations of complicated data. Naturalists and others who write personally about nature can be more inventive and more fanciful than their scientific peers.

As a nature writer you can *anthropomorphize*, giving natural phenomena human attributes or interpreting the phenomena in human terms, a taboo technique in much scientific writing. Thus Dillard humanizes chloroplasts when she looks at a quarter-inch elodea leaf under a microscope: "They wandered, they charged, they milled, raced, and ran at the edge of apparent nothingness, the empty-looking inner cell; they flowed and trooped greenly, up against the vegetative wall."

Or you may, more rarely, so fully identify with the natural world that you imagine an animal's perspective, which Thoreau occasionally recreates in *Walden*, claiming that people who spend "their lives in the fields and woods [become] a part of Nature themselves":

> Once or twice . . . while I lived at the pond, I found myself ranging the woods, like a half-starved hound, with a strange abandonment, seeking some kind of venison which I might devour, and no morsel could have been too savage for me. The wildest scenes had become unaccountably familiar.

Cosmic awareness.   More frequently nature writers, Thoreau included, imaginatively relate the natural world to the spiritual and endow what they encounter on earth with cosmic significance. Indeed, by virtue of the author's penetrating philosophical vision, Walden has become situated not only in Massachusetts but in the heart of America and in the center of the universe. No one can tell you what you'll find if you explore the reciprocal relationship between "where I lived and what I lived for," as Thoreau did when he analyzed every action and every phenomenon, natural or man-made, to show its cosmic implications that he encountered during his two years at Walden Pond. Chances are that such an intensive scrutiny of yourself and your relation to the universe will lead you to ask essential questions (such as Who am I? What is my purpose in life?) and to make a start toward, as Hubbell says, "living the questions," and getting the answers. If you use the natural world as a place to explore or to explain your philosophy of life, much of its symbolic meaning will emerge through the physical and sensory details that you supply.

Sense of moral superiority and physical well-being.   The nature writer's perspective, with head in the cosmos and feet firmly planted in the microcosm, often leads even the most self-effacing to feel morally superior to anyone who doesn't equally revere and respect nature. Ann Zwinger sees designated wilderness areas as "sacred ground," "land my culture has deemed important enough to leave alone." "It's an organism unto itself," she says. "I know I am safe there . . . from encroachment, from public harassment." Nature writers, at one with nature, will preserve and protect it from those who would destroy it. Hubbell's bumper sticker might read, "Save the baldfaced hornets!"

Admittedly, not a little of the nature writers' sense of superiority is derived from the physical well-being that results from strenuous outdoor activity. Student Leslie Moore captures the essence of this attitude in her essay "Reclaiming Pastures":

> While my friends spend their summer vacations scuba diving in the Caribbean, bicycling on the Cape, or sailing off the coast of Maine, I stay at home quite happily making my pastures. It's good to be outside, it's good to get the exercise, it's even good to feel the ache in my muscles that spreading a half ton of lime leaves. My brother spends $66 a month to work out in a fitness center. He says he's working on six muscle groups: back and biceps, shoulders and legs, chest and triceps. I don't really concentrate on the muscle groups that forking wet hay into the wheelbarrow work, but I do know that the jeans I bought to fit tight at the beginning of the summer hang loose from my hips now.

Moore can't resist wrapping up her essay with a bit of ironic smugness: "Who's to know whether my svelte new lines came from pumping a fancy step machine or pushing a rotary lawnmower."

Places as Contexts for Social Criticism

You may choose to write about an ugly or depressing place from the same motives that stimulated the "Ash Can" school of painters, who find beauty, strength, power, and inspiration in scenes of decaying buildings, dismal streets, or junk-filled alleys. As a contemporary writer, however, you're more likely to use extended discussions of such settings as the basis for social criticism. A description of such a place, with sordid details emphasized, could imply questions such as, Why aren't the buildings kept in better repair? the streets better lighted? the alleys cleaned up? How can people live safely and happily in such miserable circumstances?

Social criticism of a place serves a number of functions. You may write critically simply to express your attitude about it or to ventilate your feelings. You may want, in addition, to call attention to a problem or problems inherent in or created by the place. Moreover, you may also want to imply that action should be taken or even to propose specific solutions to the problems you've pointed out.

Techniques for Writing Social Criticism

When you write social criticism of places, you expect your readers to trust your perspective and your interpretation and to assume that your judgment is accurate. To ensure that your readers see it your way, you'll need to carefully control the tone, point of view, and selection of details.

Tone.   Make sure your words have appropriately negative connotations, or that readers will interpret more neutral words negatively in the context in which they appear. Sometimes the words themselves are overtly denigrating, as in Joe Eszterhas's arrogant perspective of Harrisonville, Missouri: "Except for the twisters, the horse-thieves and the velvetleaf, it is like any other tacky, jaundiced Southern town." Sometimes innocuous or neutral words derive their negative connotations from their context, as they do throughout Joan Didion's "Some Dreamers of the Golden Dream," where even advertising slogans and business names have sinister connotations: "Past the motel that is nineteen stucco tepees: 'SLEEP IN A WIGWAM—GET MORE FOR YOUR WAMPUM.' Past Fontana Drag City and the Fontana Church of the Nazarene and the Pit Stop A Go-Go. . . ." You don't need lots of words, just the right ones.

Point of view.   You may be overtly critical, though a whisper of criticism is usually more effective than a diatribe. Sometimes a simple presentation of unadorned but damning facts without authorial commentary is sufficient. William Warner devotes a concluding chapter of *Beautiful Swimmers* to speculation about the future of the Chesapeake Bay's natural environment. He quotes the view of the watermen that the bay "is everywhere getting a little tired. Each summer there are more fish kills and in winter you can sometimes see strange little red dots suspended in the water."

At other times you may wish to be ironic, to pretend neutrality or even approval while your evidence demands disapproval from readers with common sense (see Didion's descriptions of the San Bernardino Valley). Your attitude should be consistent to avoid sending your readers mixed signals.

In *Rachel and Her Children: Homeless Families in America,* Jonathan Kozol presents, often without comment, a great deal of information about New York City's welfare hotels. He counts on his intended readers— white, upper- and middle-class—to judge the accommodations according to their standards of how people, in this case, mothers with young children, ought (and ought not) to live:

> The crumbling plaster in the Martinique Hotel is covered with sweet-tasting chips of paint that children eat or chew as it flakes off the walls. . . . The bathroom plumbing has overflowed and left a pool of sewage on the floor. A radiator valve is broken. It releases a spray of scalding steam at the eye level of a child.

Selection of details.   Whether you use understatement, neutrality, or overstatement, all the details you select should reinforce your point of view. In a writing of social criticism, even trivia such as glue dripping on a millionaire's cherry table, can be symbolic, portentous. You can juxtapose seemingly neutral details to imply negative relationships among them, as Didion does in "Some Dreamers of the Golden Dream" when she characterizes the San Bernardino valley: "Here is where the hot wind blows and the old ways do not seem relevant, where the divorce rate is double the national average and where one person in every thirty-eight lives in a trailer." Although there may not be a necessary connection between the "hot wind" and the irrelevance of "the old ways" or between a divorce rate "double the national average" and the fact that "one person in every thirty-eight lives in a trailer," the juxtaposition of these details implies a logical connection as well as the writer's negative attitude toward the place.

Calling Attention to Problems

Even a place that outsiders see as bland or perhaps beautiful can look ugly to you as a social critic if its conspicuous features provide the basis for your negative interpretation. You can emphasize details that are either intrinsically unaesthetic or that, according to your standards, signify the tawdry values or sordid actions of the people who live there. Joan Didion emphasizes both kinds of details in "Some Dreamers of the Golden Dream." She describes California's San Bernardino valley, "an alien place," as

> not the coastal California of the subtropical twilights and the soft westerlies off the Pacific but a harsher California, haunted by the Mojave just beyond the

mountains, devastated by the hot dry Santa Ana wind that comes down through the passes at 100 miles an hour and whines through the eucalyptus windbreaks and works on the nerves. October is the bad month for the wind, the month when breathing is difficult and the hills blaze up spontaneously. There has been no rain since April. Every voice seems a scream. It is the season of suicide and divorce and prickly dread, wherever the wind blows.

The inhabitants of "this ominous country" deserve what they get, Didion implies. They are uncultivated and narrowly religious: "This is the California where it is possible to live and die without ever eating an artichoke, without ever meeting a Catholic or a Jew." These people have come to this godforsaken corner of southern California, the literal and figurative "last stop for all those who come from somewhere else," to "find a new life style." But because they are without history, without roots, the only places they think to look for a way to live are "the movies and the newspapers." Didion wants her readers to recognize the arid superficiality and false values of life in the San Bernardino valley,

the country of the teased hair and the Capris and the girls for whom all life's promise comes down to a waltz-length white wedding dress and the birth of a Kimberly or a Sherry or a Debbi and a Tijuana divorce and a return to hairdressers' school. "We were just crazy kids," they say without regret, and look to the future, [which] always looks good in the golden land because no one remembers the past.

Promoting Corrective Action

George Orwell says in "Why I Write" that he writes about places and people "because there is some lie that I want to expose, some act to which I want to draw attention, and my initial concern is to get a hearing." Through fusing "political purpose and artistic purpose into one whole," Orwell wants to move his readers to change society. Understanding the problems he identifies is the first step toward solving them.

From this motive he wrote "Marrakech," which illustrates the angry thesis that "all colonial empires are sustained by the dehumanization of the poor, nonwhite natives." White residents and visitors to such countries as Morocco are aware of the dry and desolate land: "Huge areas which were once covered with forest have turned into a treeless waste where the soil is exactly like broken-up brick." Whites are aware of the overloaded, scrawny beasts of burden in these countries: "The Moroccan donkey is hardly bigger than a St. Bernard dog, it carries a load which in the British Army would be considered too much for a fifteen-hands mule, and very often its pack-saddle is not taken off its back for weeks together."

Yet most whites are unaware "that for nine-tenths of the people . . . life is an endless, back-breaking struggle to wring a little food out of an eroded soil." Because the natives appear "a kind of undifferentiated brown stuff, about as individual as bees or coral insects," whites don't see them or the abuse they suffer as beasts of burden, their "poor old earth-coloured bodies, bodies reduced to bones and leathery skin, bent double under the crushing weight" of heavy loads of firewood. When the downtrodden recognize their common humanity, Orwell predicted in 1939 when he wrote "Marrakech," they will with justice "turn their guns" on their insensitive white overlords, not only in Morocco, but in colonial empires throughout the world. Orwell claims that whites should act to remedy social justice everywhere in the world for humanitarian reasons, before it's too late.

Another effective way to make a case for reform, whether of the environment or of the condition of its people, is to structure your essay or longer work the way Warner structures *Beautiful Swimmers*. You can use most of the piece to set a beautiful scene and then write a short, sharply drawn conclusion in which you explicate the problem or threat to the setting your readers have come to know intimately and to love. Warner spends the first nine chapters of his book discussing the ecology, the flora and fauna, the people, and the economy of the Chesapeake Bay during different seasons. Then, in the last chapter, he pleads for preservation of the bay instead of the destruction that he sees as imminent. Warner uses negative description to characterize the banks and the waters of Virginia's historic James River; three nuclear power plants, raw sewage, the waste of "much heavy industry" that contribute to the "leaden and gray water." His words carry an implied plea for cleaning up the water, preserving the fragile ecology, and preventing "general eutrophication"—a "very one-sided imbalance [in the water] that produces a suffocating pea-green plant organism at the expense of nearly all others. General eutrophication is Lake Erie. Simple as that."

Places as Contexts for Adventure and Exploration

Exploring the Amazon jungles. Traveling on the Orient Express. Scaling Mt. Everest. Searching for the Northwest Passage. Trekking west by covered wagon. Floating down the Mississippi on a raft. Accounts of such adventures on a grand scale, which focus on places unusual or exotic, are particularly appealing to Western European and American readers, who have a heritage of discovery, conquest, and settlement of new territories. Although for Americans, many frontiers have vanished—except the seas, the tundra, and outer space—adventure lies in the minds and spirits of those who encounter new terrain. Thus every place we haven't seen before, or every familiar place seen from a new perspective—such as a supermarket, a storefront church, or a neighborhood bar—becomes a possible site for exploration and a suitable subject for writing. If the adventure leads to self-knowledge or spiritual or psychological insight, so much the better.

Writing About Adventure and Exploration

In writing about places as contexts for adventure and exploration, you'll need to be particularly concerned with focus, pace and style of travel, and scene setting.

Focus.   Do you want to focus on the phenomenon or process of the adventure, strictly on the place or places explored, or on yourself as an adventurer? In traveling toward something, are you escaping something else? Your focus will determine how much space you devote to discussing matters such as motives for travel, choice of route (scenic, fast, out-of-the-way), destination, mode of transportation (car, foot, bike, balloon, camel), supplies, and traveling companions (intentional or accidental). Your focus will determine whether you write about places because of their scenery, climate, history, or contemporary culture; whether you concentrate on people as a nation, a community, or as individuals; whether you look at economy; or whether you examine the place's role in world affairs. You can offer an overview of many of these aspects, as articles in *National Geographic* often do, or you can single out one or more aspects for extended discussion. If the journey—whether to the cabin in the woods, the beach at Bar Harbor, or even to the suburban shopping mall—has become a source of self-knowledge or of spiritual or psychological insight, you may decide to emphasize its personal meaning. You can structure your writing to reinforce the emphasis you want by using a chronological, a geographical, a topical or a psychological pattern of organization (see pages 121–22).

Pace and style of travel.   Will you proceed at a rapid, moderate, or leisurely pace? Will you travel steadily according to a predetermined plan or take time out for detours, literal and metaphorical? Do you seek the safe and secure route, or are you a risk taker in search of the unbeaten path that requires resourcefulness, ingenuity, and daring? Will you bear with you the heavy baggage of your own civilization, or will you live out of a backpack and off the land?

Scene setting.   Your readers will be looking over your shoulder as you plan the trip, and you'll be taking them with you to the places you visit. You'll introduce them to the people you meet, who may be typical or atypical, commonplace or bizarre. You'll sketch their physical details, accents, actions, and their interaction with you. By candidly presenting specific scenes, vignettes, portraits, and physical or geographical description, you'll enable your readers to see what you see exactly as you see it, to share your prejudices and predilections, to enjoy (or be repelled by) the food at your restaurant table or over your campfire, to move along the path of adventures with your rhythm and pace. After your readers experience your trip as armchair adventurers, they can then decide whether they want to travel themselves.

Exploring a Place for Adventure

Eudora Welty, who has lived most of her long, creative life in her parents' house in Jackson, Mississippi, declares that "a sheltered life can be a daring life . . . for all serious daring starts from within." Nevertheless, it's part of the American tradition to hit the road for adventure. The motto for inveterate travelers who crave "the poetry of motion" is Paul Theroux's claim that "the journey, not the arrival, matters." Although travel itself, says the peripatetic Theroux, is "a vanishing act, a solitary trip down a pinched line of geography to oblivion," the travel writer's account of the trip is the opposite," the loner bouncing back bigger than life to tell the story of his experiment with space." Travel writers commonly adopt one of three points of view. The first point of view is that of a stranger in a strange land or someone encountering a place for the first time. It lends itself to wonderment if the place exceeds the traveler's expectations, to irony if it doesn't, and in either case to comparisons with the place from which the traveler comes. Another point of view is that of a person returning to a place after a long absence. It usually includes a mixture of pleasure, disappointment, or nostalgia and a comparison of then and now. The third common point of view is that of an intimate or an habitué who takes readers by the elbow and guides them down the byways and backstreets and into other peoples' houses.

The viewpoint of a stranger in a strange land is the most conducive to adventure writing because the traveler continually meets with surprises and other unknown phenomena that ultimately must be interpreted for the reader. In *Old Glory: An American Voyage,* a typical work of this genre, English travel writer Jonathan Raban explores what for him is a new frontier. He describes his 1979 trip, inspired by Huck Finn, down the Mississippi River from Minneapolis to New Orleans in a sixteen-foot motorboat. He decided in advance that

> the book and the journey would be all of a piece. The plot would be written by the current of the river itself. It would carry me into long deep pools of solitude, and into brushes with society on the shore. Where the river meandered, so would the book. . . . I would try to be as much like a piece of human driftwood as I could manage. Cast off, let the Mississippi take hold, and trust to whatever adventures . . . the river might throw my way. It was a journey that would be random and haphazard; but it would also have the insistent purpose of the river current as it drove southward and seaward to the Gulf of Mexico.

Raban devotes much space to the place itself, to the river and its surrounding terrain, gorgeous in Wisconsin with a "tesselated pattern of islands and slackwaters" and "cold, dangerous and ugly" near southern Mississippi. Raban identifies his route—readers could plot it on a map—and shares his discoveries. He characterizes river cities and towns; Muscatine, Iowa, is a classy, "intricate, substantial place of oxblood brickwork and terra-cotta streets"; Cape Girardeau, Missouri, is "an amnesiac city . . . littered with things absentmindedly discarded. It had left the river behind."

Raban sketches the people he meets on the river—barge pilots, sailors, casual fishermen, lock operators—and those he meets in the river towns—in bars and churches, in old age homes and decaying riverfront hotels, on political campaigns, and at barbecues. He lives for a time with a slender St. Louis woman, "full of static electricity" and adorned with, yes, diamond rings. Each encounter, brief or extended, is an adventure and a way of defining the place in which it occurred. Down the center of America, Raban cuts a swath with multiple and variegated layers like a geological core sample. And when his trip is over, he writes a book about it, recounting in Paul Theroux's words, "the progress from the familiar to the slightly odd, to the rather strange, to the totally foreign, and finally to the outlandish."

Exploring a Place for Self-Knowledge

Like Jonathan Raban and Paul Theroux, writer Mary Morris is a "journeywoman, a wanderer of the planet." But the emotional heart of Morris's journey to Central America narrated in *Nothing to Declare: Memoirs of a Woman Traveling Alone* is the voyage to the center of her soul. Her explanation of why she travels is typical of many adventure or exploration writers. She is on a compulsive quest for adventure, "the obvious proof is that you can't stop." She loves maps, "I love to figure out where I am going and how I am going to get there, what route I will take." She constantly expects adventure, "even though I know that the journey is never what we plan for; it's what happens between the lines." Typically, Morris decides where to go by following the "maps of my own inner landscape . . . [which] guide me as surely as any by Rand McNally would."

Like other inveterate travelers, Morris has confidence that she will land on her feet wherever she is, both through her intuitive sense of physical direction and the fact that "nothing terrible has ever happened to me." Yet like all adventurers, she loves to take risks, and much of *Nothing to Declare* narrates her flirtations with danger and with strangers, which are seen as one and the same for women traveling alone. "I wander the world," she says, "drifting between places and people . . . yet I always find those men who cannot love, the ones I care for with a deep passion." Narrow escapes are de rigueur for Morris as for other travelers, who never share a beer at the end of a hard day's journey and rejoice at what a safe trip they've had. Instead they brag, as Morris does, "I have had close calls, but I have never been raped or wounded or kidnapped or tortured." Perhaps, however, it is only women travelers on quests of self-discovery who can admit their vulnerability in print. Thus Morris adds, "But I have been left and betrayed, bewildered and afraid."

Nevertheless, books about journeys to self-knowledge are ultimately success stories written by people who may have wandered temporarily into a maze but who ultimately emerge with newfound power and understanding. Morris travels to overcome her experience of betrayal, symbolized by the barely concealed black eye with which she arrives in Mexico. She explains that she has lost her way, "somewhere between the Midwest and Manhattan, childhood and old age, between college and life." So she moves paradoxically from one location to another—throughout Mexico, Guatemala, Honduras, even war-ravaged Nicaragua—to regain her sense of self-direction. Ever in search of the moment of truth "when I would understand what I had not understood before," she finally realizes "that growth comes over time, . . . in small, imperceptible ways." Her new power is symbolized the next day when, swimming far out to sea alone, "something I knew I shouldn't do"—but of course travelers sometimes do court danger—she outswims a gigantic pursuing barracuda. Although she expects it "to rip through the muscle of my calf or tear off my heel," she safely reaches the shore. Finally, Morris discovers the strength of will and character to survive on her own, without the distractions of tourists, friends, or lovers. Her quest is at an end: "Like a person about to die, I felt my life come rushing back to me." She can return in triumph, not only to write about her adventures but to imply that such daring exploits will be the readers' salvation, as well.

Writing a Guide for Travelers

Travel literature is, for most readers, an agreeable form of escape from wherever they are, whether or not a trip to Katmandu, Kenya, or the Grand Canyon is more a wish than a reality. For some, reading about a trip is an inspiration to make it happen. For others, reading about a trip is just as satisfying as actually taking the trip.

As the writer of a travel guide, in essay form or longer, for a particular place, you can assume (in the absence of contrary evidence) that your readers don't know very much about the place, that they haven't been there for a while, or that they're looking for a new route to take over familiar terrain. As the writer, you take on the roles of expert and interpreter. Without being patronizing, you make sense of the place for the uninitiated by answering the journalistic questions: What? Why? Where? When? and How? The answer to who should go to the place is self-evident—the reader.

Where is the place?   Your identification of where to find the place can be precise and factual. A map or diagram might help, as would locating the place in relation to other places the readers might know. Or you can identify especially historical, picturesque, or otherwise significant places within the larger area. In the first paragraph of *The World of Venice,* James Morris (now Jan Morris) provides a fittingly nautical introduction to his island subject that combines information about its location and its moody marine atmosphere:

> At 45 14′N., 12 18′E., the navigator, sailing up the Adriatic coast of Italy, discovers an opening in the long low line of the shore; and turning westward, with the race of the tide, he enters a lagoon. Instantly the boisterous sting of the sea is lost. The water around him is shallow but opaque, the atmosphere curiously translucent, the colours pallid, and over the whole wide bowl of mudbank and water there hangs a suggestion of melancholy.

What are the notable features?   Why should one go to this place? Although you'll have to be selective since you can't cover everything, what you emphasize will depend on your own interests or on the concerns of your readers. In *Iberia: Spanish Travels and Reflections,* world traveler James Michener offers an unusually thorough and eloquent guide to a fascinating country. His book is still valuable for its breadth and humanity despite its publication in 1968; most travel books need frequent updating. His account assumes that travelers to Madrid, like travelers to any other city or country, might want to better understand characteristic features such as its history, religion, politics, people, and culture. They may also want to know about recreation, entertainment, and shopping.

History.   History can be found in plazas, churches, statues, and buildings, such as "El Escorial" in Michener's Madrid:

> [The Slag Heap], a strange pile of gray-black stone set among foothills . . . representative, in its heaviness and simplicity, of the essential Spanish characteristics. . . . Four things, interrelated and enclosed within common walls: a palace from which kings ruled Spain; a grandiose mausoleum holding the sarcophagi of many kings; a monastery; and an enormous church.

Religion.   Michener discusses Spanish Catholicism and its effects on the indigenous population and on Spain's international politics. In the process he dispels myths such as "The Black Legend," which claimed that repressive Spanish "Catholicism intended to enslave the world" by means of the Inquisition.

Politics.   Michener considers the question "After Franco?" at length, beginning with a Spanish friend's observation to clarify the subject for American readers, "'We Spaniards are utter bastards to govern. We are Texans cubed.'"

Notable or typical people.   Michener sketches portraits of Madrileños he met by chance or intention, including authors, artists, political leaders, socialites, businessmen, and bullfighters. He also provides accounts of the lives of representative historical figures.

Culture.   Culture is revealed in all of the preceding categories, but Michener specifically discusses it in describing how the Madrileños live. For instance, he says of Madrid's public transportation, traffic jams, newspapers, television, and mores:

> *Then* [in 1950] Madrid was a puritan city, with police watching for any display of modern life such as short dresses on women, or hand-holding between lovers. . . . I saw English women thrown out of churches because their bare elbows showed. . . . *now* [in 1965] . . . young people in love kiss openly, girls wear pretty much what they want, and the only women who bother about covering their heads when visiting churches are self-conscious American Protestants.

Recreation and entertainment.   You can look at orchestras, museums, sporting events (in Spain, *jai alai,* soccer, bullfighting, betting pools), festivals, theaters (in Spain, special ones feature the *zarzuela,* "a playlet, half spoken, half sung, with dancing, comedy and delightful music." Be sure to give details about days of the week and times of opening and closing; prices, including group and special rates or free days. You could also give information about tours (such as walking or bus tours), indicating tour routes and particular points of interest.

Shopping.   Discuss what to buy, such as typical native arts, crafts, or manufactured products, and where to buy it; and identify particularly good bargains. Michener observes, "*Then* prices for things like men's suits, women's gloves, leather goods . . . were low and represented the best buys in Europe; *now* there are no bargains but quality is good and what you pay for you get." Unless your writing is short-term or will be updated frequently, avoid giving specific prices because they date your work.

How can one get there?   Identify the best routes to a place (the most direct or the most scenic) by car, ship, or plane. Point out any travel bargains that are available to get to a place and to get around in it. Travelers also appreciate information about the local modes of transportation. James Morris describes the various Venetian crafts that ply the "streets full of water":

> If you take an aircraft over Venice, and fly low over her mottled attics, you will see her canals thick with an endless flow of craft, like little black corpuscles. Every kind of boat navigates the Venetian channels, for every kind of purpose, and many are unique to the place. There is the *gondola,* of course ["the queen of the canals"]. . . . There is the *vaporetto,* which is the water bus. . . . not to speak of . . . frisky outboards, or sleek speedboats, or dustbin barges, or parcel-post boats, or excursion launches, or car ferries, or canoes. . . .

Where can one stay? What's good to eat?   In describing food and lodging, you'll need to supply basic information about location, decor, price range, cleanliness (only if it's not), and quality of service. Readers will want to know a restaurant's specialties, its ambience (Is it a family restaurant or a more formal—and pricey—establishment?), and its notable personnel (a famous chef). They will want information about a lodging's special features, such as guarded parking, a pool, exercise facilities, babysitting, and breakfast.

You can transform such information from a mere list into an interesting essay by interpreting it in a context. In *New York: Places and Pleasures*, Kate Simon coveys the atmosphere of a typical New York luncheonette:

> Beyond [the mob at the entrance] is the genie who frantically fills and seals coffee jars and wraps sandwiches delivered to him with loud announcements by a distant assistant (with speed and sureness, he also pours milk, cuts pie, mixes sodas, ladles soup—less like a man than a perspiring octopus). . . . [To get a seat,] as you make your way down the counter, examine each plate. . . . When you see a near-finished piece of pie, or a cup of coffee tilted fairly high, make your move. Take a stand behind the tilter and don't budge. . . . How close can you stand without annoying your enthroned predecessor or tripping him as he slides off the stool?

Simon follows this advice with specific suggestions on how to get the most for your money, such as eating your larger meal at midday, when prices are lower.

When is the best time to visit?   Readers will want to know the temperature range, typical weather, and appropriate clothing to bring during likely seasons for visiting, as well as the dates of holidays, festivals, or other recurring events of note (the Calgary Stampede, the Indy 500, Mardi Gras). James Morris says of the seasons in Venice,

> She lives for the summer, when her great tourist industry leaps into action, and in the winter she is a curiously simple, homely place . . . her Piazza deserted, her canals choppy and dismal. . . . A harsh, raw, damp miasma overcomes the city for weeks at a time, only occasionally dispersed by days of cold, sunny brilliance. The rain teems down with a particular wetness, like unto like. . . .

What other important things should travelers know?   Give important information such as the names and rates of exchange of local currency; hours that banks, stores, and subways are open; how and where travelers can find emergency medical help; local customs (such as how much and whom to tip); what languages are spoken. Ved Mehta in *Portrait of India* says of India's languages,

India teems with languages. There are fourteen officially recognized regional languages, two hundred and fifty major dialects . . . many completely unrelated to one another. English . . . has never been understood by more than three percent of the population. The closest thing to a national language is Hindi, yet it is understood by only forty per cent—or at most, fifty per cent—of the population. Most Indians can understand only one language—that of the place in which they were born.

Feel free to add anything else of particular interest that strikes you as significant. Your readers depend on your information to help them have a good time—and to avoid disasters.

Checklist for Writing About Places

1. Do I know the place I'm writing about firsthand? intimately, as an inhabitant? impressionistically, as a visitor?

2. Have I selected a place to write about to which I react strongly, either positively or negatively?

3. Why am I writing about this particular place? Is my purpose clear? Is my subject sufficiently limited so I can handle it adequately in the space I have?

4. Do I have an unusual perspective to view it from or something original to say about it? In what ways does my treatment of a familiar place depart from the hackneyed, the conventional? In what ways is it familiar to my readers? Should it be?

5. What kind of character do I appear to be in this writing? Do I appear as I want to? Is my character consistent? Does it change as a result of the experiences I narrate?

6. Do I provide enough specific details, vignettes, and other descriptions of the inhabitants and the ambience of the place to put my readers on the scene? Do I let the details demonstrate the essence of the place and my view of it rather than overtly belabor my interpretation?

7. Am I chauvinistic? Should I be? If I dislike a place, have I anticipated the sentiments of readers who like it?

8. Does my chosen pattern of organization reinforce my emphasis?

9. Is my writing understated? (If it is overstated, how can I justify the excesses?) Is my writing unsentimental even when I love or otherwise appreciate the place? Should it be that way?

10. Will my readers want to go to the places I like? Will they appreciate them, at least? Have I made a good case for why they should avoid or be repelled by places I dislike?

Selected Reference List of Writings About Places

See also "Works Cited."

Ehrlich, Gretel. *The Solace of Open Spaces.* 1985. New York: Penguin, 1986.

FitzGerald, Frances. *Cities on a Hill: A Journey Through Contemporary American Cultures.* 1986. New York: Touchstone, 1987.

Lopez, Barry. *Arctic Dreams: Imagination and Desire in a Northern Landscape.* 1986. New York: Bantam, 1989.

McPhee, John. *Coming into the Country.* 1976. New York: Bantam, 1977.

Theroux, Paul. *Riding the Iron Rooster: By Train Through China.* 1988. New York: Ivy, 1989.

Westfall, Patricia Tichenor. *Real-Farm.* 1989. New York: Avon, 1991.

Williams, Terry Tempest. *Refuge: An Unnatural History of Family and Place.* 1991. New York: Vintage, 1991.

Works Cited

Beston, Henry. *The Outermost House: A Year of Life on the Great Beach of Cape Cod.* 1928. New York: Penguin, 1976. 113, 162.

Dickens, Charles. *American Notes and Pictures from Italy.* 1842. London: Oxford UP, 1957. 87, 122, 171–72.

Didion, Joan. "Some Dreamers of the Golden Dream." *Slouching Towards Bethlehem.* 1968. New York: Farrar, 1968. 3–4.

Dillard, Annie. *Pilgrim at Tinker Creek.* 1974. New York: Bantam, 1975. 2, 3, 5, 75, 85, 128–29.

Eszterhas, Joe. "Charlie Simpson's Apocalypse." *The New Journalism.* Ed. Tom Wolfe and E. W. Johnson. 1972. New York: Harper, 1973. 127–60.

Geertz, Clifford. *Works and Lives: The Anthropologist as Author.* Stanford, CA: Stanford UP, 1988. 2.

Hubbell, Sue. *A Country Year: Living the Questions.* 1986. New York: Harper, 1987. 94–95.

Kozol, Jonathan. *Rachel and Her Children: Homeless Families in America.* New York: Crown, 1988. 102–03.

McPhee, John. *The Pine Barrens.* 1976. New York: Vintage, 1978. 81, 83, 84.

Mehta, Ved. *Portrait of India.* New York: Farrar, 1970. 458–59.

Michener, James. *Iberia: Spanish Travels and Reflections.* New York: Random, 1968. 330, 332, 370, 373, 390.

Morris, James. *The World of Venice.* New York: Pantheon, 1960. 23, 135, 203.

Morris, Jan. *Journeys.* New York: Oxford UP, 1984.

Morris, Mary. *Nothing to Declare: Memoirs of a Woman Traveling Alone.* 1987. New York: Penguin, 1988. 22–23, 37, 175, 211, 212, 242.

Orwell, George. *Down and Out in Paris and London.* 1933. New York: Harcourt, 1961.

———. "Marrakech." *An Age Like This 1920–1940.* Vol. 1 of *The Collected Essays, Journalism and Letters of George Orwell.* Ed. Sonia Orwell and Ian Angus. 4 vols. New York: Harcourt, 1968. 187–93.

————."Why I Write." *A Collection of Essays*. San Diego: Harcourt, 1953. 309–16.

Payne, Tim. "On the Beach at Bar Harbor." *The Essay Connection: Readings for Writers*. 3rd ed. Ed. Lynn Z. Bloom. Lexington, MA: Heath, 1991. 232–35.

Raban, Jonathan. *Old Glory: An American Voyage*. 1981. New York: Penguin, 1982. 16, 126, 192, 273, 295–96.

Simon, Kate. *New York: Places and Pleasures*. 4th ed. New York: Harper, 1971. 140, 143.

Theroux, Paul. *The Old Patagonian Express: By Train Through the Americas*. 1979. New York: Washington Square, 1980. 3, 6–7.

Thoreau, Henry David. *Walden*. Ed. William Howarth. New York: Modern Library, 1981. 81, 118, 122.

Trecker, Janice Law. "Reaping late summer's sweet bounty." *Hartford Courant*. 16 Aug. 1992: C3.

Walton, Izaak. *The Compleat Angler*. London: Nonesuch, 1936. 33.

Warner, William. *Beautiful Swimmers: Watermen, Crabs and the Chesapeake Bay*. 1976. New York: Penguin, 1979. 257, 261.

Welty, Eudora. *One Writer's Beginning*. Cambridge, MA: Harvard UP, 1984. 104.

Williams, Terry Tempest, and Robert Finch. "Landscape, People, and Place." *Writing Natural History: Dialogues with Authors*. Ed. Edward Lueders. Salt Lake City: U of Utah P, 1989. 38–65.

White, E. B. "Once More to the Lake," "The Ring of Time." 1941, 1956. *Essays of E. B. White*. New York: Harper, 1977.

Zwinger, Ann, and Gary Paul Nabhan. "Field Notes and the Literary Process." *Writing Natural History: Dialogues with Authors*. Ed. Edward Lueders. Salt Lake City: U of Utah P, 1989. 67–117.

6

WRITING ABOUT PERFORMANCE

People go to spectator sports to have fun and then they grab the paper to read about it and have fun again.

— Red Smith

The English [theatre goers] do not know what to think until they are coached laboriously and insistently for years, in the proper and becoming opinion. For ten years past . . . I have been dinning into the public head that [as a drama critic] I am an extraordinarily witty, brilliant, and clever man.

— George Bernard Shaw

Young critics tend to enter the field full of grand visions for the betterment of the musical world. They are much tougher than the older, more experienced ones. Later all critics come to realize that they are not going to revolutionize music. . . . Critics don't make careers. Artists make careers.

— Harold C. Schonberg

If everybody is talking about [the movie], don't go.

— John Leonard

Love and the Reviewer

Behind every good review is a passionate reviewer, even though most of that love, like most of what you know about the subject, may not show on the surface. This doesn't mean that you have to love, or even like, every performance, every performer on which you comment. If you admire everything indiscriminately, your readers won't be able to trust your continually charitable perspective. This does mean, however, that you have to love the medium you write about.*

Love keeps reviewers knowledgeable. For only love will motivate the true devotee to read the mediocre and bad books as well as the good, to watch every game of the local Little League, to become familiar with all facets of a subject to satisfy other devotees as well as more casual readers. You don't have to be an expert; if you were you might be on stage instead of on the aisle. But in order to write convincingly about the performance at hand, or the subject in general, you do have to understand the rules of the game, the skills of the craft, and current significant developments in the medium. If you love a subject, acquiring the knowledge necessary to write about it is fun, not work; you pick it up by hanging around backstage, in the concert hall, or on the field, and by reading, reading, reading. To love a subject is to know it; to know it is to love it.

Knowledge keeps reviewers credible as well, for it keeps them convincing. Thus when John Lahr, *New Yorker* critic, begins a review of *Oleanna* with "David Mamet understands that envy is the gasoline on which a competitive society runs, and no modern American playwright has been bolder or more brilliant in analyzing its corrosive social effects," we believe him; he must know most, if not all, contemporary American playwrights to make that comparison. Although we allow the reviewer some poetic license—he can mean *nearly all* rather than *every single one*—we have no doubt, if we think about his credibility at all, that Lahr has seen enough plays to make that generalization. We are more likely, simply, to trust him, and to look for his subsequent commentary.

---

* *Performance* is used throughout this chapter in two senses. One sense implies performance as in performing arts, a body of created works, events, entertainment, or other activities performed for a public audience. *Fact and Artifact* expands this definition to include not only the fine arts—music, art, dance, and literature (fiction, poetry, drama, literary nonfiction)—but also entertainment—television, restaurants, sports events, and the performers themselves. The other, more restricted sense of performance refers to a single work, event, or performing activity.

Although reviews represent the most common writing about performance, usually in the more restricted sense, there are many other kinds of writing about performance—longer interpretive and critical commentaries on individual works (much literary criticism), performers (such as studies of musicians, writers, chefs, or athletes), or groups (an orchestra, a team, a television series). For simplicity, *reviewer* or *commentator* will be used to identify the writer of performance used in either sense. As you read, feel free to expand or restrict the scope of the discussion to refer to the type of writing you're concentrating on.

Love of a subject keeps reviewers hopeful, eager to believe that a performance will be very good, if not superlative, or, if all else fails, very interesting. One of America's most distinguished, delightful sportswriters, Red Smith, explains why covering baseball every day never got dull: "It becomes dull only to dull minds. Today's game is always different from yesterday's game. If you have the perception and the interest to see it, and the wit to express it, your story is always different from yesterday's story." Smith's observations apply to writing about any kind of performance at any time, under any circumstance.

Love of a subject keeps reviewers caring, tolerant, and positive in most of their public commentary. Unless you have or want a reputation as a curmudgeon, you'll want your commentary to be generally upbeat. Although you may not like two out of three books you read or restaurants you investigate, you don't have to review all the bad ones, although as a sportswriter you are obliged to cover every last game of a losing season. You may do your readers a favor if you let the greasy cuisine of the Viaduct Restaurant or the awkwardly written *Montgomery, Alabama's First Lady of the Violin* disappear without notice. But if the work, event, or performer, is well known, readers will expect to see a review.

Guidelines for Writing Reviews

When you write a review or commentary, you become a fearless interpreter of your subject, whether it's a book, recording, play, concert, film, television program, art show, restaurant, or a sports event. You also become a subtle showoff because your writing conveys with every measured syllable and metaphor a sense of your personality, your authority. Every time you write with perception and wit you earn your readers' trust; every time the readers return to your commentary, they give your work a vote of confidence whether or not they agree with your judgment.

Readers also appreciate wit with wisdom, so if your review can entertain as well as enlighten, so much the better. The beginning of William Kennedy's review of the 1992 Broadway revival of *Guys and Dolls* delights readers with stylized high praise that echoes the language of its creator's 1930s gangsterese: "which I am offering six-to-five is the best musical ever created—bet me." Indeed Kennedy, a noted novelist, captures the comic joy of Damon Runyon's "invented tongue," the "language of gamblers, hoodlums, chorus girls and cops," throughout his review by writing in a modified version of the language. His witty conclusion complements the beginning, a neat closure for any review: "These odds [that Runyon's work will endure] are just enough to keep you interested: six-to-five, a nice price. Bet me."

As a reviewer you don't have to create an audience; the bookworms, opera buffs, sports fans already exist. This makes your task both easier and harder. You can capitalize right from the start on your readers' interest, whether passionate or casual, but remember that they are also likely to know a great deal about the subject. You can't make the factual mistakes that you might make with a less knowledgeable and more forgiving audience—the Trekkies will know whether or not you have been a regular passenger on the *Starship Enterprise*. Your commentary will have to sustain the readers' interests by satisfying the major reasons that they read reviews: for information, interpretation and evaluation, and entertainment.

Conventions of Reviews

The best reviews exhibit the conciseness, self-containment, and unity—which comes from both structural and stylistic integrity. Wit is a bonus.

Conciseness.   Life, said pessimistic philosopher Thomas Hobbes, is nasty, brutish, and short. Although reviews may or may not be nasty and brutish, they are usually short. Reviews are rarely allocated more than two thousand words and sometimes fewer than five hundred. Clarence Olson, for two decades book editor of the St. Louis *Post-Dispatch,* advises, "A review should be as succinct as possible; the ideal review is almost uncutable because the loss of a sentence or even a word would hurt." So you have to be selective to convey the essence of a four-hour television special, a double header, a six-hundred page novel; there's no room for scene-by-scene descriptions, long quotations, or elaborate analyses.

Self-containment.   Although you write for an audience of devotees of your subject, you must assume that most of them are unfamiliar with the particular work, performance, or game you're discussing. They read your review to learn about it. Because most reviews are read casually, perhaps over the breakfast coffee, on the subway, or before bedtime, you should assume that readers have a certain amount of inertia; even though they may know a lot about the subject, they don't want to look up anything (such as allusions, statistics, or references to past performances) as they read. Include enough information so they won't need to.

Unity.   "There should be unity to a review," says Olson, "a beginning in which a theme is established, a middle in which this theme is fleshed out with details and supported by logical arguments, and an end that returns to the basic theme or offers a summary conclusion." Often, you can enhance this unity by weaving a symbol, a metaphor, or another stylistic device through the review, particularly at the beginning and the end.

Let's see how student Mary Roberts attains these qualities of conciseness, self-containment, and unity in a review of Alice Walker's *The Color Purple.*

Wit. Although it's not easy to be witty on command, readers appreciate the elegant turn of phrase, the subtle echoing of a theme or phrase from the original work in the analysis of it. Such precise language implies that the reviewer understands the subject's spirit as well as its substance and is therefore a fitting commentator. Witty writing also compliments the readers, for the writer assumes they'll recognize and appreciate such understated word play. Note, for example, the reflections on colors that illuminate the beginning and ending of the review of *The Color Purple* that follows.

Painted boldly on the bare canvas of aliveness, *The Color Purple* is pure. 1
Like the deceptively simple brush strokes of an oriental watercolor, the crude, spare words of Alice Walker's novel, told through letters written in Black Southern dialect, come together as poetry. The experience of her characters is real, springing from the energy of their rural, ghetto culture which Walker has tapped. The result is power.

Celie and Nettie are sisters biologically, spiritually, and experientially. Born 2
into a world of hardship and oppression, they are separated early. Celie's stepfather forces her into two apparently incestuous pregnancies, gives away her babies, keeps her ignorant and ugly, beats her, and marries her off at twenty to Mr. _____ (she never names him until the very end of the novel), who treats her with comparable callousness for many years of the novel's thirty-year span. She is a tireless worker with a generous spirit; she rears Mr. _____'s children by a previous marriage, does all the housework and most of the heavy farm labor, and endures sex. With no one to talk to on earth, Celie writes letters to God. These are misspelled but heartfelt accounts of her life, and reflections on man-woman relations, love, friendship, racism, maternity, and woman's fate, among other topics.

Her husband spends much of the time mooning over the love of his life, 3
Shug (for Sugar) Avery, a jazz singer, "the most beautiful woman" Celie ever saw, with whom Albert, as Shug dares to address Mr. _____, carries on intermittent affairs. Celie's generosity, the essence of *caritas,* enables her not only to welcome the dying Shug when Albert brings her home, but to nurse her to health and creativity.

Albert and Celie agree, "Hard not to love Shug. . . . She know how to love 4
somebody back." For Shug is the earthy essence of sex and love, and teaches Celie about both. (Walker handles their own lovemaking decorously):
— God don't think [sex] dirty? I ask.
— Naw, Shug say. God made it. Listen, God love
everything you love—and a mess of stuff you don't.
But more than anything else, God love admiration. . . .

> Not vain. Just wanting to share a good thing. I think
> it pisses God off if you walk by the color purple in a
> field somewhere and don't notice it.

To escape Celie's marital fate, pretty, better-educated Nettie seeks work with   5
a missionary couple, who take her with them and their two adopted children
(Celie's, though they don't know this) to Africa to aid the Olinka, whose native culture is threatened and eventually destroyed by white plantation own-
ers. Shug discovers the cache of her letters, mailed over the years, that Albert
has hidden from Celie. This further cements the allegiance of Shug and Celie,
though their love is scarcely exclusive, for Shug soon marries one of her many
male lovers.

Yet *The Color Purple* is not a story in black and white. Walker reveals new   6
depths and beauty in the gradations of shades of black, though the few white
characters are uniformly monochromatic—and ugly. Walker's medium is her
own culture; her narrative is sometimes shocking and brutal, sometimes warmly
funny, and often exquisite, but never narrowed by anger or evangelism. Her
awareness and portrayal of relationships is so keen that she is able to transform hate into love, without missing a nuance.

The Color Purple could be considered a revolutionary black feminist work.   7
That it is a deep, intense study of sisterhood is certainly true, but to stop there
would surely "piss God off." Once Celie learns love, and gains self-respect and
ultimately financial and emotional independence (she goes into business de-
signing and making perfect pants, for women and for men), she can love not
only women and children, but humanity. And they can love her—and each
other—back. Indeed, the book ends with a family reunion, a day spent "cele-
brating each other." The novel's humanity transcends its feminism. *The Color
Purple* is pure, the color purple is love.

In spite of the review's short length, about 640 words, Roberts tells us a
great deal, supplying enough essential information to make the review
concise and self-contained. Typical of a well-mannered review, every character is introduced at the first meeting and every major relationship is
indicated immediately, by a few representative specific details or actions.
At the outset, Celie is "ignorant and ugly," a "tireless worker with a generous spirit"; Albert, "Mr. _____," is Celie's husband and Shug's lover; and
so on.

Operating under the somewhat contradictory constraints of the reviewer's
need to be both concise and self-contained, Roberts sketches the broad outline of the plot, emphasizing some aspects, subordinating others, and omitting still others to satisfy the readers' need to know right away who's who,
what's what, and why the characters behave as they do. Yet in deciding what
to emphasize and what to omit, she also makes judgments about the relative
importance of major and minor themes, characters, and plots in the novel,
knowing that her readers will be testing these judgments against their own
as they read the book itself.

Paragraphs 2 and 3 concisely explain the *main plot,* which centers around the loveless and exploitative relationship of Albert to Celie and the loving and humanly fulfilling relationship between Celie and Shug. Roberts wisely devotes more than twice as much space to the main plot as she does to the *subplot,* Nettie's adventures as a missionary among the Olinka. This proportion reflects the emphasis of the novel itself and the readers' likely interest. Readers need to know much more about the central phenomena of the novel, particularly the changing relationships in which Celie is involved, than they do about the less significant subplot. Space limitations prevent Roberts from discussing still other, less salient aspects of the plot such as Nettie's marriage, relationships among other family members not identified in the review, and various ways in which the bigoted white characters (alluded to in paragraph 6) systematically exploit the blacks.

In paragraph 7, in the course of assessing the novel's themes, Roberts implies the *outcome* of the plot, necessary in this case (despite the taboo on this for mystery and drama reviews) because of the novel's extended, highly moving conclusion that celebrates love and family union—two of the book's *major motifs.* Because the plot exemplifies as well the motifs of racism, the relations between men and women, friendship, and women's fate, the reviewer appropriately and economically identifies these themes while discussing the plot instead of treating them separately.

The review is unified by imagery in the first and the concluding paragraphs that relates memorably and immediately to the novel's title. Roberts rings changes on *The Color Purple,* referring at the beginning and end to the "pure" color and specifying at the end (in a significant variation on the beginning) that the nature of that color is "love." Roberts ends with this extremely strong word to mirror the novel's strength and emphasis. Her only extensive quotation, in paragraph 4, explains the symbolism of "the color purple." She has the daring to echo its earthy phrase "pisses God off" in her final paragraph, a risky use of potentially offensive language that is nevertheless a dynamic unifying device. In paragraph 6 Roberts provides additional unity through symbolically equating the characters with colors that are "gradations of shades of black" and "monochromatic—and ugly" white—witty writing that reflects the title.

Roberts concisely includes other essential information in her review. She identifies the book's *type,* an epistolary novel, not by using the technical term that some readers might not understand, but by referring to the book's letter format. She alludes to *settings,* the southern "rural, ghetto" and the Olinka tribal setting in Africa. (The novel itself is not more specific.) She tells us that the book's *language* is "Black Southern dialect" and later verifies this with the dialect quotation in paragraph 4, which also conveys the novel's *tone.* Furthermore, because Roberts likes the book, she leaves us happy with her strong praise; it's satisfying to leave the review resonating with language of the last sentence, "the color purple is love."

Information in Reviews

The emphasis of a review or sports writing depends, in part, on the nature of the performance. If readers can buy it (such as a book or a recording) or attend it (such as a play, film, restaurant, sports event), then you need to provide enough information for them to decide for themselves whether to do so, regardless of your opinion. If, on the other hand, you review a unique performance (such as a concert or a ball game), which is over and done with by the time readers encounter your review, your commentary may be more analytic. Nevertheless, your review will influence readers the next time the home team is in town or Zubin Mehta conducts.

Foreground Information

Whatever its emphasis, a review needs to answer some or all of the questions that follow. This information can be brief where a word, a phrase, or a figure suffices, leaving space for what you want to emphasize in greater detail. In organizing this information, start with the first thing that readers need to know in order to understand the next piece of information (the title, perhaps), then add the second most essential fact (its genre or author), and so on. You can skip what you think your readers already know (a plot summary of *Hamlet,* identification of Beethoven), for you don't want to talk down to them. But if you have any doubts about their level of understanding, it's better to include more information than too little.

What is the specific event, performance, or work?   Tell your readers what you are reviewing: the finals of the 1995 Davis Cup matches, the 1950 production of *Guys and Dolls,* its 1992 revival, or some other production on or off Broadway. If you are reviewing a performance, specify its exact date and place: the revival of *Guys and Dolls* that opened Tuesday, April 14, 1992 at the Martin Beck Theater in New York, directed, as William Kennedy notes, "by the three-time Tony winner Jerry Zaks, a very valuable citizen of Broadway. . . ."

What is the genre? the mode?   You'll need to identify the genre and mode of unfamiliar works as specifically as you can. Although a music review could focus on heavy metal, country and western, madrigals, reggae, rap, or grand opera, each review would attract a potentially different audience.

What happened?   Readers who haven't read the book or seen the play or film will want to know the plot—though the reviewer should never give away the ending, especially to tell whodunit. Although devotees who haven't attended the game or the race might want a play-by-play description, they can get this only from on-the-spot commentary while the event is in progress. A written review gives readers a selective account of what happened, focusing either on the highlights or the most controversial events, or on some lesser points that the reviewer has enough wit to render utterly fascinating.

In "Comedy's Greatest Era," James Agee summarizes the major action of *Safety Last,* a silent "comedy of thrills," by identifying the major complications of the plot. In the process, he analyzes the comic technique of Harold Lloyd in the star's repeated but unintentional brushes with danger and equally unwitting but hairbreadth escapes:

> In *Safety Last,* as a rank amateur, [Lloyd] is forced to substitute for a human fly and to climb a medium-sized skyscraper. Dozens of awful things happen to him. He gets fouled up in a tennis net. Popcorn falls on him from a window above, and the local pigeons treat him like a cross between a lunch wagon and St. Francis of Assisi. A mouse runs up his britches-leg, and the crowd below salutes his desperate dance on the window ledge with wild applause of the daredevil. A good deal of this full-length picture hangs thus by its eyelashes along the face of a building. Each new floor is like a new stanza in a poem; and the higher and more horrifying it gets, the funnier it gets. . . .
>
> [In the climactic gag] Lloyd is driven out to the dirty end of a flagpole by a furious dog; the pole breaks and he falls, just managing to grab the minute hand of a huge clock. His weight promptly pulls the hand down from IX to VI. That would be more than enough for any ordinary comedian, but there is further logic in the situation. Now, hideously, the whole clock face pulls loose and slants from its trembling springs above the street. Getting out of difficulty with the clock, he makes still further use of the instrument by getting one foot caught in one of these obstinate springs.

What major works were performed or exhibited?   In a review of a concert or art exhibit, you'll want to concentrate on the highlights. But to convey the flavor of the entire program you'll need to identify the range or type of the lesser offerings as well. To avoid lists, which quickly become monotonous, you can integrate the necessary factual information with your analysis of specific works. Thus Agee embellishes his list of Lloyd's comic techniques with enough interpretive details to disguise it. In a restaurant review you'll want to discuss a sampling of the chef's specialties as well as the standard fare. Provide a sufficient survey of the menu to give prospective diners a taste of what they'll order.

Student Shawn Springer combines an overview of the program with interpretive comments in reviewing a concert of traditional Japanese music performed for an American audience unfamiliar with the music, instruments, and performers:

> Many of the selections represented stories or legends. "Wandering Bell" tells the legend of the disciple of a wandering priest who carried a bell to attract fol-

lowers. "Evening Faces and Night-Blooming Flowers" described musically the tale of a ladies' man who while having a romance with one woman becomes interested in another. Other selections represented moods. . . . A shakuhachi duet entitled "Distant Sound of Deer," played by the Master, Seibi Sato, and another elderly musician, represented the cries of the male and female deer and the feelings of loneliness these inspired in a priest overhearing them.

Who are the principal people?   Important people may include the author, composer, conductor, director, coach, manager, soloists, star players, or outstanding members of the supporting cast. If your readers are familiar with the person's characteristic style or method of performance (say, the comic styles of Charlie Chaplin, Groucho Marx, or Roseanne Arnold), you won't need to describe it in detail unless you have something new to say.

Background Information

Background information helps readers put a particular game or performance into its historical, intellectual, artistic, social, or political contexts. You can use such information to show how the current work or event evolved or to clarify meaning, technique, of your interpretation. Although there is no single optimum ratio between background and foreground information, unless your emphasis is on an historical perspective you'll want to keep background subordinated. Use the questions that follow to decide what information is appropriate for your review.

What background information is available?   Is it interesting? Is it useful in interpreting a given performance in relation to the performer's other work? Would it help readers better understand the work or avoid misinterpretation? In many instances, a brief mention of crucial information will suffice. For instance, in reviewing a biography, you'll usually need to weave in the subject's birth and death dates because readers need that grounding in time.

In writings with a historical or evolutionary emphasis, you'll need to include more background material and give it a more prominent position in the work. In his classic and rare piece of sports commentary, "Hub Fans Bid Kid Adieu," John Updike explains the significance of Ted Williams's retirement from baseball through analyzing what Williams meant to the Boston Red Sox and to fans during his twenty-year career. The essay is necessarily long because of the complicated history of Williams's long career:

> The affair between Boston and Ted Williams has been no mere summer romance; it has been a marriage, composed of spats, mutual disappointments, and, toward the end, a mellowing hoard of shared memories. It falls into three stages, which may be termed Youth, Maturity, and Age; or Thesis, Antithesis, and Synthesis; or Jason, Achilles, and Nestor.

First, there was the by now legendary epoch when the young bridegroom came out of the West, announced "All I want out of life is that when I walk down the street folks will say, 'There goes the greatest hitter who ever lived.'" The dowagers of local journalism attempted to give elementary deportment lessons to this child who spake as a god, and to their horror were themselves rebuked. Thus began the long exchange of backbiting, bat-flipping, booing, and spitting that has distinguished Williams's public relations. . . . spitting incidents of 1957 and 1958 and the similar dockside courtesies . . . extended to the grandstand should be judged against this background. . . . Greatness necessarily attracts debunkers, but in Williams's case the hostility has been systematic and unappeasable. His basic offense against the fans has been to wish that they weren't there. Seeking a perfectionist's vacuum, he has quixotically desired to sever the game from the ground of paid spectatorship and publicity that supports it. Hence his refusal to tip his cap to the crowd or to turn the other cheek to newsmen. It has been a costly theory—it has probably cost him two Most Valuable Player awards, which are voted by reporters—but he has held to it from his rookie year on. While his critics, oral and literary, remained beyond the reach of his discipline, the opposing pitchers were accessible, and he spanked them to the tune of .406 in 1941. He slumped to .356 in 1942. . . .

This is only the beginning, about Williams's rookie years. There's more, much more.

What controversies, trends, or values are involved?   What does this event, place, work, creator, performer, or group represent? Innovation and independence among artists, writers, ballplayers, provoke controversy if the status quo or conventional values are threatened. The example of Ted Williams illustrates the difficulty fans and reporters had in separating their reactions to a player's unconventional public personality from their assessments of his performance. From an artistic perspective, you could discuss the phenomenon of Dadaism, or the metamorphosis of James Joyce's *Ulysses* from a banned book to a classic within 40 years. You could discuss political controversy, such as whether or not the 1936 Olympic games should have been held in Nazi Germany or whether or not books advocating apartheid should be sold in South Africa. Or you could discuss fads, such as stock car racing in the 1950s and 1960s, jogging in the 1970s and 1980s, or roller-blading in the 1990s, as social as well as athletic issues.

What is the prevailing atmosphere?   When writing about an event, ask: What is the atmosphere during rehearsal? In the audience? in the locker room? in Louisville on Derby Day? On the assumption that a restaurant's environment reflects the food quality and is part of the total dining experience, many restaurant reviews begin with the decor, as in the following introduction to Richmond's Tobacco Company restaurant by student Jim O'Neal:

Why would nonsmokers, or smokers, for that matter, want to eat in a converted tobacco warehouse? If you found yourself at 1201 E. Cary Street in Richmond's renovated warehouse district, the answer would be easy—because the building itself looks so inviting. When you walk through the frosted glass doors of this Victorian style brass-and-brick emporium, your eye is immediately drawn to the skylighted ceiling and to the pots of flowers and tubs of plants suspended from it at varying heights by pulleys (so they can be raised or lowered for watering). Each of the two upper floors is arranged in an open quadrangle, with wrought-iron railings separating the diners' bent wood chairs and old fashioned tables from the large, sky lighted central air shaft in which the plants hang—like a patio without floors, suspended over the equally inviting bar that occupies most of the first floor. Your reception will be as pleasant as the decor.

Interpretation and Evaluation

People often read reviews to help them decide which available recreation or entertainment best suits their wishes and their pocketbooks. As they decide whether to pursue the subject any further, they use the reviewer's information and evaluation to make a *cost/benefit analysis*. Is the subject worth the time? the money? the effort to get to, to understand, to appreciate? What are the alternatives? There are no absolute answers to questions of personal preference, but what you say can give your readers reasons for making up their own minds.

Helping Readers Make Informed Choices

Readers of reviews about a particular subject consider matters such as *identification* (What is the specific topic? Is *The Lives of a Cell* about biology? or the Communist party?), *relevance* (Will it interest me?), *level of difficulty* (Will it be too complicated for me to understand?); *familiarity* (Have I already been there, done that? Is it too innovative for me to cope with?), and *appropriateness* (Is it too sexy for my little sister?).

Readers contemplating a night on the town use answers to these questions and the information you provide to match up their time, money, and taste. For laughs, should we go to *Plan 9 From Outer Space* (which was voted "the worst movie of all time," according to film critic David Ansen) or to *The Taming of the Shrew?* Should we eat a long, luscious meal instead? But where? At Landini Bros., "a home style restaurant," says reviewer Phyllis Richman, with "zesty" food and "waiters that are likely to befriend you, bone your fish and advise you how to reheat the leftovers"? Or should we go to Maxine's, where "the menu is Swiss and small and. . . . the dense and crusty country style bread hints of mountain villages"? A reviewer's answers to some of the questions that follow can help readers make informed choices.

Why comment on this particular work, event, or performer?   Why play down or ignore others? A subject may have *national or international significance*. The press reviews all revivals or new films by major directors such as Ingmar Bergman, Federico Fellini, and Woody Allen, regardless of the film's quality or the director's personal notoriety. *Regional relevance.* Rodeos get more extensive coverage in western states, where they're popular events, than they do in the east, where they seldom occur. A subject may have *local interest*. Parents, relatives, friends, and the performers themselves devour accounts of school plays and athletic events. The home team always warrants more emphasis than the out-of-towners. A subject may represent the reviewer's *personal preference*. Every review is an argument, overt or implied, to justify the reviewer's preference (dissenters would say prejudice), perhaps for Ben and Jerry's chocolate ice cream over Borden's, for why Michigan should have beaten Ohio State, for vacationing in Sanibel rather than Key West.

How well done is a given work or event?   The quality of a performance depends on the standards by which it's judged. If you make your standards clear, even if readers don't agree with your evaluations, at least they'll understand why you made them. Your standards will probably be influenced by some or all of the criteria that follow.

Reviewer's level of knowledge.   The reviewer's motto should be, "Don't get in over your head." You don't have to be an expert on a subject to write a good, accurate, reliable review. However, just as no noteworthy performance occurs in a vacuum, no noteworthy review is written in one. The more you know, the better your review will be, especially if you're writing for publication. Knowledge gives you the power to make accurate interpretations and thoughtful judgments and the authority to convince your readers that you're right.

The creator's or performer's level of professionalism.   You expect more from professionals than from amateurs, more from veterans than from novices, more from adults than from children, prodigies excepted. Yet, for a variety of reasons, you may be more indulgent in evaluating the work of members of your own family, hometown folks, or performers who have overcome handicaps.

Aesthetic aspects.   You'll want to consider features such as the harmony of Mozart's Clarinet Quintet in A, K. 451; the assonance, however intentional, of P. D. Q. Bach's Schleptet in E Flat Major, S.O.; the memorable characterization of Willy Loman, Mrs. Dalloway, or Beloved; the commercial packaging of Madonna or Prince.

Technical quality.   You'll comment on technical aspects such as a skater's flawless (or flawed) double axel or a violinist's nimble and accurate playing of a Paganini cadenza. Reviewer David L. Kirp criticizes Richard Rodriguez's

Days of Obligation: An Argument with My Mexican Father, in part, on technical grounds:

> [It] can be maddeningly presumptuous and determinedly obscure. Rodriguez's prose was spare and lucid in *Hunger of Memory,* but in his new book the language is sometimes as ornamental as a five-tiered wedding cake, as if what really matters is the flood of words and not their meaning. The technique of constantly changing the subject, seemingly intended to display the writer's post-modernist credentials, can resemble an MTV video—quick, clever and forgettable.

Adherence to cultural, community, or moral norms.   A preference for French, Japanese, or Southern cooking may depend more on the taste of the reviewer's culture than on the taste of the food. The Victorian audience, reviewers and readers alike frowned on literature that would "bring a blush to the cheek of the young person." Contemporary commentators reflect contemporary values. Barbara Grizzuti Harrison rates the Olympic performance of fourteen-year-old Romanian Nadia Comaneci a perfect 10, which "combined an exquisite elfin fragility with tensile strength." By age twenty-eight, however, in Harrison's judgment, the former gymnast has become a "prototype of zero," stupid, sleazy, a voracious bulimic whose "rank, feral" smell symbolizes her degradation.

Political and social perspectives.   These angles of vision include feminist, Marxist, and democratic (or Democratic), among many others. John Russell writes indignantly about a 1989 exhibition of Frederic Remington's Western paintings and sculpture at the Metropolitan Museum of Art:

> Remington has traditionally been regarded as a popular favorite whose work is of no esthetic interest whatever. He is associated, moreover, with a macho, pre-Freudian and blatantly racist conception of American manhood. . . . Shooting and scalping were the things that most excited him in life. . . . [He was] possessed by hatreds that skewed his whole vision . . . [violent prejudices against] "Jews—injuns—Chinamen—Italians—Huns, the rubbish of the earth."

How, Russell snarls, can we admire someone "who not only painted despicable pictures" but also held such a racist view of the world?

What are the best and worst features?   You're likely to remember both extremes most vividly, but what you discuss first establishes the tenor of your review. Student Cathy Lafferty expected the movie *The World According to Garp* to be as enjoyable as the book, but she was sadly disappointed:

> Which came first, the movie or the book? After watching *The World According to Garp,* it is obvious that the book did. The movie, constructed with a brilliant collection of scenes, remains only that—a collection of scenes.

For anyone watching *Garp* for the first time, the production must seem a jumbled, disjointed mess. It is funny, it is sad. It is simultaneously shocking and innocent. But there is simply too much book for one two-hour movie to cover. Because of this, only the highlights are used, and they are excellent. However, chopping out over two thirds of the novel makes the movie's story line lurch along, even if the viewer is lucky enough to know what's happening.

How does this work or event compare with others?   Comparisons are particularly common in music reviews and sportswriting where a newcomer's work can be quickly described—and assessed for better or worse—by reference to the work of better-known performers. Thus *New York Times* pop music reviewer John Pareles introduces Mary-Chapin Carpenter's concert of November 17, 1992, with the observation that her "confessional songs with rock and country roots . . . can stand alongside the best efforts of Bonnie Raitt and Linda Ronstadt. Unlike them, Ms. Carpenter writes most of what she sings." Her band "often sounded like Bruce Springsteen's E Street Band relocated to mid-1970s Los Angeles. The musicians were at home with Byrds-style folk-rock and lighty chugging, countrified Chuck Berry licks."

Every day new assessments examine new performances. The wise reviewer tempers Sunday's superlatives to avoid looking foolish in Monday's clear dawn, while commentaries on classic performers and performances are often written months or years after the fact. For instance, novelist Joyce Carol Oates's "On Boxing" interprets each boxing match as "a story," the "remnant of another, earlier era when the physical being was primary and the warrior's masculinity its highest expression." From this dramatic perspective she hits the high points of the careers of boxers such as Gene Tunney, Carmen Basilio, Muhammad Ali, and Mike Tyson.

Does a work or a performance fulfill expectations?   Your answer implies that you've determined the potential in advance. Student Bruce Carlton answers an unequivocal "Yes" to Sergei Eisenstein's film, *Potemkin* (1925). Carlton's review shows how Eisenstein translated the didactic message "that an abused and repressed people should, and inevitably will, overthrow their oppressors, overcoming much hardship and suffering in the process" into one of the greatest films of all time. Carlton contends that Eisenstein's unsurpassed editing techniques not only fulfilled but also expanded the potential of filmmaking in that era. To support this view, Carlton focuses on Eisenstein's skillful use of diverse camera angles, and film speeds, and montage:

> Eisenstein links two unrelated images to create a new single concept. He uses a simple sequence of shots to show how the church is allied with the Czarist regime in oppressing the people. The first group of shots shows an old priest slamming a crucifix into the palm of his hand. Next we see a lieutenant fin-

gering the pommel of his revolver. Then Eisenstein cuts to the cannons of the *Potemkin* so we are looking directly down their barrels.

Is a performance appropriate to its medium, aims and audience?   In "Bard Times at the Folger Theater," Michael Kernan reviews a festival of excerpts from Shakespeare's plays performed by fourth to sixth graders to commemorate Shakespeare's 416th birthday.

> We missed the Murch School version of "Macbeth" with six Witches (everyone always wants to be a Witch) but did catch the Haycock School's opening scenes from the play. We can report that King Duncan's voice is changing and that Lady Macbeth looked smashing in a black gown with pearls, striking sparks in her scene with Macbeth, who wore horn-rimmed glasses like a power-mad executive.
>
> Carderock Springs School presented a brisk "Romeo and Juliet" in a shade over 21 minutes, cutting directly from the banishment to the tomb scene. The acting was vehement.

Partly by what he says ("The acting was vehement") and partly by what he doesn't say, Kernan implies that the performances are less than superb. He comments on the costumes of Macbeth and Lady Macbeth, notes that "Duncan's voice is changing," but utters not a word about the acting. Readers can draw their own conclusions about the propriety of a twenty-one-minute version of *Romeo and Juliet*. But these imperfections are tolerable because these are amateur productions, well-suited to the performers' capabilities, and to the audience—mostly parents and teachers. Kernan counts on his readers not to judge these innocents, who have "never seen, heard, or read" a Shakespeare play before, by professional standards. Neither does he. To attack the defenseless would be unfair and it would anger readers who expect to be entertained.

Reviewers' judgments vary, as do their reasons for making them. As we've seen, professional and amateur performances warrant different standards of evaluation. Different audiences likewise require different degrees of technicality or simplicity of explanations in reviews. Even restaurant reviews, presumably all intended for people who like to eat, assume that readers have varying degrees of knowledge about food. For instance, Phyllis Richman's review of La Bergerie, a French restaurant in Washington, D.C., provides an appetizing overview of the menu, understandable to even a casual supermarket browser:

> Basque dishes in a French restaurant are rare. For those alone, La Bergerie merits distinction among Washington's French restaurants. It serves piperade, that pepper-tomato-onion omelet topped with ham, a Basque seafood platter that tastes of its Spanish borders in its garlicky tomato sauce, and preserved duck sautéed with potatoes and mushrooms.

In contrast, Mimi Sheraton's review of La Côte Basque is intended for serious cooks and serious eaters:

> Few restaurants of any age could match the celestial soupe de pêcheur, a brick-red Provençale fish soup thickened with julienne strips of vegetables and adrift with tiny scallops, shrimp and coral chunks of lobster, all burnished with the pink garlic-and-cayenne-flavored sauce rouillé. . . . Pâtés and terrines are also exceptional, most especially the gentle pâté of sweetbreads, the lustier pâté de campagne and the game pâté. . . . Among the few disappointments in the charcuterie selection . . . was the salty, dry domestic prosciutto, misleadingly billed as jambon Bayonne.

Most readers, even those who can't cook, can recognize all of Richman's culinary terms (*omelet, sautéed*) with the possible exception of *piperade,* which is defined immediately after using it. But Sheraton assumes that her readers know a great many cooking terms and food names, because the only food she defines is *soupe de pêcheur.* To write a review as sophisticated as Sheraton's, you will need to be a well-informed cook, aware of how to make sauce rouillé and game pâté, and the differences between prosciutto (domestic and Italian) and jambon Bayonne, pâtés, and terrines.

Even the most knowing and dazzling reviewers, however, don't oblige the readers to agree with their judgments. As long as you present enough evidence to illustrate your opinions and support your inferences, readers can recognize the basis of your judgment and use it to decide for themselves whether or not they want to agree. Winning agreement is much less important than winning attention. Whether you write one review or a thousand, you'll want the readers to hear you out and give serious thought to your opinions. Because readers' tastes and judgments vary widely, you can't expect to convince everyone, but you can make your own preferences and biases apparent so readers can allow for them.

Reviewing Techniques

In writing reviews and commentaries, you'll need to determine the best way to convey your opinion and the most appropriate organizational format, and to be aware of the stylistic conventions that apply to your medium.

What's the best way to convey my opinion?   Restraint is generally preferable to overkill. You can communicate your opinion through tone, symbolism, and specific details from the work or event rather than flatly pronouncing on its quality. The wit, precision of language, and good humor of Mary Roberts's review of *The Color Purple* mirror Alice Walker's own techniques and convey with restraint the reviewer's high opinion of the book. If readers trying to decide whether to attend a performance of "Carter the Unstoppable Sex Machine" don't take their cue from the group's name, the reviewer's language provides abundant connotations: "Technosarcasm and sugarcoated bile from the guitar-playing London duo who call themselves Fruit Bat and Jim Bob and who play to the accompaniment of throbbing prerecorded tapes . . . the boys in Carter U.S.M. are this moment's masters of peppy moping." Such commentary leaves readers with the sense that they're making up their own minds rather than being preached at. If readers themselves make the ultimate judgments they'll remember them longer.

Exceptions: short, capsule reviews are common in interpretive listings of cultural events or annotated bibliographies, when you don't have the space to *show*, but only to *tell*—contrary to the usual practice. The *New Yorker's* two-sentence assessment of an art show by Ellsworth Kelly makes readers want to see it, or see it again:

> Kelly, a supreme abstractionist, is also one of the best things ever to have happened to the plant kingdom: his botanical sketches are truly exquisite—as piercingly simple, crystalline, and intense as his nonobjective paintings. Ruskin's advice to young pre-Raphaelites—to look at the world as if through lidless eyes—could plausibly have been the credo of this sixty-nine-year-old Yankee literalist.

It's also appropriate to be explicitly succinct when warning readers away from a bad performance, unless you want to prolong your discussion for laughs. Walter Kerr identifies *Hook 'n' Ladder* as "the sort of play that gives failures a bad name." Or, you can spell out the praise when you want to give a performer or a work an extra boost: it's nice to know that Mary-Chapin Carpenter is "a performer with brains, humor, determination, insight, resilience and a voice that can express them all."

What organizational formats work best?   No single format will guarantee a good review, but two of the most effective are chronological and comparison and contrast. On the other hand, reviews dominated by statistics are often formulaic and—let's face it—dull except to devoted diehard fans.

Chronological format. In a chronological format, the reviewer describes the performance or narrative of a novel or film in the order in which events take place. Or, the reviewer provides a brief overview of the performance and then analyzes whatever is most prominent among its strengths or weaknesses. Mary Roberts's review of *The Color Purple* follows a chronological format.

In reviews, as in other writing, the lead paragraph or section is the most important. It should be appealing and informative and should set the tone for what follows, as does Roberts's opening line: "Painted boldly on the bare canvas of aliveness, *The Color Purple* is pure." If a performance is unusual or highly innovative, the review can either establish a norm against which to discuss differences or introduce the innovation before describing the more conventional aspects of the performance, as does the beginning of Paul Hume's review of a flute concert:

> Before he played a single note, James Galway had the National Symphony's audience in his pocket Wednesday night. When it was time for the Mozart D Major Flute Concerto, Galway came onstage, his golden flute over his shoulder. When he reached the center of the stage, he shook hands with the two first-chair violinists, then bowed to the audience. The formalities over, he turned and pointed his flute straight at the oboe, asking for the official "A."

Having established Galway's unusual, though professionally assured, stage presence, the reviewer then describes the concert in the order in which the works were performed.

Comparison and contrast format.   Reviews can be organized by comparing and contrasting the current performance either with previous ones by the same artist or team or with a rival performance. Is this one the best or the worst of the season, of your memory, or of all time? Or is it essentially mediocre in comparison with others?

Comparisons and contrasts are inevitable with a remake of or a sequel to the original work. Except in rare cases when the works are seen as similar in quality, reviewers either begin or conclude by asserting the superiority of one version over the other. Thus The *New Yorker*'s review of Gary Sinise's 1992 remake of *Of Mice and Men* begins with a comparison to the 1939 version: "Lewis Milestone's version of John Steinbeck's tragic fable, with Burgess Meredith as the shrewd ranch hand George and [Lon] Chaney as the simple giant Lennie, is a wonderfully wrought classic." Reviewer Michael Sragow says that in the new movie "the cast acts with self-conscious, surface physicality." Sinise as George "edges his profile into every shot as if he were a model in a rustic-clothing catalogue" and John Malkovich as Lennie "carries on like a further infantilized Tommy Smothers (his upper register recalls Tweety Pie)." "The only restrained performance," notes Sragow, "is given by Lennie's pup." The more numerous and detailed such comparisons become, the more knowledgeable and specialized the reviewer assumes the audience to be. These audiences are the avid fans who savor a review of the genre and a recapitulation of the records or crave the comfort of a familiar litany.

Statistical format.   Sports writers love to use statistics, either to compare one player's or team's record with others or in a resumé of a team's or individual player's record. Recite statistics with caution, for such commentary quickly becomes mechanistic and formulaic. In "Soccer players win awards," an anonymous article from the University of Connecticut's *Daily Campus*, the writer announces that "UConn junior midfielder Karen Ferguson and graduate student forward Denise Swenson were named to the 1992 Northeast All-Region Women's Soccer First Team." The article then presents paragraphs of statistics, of which the following is typical:

> In 1992, Swenson led the 15-5-1 Huskies in scoring with 12 goals and four assists for 28 points. Swenson finished off her collegiate career as the seventh leading scorer in UConn women's soccer history with 32 goals and seven assists for 71 points. This year's Northeast All-Region honor is Swenson's second such award. Swenson was named to the 1990 northeast All-Region First Team.

Such writing could be generated by a machine. Insert the type of sport in one slot; the school, team, or player in another; the player's or team's current year record in still another; the past year's (or period of time desired) record in yet another slot; and plug in the figures. These articles might as well be anonymous. Such writing is easily forgettable, because it lacks distinction of style and point of view.

So, beware! The amount of statistics is a matter of taste. But, as in using expletives, less is better. Stop before you become a statistical exhibitionist and find yourself making comparisons or allusions simply for their own sake rather than to advance an argument or illuminate an analysis.

What are the stylistic conventions?   The only stylistic convention that is uniformly observed in reviews of written media, current performances, and restaurants is that of writing in the present or the present perfect tense. Reviews of past events such as games already played or concerts already performed generally use the past tense.

There is no consensus among reviewers about whether to write in the first person "I" or "we"; in the impersonal "one"; in the submerged personal "this reviewer"; or, as Tom Wolfe sometimes refers to himself, as "the man in the Borsalino hat." Or you can avoid referring to yourself altogether, as do many of the reviewers in this chapter. Whether or not you do so, readers will automatically identify the opinions expressed as yours, and not messages from God, though some reviewers might wish otherwise. Whatever form of address you prefer, remember that readers look at a review for commentary about the subject, not for the reviewer's autobiography.

Although clichés often clutter even professionally written reviews, they trivialize the writing and make it sound amateurish. It's easy to avoid them if you disregard the knee-jerk language and the first adjectives, metaphors, or other figures of speech that come to mind. Frank Sullivan's character, Mr. Arbuthnot, the Cliché Expert, converses exclusively in the clichés of the subject he discusses. Here this "battle-scarred veteran of not a few first nights" comments on drama:

Q—What kinds of plays are there?

A—Oh, their number is legion. There are dramas of frustration and dramas of extramarital love, or the eternal triangle. There are plays that are penetrating studies and plays that are valuable human documents. . . . Tragedies should, of course, be stark, and melodramas lurid. . . . farces must be rollicking, and comedies must be either of ancient vintage or sophisticated.

Adapting Reviews to Particular Types of Performance

When you review a performance of a particular medium, place, or game, no matter which format you choose, you'll want to consider the relevant aspects of each type. What you choose to discuss or omit will depend on your emphasis and purpose.

BOOK

- Theme(s); moral, social or other issues; values
- Plot, subplots (including conflicts, crises, resolution)
- Characters—major, unless the minor roles are notable
- Language—the author's, the characters'
- Settings
- Typical or atypical features of the mode (mystery, romance, stream of consciousness)
- Comparison of this work to the author's other works

PLAY, FILM, OR TELEVISION PROGRAM

- Theme(s), major points
- Plot, subplot(s)
- Characters
- Characters' speech
- Setting(s), staging
- Costumes
- Music, sound, and lighting effects
- Quality or conspicuous features of the editing or direction
- Audience reaction
- Comparison of this work to author's, actor's, director's other works

MUSICAL PERFORMANCE, ART SHOW, ENTERTAINER, OR LECTURER

- Selections performed or displayed—variety, balance, traditional elements, innovation
- Musical direction, arrangements, interpretation
- Artist's or performer's technical mastery, artistry, style(s), virtuosity,

effectiveness in performing individually or as a group; relation to past performances or showings
• Audience reaction

RESTAURANT, BAR, OR NIGHTCLUB

• Physical setting—location, ambience, decor
• Intended patrons—family, singles, business people or workers
• Type(s) and variety of food and beverages served, representative or specialty dishes
• Quality of food and cooking
• Names of notable chefs and conspicuous service personnel
• Quality of service
• Kind and quality of music or entertainment
• Price range

SPORTS EVENTS OR INDIVIDUAL ATHLETIC PERFORMANCE

• Highlights of an individual game, of a season, or of another segment of a team or individual performance
• Low points, blunders
• Opponents' performance, behavior
• Colorful sidelights
• Setting, weather, audience reaction
• Relation of this event or performance to the athlete's or team's characteristic performance (Is this one better, worse? For what reasons? Is it typical or atypical? In what ways?)

The Reviewer's Styles and Persona

Reviewing is, like other types of writing discussed in this book, an act of self-assertion. Over time the devotees of your subject, through reading your reviews regularly, will form opinions about your authorial persona, identifying you as someone who can be counted on to make either wise and reasoned judgments or wrong ones, if they consistently disagree with you.

Readers will also identify your distinctive style which, like seasoning judiciously used, should be sufficiently subtle so that it enhances but does not overpower the subject. However individual your style may be, it will nevertheless be influenced by where your writing will appear. Course papers and magazine essays permit the luxury of long paragraphs and longer sentences than newspapers do, for the length of newspaper paragraphs is determined as much by sight as by substance, with breaks coming every column inch. Short paragraphs dictate short sentences.

The nature of your subject will also influence your writing style. Sports stories are written in crisp, sometimes pungent, uncomplicated language. Reviews of grand opera and serious books are themselves serious and formal. Reviews of pop music and detective stories sometimes imitate the language of the subject as does Robert A. Hull's commentary on "bubblegum" music:

> Bouncing from the radio in '68 and '69 with a smacking resiliency, bubblegum music hit the charts at a time when the kids were grooving to the perpetual doodling of the Grateful Dead. . . . "Super Bubble" erases the esthetic snobbery that has tried to squelch the bubblegum style throughout the years by simply being jam-packed with skip-a-rope dynamics . . . [including] Ohio Express' "Yummy, Yummy, Yummy" and "Chewy, Chewy." . . . bubblegum rock created the sensation of carefree playfulness, expanding like a gigantic bubble being blown by Bazooka Joe.

Kids, grooving, squelch, jam-packed, are casual terms that the bubblegum fanciers themselves might use. *Bazooka Joe* is, likewise, a reference that bubblegum chewers will savor particularly, though even the uninitiated can enjoy the *gigantic bubble* simile. Hull invents *skip-a-rope* to capture both a particular rhythm and a particular mood of "carefree playfulness." However, the writer characteristically exhibits more knowledge and control than do the habitual users of this language. He sprinkles in enough bubblegum language to convey the music's flavor and bounce but distances himself through more formal vocabulary (*resiliency, esthetic snobbery*) and an objective tone to analyze the phenomenon in a way that real bubblegum rockers are not likely to do.

You may occasionally want to use the language and mode of one kind of performance to review another, commenting for instance on grand opera in the language of sports. The incongruity between language, mode, and expectation is usually humorous, as is student Pam van der Leeden's analysis of Introductory Biology as a dramatic production:

> "Bio 101" reopened to mixed reviews yesterday in the recently refurbished Millington Theatre, in the seventeenth year of its run. "Bio 101" requires virtuoso performances from actor and audience alike, for it is a one-man play, difficult to act and even more difficult to sit through. The audience seemed intimidated by the high-powered style of delivery and retreated beyond the fourth row, although the rest of the house was packed and overflowing into the aisles.
>
> "Bio 101" managed to hold the attention of the audience, although it was unclear to this reviewer whether they were listening from interest or from fear of being thought ignorant. The play's reliance on scientific, highly technical monologues restricts its audience to the intellectual elite. . . .

Writing a review that imitates your subject's style dramatizes the subject's stylistic individuality. Whether your imitation is the sincerest form of flattery or an indirect form of criticism, it calls attention to the distinctiveness of the original and to the reviewer's cleverness, as well. The most skillful imitations reflect the substance as well as the style of the original, as does student Audrey Guengerich's appreciative but tongue-in-cheek review of Gertrude Stein's *The Autobiography of Alice B. Toklas,* which despite its title is really Stein's own autobiography. Unlike many other reviews, however, this kind of imitation depends on the audience's familiarity with the original to savor the reviewer's stylistic and intellectual finesse:

> The good Alice B. Toklas had a heluva good life. She was born in California but her true existence did not really begin until she was twenty-six and she met Gertrude Stein in Paris. This was the year 1907 and the good Alice was immediately drawn and later devoted to the genius Gertrude Stein although she was not drawn and later devoted to the two other geniuses of her acquaintance, Pablo Picasso and Alfred North Whitehead. Yet she was devoted to Gertrude Stein and her devotion is but one reason why the good Alice can be called good. There are also other reasons for Alice's esteemed goodness and those reasons are established in *The Autobiography of Alice B. Toklas* written by Gertrude Stein.
>
> Some might suggest that *The Autobiography of Alice B. Toklas* could just as well be called *The Autobiography of Pablo Picasso* or, for that matter, *The Autobiography of Helene the Maid,* and it would come to the same thing as long as Gertrude Stein is its author and she has space to write about what she really wants to write about which is of course Gertrude Stein. But that accusation is simply not so. For one thing, without the first three pages and the last two pages the book would have been another work entirely. These five pages are devoted almost exclusively to treatment of the Good Alice with only casual reference made to Gertrude Stein. . . .

Using Gertrude Stein's distinctive, highly coordinated ("and," "and"), cheerfully colloquial ("a heluva good life") style, Guengerich immediately captures the spirit of Stein's self-portrait. With mild satire, whose meaning is contingent on the readers' recognition of the original *Autobiography,* Audrey demonstrates Stein's egotism. Alice is good because Alice recognizes Gertrude Stein's genius and because Alice is "devoted to the genius Gertrude Stein," as is Stein herself. Guengerich calls attention to Stein's egotistical ruse of pretending to write Alice's autobiography by citing the actual number of pages "devoted almost exclusively" to the good Alice (5 whole pages!), yet even these make only "casual reference to Gertrude Stein." And so on. Although Guengerich pokes fun at Stein's tricks, she also appreciates Stein's ability to write with bravado and to get away with it.

You may on other occasions write a review intended to devastate a subject by blazing away at it with sarcastic wit. In such instances, you assume that the performance under consideration is too bad, too commonplace, or too trivial to warrant serious treatment, and you assume that your audience will agree. This justifies committing what in other reviews would be two unthinkable acts, shifting the focus from the work to yourself and, in the process, shooting at a mosquito with an elephant gun. Be forewarned! A review intended to show off your dazzling wit can also provoke disagreement. Are you willing to risk antagonizing your readers?

Dorothy Parker, a consistent show-off, occasionally wrote reviews of this kind for the *New Yorker*. The fact that they are still savored and imitated 65 years later testifies not to the timelessness of the bad books she reviewed, for these have long since been forgotten, but to her skill as a writer. Parker continues to entertain us with her semihelpless but devastatingly witty persona who invariably says the right thing at the wrong time. Parker's review of July 21, 1931, "The Grandmother of the Aunt of the Gardener," does not even mention the title of the volume under consideration until halfway through the review—a clue to her self-centered focus. The book is merely her excuse for having fun:

> . . . How am I not to be bitter, who have stumbled solo round about Europe, equipped only with "Non, non et non!" and "Où est le lavabo des dames?" How shall I leash my envy, who have lived so placed that there were weeks at a stretch when I heard or saw no word of English; who was committed entirely and eagerly to French manners, customs, and abbreviations, yet could never get it through the head that the letter "c" on a water-faucet does not stand for "cold"? . . . .

> I have here before me a small green book called *The Ideal System for Acquiring a Practical Knowledge of French* by Mlle. V. D. Gaudel. . . . Well, everything might have been all right if Mlle. Gaudel . . . had not subtitled her work *Just the French One Wants to Know*. Somehow, those words antagonized me, by their blandness, so that I forgot the thirst for knowledge and searched the tome only for concrete examples of just the French one will never need. . . .

> Now you know perfectly well that at my time of life it would be just a dissipation of energy for me to learn the French equivalent of "Either now, or this afternoon at five." It is, at best, a matter of dark doubt that . . . it will be given me to slide gently into a conversation with "I admire the large black eyes of this orphan." . . . or that I swing into autobiography with the confession: "I do not like to play blindman's buff." . . .

> It might occur that I must thunder: "Obey, or I will not show you the beautiful gold chain." But I will be damned if it is ever going to be of any good to me to have at hand Mlle. Gaudel's masterpiece: "I am afraid he will not arrive in time to accompany me on the harp."

> Oh, "Just the French One Wants to Know" *mon oeil*, Mademoiselle. And you know what you can do, far better than I could tell you.

Checklist for Writing About Performances

1. Do I know well what I'm reviewing?

2. Do I like the subject under consideration, if not the particular work or event?

3. If the answer to questions 1 or 2 is *no,* why am I writing the review? or commentary?

4. Do I know enough about the subject to explain it knowledgeably to someone who doesn't know much about it? to someone who does?

5. Who will read this review or commentary? What will they be looking for?

6. How long is the review? What information and evaluation are essential? What are less essential? On what bases will I decide what to emphasize, subordinate, and omit?

7. How does the organization reinforce my emphases and my interpretation of the subject?

8. How technical, specialized, or general is my language? how colorful?

9. What is the tone of this review? Am I creating a particular authorial persona for this review? If so, how do the tone and persona relate to my subject and point of view?

10. Do I enjoy writing this review or commentary? Would I enjoy reading this review if someone else had written it? If not, what can I do to make it more appealing?

Selected Reference List of Writings About Performance

Books and Literature

Lawrence, D. H. *Studies in Classic American Literature.* 1923. New York: Viking, 1977.

Rich, Adrienne. *Blood, Bread, and Poetry: Selected Prose 1979–1985.* New York: Norton, 1986.

Updike, John. *Odd Jobs: Essays and Criticism.* New York: Knopf, 1991.

Woolf, Virginia. *The Common Reader,* 1925. New York: Harcourt, 1984.

———. *The Second Common Reader,* 1932. Harcourt, 1986.

Drama

Bentley, Eric. *What Is Theatre?* 1968. New York: Limelight, 1984.

Shaw, George Bernard. *Shaw on Shakespeare.* Ed. Edwin Wilson. New York: Dutton, 1961.

———. *Shaw's Dramatic Criticism (1895–98)*. Sel. John F. Matthews. New York: Hill, 1966.

Simon, John. *Uneasy Stages: A Chronicle of the New York Theater 1963–1973*. New York: Random, 1975.

Films and Television

Kael, Pauline. *Movie Love: Complete Reviews, 1988–1991*. New York: Plume, 1991.

Mast, Gerald, and Marshall Cohen, eds. *Film Theory and Criticism: Introductory Readings*. New York: Oxford UP, 1985.

Reed, Rex. *Rex Reed's Guide to Movies on TV and Video*. New York: Warner, 1992.

Simon, John. *Reverse Angle: A Decade of American Films*. New York: Clarkson, 1982.

Food

Fisher, M. F. K. *The Art of Eating*. New York: Macmillan, 1990.

Liebling, A. J. *Between Meals: An Appetite for Paris*. San Francisco: North Point, 1986.

Stern, Jane, and Michael Stern. *Roadfood*. 1977. New York: Harper, 1992.

Music

Feather, Leonard. *The Pleasures of Jazz*. New York: Horizon, 1976.

Gould, Glenn. *The Glenn Gould Reader*. Ed. Tim Page. New York: Knopf, 1984.

Schonberg, Harold. *Facing the Music*. New York: Summit, 1981.

Shaw, Arnold. *Black Popular Music in America; From the Spirituals, Minstrels, and Ragtime to Soul, Disco, and Hip Hop*. New York: Schirmer, 1986.

Sports

Angell, Roger. *Once More Around the Park: A Baseball Reader*. New York: Ballantine, 1991.

———. *The Summer Game*. 1962. New York: Penguin, 1990.

The Best American Sports Writing 1993. Series ed. Glenn Stout. Boston: Houghton, 1993.

Smith, Red. *The Red Smith Reader*. Ed. Dave Anderson. New York: Random, 1983.

Works Cited

Agee, James. "Comedy's Greatest Era." *Agee on Film*. 1958. Rpt. in *Humor in America*. Ed. Enid Vernon. New York: Harcourt, 1976. 281–96.

Ansen, David. "Films So Bad They're Good." *Newsweek* 28 Apr. 1980: 97.

"Carter the Unstoppable Sex Machine." *New Yorker* 2 Nov. 1992: 27.

"Ellsworth Kelly." *New Yorker* 23 Nov. 1992: 30.

Harrison, Barbara Grizzuti. "Nadia Comaneci." *The Astonishing World*. New York: Ticknor, 1992. 204–221.

Hull, Robert A. "Here's to Bubblegum and Girl Groups." *Washington Post* 27 Apr. 1980: M8.

Hume, Paul. "Galway's Golden Flute." *Washington Post* 16 May 1980: D4.

Kennedy, William. "The Runyonland Express Is Back in Town." *New York Times* 15 Apr. 1992: D:1, 28.

Kernan, Michael. "Bard Times at the Folger Theater." *Washington Post* 24 Apr. 1980: D13.

Kerr, Walter. Quoted in *The Passionate Playgoers*. Ed. George Oppenheimer. New York: Viking, 1958.

Kirp, David L. "Beyond Assimilation." *New York Times Book Review* 22 Nov. 1992: 42.

Lahr, John. "Dogma Days." *New Yorker*. 16 Nov. 1992: 121–25.

Oates, Joyce Carol. "On Boxing." *On Boxing*. 1987. New York: Dutton, 1988.

Olson, Clarence. Letter of instructions to book reviewers. 5 Apr. 1983.

Parker, Dorothy. "The Grandmother of the Aunt of the Gardener." *The Portable Dorothy Parker*. Ed. Brendan Gill. 1973. New York: Viking, 1991. 545–47.

Pareles, John. "Country on a Road Through Suburbia" *New York Times* 18 Nov. 1992: C19.

Richman, Phyllis. "La Bergerie: Dining Guide." *Washington Post Magazine* 14 Oct. 1979: 48.

———. "Richman on Restaurants: Landini Bros., Inc." *Washington Post Magazine* 20 Apr. 1980: 45.

———. "Richman on Restaurants: Maxine's." *Washington Post Magazine* 27 Apr. 1980: 56.

Russell, John. "Remington's War and Old West." *New York Times* 16 Feb. 1989: 10.

Sheraton, Mimi. "Restaurants: An Old Favorite Returns in Style." *New York Times* 2 May 1980: C14.

Smith, Red. "I'd Like to Be Called a Good Reporter." *The Red Smith Reader*. Ed. Dave Anderson. New York: Random, 1982. 3–16.

"Soccer players win awards." *The* [University of Connecticut] *Daily Campus*. 2 Dec. 1992: 16.

Sragow, Michael. "*Of Mice and Men*." *New Yorker* 9 Nov. 1992: 34.

Sullivan, Frank. "The Cliché Expert Testifies on the Drama." *The Night the Old Nostalgia Burned Down*. Boston: Little, 1953. 131–45.

Updike, John. "Hub Fans Bid Kid Adieu." *Press Box: Red Smith's Favorite Sports Stories*. Ed. Red Smith. New York: Norton, 1976. 68–81.

7

━ . ⏑

WRITING HUMOR

*I can't tell a joke. I don't know any jokes. I forget them . . . because comedy
for me comes out of character.*

—Wendy Wasserstein

Humor is emotional chaos told about calmly and quietly in retrospect.

—James Thurber

Everything is funny as long as it is happening to somebody else.

—Will Rogers

*Humor is what you wish in your secret heart were not funny, but it is, and you
must laugh. Humor is your own unconscious therapy.*

—Langston Hughes

Purposes of Humorous Writing

If laughter is the emotion closest to tears, then the epigraphs for this chapter convey that catch in the throat, the intermingling of innocence and experience, wit and wisdom. Although some forms of humor—many puns, jokes, parodies, and tall tales—exist mostly for fun, other forms exist to help us cope with "emotional chaos," anger, disorder, defeat, and disaster. If we didn't laugh, we'd cry, fall apart, or become apoplectic. As readers and as writers, humor becomes our "unconscious therapy."

Your purpose as a humorist is, if nothing else, to capture your readers' attention, preferably near the beginning of your writing. Once you have it, you'll want to win readers to share your viewpoint—whether benign, cockeyed, or critical—and consequently, to share your attitude toward the subject as well. Humorists have no obligation to play fair or to provide a balanced perspective of the issue; and only their own taste or a strong sense of social taboos will keep them away from some sensitive subjects. Everything else is fair game. But beneath the idealism of the humorist, the benevolence of the writer of good-natured essays, lurks a core of realism. You know you can't win 'em all, especially if you're stalking your readers' sacred cows, whether you use a blowpipe or a blunderbuss. You'll fulfill your comic function as long as you elicit a response from your audience. The more emphatic the reaction the better, whether a knowing smile, a giggle, a guffaw, a grimace, an eruption of outrage, or a promise of reform. Some humor provokes laughter; some humor simply provokes.

In this section, we'll look at some specific purposes of humorous writing.

To Celebrate Joy

Benign humor helps writers and readers alike to savor the pleasant aspects of life, to recapture good times past—a simpler world, an innocence untainted by the cynicism of age or the disappointments of experience. Mark Twain's succulent, three-sentence description of the pleasures of picking a watermelon, cooling it, anticipating the dénouement, and finally eating the delicious fruit not only recreates a blissful childhood, but also suspends adult morality in favor of juvenile pranks that acquire the melon "by art":

> I know how a prize watermelon looks when it is sunning its fat rotundity among pumpkin vines and "simblins"; I know how to tell when it is ripe without "plugging" it; I know how inviting it looks when it is cooling itself in a tub of water under the bed, waiting; I know how it looks when it lies on the table in the great floor space between house and kitchen, and the children gathered for the sacrifice and their mouths watering; I know the crackling sound it makes when the carving knife enters its end, and I can see the split fly along in front of the blade as the knife cleaves its way to the other end; I can see its halves fall apart

and display the rich red meat and the black seeds, and the heart standing up, a luxury fit for the elect; I know how a boy looks behind a yard-long slice of that melon, and I know how he feels; for I have been there. I know the taste of the watermelon which has been honestly come by, and I know the taste of the watermelon which has been acquired by art. Both taste good, but the experienced know which tastes best.

Twain prefaces this account with the wry assertion, "When I was younger I could remember anything, whether it had happened or not; but my faculties are decaying now, and soon I shall be so I cannot remember any but the things that never happened." Whether or not this narration, then, represents an actual experience or is an idealized recreation of an Edenic childhood doesn't matter. What does matter is Twain's good-humored recollection of the good old days that readers can share vicariously even if their watermelon always comes wrapped in supermarket plastic.

To Provide Comic Relief

A comic perspective makes more palatable the bittersweet medicine of life. The very act of writing about the humorous aspects of a painful subject helps the writer to distance the pain and thereby to understand, interpret, and cope with it. Suzanne Britt, who describes herself as "stately, plump," copes with corpulence and offers some relief, comic and cheering, to others of her proportions in "That Lean and Hungry Look," a series of invidious comparisons between thin and fat people:

> Thin people make me tired. They've got speedy little metabolisms that cause them to bustle briskly. They're forever rubbing their bony hands together and eying new problems to "tackle." I like to surround myself with sluggish, inert, easy-going fat people, the kind who believe that if you clean it up today, it'll just get dirty again tomorrow.
>
> Some people say the business about the jolly fat person is a myth, that all of us chubbies are neurotic, sick, sad people. I disagree. Fat people may not be chortling all day long, but they're a hell of a lot *nicer* than the wizened and shriveled. Thin people turn surly, mean and hard at a young age because they never learn the value of a hot-fudge sundae for easing tension. Thin people don't like gooey soft things because they themselves are neither gooey nor soft. They are crunchy and dull, like carrots. They go straight to the heart of the matter while fat people let things stay all blurry and hazy and vague, the way things actually are. Thin people want to face the truth. Fat people know there is no truth.

Britt deals not in individual personalities, which could result in a vicious, if not libelous, attack, but in stereotypes, creating antistereotypes to combat the negative reactions of a thin society toward its fat members.

Indeed, the possibilities are legion for pitting opposites against one another and exaggerating the positive features of one in symmetrical contrast to the negative features of the other. Britt has also written, for example, "Neat People vs Sloppy People." Guess whose side she's on! She identifies herself as a member of the group she defends; her tone is good-natured and her examples are benign. Through these means she controls her subject and her readers' reaction to it—even if she can't control her weight.

To Take the Sting Out

Humor can take the sting out of an astringent experience or mitigate its bitterness. Writing with humor about an experience or relationship that was unhappy, frustrating, or tension-producing can provide the "unconscious therapy" of which Langston Hughes speaks. Humor can transform the fall guy, the victim, the klutz into the survivor of life's adversities or his own ineptitudes and mistakes who can expect sympathy from readers both for surviving and for the good grace with which he regards his past history. Thus from her perspective as an experienced and confident driver of several years, in "Learning to Drive," student Ann Upperco Dolman looks back with amused amazement on her near misses as a new driver:

> One day while driving on the highway, I drifted dangerously close to a car in the lane to my right, almost scraping the shiny chrome strip right off its side. Dad [Dolman's patient instructor] looked nonchalantly into the terrified face of the other driver—a mere six inches away—then turned back to me and said, "You might want to steer to the left a bit; you're just a little close on this side." A mile further down the road, Dad chuckled and said, "I think you gave that poor lady a scare—her eyes were as big as golf balls!" Here was he, not only unperturbed, but actually amused by the whole incident while I watched my whole life pass before my eyes.

To Add Pep, To Provide a New Perspective

Humor can pep up the mundane or provide a new look at ordinary life. Repetitive, predictable, boring tasks or activities that the writer has come to loathe through sheer familiarity take on a new life if viewed through the distorting lens of a comic perspective. Because readers are likely to feel the same way about such activities as housework, lawnmowing, commuting, perhaps walking the dog at 6 A.M., the writer can count on a sympathetic audience from the outset. The attitude of Betty J. Walker, a student who held a full-time job while also managing a busy household, speaks for millions:

> HOUSEWORK—Housework—I hate it. I have tried for the past 20 years to learn to like it but to no avail. It is so boring. It is repetitive and stagnates the mind. Anyone can do it; it requires no real talent except the willingness to do the same thing over and over again.

> Now take dusting . . . an exercise in sheer futility. You take a cloth and spray some type of polish on it. You move it around on the surface of the table or chair or whatever and pick up the dust on the rag. You move around the room, dusting whatever level surface there is available that does not move. You move on from room to room. After a lapsed period of perhaps 20 minutes, you return to the room you dusted first. What do you find there—dust!

After this point Betty's self-deprecating persona emerges. This keeps her recitation of housekeeping chores from becoming whiny or self-pitying, either of which would destroy the humor. This persona, who readily admits personal failings and even exaggerates them, establishes an intimate relationship with her readers. Readers relax sufficiently in her unbuttoned presence to sympathize with her predicament and to acknowledge their own shortcomings, if only to themselves:

> Lest you form the opinion that I am lazy, let me reassure you—I am. I will work all day at something I enjoy doing. Writing or sewing or creating something keeps me interested and busy and I am never bored. But the repetitive things drive me up the walls. The trouble with housework is that once you have it all done and the house is all clean and shining, six months later you have to do it all over again.

Who hasn't felt that way? Why dust when the surf's up—or anything else, for that matter? You'll find that this familiar theme has many variations if you try writing about your own particular source of irritating boredom.

To Call Attention to the Unusual

Humor can call attention to the paradoxical, quixotic, irritating, bizarre, and unpredictable aspects of human behavior or society, either to laugh at weirdness for its own sake, to express the author's irritation with the subject, or to promote change or reform. Humorists function as authenticators of the incongruous, voyeurs of the absurd, inviting readers to have a look and a laugh, too—as when one of Oscar Wilde's characters acidly observed of a recent widow, "I understand her hair has turned quite gold from grief."

Sometimes all you have to do as a humorist is to point out a situation, phenomenon, personal trait, or incongruity and let readers draw their own conclusions about whether to put up with the situation or phenomenon, or to try to change it. Tom Wolfe's freewheeling, flamboyant social commentary is evident even in the titles of some of his best-known works: "The Life and Hard Times of a Teenage London Society Girl," "Mau-Mauing the Flak Catchers," and *The Electric Kool-Aid Acid Test.* "Radical Chic" is Wolfe's comic analysis of a social and political incongruity—a 1966 fund raiser for the social revolutionary (some would say anarchistic) Black Panthers held by New York Philharmonic conductor Leonard Bernstein and other Park Avenue socialites. Although Wolfe wasn't there, he sets scenes and recreates dialogue as if he had been on the spot. Indeed, because so much humorous writing is exaggerated, humorists seem to be exempt from the fidelity to the truth that governs most other nonfiction writing:

> Mmmmmmmmmmmmmmmm. These are nice. Little Roquefort cheese morsels, rolled in crushed nuts. Very tasty. Very subtle. It's the way the dry sackiness of the nuts tiptoes up against the dour savor of the cheese that is so nice, so subtle. Wonder what the Black Panthers eat here on the hors d'oeuvre trail?

When you write humor to demonstrate your irritation with the subject, and in the process to show off how smart you are, your writing will gain in wit if you can imply your own superiority or expertise—real or feigned—with which you invite your readers to ally. Humorists adopting this stance, as Wolfe does throughout his work, would never acknowledge that they may be part of the problem they describe. Although they can point out solutions, these are generally unreal and not likely to be adopted. If anyone would or could stamp out the subjects of their sarcasm, the Wolfes of this world would only find others to criticize—perhaps getting closer and closer to home. But not to worry, Suzanne Britt, Garrison Keillor, or some other humorist will come to the rescue.

To Be Daring, Defiant, or Vengeful

Humor gives the writer the chance to commit an act of daring, of defiance, perhaps even of revenge, by throwing the verbal snowballs that knock off the pompous passerby's top hat. Through humor the little guys can attack the privileged and the powerful, the oppressors and the overlords, and can thereby find a socially acceptable release for their own aggression and hostility and, sometimes, for the collective anger of the society they represent. Such humor is always written from the point of view of the underdog, who automatically evokes the readers' sympathy because, although they may laugh at the wit of the writing, they share the writer's anger at the situation.

"I Want a Wife" is Judy Brady's classic interpretation of the lives of many women who feel oppressed by the myriad of selfless duties a male-dominated society expects them to perform as wives and mothers. Although this particular wife is married to a student, there are infinite alternative possibilities in this consciousness-raising scenario:

> I want a wife who will work and send me to school. And while I am going to school I want a wife to take care of my children. I want a wife to keep track of the children's doctor and dentist appointments. And to keep track of mine, too. . . .
> I want a wife who will take care of *my* physical needs. I want a wife who will keep my house clean. . . . I want a wife who cooks the meals, a wife who

is a *good* cook. . . . I want a wife who will care for me when I am sick and sympathize with my pain. . . .

I want a wife who will not bother me with rambling complaints about a wife's duties. . . .

When I am through with school and have a job, I want my wife to quit working and remain at home so that my wife can more fully and completely take care of a wife's duties. My God, who *wouldn't* want a wife?

Whether or not Brady's satiric attack on the traditional family system has promoted greater equality between husbands and wives is a matter of conjecture. It is nonetheless true that the most serious purpose of the most devastating sort of humor, satire, is to promote change or reform in an area that the writer considers a serious problem. For humorists, like all serious writers, care deeply about their subjects. The satirists' profound concern is the index of their profound desire for reform, whether their corrective laughter is gently sympathetic or bitter with the anger of moral outrage. (For more about satire, see pages 203–5.)

Guidelines for Writing Humor

"One man's Mede is another man's Persian," the punning paraphrase of "One man's meat is another man's poison," is a fitting reminder that one person's process for writing humor won't necessarily work for someone else. James Thurber writes from his experiences "at parties" and "during dinner." Theodore Geisel, the late "Dr. Seuss," wrote from his imagination, in isolation in a glorious tree house. You're probably already well aware of where and how you write in general. The points made in the following guidelines to writing humor will be discussed in this chapter.

1. Find a subject that has possibilities for a comic or ironic narrative, portrait, criticism, parody, or satire. You should feel strongly about it, favorably or negatively; it's hard to provoke laughter or scorn for a subject about which you are neutral.

2. Make sure you know your subject well enough to depict—and perhaps exaggerate or diminish—its major and minor attributes, its nuances as well as its broad outlines.

3. Determine your purpose(s). Among others, these may be:

- to celebrate, to savor the pleasant aspects of life
- to provide comic relief, to help you or your readers cope with a problematic subject
- to mitigate bitterness or unhappiness
- to pep up the mundane or to provide a new perspective of ordinary life
- to call attention to an amusing subject

- to demonstrate irritation through defiance, revenge, or a plea for change or reform

4. Determine your audience and figure out how you want them to react to the subject, purpose, and techniques of your writing.

5. Decide on the comic form (such as narrative, portrait, criticism, parody, or satire) and techniques that will enhance your purpose and that you can use with skill.

6. Figure out ways to exploit these techniques to give you maximum control over your writing, including its characterization, tone, and language. You'll want to control its structure, strategically placing miniclimaxes and plateaus, and positioning the climax at or near the end. You'll need to control yourself, too; don't laugh overtly at your own jokes or wit.

7. Know when to stop. Don't prolong either the joke or the emotion your writing arouses beyond the point of maximum response.

Comic Personae and Characters

You can present your subject as a comic persona, a created character who is often a caricature or stock figure in the story being told. Three common characters among a host of possibilities in contemporary humorous writing are the incompetent, the helpless victim of circumstances, and the innocent. Among other comic characters are personified animals and recalcitrant or malfunctioning machinery.

The incompetent.   The incompetent is often a caricature or stock figure, identifiable by several exaggerated characteristics, and usually seen from the outside rather than the inside. Erma Bombeck's slightly cynical, overweight housewife is forever trying to cope with difficulties, often absurd problems, that are always out of hand; we've already met her alter ego, Betty J. Walker (pages 178–79). From this perspective Bombeck discusses her most common topics: indifferent housekeeping ("ironed sheets are a health hazard"), her excess weight ("I have dieted continuously for the last two decades and lost a total of 758 pounds"), and her difficulties with childrearing ("'Did you know you have gym shoes under your bed that have rusted? A three years' supply of crumpled nose tissue in your sock drawer?'"). For these characters, victories, if achieved at all, are temporary and transient, because Bombeck, like many of her readers, is forever subject to the plagues of dust, dumpiness, and disobedience.

The helpless victim of circumstances.   We've all suffered from circumstances beyond our control—as victims of insensitive bosses, arrogant waiters, rude salesclerks, machinery that breaks or that we can't operate, arguments that escalate, or other situations beyond our control. Victims of circumstances cannot cope with the expectations of an otherwise competent world where everybody else seems to know what to do, how to do it, and is in control. We and our readers can immediately identify with such characters as the antihero, the klutz, the sap, the fool, and the fall guy. In the immortal words of Ann Landers, we've "been there, honey."

Many of James Thurber's characters are ineffectual people, such as Walter Mitty, the harassed, henpecked husband and universal wimp. The comic persona of Thurber himself is presented in "University Days" as a meek, dreadfully nearsighted student, well-intentioned but not too bright. This persona explains, deadpan, that he could "never pass botany . . . [because he] could never see through a microscope":

> This used to enrage my instructor. He would wander around the laboratory pleased with the progress all the students were making in drawing the involved and, so I am told, interesting structure of flower cells, until he came to me. I would just be standing there. "I can't see anything," I would say. He would begin patiently enough, explaining how anybody can see through a microscope, but he would always end up in a fury; claiming that I could *too* see through a microscope but just pretended that I couldn't. "It takes away from the beauty of flowers anyway," I used to tell him. "We are not concerned with beauty in this course," he would say. "We are concerned solely with what I may call the *mechanics* of flars." "Well," I'd say, "I can't see anything." "Try it just once again," he'd say, and I would put my eye to the microscope and see nothing at all, except now and again a nebulous milky substance—a phenomenon of maladjustment. You were supposed to see a vivid, restless clockwork of sharply defined plant cells.

After taking a deferral for a year, Thurber, who must pass botany in order to graduate, tries again and encounters at last, "to my pleasure and amazement, a variegated constellation of flecks, specks, and dots," which in hasty excitement he draws, only to further infuriate the instructor. "His head snapped up. 'That's your eye!' he shouted. 'You've fixed the lens so that it reflects! You've drawn your eye!'"

Thurber the student may not be able to see cells through a microscope, but Thurber the humorist turns that defeat into a comic triumph. As he exploits the limitations of the subject, he escalates the humorous pitch with each repetition that his persona is unable to "see cells." In the culminating scene, he gains control over his ineptitude and over his antagonist, who loses self-control as the Thurber persona gains assurance and has the last laugh on the enraged professor: "'That's what I saw,' I said. 'You didn't, you didn't, you didn't!' he screamed, losing control of his temper instantly." In this scene, the culmination of a perverse victory, the underdog becomes top dog.

Morally naive or innocent persona.   Naive characters are children, country bumpkins, or other apparent innocents, presumably unaware of the comic or moral implications of the behavior they exhibit or the values they condone. In reality, of course, such characters are well aware of the meanings as well as the consequences of their actions, and they often use their naive facade as a way to manipulate other characters. Readers can be counted on to understand who such a character really is; they share the last laugh as they collude with the character to put something over on a more vulnerable (and sometimes wrong or evil) character.

In his *Autobiography* the adult mark Twain recollects how he, as a supposedly innocent child, played tricks on his mother:

> Often I brought [bats] home to amuse my mother with. It was easy to manage if it was a school day, because then I had ostensibly been to school and hadn't any bats. She was not a suspicious person, but full of trust and confidence; and when I said, "There's something in my coat pocket for you," she would put her hand in. But she always took it out again, herself; I didn't have to tell her. It was remarkable, the way she couldn't learn to like private bats. The more experience she had, the more she could not change her views.

Twain the child knew very well what he was doing in taking advantage of his trusting mother; he not only had the bat in his pocket, but also the ace up his sleeve. The more he tricked his mother and got away with it, the better the joke. But both as a child and as an adult humorist creating a character, Twain observed a cardinal rule: *Humorists shouldn't laugh at their own jokes.* Self-conscious humor is embarrassing to observe, and to read. Instead, deadpan humor, sufficiently low-key so that the joke dawns gradually on the participants if not on the readers (who may be cued in to the humor right from the start) conveys memorable wit with subtlety.

Animals, machinery, or equipment.   These "characters" can be central figures in a comic tale or supporting members of a comic cast. Sometimes animals are personified, such as the animals in satirical allegories ("Reynard the Fox"), fables (Bre'r Rabbit), comic strips (Hobbes the tiger), and other comic tales. Such animals can talk and think; their motivations and psychology are excruciatingly human. Although they can be tragic figures, as is Kafka's human character metamorphosed into a giant cockroach in "Metamorphosis," long tradition and their essential nature usually make animals comic figures. Thus Don Marquis's archy the cockroach, who types in lowercase because he's not strong enough to work the shift key, explains his human capability and insect perspective:

> expression is the need of my soul
> i was once a verse libre bard
> but I died and my soul went into the body of a cockroach

it has given me a new outlook upon life
i see things from the under side now

The essential joke that such works exploit throughout is the parallel between the animal and its human analogue; although we may respond to the animal as an animal, we understand it as a human.

Recalcitrant or malfunctioning machinery or equipment can be the focus of a comic tale. In humorous writing, complicated machinery often develops a personality of its own, outwitting, thwarting, or otherwise frustrating an inept or timid human operator. The machine may be a computer, an answering or FAX machine, a VCR, or any implement designed to make one's life simpler and more fun but in actuality making it more complicated and more harassing. It's funny when the nominal master becomes dominated by the intended servant. Since the victim may be writing the piece, the fact that the writer has survived not only to tell the tale but to recognize its humor gives the readers license to laugh, as well. Such is the case in Ann Dolman's description of her first attempts to drive a shift car:

> Once out on the street (after a bristly encounter with the forsythia bush which unfortunately stood at the end of the driveway), I embarrassed myself completely. To keep from stalling, I'd rev the engine while I tried to slip the clutch. I couldn't even pretend to be a racing driver; the car didn't have the decency to sound like a high-powered race car, it just roared like an outraged lion with a thorn in its paw. Feeling conspicuous about making all this noise, I let the clutch out too soon, which either stalled the car, or, worse still, made it jerk down the street like a bucking bronco. The poor car looked like a see-saw with the front end first taking a nose-dive while the rear-end flew up, then leaping into the air as the rear end came back down. Jolting around the block with tires screeching and rubber burning, I provided my neighbors with the best free entertainment they'd seen in a long time, since the days when my brother was learning how to drive that beastly little car.

Comic Structure

Situation comedy.   In a situation comedy, characters are immersed in and then escape from difficult, painful, or otherwise horrible situations. "Humor has an intimate relationship with pain—somebody else's pain," explains Doug Marlette, Pulitzer Prize-winning creator of the comic strip *Kudzu*. In *In Your Face,* he says, "Sitting on a whoopee cushion may be humiliating if it happens to you, but it's hilarious when it happens to someone else. All situation comedies—from *I Love Lucy* to *The Cosby Show*—are based on putting characters we identify with into horrible situations so we can watch them squirm and writhe their way out."

But you're unlikely to start writing humor with a full-grown situation comedy. As with other subjects, you'll probably begin by writing about what you know—a painful or problematic period in your life or the life of someone close to you, or perhaps the difficulties of your family or a larger group. In order to gain a humorous perspective, you'll have emerged from this period, either by solving the difficulty or by outgrowing it. Marlette comments, "No one really enjoys going through adolescence, but watching someone else's teenage years can be uproariously funny. You could say I was an expert on the subject because my adolescence was one long, sustained whoopie cushion." Survivors can laugh in ways that people still involved in the problem situation cannot, as many of the student writings in this chapter illustrate.

Building to a climax.   Although you can milk problems for laughs, once the solution comes, the joke is over. Consequently, structure your work to have a long buildup and a brief climax. In much humorous writing, you'll want to build, build, build from the innocuous observation or phenomenon to the mildly funny one, escalating progressively to the comic knockout. But readers can't tolerate an ascension that goes straight up; they need to pause to catch their breath. With this in mind, whenever playwright George S. Kaufman "saw three straight funny lines in a play he was directing, he cut the first two." If you're stringing comic anecdotes on a narrative thread, arrange them according to this principle. You can provide resting spaces through longer descriptions or through repetition of the key elements that culminate in the comic punch.

James Agee recognized this principle when he categorized four types of laughter in "Comedy's Greatest Era":

> In the language of screen comedians four of the main grades of laugh are the titter, the yowl, the belly laugh and the boffo. The titter is just a titter. The yowl is a runaway titter. Anyone who has ever had the pleasure knows all about a belly laugh. The boffo is the laugh that kills. An ideally good gag, perfectly constructed and played, would bring the victim up this ladder of laughs by cruelly controlled degrees to the top rung, and would then proceed to wobble, shake, wave and brandish the ladder until he groaned for mercy. Then, after the shortest possible time out for recuperation, he would feel the first wicked tickling of the comedian's whip once more and start up a new ladder.

Agee illustrates an "old, simple example of topping," in which "an incredible number of tall men got, one by one, out of a small closed auto. After as many have clambered out as the joke will bear, one more steps out: a midget. That tops the gag. Then the auto collapses. That tops the topper." Other examples of "topping" include Harold Lloyd's film, *Safety Last,* which Agee describes (page 155), and Thurber's fruitless attempt to "see cells," culminating in his teacher's outrage (page 185).

Creating categories with repeated internal structures.   You can organize your humorous writing about a subject by dividing the subject into weird or arbitrary categories. Fran Lebowitz, a cantankerous social critic who thinks of her writing "as an organized and rarefied form of a tantrum," assumes the posture of someone who never gets used to anything, experiencing customs and situations as if they were created on purpose to annoy her. She begins "The Sound of Music: Enough Already" with the preemptive strike of the chronic victim:

> First off . . . in instances where I have not personally and deliberately sought it out, the only difference between music and Muzak is in the spelling. Pablo Casals practicing across the hall with the door open—being trapped in an elevator, the ceiling of which is broadcasting "Parsley, Sage, Rosemary, and Thyme"—it's all the same to me. Harsh words? Perhaps. But then again these are not gentle times we live in . . . .

She personifies "music," the object of her attack, treating the phenomenon as if it were human and had a mind of its own. To illustrate her point— "so that music might more clearly see the error of its ways"—she invents categories of irritating phenomena; some of the humor lies in the very categories themselves: "Music in Other People's Clock Radios," "Music Residing in the Hold Buttons of Other People's Business Telephones," "Music in Public Places such as Restaurants, Supermarkets, Hotel Lobbies, Airports, etc."

Like Suzanne Britt, James Thurber, and many other humorists, Lebowitz establishes a pattern in her first category that she follows in the others; part of the punch of any joke lies in the anticipation. Once readers find a particular technique or point appearing in two successive categories, they look for it in the rest as well, prepared to laugh again at what they already found enjoyable. Thus at the end of the first category, "clock radios," Lebowitz claims, "I do not wish to be awakened by Stevie Wonder and that is why God invented alarm clocks." At the end of the second category, "hold buttons," she claims that God was referring to the "good" silent hold buttons on telephones (and not the "bad" musical hold buttons) "when he said 'Forever hold your peace.'" And so on. Though of dubious theological value, the Bible According to Lebowitz has its comic place, at the end of the punchline.

Narrative, meandering to an implied point.   Of course, not all humor is structured according to climaxes and categories. E. B. White's essays (see pages 197–98) and many of Garrison Keillor's narratives flow gently along, eddying into occasional backwaters, following the conduits of an obscure channel, proceeding inexorably to a predetermined end but with sufficient subtlety concealing their tight structure so that readers are not overtly aware that the humorous or good-natured tension is escalating.

Comic Language

Humorous language, like any language, derives much of its meaning from the context in which it occurs. An ironic or sarcastic tone, a wink, a grimace, a shrug of the shoulders establishes a counterpoint that undercuts the literal meaning of the words. Because so much humorous writing derives its humor from the dissonance between the words and their accompanying context, one of the humorous writer's continuous tasks is to convey the tone—and, consequently, the meaning—without the winks and the nudges that signal "Joke!" or "Ha ha!" Whether you do this in a subtle or blatant manner will be determined partly by your use of some of the types of comic language discussed here—comic irony, comic dialogue, and other funny language—proper names, mottoes, and plays on words.

Comic irony.   In verbal irony, the words are at odds with the music. When you write ironic humor, you use understatement or overstatement—hyperbole or burlesque—or you juxtapose unlike images or concepts to create an ironic commentary of one on the other. The restraint of your expression and the tightness of your stylistic control belie the intensity of your involvement with the subject.

Understatement.   In this form of verbal irony, less is more. In "Goodbye to All T--t!," novelist Wallace Stegner pleads for restraint in writing on the grounds that understatement and allusiveness are more stylistically effective than sexual or profane explicitness. He illustrates his point with a climactic anecdote:

> I remember my uncle, a farmer who had used four-letter words ten to the sentence ever since he learned to talk. One day he came too near the circular saw and cut half his fingers off. While we stared in horror, he stood watching the bright arterial blood pump from his ruined hand. Then he spoke, and he did not speak loud. "Aw, the dickens," he said.
>
> I think he understood, better . . . than some novelists, the nature of emphasis.

When you represent a subject as less important or less significant than it really is, you count on your readers to draw on outside knowledge to assess its true meaning and to appreciate the implied contrast between things as they seem and things as they are. In his *Autobiography,* Mark Twain presents himself as a bat-lover from childhood. He used to play hookey from school to explore in the bat caves near his hometown of Hannibal, Missouri, and would bring bats home, secreted in his trouser pockets, to torment his unsuspecting mother. When he says, "I think a bat is as friendly a bird as there is," he can count on his readers to know that a bat isn't a bird. Our appreciation of that subtle joke occurs simultaneously with our acknowledgment that many people are frightened of bats.

Whether the comic ironist has an ace up his sleeve or a bat in his pocket, the reader knows it's there. Consequently, even if we readers fear bats, we're Twain's allies in his prank because we know something his mother doesn't. So we wait in anticipation to see how she will react when he tricks her into putting her hand into his pocket. Sure enough, when Twain says that his mother "always took [her hand out] again, herself" after feeling the bat, he never says that she was terrified, nor does he indicate the speed with which she removed her hand. He doesn't need to; readers' imaginations fill in the details as Twain adds "It was remarkable, the way she couldn't learn to like private bats." "Private bats" is another joke between Twain and the readers, who rightly doubt that she'd have liked public bats any better.

In a similar manner, *New Yorker* writer Lillian Ross can count on her sophisticated readers to supply a great deal of understanding and background information that her naïve subject lacks. The interplay between what Ross and her readers know and take for granted and what her subjects don't know allows her to write with ironic understatement "The Yellow Bus," a quintessential initiation story of the first trip to New York by eighteen members of the class of 1960 Bean Blossom (Indiana) Township High School, and two chaperones. With deadpan delivery Ross supplies a myriad of details to establish a minute-by-minute account of a classic comic situation: the experiences of innocents abroad, rural folk from a village of "three hundred and fifty-five inhabitants and a town pump."

Not knowing where to stay, the group takes the advice of their bus driver, also from Bean Blossom, and checks in at "the Hotel Woodstock, on West Forty-third Street, near Times Square." Not knowing where to eat, they follow his recommendation for their first and many a subsequent meal, "Hector's Cafeteria, around the corner from the hotel," where the "stern-voiced manager near the door" shouts "'Take your check! Take your check!,'" giving the Indiana group "the same sightless once-over he gave everybody else." Feeling "puzzled, fearful, and disheartened," and harassed by the counter-man, all follow the lead of class president Mike Richardson and "quickly and shakily" fill their trays with "fish, baked beans, a roll, iced tea, and strawberry shortcake." Sweating, bumping their trays and elbows against other trays and other elbows, they find seats. "Then, in a nervous clatter of desperate and noisy eating," stuffing their food down, they echo Albert Warthan's observation,

> "My ma and pa told me to come home when it was time to come home, and not to mess around," Albert said. "I'm ready to chuck it and go home right now."
> "The whole idea of it is just to see it and get it over with," Mike said.

"The general effect of Hector's Cafeteria," says Ross, is "to give the Bean Blossom Class of 1960 a feeling of unhappiness about eating in New York," and to strengthen their faith in "the superiority of the Big Boys [a hamburger drive-in chain] back home."

Throughout an extremely long and detailed recreation of their "two day and three night visit," Ross writes as an ironist whose fund of knowledge is far superior to that of her subjects. Although she never identifies any alternatives, the details she presents, the dialogue she quotes make her subjects look foolish. She knows New York intimately, in a myriad of ways that the Bean Blossom contingent doesn't. She knows where to stay, where and what to eat (and, by implication, how to stand up to bullying restaurant managers and counter help), how to behave in the big city. She knows the folly of relying on a naive out-of-town bus driver for travel information, of staying at the Woodstock (or perhaps at any Times Square hotel), and of eating at crowded unpleasant places with bad food. From a broader perspective, Ross knows, too, the limitations of having Bean Blossom, Indiana, as the focal point of one's universe and the frame of reference to judge everything else.

Ross has written a piece, humorous to other readers, New Yorkers or not, who share some of her knowledge and values; they will accept the author's implication that her judgment is superior and right. Those who do not may miss the irony. Yet even readers who appreciate Ross's ironic style might remain unconvinced that the Big Apple is superior to Bean Blossom. Or they might be kinder than she is and feel compassion for these teenagers from America's heartland (or any other victims of supercilious wit), whether or not they long for the country life.

Overstatement.   To create humor through overstatement you stretch or exaggerate your subject's emotions, state of mind, physical characteristics, behavior, typical mannerisms, gestures, clothing, or manner of speaking. You can make simple actions more complex, speed them up or slow them down, inflate their cost (in time, money, or effort), or dramatize their negative or positive effects. When you exaggerate, you count on your readers to be aware of the norm against which to measure the extent of your overstatement, for their recognition of the discrepancy between the two will cause them to laugh. The overstatement of *Dave Barry's Only Travel Guide You'll Ever Need* actually reinforces the fears of the Bean Blossom visitors and in the process satirizes them—and any other fearful tourists, natives—and travel guides, as well:

> Here are some tips for getting maximum enjoyment from your trip to New York:
> 1. Cancel it immediately.
> Ha ha! We are just kidding, of course. New York is in fact a major tourist destination, drawing millions of visitors each year, the majority of whom are never robbed and stabbed and left on the sidewalk to bleed to death while being stepped over by enough people to populate the entire state of Montana.

Their secret? They follow certain commonsense New York City safety rules, such as 'Always walk at least 30 miles per hour.'

Student Don Aker often explores the pleasures and pitfalls of parenting very young children. In "Do You Remember Sex?," he adopts the persona of a chronically exhausted father. How exaggerated this appears may be a function of how removed the reader is from the experiences Aker describes:

> Recently I read the results of a survey that indicated Canadian couples have intercourse approximately 2.4 times per week. The couples surveyed were either childless or liars. . . .
>
> It's not that children kill sex. They just put it on hold. At the end of the day, my wife and I lie in each other's arms and moan, but rarely from passion—usually her feet are aching and my back feels like it's done double duty as a playground for pygmies. We've discovered a different kind of sex, a spiritual bonding that occurs as we cling to each other in similar states of exhaustion and groan. A few weeks after we brought our first baby home from the hospital, a neighbour took a picture of us which, at the time, made us look like we'd been held hostage by psychotic sleep-deprivation scientists. Now I wish we looked—and felt—that good.

Readers are generally not meant to take such exaggeration literally. Although we may be convinced that the Akers find themselves exhausted by childrearing and preoccupied with their children's activities, the essay shows that they have a social life with other adults. From our own everyday lives—the norm against which we measure the Akers—we supply a corrective to Aker's nine paragraphs of exaggeration. In the conclusion, Aker does too, expressing his true attitude toward parenthood in a tone very different from the weary resignation of the rest of the essay:

> Children have a way of putting things in perspective. The other day as I was making a compost bin in the backyard, two little bodies pressed against me, noses poised an inch above the nail as I hammered, and my four-year-old said, "Daddy, you do good work." Turning to look at my daughters, I could see she was right. And that, as Frost wrote, has made all the difference.

Yet even here, Aker exaggerates; it would be impossible for him to hammer if his daughters' noses were really "poised an inch above the nail." As readers, once again we supply the corrective automatically.

Burlesque.   This variety of overstatement is characterized by ridiculous exaggeration, and distortion of the subject or real point in order to call attention to it. Like a handsome actor altered by age and obesity, the original shape shows through the changes, in recognizable and ironic contrast to the original. Burlesque elevates a trivial subject out of all proportion to its merits, grossly diminishes an important subject, sentimentalizes honest emotions, dignifies the ridiculous, or makes the bad worse. In burlesque there is always a critical *discrepancy between subject and style* so conspicuous that the readers can't miss it.

Student Richard Loftus, an experienced chef, burlesques his mother's cooking by quoting a typical, emblematic recipe "Green Bean Surprise Casserole," and commenting on it:

> 1 can green beans, drained
> 1 can cream of mushroom soup
> 1 box cheez-bits
> Layer ingredients—beans, then soup, then cheez-bits—in greased casserole. Place casserole in preheated 350 oven. Bake forty-five minutes. Serve.

> I'm telling you something I've never told anyone. Never, through the long years of dinners made possible by the invention of the electric can opener and the publication of Peg Bracken's *I Hate to Cook Cookbook*. Never, though the mention of meat loaf conjures images of a dark, brick-like thing, ketchup-glazed and gurgling angrily in a sea of orange drippings in a pyrex baking dish. Never, even when her mantra spun in my brain like an old forty-five: "Some people live to eat, Richard (my name spoken with accusative gravity), *I* eat to live." Oh Mom, was there ever a worse cook than you?

Loftus's mother may not be the worst cook in the world. Her meat loaf may, to less critical ears, be sizzling in the oven rather than "gurgling angrily"; its ketchup glaze may, in fact, taste good. Her "Green Bean Surprise Casserole," though a recipe no gourmet cook would allow in the kitchen, is recommended by the (you guessed it) cheez-bit manufacturers. In expanding on the trivial, in making the bad worse, Loftus gets his point across. Our common sense tells us he's exaggerating, our common sense lets us laugh at his burlesque (unless we're bad cooks, identify with the victim of this satire, and see nothing funny in it at all).

Comic dialogue.   "Clichés are like cops," says humorist Peter De Vries, "in that you can never find one when you want one." He continues, "This applies to trite questions as well as to trite statements. I have been waiting since 1948 for some poor devil to ask, 'What does a woman want most in a man?' so that I can come back, quick as a flash, with 'Fiscal attraction.'" If you want to write like De Vries or other humorists who believe that if they pay attention to the sound the sense will take care of itself, you'll need to listen carefully to what people say and how they say it. Through reproducing the intonation, emphasis, dialect, clichés, and jargon of ordinary speech— and sometimes through understating or exaggerating these features—you can often let your subjects speak for themselves, to the amusement of yourself and your audience.

Humorous mundane speech.   Mundane speech lends itself well to deadpan humor. Lillian Ross records with apparent fidelity the dialogue of the disgruntled, disillusioned Bean Blossom High School students as they eat their first New York meal in Hector's Cafeteria. Although the language is itself unremarkable, the students reveal their provinciality with every sentence they utter: "The whole idea [of coming to New York] is just to see it and get it over with." Because Ross and her readers take for granted that the whole idea of any sightseeing trip is never "just to see it and get it over with," the remark becomes both foolish and funny.

In a like manner, E. B. White uses an understated phone conversation to recreate the anxieties he experienced as a teenager getting up enough nerve to ask a girl for his first date:

> I had rehearsed my first line and my second line. I planned to say, "Hello, can I please speak to Eileen." Then when she came to the phone I planned to say, "Hello, Eileen. This is Elwyn White." From there on I figured I could ad-lib it.

White expects his readers to be amused by his boyhood rehearsal of the mundane conventions of phone etiquette, and, drawing on their common sense of how to act in similar circumstances, to be equally amused at his failure to practice what should be the more original portions of his imagined conversation.

Imaginary dialogue in unlikely situations.   Anything goes, as long as the reader gets the point. Don Aker describes his experience in the hospital awaiting minor surgery and fearing the worst—a general situation readers can identify with despite the nature of this particular operation—a vasectomy. Indeed the modest Mr. Aker (though not too modest to write about it) is most upset at "the prospect of lying naked, spread-eagled on an operating table before a group of strangers." "I preferred," he says,

> to be unconscious during the event—the alternative of being awake during the operation appalled me. . . . I could hear it all in high-fidelity stereophonic digitally-reproduced sound: "Well, Mr. Aker [slice], what do you [slice] do?" "I'm a [snip]—I'm [snip]—I'mateacher." "How long [snip] have you [snip] taught?" And the answer would no doubt elude me as I concentrated all my energy on looking nonchalant with knees raised, legs apart, and face scarlet.

Parodies of jargon.   When you recreate jargon with exaggerations slight or more substantial, you call attention to the speakers' values, occupations or professions, activities, or states of mind that influence their speech, though they are oblivious to how ridiculous they sound to listeners who share neither their values nor their vocabulary. Jim Smith, a student, satirizes his first day in Air Assault School by quoting the drill sergeant's commands and the recruits' replies, which grow less tentative as their indoctrination proceeds:

> "Here at the Air Assault School, you WILL BE motivated at all times. YOU WILL conduct yourselves in a professional manner at all times. You WILL re-

main alert at all times. You WILL address me and the other cadre as Air Assault Sergeant. Is THAT CLEAR?" "Clear, Air Assault Sergeant-t-t." "WHAT?" "CLEARAIRASSAULTSERGEANT!" "That's more like it. You will double-timeeverywhereyougoandshout a LOUD and VIGOROUS AIR ASSAULT everytimeyourleftfoothitstheground. Is THAT CLEAR?" "CLEARAIRAS-SAULTSERGEANT!!"

Through capital letters and runtogether words Smith captures the emphasis, intonation, and terseness of the commands. The cliches, jargon, and repetitive format of the drill sergeant's language reinforce the image of military precision and conformity. They also emphasize the ridiculousness of a situation against which Smith wishes to protest.

Imitations of dialect.   Imitations can be the source of good-natured humor if the nuances of conversation are captured with precise attention to their flow and interchange. Garrison Keillor, a master of this art, tells all his tales from Lake Wobegon, the imaginary town in Minnesota where "all the women are strong, all the men are good looking, and all the children are above average," in conversational language that imitates what a variety of characters think and say, read and write. In this typical passage he reminisces about his early elementary school days:

> Mrs. Meiers had a Reading Club on the bulletin board, a sheet of brown wrapping paper with a border of book jackets, our names written in her plump firm hand and after each name a gold star for each book read. . . . Daryl Tollerud has read two books, Mary Mueller has read sixty-seven, and her stars are jammed in tight behind her name. In the encyclopedia, I'm up to Customs of Many Lands and she is up to Volcanoes. She is the queen of Reading Club and she knows it. Girls want to sit next to her at lunch. Her close friends believe that Mary writes her book reports from book jackets. *Look at this:* "*Little House on the Prairie* is a book about the Ingalls family living in South Dakota. . . .*" She didn't read that book, the big cheater.* Marilyn Peterson put a slip of paper in a book in Mary's desk. It said, "You big cheater," she put it in at the end of the book. Mary didn't say anything about it. "See?" Marilyn said. "She didn't read that book."

After the first sentence, with its literary "plump firm hand," the language gets more conversational—"her stars are jammed in tight behind her name." Then comes "Customs of Many Lands," resonant of the language of a children's encyclopedia. From there on, the language is an amalgam of girls' dialogue, quoted directly ("*She didn't read that book, the big cheater.*") and indirectly ("she put it in at the end of the book"), perfectly ordinary-sounding but convincingly recreated to convey the generally mellow mood of the reminiscence and punctuated with the jabs and snipings of the girls' gossip. To decide whether you've got the words right, say them out loud, and listen to the sentence rhythm and length, repetition of key words and phrases, and where the pauses and emphases come. These will tell you whether the words match the music.

The humor can be less gentle, more raucous if the language is colorful and somewhat different from your own language, or that of your readers, particularly if the speakers of the dialect are themselves colorful and different from the readers in age, geographic location, or social or economic status. For examples of dialect, see the excerpts from Dudley Bass's essay in Chapter 2.

Funny proper names.   Humorous proper names, of people, places, products, and organizations, were meant to be exploited. We have fun just thinking of people with names such as Virginia Ham, Ima Hogg (sister of Ura), and the mail carrier Walker Miles. Adam's Rib Restaurant and Bah, Humbug! Exterminators beckon from the phone book, while Foggy Bottom, Bald Knob, and Short Pump enliven the maps they grace.

When you use such names, real or invented, you expect your readers to share your sense of the ludicrous connotations, and to judge the characters, places, or objects accordingly. You can use humorous names to emphasize the eccentricity of bizarre figures, to make them memorable, and to reinforce or satirize the stereotypes of their connotations. We know when we first encounter the satiric names of Art Buchwald's creations—Congressman Michael O'Lobby from the State of Indignation and Professor Heinreich Applebaum, director of the Computer Proliferation Center at Grogbottom— that neither they nor their activities will be treated seriously.

Mottoes, advertising appeals, political slogans.   You can use mottoes, advertising appeals, or political slogans for satiric purposes, often as ironic commentaries on the products or situations to which they pertain. Joe Eszterhas uses these to reinforce his snobbish interpretation of Harrisonville, Missouri:

> Life should be staid and bucolic, a slumbering leftover of what everyone who buys the $3.00 Wednesday-night Catfish Dinner at Scott's Bar-B-Q calls Them Good Old Days. But it isn't like that anymore. . . . [in spite of the fact that] the American Legion Building at 303 Pearl Street, a mausoleum of cigar butts, housed a nightly clap-happy gospel meeting—"Do You Want to Be Saved?". . . . and The Chamber of Commerce announced "real-big, real-good" news—the long-delayed acquisition of a shiny new cherry-topped . . . ambulance.

As with comical proper names, never explain. Humorous slogans and mottoes speak for themselves. You provide the context and set the tone for the readers' interpretation.

Plays on words.   All writers play with words; humorists have more conspicuous fun doing so. Tempting as it may be, you can't compose a whole essay exclusively of *bons mots;* though witty words can provide the spice that enlivens the matrix. As with spices, a hint is better than a handful. Some of the more common word plays are puns, spoonerisms, reversals, and non sequiturs.

Puns.   Puns use words humorously in more than one sense. Adlai Stevenson said when campaigning, "Your public servants serve you right," a modern application, perhaps, of Sir Henry Wotton's observation that "an ambassador is an honest man sent to lie abroad for the commonwealth." If you're a chronic punster, beware: some readers find puns the caterpillars of the world of words, the "lowest form of wit." But consider the caterpillars' potential!

Spoonerisms.   In the grand tradition of their namesake, the Reverend William Spooner, spoonerisms reverse the initial sounds of paired words, as in the church usher's whisper to the astonished parishioner, "Let me sew you to your sheet" instead of "Let me show you to your seat."

Reversals.   In reversals or other unconventional turns of conventional phrases, you begin a phrase in a conventional manner and slip in the alteration when readers are least expecting it. Thus Dorothy Parker observed in a drama review that a well-known actress "ran the gamut of emotions from A to B." The change, in this case the use of *B* rather than the predictable *Z,* causes readers to do a double take and to laugh as the shock of the unexpected hits them.

Non sequitur.   In a *non sequitur,* the humorist follows a logical premise with an illogical, unexpected, and perhaps ridiculous conclusion. The surprise startles readers into laughter: "No wonder academic politics are so vicious—the stakes are so small." Oscar Wilde is the master of such *bons mots.* Among his most startling and most funny are these, pungent and true: "A man cannot be too careful in the choice of his enemies" and "I can resist everything except temptation."

Common Comic Forms

The range of comic forms is as long as your funny bone, as wide as your grin. Humorous writing can range from gently amusing narratives to bitter satires, with a variety in between, including humorous portraits, social criticism, and parodies.

Humorous Narrative

When you're beginning to write humor, it's far easier to write an amusing account of something funny—or even simply pleasurable—than to strive to demolish a detested subject with elegant rapier wit. Everyone loves a good story; you've probably had plenty of experience in recounting such narratives for the pleasure of yourself and your audience.

Initiations are often good subjects; although they may strike the participants as painful at the time they happen, in retrospect the experiences grow less threatening and more comical. The discrepancy between the superior knowledge of hindsight (always 20/20 vision) and a character's myopia during the experience gives perspective and panache to Ann Dolman's account "Learning to Drive" (pages 178, 185), to E. B. White's recollection of making his first date (page 193), and to Don Aker's initiation into parenthood (page 191). The juxtaposition of the past and present point of view provides a naturally triumphant perspective. You've not only survived but prevailed through the very act of expressing wisdom with wit in exploring the comic possibilities of a situation that was once problematic. Or you may want to write about a subject intrinsically pleasurable (such as Mark Twain's account of the childhood joys of eating watermelons obtained "by art"), or one which you have come to appreciate more over time as your increased maturity and experience help you to understand it better.

Whatever the subject, you'll want to establish yourself as a credible narrator, find a structure that enhances your story, and choose language that reinforces your tone and your point. You'll appear credible, even though, like Twain, you "remember the things that never happened," if you *show* people, places, events in highly specific detail rather than simply *tell* about them. If you're a character in your own story, show yourself in thought (from inside your mind) and in action, behaving naturally. If you're recollecting an actual experience, edit your memories to reinforce the point of your narrative. Although James Thurber probably studied more aspects of botany than cells under a microscope, in "University Days" he focuses—literally—on the latter for its comic effect. The most logical arrangements of a comic narrative are either sequential, according to stages of the process or actual sequence of events (as in Dolman's "Learning to Drive"), or topical, starting with a low-key subject or event and moving toward the funniest or most outrageous. For most comic narratives, conversational language is best suited to the subject and to the authorial persona.

In "Once More to the Lake," E. B. White examines his return as an adult to the lake in Maine where he had spent summers with his father—this time with his own young son in tow:

> Summertime, oh summertime, pattern of life indelible, the fade-proof lake, the woods unshatterable, the pasture with the sweetfern and the juniper forever and ever, summer without end; this was the background, and the life along the shore was the design, the cottages with their innocent and tranquil design, their tiny docks with the flagpole and the American flag floating against the white clouds in the blue sky.

White's description is easy, gentle, rhythmic—characteristic of the essay's overall organizational pattern. The short tranquil segments of this sentence convince the reader with their specificity, lull the reader with their rhythm, like rocking in a hammock. White's mood and language are good-humored; he's not trying to make readers laugh, but to help them feel comfortable and relaxed as a consequence of his own easy attitude. If they smile with an appreciation of the moment, so much the better; a more raucous reaction would be out of keeping with White's treatment of the subject.

In this essay White also explores the significance of the continuity of generations, a topic which has been treated with utmost solemnity by poets, philosophers, and social scientists, among others. Yet White, ever mindful of his own childhood experiences in the same spot, avoids somberness because of the very pleasant nature of the activities he and his son enjoy, and their obvious pleasure not only in what they did, but in the fact that they did these things together:

> After breakfast we would go up to the store and the things were in the same place—the minnows in a bottle . . . the fig newtons and the Beeman's gum. . . . We would walk out with a bottle of pop apiece and sometimes the pop would backfire up our noses and hurt. We explored the streams, quietly, where the turtles slid off the sunny logs and dug their way into the soft bottom; and we lay on the town wharf and fed worms to the tame bass. Everywhere we went I had trouble making out which was I, the one walking at my side, the one walking in my pants.

Although a generation has passed, nothing has changed. Father and son go to the same store White and his own father went to thirty years before; it sells the same cookies and gum arranged in the same way, and the same soda pop still fizzes in the same painful fashion, though the pain is so predictable and so mild that it doesn't really hurt. In looking at his son, White as father sees his own image superimposed; the identity is born of love and again reinforces the essay's good humor, calculated to make readers smile with appreciation of its universal subject. This subject, we are to believe, was comfortable for White both when he experienced it and when he wrote about it later on. His ease with his topic contributes to the readers' enjoyment.

Comic Portraits

People make good subjects for humorous essays. *Character types* (the scold, the overbearing man, the garrulous fellow, are as old as classical antiquity); *people in familiar roles* (the country maid, the schoolboy, the henpecked husband); *free spirits;* and *people with bizarre, unusual or particularly strong personalities, fixed ideas, or eccentric occupations* are especially suitable. Humorous essays can also be narratives centering on comic personae, such as the helpless victim of circumstances or the innocent (see pages 182–85).

In Chapter 4, Writing About People, we discussed the essentials of writing portraits of anyone, comic or not. It's important to convey the relevant aspects of a subject's personality, behavior, manner of speaking, dress, relations with family, peers, or friends. In comic portraiture you'll want to emphasize and perhaps exaggerate those features that contribute to the subject's uniqueness or eccentricity. Your own attitude toward the subject will determine whether you treat the features with respect and sympathy or with ridicule, parody, or satire.

If you approve of your subject, you may simply wish to present information without commentary. If you disapprove of your subject, you can indicate this by emphasizing negative or ridiculous features and by exaggerating these to the point of caricature. You can quote damning excerpts from the subject's speech or writings that reveal hypocrisy, mean or unethical motives, stupidity, or unintentional self-parody. You can show the subject behaving foolishly or keeping company with boors, fools, inane people, or villains. You can comment negatively on what you find, or you can quote others' critical views. The main caution is not to pick on someone defenseless and so evoke pity for the underdog. The bigger the subject, the more significant the consequences of a fall from glory, the more satisfying it will be for you to provide the comeuppance and for your readers to enjoy the dénouement.

The *Washington Post* knew, in May 1987, that it had a very big subject indeed in "polyester" televangelist Jim Bakker, who, in 1986, paid himself $1.6 million in salary and bonuses to run the PTL—People That Love—Ministry. While then-President Ronald Reagan was praising the PTL network, its "religious-oriented talk show" carried on two hundred television stations, Jim and Tammy Faye Bakker "became pop icons to millions of born-agains." In the Bakkers' heyday, say reporters Art Harris and Michael Isikoff, "Tammy Bakker's tears rolled down like a mighty stream as Jim Bakker implored viewers and 'partners'" for funds, representing his ministry as teetering on the brink of financial disaster. These stratagems netted PTL $100 million a year, which enabled the Bakkers to:

> revel in an extravagant, go-go life style more akin to "Dynasty" than Christian ministry. Tammy wore mink. . . . They cruised about in one of three black Cadillac limousines, bought a houseboat, a vintage $62,000 Rolls, a Corvette, an $800 Gucci handbag, and vacationed in $350-a-night hotel suites in Hawaii. They built a heated and air-conditioned dog house for Tammy's pooches, and flew in $9,000 worth of truffles from Brussels for a party.

Bakker swam in an indoor pool, "relaxing under the powerful hands of a blind masseur named James. In his dressing room, he installed gold-plated bathroom fixtures and an $11,000 sauna and Jacuzzi that staffers called 'the floozie Jacuzzi.'"

Tammy Faye, the eldest of eight children, grew up "with an outdoor privy." Although she had never worn lipstick before she was married, after marriage she slept with it on. "Fans loved her style . . . dolloped with diamonds, thick, iridescent makeup that streaked as she wept . . . and praised the Lord in leopard-spotted pantsuits and four-inch spike heels, pitching herself as a prototype for the modern Christian woman."

"'My shoppin' demons are hoppin,'" she'd announce to friend Karen Paxton after the show, and, reported Paxton, "'All we did was eat and shop, eat and shop.'" As Tammy felt neglected, over time, "she went on more shopping binges, fought to rein in her sweet tooth and had her breasts enlarged" at PTL's expense. "Courting what Paxton recalls as her 'Marilyn Monroe image,' she wore a transparent red silk blouse to a big road race in Charlotte. 'She showed 'em off,' recalls Paxton. 'I touched 'em and they felt very natural. It was a great job.'"

In portraying—and implicitly condemning—the Bakkers, Harris and Isikoff use details to illustrate the Bakkers' philosophy of life, how their work and leisure time manifest their true values, where they live, what they look like, how they talk, how they dress. Like the portraitists of more neutral or genuinely lovable characters, the authors can count on their readers to share their standards of conduct, ethics, manners in judging the characters they portray. Red Eubanks and Homer Alumbaugh (Chapter 4), for instance, rate a high pass. However, because they are clergy, the Bakkers are subject to extra-strict standards, and they flunk them all. The hypocritical Jim and Tammy Faye, cruelly comic embodiments of the seven deadly sins, are not holier than anybody. Readers—who might themselves be among the Bakkers' victims—can appreciate the justice of their fall. Indeed, writers' and readers' judgments are confirmed by the fact that since late 1989 Bakker, convicted on charges of fraud and conspiracy, has been serving a forty-five-year federal prison term.

Humorous Social Commentary and Criticism

The contemporary social scene, like its inhabitants, is fair game for humorous writing, particularly if you focus, as Joan Didion or Lillian Ross do, on manners, mores, or customs. Humorous social commentary, benign or more critical, can be presented through comic portraits, including those of Red Eubanks or Jim and Tammy Faye Bakker. It can appear in narratives, parodies, and satires, discussed separately in this chapter. Humorous social commentary can appear in straightforward topical essays, where the amusing nature of the subject itself and the author's appreciation of it provide the fun, as in most of E. B. White's work.

Or the commentary can be more satiric. Student Craig Swanson uses exaggeration and sardonic language to criticize video games and game parlors in "It's the Only Video Game My Mom Lets Me Chew":

> Even before I walk into the room, I feel the electronic presence sink into my bones. The beeps, twoozers, fanfares, and fugues of the video games compete for dominance, heralding my approach. Entering the game room, I notice how much the machines look like urinals, with a patron standing in front of each, his back to the crowd, likewise engaged. . . .
>
> In goes my quarter. The machine sings out its familiar song of thanks, remarkably similar to Bach's "Toccata in D-Minor." I am then attacked by spider-like "grid bugs," an army of tanks, zooming "light cycles," and descending blocks that disintegrate me into a rainbow of dust particles. Where are the bonus gobblers, shooters, racers, fighters, markers, flippers, diggers, jugglers, rollers, or airships I need to win a free game? Where is the computerized paean of praise? Instead, the machine tells me the game is over by casting out the celebrated raspberry, then slowly droning "Taps."
>
> I stop. My pockets are quarterless, my vision is distorted, and I am devoid of all intelligent thought. I stumble out, ready to avoid reality for another day.

Swanson's sardonic title and his opening metaphor of the video game parlor as men's room are initial clues to his attitude toward video games. This is confirmed by the exaggerated list of bonuses and the mention of computer game's insulting music. If we accept Swanson's authorial stance, we also accept his regret at being seduced by a mindless game that is hard on the eyes and harder on the wallet. On the basis of his experience, we are expected to generalize about video games and their numbing effects on all addicted players.

Are there any subjects that can't be treated humorously? In theory, probably not. Swift pushed satire to its tolerable limits in "A Modest Proposal," with its themes of infanticide and cannibalism. With equally scathing comedy, Edward Albee exposed the devastating relations between husbands and wives in *Who's Afraid of Virginia Woolf?* and between parents and children in *The American Dream*. In a critically comic mode, many of Charles Dickens's novels explored the motifs of poverty, starvation, child exploitation, and orphanhood. Even sacred subjects can be treated with irreverence, as attested by George Bernard Shaw's *Adam and Eve* and *Man and Superman*.

Yet in practice humor, especially if critical, is bound to offend not only some of its victims but people who respect or admire its subjects. Not everyone appreciates jokes about religion—especially their own—though who today will defend Jim Bakker and Tammy Faye? Fewer readers still, for humanitarian reasons, would find funny humorous treatments of leukemia, AIDS, genocide, starvation, concentration camps, or total wartime destruction. But there are always exceptions, as in Stanley Kubrick's renowned satire on nuclear warfare, *Dr. Strangelove: or, How I Learned to Stop Worrying and Love the Bomb.* Moreover, insane asylums and their inhabitants are perennial subjects of humor, from *Marat/Sade* to *The King of Hearts* to *One Flew Over the Cuckoo's Nest.* The premise of each rests on the tenuous distinction between the sane and the insane: who is which? And who is ultimately capable of making that distinction?

Parody

A parody, like other imitations, may be the most sincere form of flattery or the most devastating type of criticism of the original. If you enjoy reading and are well-steeped in the works and style of a particular author, it's easy to write humorously by exaggerating the subject matter, philosophy, characters, language, style or other features of a given author or a particular work (see Audrey Guengerich on Gertrude Stein, page 170). Such imitation inevitably calls attention—perhaps admiring—to both versions; sometimes it implies through ridicule that the original is badly done or needs improvement, or both. Parody derives much of its humor from the double vision of the subject that writer and readers share. Any literary mode, any author, any work, is fair game so long as readers recognize the original and can make the implied comparison between it and the exaggerated or otherwise contorted version.

In *Dave Barry's Only Travel Guide You'll Ever Need,* the parody is triple-edged as Barry parodies the substance of travel guides, their style, and their readers, the travelers themselves.

> **What to Do in Switzerland**
>
> You should open a **Swiss bank account,** because (a) you get a **toaster** and (b) you never have to pay **income taxes** again. The Internal Revenue Service has no jurisdiction in Switzerland. When you fill out your tax return, you just write, "**Ha ha,** I have a Swiss bank account and just TRY TO GET IT, YOU SUCKERS!" and all the IRS can do is gnash its **teeth.**

From the vantage point of an experienced traveler's alleged superiority Barry writes this parody, parodying even his own alleged advice in the process by commenting on it: "You can trust us when we tell you this. We're a **guidebook.**" Barry ridicules the **boldface** that emphasizes key words (**toaster, income taxes, Ha ha**), the guidebooks' preemptory tone ("You should open . . ."), and the apparent ease and simplicity of the activities such books recommend. Yet he doesn't expect his humor to change anything, neither the formulaic writing of travel guides nor their readers; they are what they are.

In contrast, student Martha Bennett Stiles's parody, "The Saxon Beauty and the Three Black Bears," is written not only for fun, but also to demonstrate an appreciation of the original—William Faulkner's style and general subject matter:

Once in the middle, center of the Okeyouchokee Forest lived three black bears where Father Bear (a tall, silent, but not overly silent, either; speaking up when Mother Bear had the porridge too hot or someone had rumpled the cushions on his pet chair: chair made by his grandfather who had been part red bear, part black zoo captive, in those days when the black bear's position had been less desirable perhaps, perhaps more circumscribed but possibly not, but less equivocal too than now, now that a bear was free but had to keep to the woods or get shot by men, bear) had built them a house, with window boxes and such; where they could be bears and never see any men to remind them that they were, after all, bears not men.

Though part of the humor of this parody lies in its implicit comparison with "Goldilocks and the Three Bears," much of the joke lies in the exaggerated Faulknerian characteristics, which even in the original are exaggerated. Readers familiar with Faulkner's work will recognize his typical setting in the Southern backwoods and his silent, brooding, isolated characters of ambiguous race, uncertain and complicated ancestry, and troubled social status, who are forced into exile by alien invaders, the white men. They will also recognize Faulkner's complicated, convoluted syntax. Stiles's entire paragraph, like many of Faulkner's, is a single sentence, replete with a lengthy parenthetical aside, elaborate grammatical subordination, and a superfluity of adjectives and adverbs and modifying phrases. Yet Stiles's imitation is indeed the sincerest form of flattery. She is not implying that Faulkner's writing is bad or that he should change either his style or his subject, she just wants readers to appreciate the wit of the implied comparison.

Satire

Satirists are idealists. Unlike some parodists, satirists are intolerant of detachment and care deeply about their subjects, even though they may be excoriating critics of the status quo. They write from a desire to point out flaws in the subject and to promote reform, whether their corrective laughter is gently sympathetic or bitter with the anger of moral outrage. Their readers may range anywhere on a continuum from those in complete agreement with the satirist to those in total disagreement, angered and repelled by the satire, especially if they themselves are the satirist's victims. However, in Jonathan Swift's opinion, the victims may never recognize themselves, for, he said, "Satire is a sort of glass, wherein beholders do generally discover everybody's face but their own."

As a satirist you have at your disposal any of the techniques for writing humor or social criticism that you care to use—overstatement, understatement, irony, paradox, caricature, the creation of a persona or imaginary situation. The better satires are deft rather than heavy handed. They exhibit the satirist's ability, as Lady Mary Wortley Montague said, to wield "a polished razor keen/[And] wound with a touch that's scarcely felt or seen" rather than to hack the victim to bits with a broad axe. The subtlety of satire is revealed in Alexander Pope's epigram, "Engraved," said the poet, "on the Collar of a Dog which I gave to his Royal Highness":

> I am his Highness' Dog at Kew;
> Pray tell me, Sir, whose Dog are you?

The best known satirist in English, who writes with the greatest moral outrage, with "savage indignation," is Jonathan Swift. His "Verses on the Death of Dr Swift, D.S.P.D." demonstrates his concern for humanity and his typically sardonic way of expressing it:

> He gave the little wealth he had
> To build a home for fools and mad:
> And proved by one satiric touch,
> No nation wanted it so much.

The best known satire in English is Swift's "A Modest Proposal for Preventing the Children of Poor People in Ireland from Being a Burden to Their Parents or Country, and for Making Them Beneficial to the Public." Swift, a prominent Anglican clergyman in Dublin, issued this cry from the heart when many Irish tenant farmers and their families not only were starving as a result of three years of poor crops, but also were ignored by their English absentee landlords. To reform "man's inhumanity to man" Swift, in the guise of a dispassionate but public-spirited gentleman, proposes that poor mothers fatten up and sell their year-old children for food:

> I have been assured by a very knowing American . . . that a young healthy child well nursed is at a year old a most delicious, nourishing, and wholesome food, whether stewed, roasted, baked, or boiled; . . . it will equally serve in a fricassee or a ragout. [This food is especially] proper for landlords, who, as they have already devoured most of the parents, seem to have the best title to the children.

This proposal, claims Swift, would help to rid the country of its countless numbers of paupers and beggars. It would promote considerable public good "by advancing of trade, providing for infants, relieving the poor, and giving some pleasure to the rich."

Swift's proposal, of course, is not modest, but monstrous, as is its narrator, masquerading in the guise of a disinterested public citizen. For Swift to have really meant for people to condone and practice cannibalism, especially of their own children, is so depraved as to be almost unthinkable—except to uncouth Americans, as his snide allusion implies. Swift's ironic, detached tone reinforces the readers' common-sense conclusion that he must have meant the opposite of what he said. Moreover, Swift counts on his readers' own moral standards to guide them to his truth and to rally them to his cause, even if their outrage does not match his own. The portraits of Jim and Tammy Faye Bakker and Craig Swanson's video game addict may also be read as cautionary tales.

A Last Word

A final word about humorous writing. Don't nudge your reader in the ribs as if to say, "Joke on board. Get it?" Never complain if they don't, never explain if they do. Enjoy.

Checklist for Writing Humor

See also "Guidelines for Writing Humor," pages 181–82.

1. Is my subject often treated humorously? If not, why not? Is it traditionally taboo or otherwise touchy? If so, how can I present it from a new angle?

2. How are my readers likely to regard my subject at the outset? Do I have to overcome their possible objections to the subject itself? or to a comic treatment of it?

3. Does my subject or my writing depend for its humor on a private joke or private associations? If so, what information or context do I need to supply so a larger audience will find it funny?

4. What comic techniques am I using? Are these best suited to my subject and treatment of it? Are there other techniques that would work better?

5. Is the writing structured to emphasize the comical aspects of the subject? to emphasize the points I wish to make about it? to provide the main climax at or near the end?

6. Do I let my humor speak for itself, without trying to explain the jokes or subtly witty nuances? Is my humorous writing funny to anyone besides myself? Have I tried it out on others to determine their reaction? If they didn't find it funny or appreciate the wit, how can I change the writing to change their reaction? Or should I change it at all?

A Selected Reference List of Writings on Humor

See also "Works Cited."

Albee, Edward. *Who's Afraid of Virginia Woolf?* New York: Atheneum, 1962.
Baker, Russell. *There's a Country in My Cellar: The Best of Russell Baker.* New York: Morrow, 1990.

Bombeck, Erma. *When You Look Like Your Passport Photo, It's Time to Go Home.* 1991. New York: Harper, 1992.

Buchwald, Art. *Lighten Up, George.* New York: Putnam, 1991.

Didion, Joan. *Slouching Towards Bethlehem.* 1968. New York: Farrar, 1990.

Ephron, Delia. *How to Eat Like a Child.* New York: Dutton, 1988.

Gordon, Karen Elizabeth. *The Well-Tempered Sentence: A Punctuation Handbook for the Innocent, the Eager, and the Doomed.* New York: Ticknor, 1983.

Ivins, Molly. *Molly Ivins Can't Say That, Can She?* 1991. New York: Vintage, 1992.

Keillor, Garrison. *We Are Still Married: Stories and Letters.* 1989. New York: Viking, 1990.

Parker, Dorothy. *The Portable Dorothy Parker.* 1944. Ed. Brendan Gill. 1973. New York: Viking, 1991.

Perrin, Noel. *Last Person Rural: Essays.* Boston: Godine, 1991.

Pinkwater, Daniel. *Fish Whistle: Commentaries, Uncommentaries, and Vulgar Excesses.* Reading, MA: Addison, 1989.

Prose, Francine. *Primitive People.* New York: Farrar, 1992.

Shaw, George Bernard. *Pygmalion.* 1916. Many reprints.

Swift, Jonathan. *Gulliver's Travels.* 1726, and many reprints. A reliable edition: Ed. Paul Turner. London: Oxford UP, 1987.

Thurber, James. *Fables for Our Time.* 1952. New York: Harper, 1983.

———. *My World*—and Welcome to It. 1942. New York: Harcourt, 1983.

Thurber, James, with E. B. White. *Is Sex Necessary?* 1929. New York: Harper, 1975.

Trillin, Calvin. *Enough's Enough: And Other Rules of Life.* 1990. Boston: Houghton, 1992.

White, E. B. *One Man's Meat.* 1944. New York: Harper, 1983.

———. *The Second Tree from the Corner.* 1954. New York: Harper, 1989.

Wolfe, Tom. *The Pump House Gang.* 1968. New York: Farrar, 1987.

Works Cited

Agee, James. "Comedy's Greatest Era." *Agee on Film.* 1958. Rpt. in *Humor in America.* Ed. Enid Vernon. New York: Harcourt, 1976. 281–96.

Aker, Don. "Do You Remember Sex?" *The Essay Connection. Readings for Writers.* 3rd Ed. Ed. Lynn Z. Bloom, Lexington, MA: Heath, 1991. 684, 685.

Barry, Dave. *Dave Barry's Only Travel Guide You'll Ever Need.* New York: Fawcett, 1991. 91, 152.

Bombeck, Erma. "Ironed Sheets Are a Health Hazard." *I Lost Everything in the Post-Natal Depression.* 1973. New York: Fawcett, 1986. 7–21.

———. "One Size Fits All of What?" *I Lost Everything in the Post-Natal Depression.* 1973. New York: Fawcett, 1986. 53–74.

———. "Talk to Me—I'm Your Mother." *I Lost Everything in the Post-Natal Depression.* 1973. New York: Fawcett, 1986. 38–52.

Brady, Judy [Syfers]. "I Want a Wife." *Ms.* Dec. 1971: 56.

Britt, Suzanne. "That Lean and Hungry Look." *Skinny People Are Dull and Crunchy Like Carrots.* Watertown, MA: Ivory Tower, 1982. 33.

De Vries, Peter. "Laughter in the Basement." *Without a Stitch in Time*. 1953. Rpt. in *Humor in America*. Ed. Enid Vernon. New York: Harcourt, 1976. 231–35.

Eszterhas, Joe. "Charlie Simpson's Apocalypse." 1972. *The New Journalism*. Ed. Tom Wolfe and E. W. Johnson. New York: Harper, 1973. 127–60.

Harris, Art, and Michael Isikoff. "The Good Life at PTL: A Litany of Excess." *Washington Post* 22 May 1987: A1, 13.

Keillor, Garrison. *Lake Wobegon Days*. New York: Viking, 1985. 179.

Lebowitz, Fran. "The Sound of Music: Enough Already." *Metropolitan Life*. New York: Plume, 1978. 131–34.

Marlette, Doug. "Confessions of a Stripper." *In Your Face*. Boston: Houghton, 1991. 70–71.

Marquis, Don. "the coming of archy." *the lives and times of archy and mehitabel*. Garden City: Doubleday, 1950. 10–21.

Pope, Alexander. Epigram. *Minor Poems*. Ed. Norman Ault, New Haven: Yale UP, 1954, 372. Vol. 6. of *Twickenham Edition of the Poems of Alexander Pope*.

Ross, Lillian. "The Yellow Bus." *Reporting*. 1964. New York: Dodd, 1981. 11–30.

Stegner, Wallace. "Goodbye to All T--t!" *Atlantic Monthly*. March 1965:118–19.

Swift, Jonathan. "A Modest Proposal." *Irish Tracts 1728–1733*. Oxford: Blackwell, 1955. 109–18. Vol. 12 of *The Prose Works of Jonathan Swift*. Ed. Herbert Davis. 14 vols.

———. "Verses on the Death of Dr Swift, D.S.P.D." *The Complete Poems*. Ed. Pat Rogers. New Haven: Yale UP, 1983. 485–98.

Thurber, James. "University Days." *My Life and Hard Times*. 1933. New York: Harper, 1990. 221–28.

Twain, Mark. *The Autobiography of Mark Twain*. Ed. Charles Neider. 1924. New York: Harper, 1959. 3, 13, 18.

White, E. B. "Afternoon of an American Boy." *Essays of E. B. White*. New York: Harper, 1977. 157–61.

White. New York: Harper, 1977. 157–61.

———. "Once More to the Lake." *Essays of E. B. White*. New York: Harper, 1977. 196–202.

Wolfe, Tom. *Radical Chic & Mau-Mauing the Flak Catchers*. 1970. New York: Farrar, 1987. 5.

8

WRITING ABOUT PROCESSES

Trust yourself. You know more than you think you do.
—BENJAMIN SPOCK, M.D.

Anyone can use this book, whether he or she be an old hand or just a beginner. . . .
—READER'S DIGEST *FIX-IT-YOURSELF MANUAL*

All people dream: but not equally.
Those who dream by night
In the dusty recess of their minds
wake in the day to find it was vanity.
But the dreamers of the day
are dangerous people,
for they may act their dream with open eyes
to make it possible.
—T. E. LAWRENCE

This chapter has two major emphases. First we'll discuss how to write "how-to" works, the most common type of process analysis other than in scientific writing (see Chapter 9). Then we'll examine some special modes of process writing, ranging from the process of making ideas visible, to explaining process by analogy, to process as parody.

Purposes of How-To Writing

Whatever the subject, your main task as the writer of "how-to" essays or books is to help your readers to see, clearly and unambiguously, how to perform the process themselves. This is why most readers will want to read your work. Your second task is to convince your readers, as Dr. Benjamin Spock tries to do from the outset of his six-decade bestseller, *Baby and Child Care,* that they have enough knowledge and skill to perform the process you're discussing.

Americans as a people are indeed "the dreamers of the day." Even with experience to the contrary, we would like to believe that if we work long enough and hard enough we will succeed at anything we try. This is the essence of the American Dream, and to fulfill it we believe that we can learn to do almost anything ourselves. We value education, which anyone, not just a person of elite status as in many other countries, can obtain—for learning, so our credo goes, is the main vehicle to self improvement. We learn from a vast array of sources, whether "the school of hard knocks" or the educational system public and private, beginning in preschool and extending through graduate school and into retirement. We learn from teachers and tutors, coaches and trainers, mentors and gurus, therapists and clergy, interior decorators and landscape architects, and from our parents, children, and best friends. Millions of us learn from self-help books and articles, many of which are written by the teachers and the tutors, the coaches and the trainers, the mentors, the gurus. We are even willing to learn from books by self-taught amateurs who, with their flamboyant personalities buttressed by the media, become self-styled "experts." Americans, who pride themselves on their can-do spirit, are equally proud of their how-to heritage—a national legacy of ingenuity, inventiveness, and resourcefulness. In the democratic spirit of America, anyone who knows how to can do; these books both create and reinforce self-reliance.

You may want to write "how-to" essays or longer works to demonstrate the superiority of your method of "how-to" (diet, get a job, raise show dogs) over those of your rivals. You may want to establish yourself as an authority on a subject. You may want to make money, a far greater possibility for authors of Great American How-To Books than for writers of the Great

American Novel. These are all writer-oriented reasons and while they may provide incentives to write, you shouldn't allow them to obscure your focus on the readers' primary interest—how to do it.

Subjects of How-To Writing

The subject of a how-to writing can be almost anything that people can learn to do, understand, grow, make, or aspire to. More books begin with "How To" than any other title—5500 in 1992, to say nothing of the myriads of how-to books with more subtle titles. Most of the subjects can be categorized by the ultimate aim of the process identified in the title.

- How to develop a skill: *How to Write and Sell Humor*; *Guitar Playing Made Easy*
- How to produce an object or product: *Simplified Boatbuilding*; *How to Grow and Sell Christmas Trees*
- How to attain a state of mind or body: *Fitness Walking*; *The Choose to Lose Diet: A Food Lover's Guide to Permanent Weight Loss*
- How to attain a level of knowledge: *Conversational French*; *How to Study* and many other textbooks
- How to fix things: *Glenn's Complete Bicycle Manual*; *Fix-It-Yourself Manual*
- How to save, manage, or make money: *Everyone's Money Book*; *How to Get Paid What You're Worth*
- How to accomplish personal or professional goals: *How to Escape from an Unhappy Marriage*; *How to Get Happily Published*; and the all-purpose *Secrets of Power Persuasion: Everything You'll Ever Need to Get Anything You'll Ever Want*

These titles may sound familiar, for many of the subjects are of perennial interest.

- Health: *Jane Fonda's Workout Book*; *Jane Brody's The New York Times Guide to Personal Health*
- Beauty: *Color Me Beautiful*; *The Joy of Beauty*
- Love and Sex: *Living, Loving, and Learning*; *Dr. Ruth's Guide to Safer Sex*
- Parenting: *How to Raise an Adopted Child*; *When Good Kids Do Bad Things: A Survival Guide for Parents*
- Independence: *Live Alone and Like It*; *Real Men Don't Bond: How to Be a Real Man in an Age of Whiners*
- Finding a Job: *Getting to the Right Job*; *Résumés that Knock 'Em Dead*

- Power and status: *How to Win Friends and Influence People*; *Your Public Best*
- Long Life: *Life Extension*; *How to Live to Be 100 or More*

All of these topics and titles reflect components of the American Dream that never dies, and that readers believe is within their grasp if only they can learn how to do it.

Many magazines for hobbyists or general readers are full of how-to articles on similar topics of perennial interest—still other versions of the American Dream, miniaturized because of their short length. Every month *Redbook,* for example, publishes how-to articles on human relationships ("Sex and the Single Mom"), health ("Same Job, Less Stress"), food ("Should You Eat Meat?"), beauty ("Hair: A Love/Hate Affair"), fashion ("Designer Looks for Less"), and money management ("Mostly Money: How to Get Out of Debt"). Although these topics may not be new to you as a writer, they're bound to be new to some readers and to be of interest to others who can never know too much about a good thing. In short, you can write on anything you want, whether you choose a brand new subject or an old but flourishing chestnut, as long as you tell your readers how to do it.

Fundamental Assumptions of How-To Writers and Readers

Desirability of the Goal

A fundamental assumption of all how-to writings is that it is good, useful, valuable, or otherwise desirable to achieve the promised goal. Whether the goal, such as a flat stomach, breastfeeding, avoiding depression—or probate—is desirable in itself is never questioned. Writers and readers take the appropriateness of the subject for granted. This implicit validation of the subject is apparent in the 228 *Joy-of* instructional titles listed in *Books in Print* (1992) including *The Joy of—Chocolate, Cooking, Depression, Juggling, Money, Teddy Bears, Sex,* and *No Sex.* If it's joyous it's got to be good in itself or good for you.

Indeed, most "how-to" books promise satisfaction, if not joy, in either the performance or the completion of the process, or both. Harvey S. Wiener's *Total Swimming: How the Perfect Exercise Can Offer Rewards Both to the Body and to the Inner Self* promises these rewards in both the title and the subtitle. If the discussion is *Total,* what else is there to say on the topic? If the subject, swimming, is *Perfect,* what alternative exercise could possibly be better? If swimming *Offers Rewards* to the *Inner Self* as well as to the *Body,* what more can it do? Indeed, Wiener, an academician and regular lap swimmer, maintains that:

Swimming is a perfect activity for the high-pressured, competitive twentieth century, a sport to ease the mind, to release daily tensions, and to develop a body free from the demands of the battleground most of us call our lives and our jobs.

Promise of Success

A second assumption, shared by how-to writers and their audience, is that the readers can not only learn how to perform the process with relative ease, but also that they can learn to do it well enough to be successful. Some processes are for everyone, claim the authors. Wiener says, with authoritative support, that swimming is fine for the young (three-year-olds on up) and the old (no maximum age), for pregnant women, for the athletic and the sedentary, and that it's the best exercise possible for high-risk or recovering cardiac patients.

As readers become proficient in the process, they will gain control over that segment of their lives to which the process pertains, thereby fulfilling that portion of the American Dream. Many how-to writers claim that the process they teach will change the readers' lives, now and forever. As Wiener says, with full awareness that his enthusiasm may make it "seem as if swimming is Dr. Holiday's Magic Youth and Health Elixir, yours for two bits from the Medicine Bluff Drug Store":

> Having failed with so many other activities, and having won such stunning and unexpected improvements in my life after I built regular swimming into it, I'm unabashed in my prejudice. Swimming changes lives. What you learn from the water while you're developing body and self during the swim is skill to meet daily responsibilities with a new energy, attainable through no other sport I know.

Some "how-to" literature recommends strategy over skill or training. For instance, the jacket copy on Robert Half's widely read *The Robert Half Way to Get Hired in Today's Job Market* claims that the readers can "wage a winning job campaign" (that is, apply the right strategy) whether they're "too old," "too young," "over qualified," or "under qualified." In this book Half, president of a large employment agency, presents "practical, success-oriented tactics" for job hunting based on his extensive experience in finding jobs for more than 100,000 people. He contends, "knowing how to *get* a job is as important as knowing how to *do* a job"; "it isn't necessarily the most 'qualified' person who gets a particular job," but the most convincing applicant interviewed—"It could be you."

Half believes what he says, and his experience backs him up. He is not a con man. But he exudes the optimism characteristic of "how-to" writers, successful practitioners of their subject, writing for readers who probably lack the skills the author tries to impart (why else would they read the book?). Half does not dismiss the advantages provided by readers' innate talent, relevant background, and willingness to improve the quality of their professional performance. But, typically, he does downplay these qualities in his focus on successful job-seeking tactics: if readers follow the step-by-step process and play by the author's rules, they're likely to be successful, irrespective of their talent and training. The American Dream perpetuated.

For instance, although acknowledging that "nothing will have more bearing on whether or not you get hired" than your credentials, Half provides assurance that "you may have more skills than you think" to help you "get around the credentials bind." Likewise, although Half's own survey "indicates that as many as 75 percent of personnel executives will bypass a substantially overweight candidate in favor of a thinner, similarly qualified candidate," job seekers can either "go on a diet" or

> Work to counteract the prejudicial notion that because you are overweight, you are a lazy, undisciplined, or unhealthy person. Stress your attendance record at your last job (assuming it's worth stressing). Guard against appearing too lethargic.

Optimistic advice for every contingency is typical of the better "how-to" writers. They, like their readers, are pragmatic. If one method or plan of advice doesn't work, they offer alternatives. Indeed, many well thought-out books and articles present alternate routes to the pot of gold at the end of the rainbow. For instance, Jane Bryant Quinn's *Making the Most of Your Money* offers 934 pages of comprehensive advice for everyone from the "young and single" to "married couples" to the "sort of married" and "older widows." Quinn begins with "Where You Stand on the Money Cycle" and "Finding the Money" and moves on to "Paying for College," "Understanding Investing," and "Retirement Planning." Characteristically, Quinn anticipates every situation imaginable. Her advice is to the point and is presented with clarity and wit. Of job skills, for example, she says, "A wife without them is asking for trouble. Life is not fair. Death or disability occurs. Breadwinners lose their jobs. Not all spouses love each other until the end of time. As the poet said, 'Provide, provide.'" If readers still don't succeed, they can turn to some of the other "how-to" books on the same subject that offer alternatives to Quinn's advice. Hope continues to propel writers and readers alike ever toward the goal that one "how-to" book, if not another, expects to fulfill.

The Writer's Qualifications

A third assumption of how-to writing is that the writer is an expert on the subject, either by virtue of formal training or through personal experience, or is accurately reporting, as might a newspaper article or course paper, the process an expert recommends. If you wonder whether you do something well enough to tell others how to do it, consider the following questions.

1. How well can I perform the process I want to write about? Can I make the process work for me most—if not all—of the time?

2. How well can I perform the process in comparison with other people whose skill I respect, whether they're amateurs or professionals?

3. Has my performance been validated by others such as teachers or experts in the field? by employers? peers? students? awards or other forms of recognition?

4. How up-to-date is my knowledge and my information? Do I need to brush up on the current state of the art in terms, concepts, or techniques?

If you're comfortable with the answers to these questions, you're probably in good shape to start writing. If not, you can consult authorities for some of your information and supplement it with your own firsthand experience and common sense. Many "how-to" works, including newspaper and magazine articles, are written by nonspecialists (journalists, hobbyists, students, and others) who present information in a clear and interesting manner. Sometimes they are better than the experts at conveying information or advice to a general audience. Because these less-than-experts recognize what readers know and don't know, they can thereby accommodate the innocent and the unsophisticated.

For instance, in "A Personal Note on Tone," student Tim Payne, an English major studying the French horn for fun, bases his instructions on tone production on "my own struggles with the horn and my in-practice adaptations of the words and models of several instructors." He has learned enough as a student to provide an explanation that is clear and comprehensive, elegant and interesting to anyone with a rudimentary knowledge of music. His opening paragraph discusses the general parameters of the debate over bright versus dark tone. In the second paragraph Payne identifies his sources of information and the points of agreement between "bright-siders" and "dark-siders." Then he begins to discuss the actual technique of tone production.

| Payne begins not with a discussion of the process, but with an acknowledgment of the disagreement over the essence of his subject. | There is disagreement among horn players and other appreciators of the French horn as to whether the ideal sound for horn is bright or dark—what I like to call the difference between the hunting horn and the "haunting" horn. The bright-siders often say the dark tone sounds too much like a tuba, and the dark-siders respond that the bright tone sounds too much like a trombone. It can be argued that the bright sound is ideal for some settings and the dark sound for others; for instance, the bright sound is generally more fitting for a brass ensemble and the dark sound for a woodwind quintet, bright for a | Despite the technical nature of the disagreement, Payne explains it in terms that nonspecialists can understand.

However, understanding |

Payne speci-
fies that his
audience in-
cludes both
bright- and
dark-siders.

sparkling allegro, dark for a death march. I feel, however, that players and tastes . . . fall basically on one side
or the other: a dark-side player will take on, say, the soaring, heroic passages of "Jupiter" from Holst's *The Planets*
with a *brighter* darkness in his tone, but it's still a darkness at heart.

will be
greater if the
readers have
some basic
knowledge of
music.

It's necessary
to specify
Payne's bias
because this
influences his
choice in tone
and the na-
ture of the
how-to in-
structions
that will
follow.

My point here is one of forewarning and perhaps of
self-introduction—but also, I hope, of clarification: I am
a dark-sider, a "haunter"; therefore, because the comments I wish to make about tone-production are relatively specific and are based entirely on both what I've
gained from my own struggles with the horn and my in-
practice adaptations of the words and models of several
instructors, I must admit that what I have to say refers
to and hopes to facilitate the production of a dark tone.
But (before you bright-siders throw this paper to the
ground to vent your spit-valve on) not *merely* a dark tone,
but a dark good tone—emphasis on the *good*. Beyond
the bright/dark debate there are several elements of good
tone on which there is general agreement: openness, resonant or ringing quality, consistency throughout the register, consistency over the duration of individual notes
and phrases (including attacks, releases, and slurs), consistency (or control) throughout the volume spectrum,
and focus. Since the concept of sound to which I aspire
contains these widely accepted elements of good tone, I
hope that anyone, bright or dark, can find something of
interest and of use in the following practical suggestions
based on my experience.

Payne cites
his source of
knowledge.
He admits
that he's not
an expert,
and that his
preference is
based on his
limited stu-
dent experi-
ence—his
own and that
of several
teachers.

Payne as-
sumes that
his readers
can play the
horn and can
read music. Is
this assump-
tion justifi-
able? Or
would this
assumption
exclude peo-
ple who
couldn't play
the horn or
read music?

Like a good
debater,
Payne ac-
knowledges
the many
points of
agreement
between the
opposing
views.

Payne
explains a
concept,
response
adaptation,
and de-
fines it.

My first directive recalls perhaps the first instruction
you ever received on horn-playing: take the horn and find
the open note which comes most naturally and easily to
you. This will probably be the written *e* or *g* above middle *c* or perhaps even third-space *c*. Using this note, along
with your ears, your mind's eye, your concentration, and
what I will call your response adaptation, you will develop your concept of tone and your model or reference
point for this concept. Response adaptation is your physical adjustment, largely by trial and error, *toward* the re-
alization of what your ear and mind are continuously en-
visioning as better tone. This process is much like walking
in a dense fog: as you take a step forward into what little distance you can see, you are able to see that much
further, and so it is with the next step and the next, the
vision always just beyond the present location, so that
you can continue forward until you reach your destination or goal. . . .

Payne has
captured the
essence of
learning any
process in
this simile.

This is a
vivid cue of
what readers
can expect in
the next four
pages of step-
by-step in-
structions
that illumi-
nate the path
toward an ul-
timate goal.

Audience

How much your intended audience knows about a subject is critical in process writing because you have to gear your explanation so closely to its level. Although it's assumed that you (or your sources) know more than your readers about the process at hand, you'll be insufferable if you're condescending, as in the chef's immemorial advice to the novice cook: "First, stand and face the stove." If you write over their heads they're likely to stop reading unless your explanation is sufficiently interesting in itself (as Tim Payne's is) to encourage them to read just for the enjoyment of it.

In *Mind Over Machine,* Hubert and Stuart Dreyfus have identified the characteristics of four stages all learners go through as they gain in understanding and expertise.

Novice: Novices learn facts, features relevant to the skill, and rules for deciding how to act on these. The rules need to be context-free, objectively defined so the novice can recognize and apply them in any situation: "Stay one car length behind the car in front of you for every 10 m.p.h. of speed." If you write for novices, you'll need to supply an overview because novices are usually so focused on following the rules that they lack a coherent sense of the overall task. In general, don't bother identifying exceptions to the rules; readers at this stage can't cope with them.

Advanced beginner: As novices gain experience in real situations, their performance improves to the point where they can consider more than context-free facts. A good way to address such an audience is to present more sophisticated rules in the abstract and in real-life situations that will enable readers to draw on their own experience. They can note similarities between new and familiar situations and can learn to work with new information, additional concepts, contingencies, and possibilities: "In judging proper driving distance from other cars, learn to discriminate between drunken drivers and those who are impatient but alert."

Competent performer: Experienced learners recognize more and more context-free and situational elements. To keep these readers from being overwhelmed by too much information, present a plan to help them organize what they need to know next and to concentrate on only its most important features: "To judge the appropriate distance to keep away from other cars, consider traffic density, weather conditions, etc." Competent readers will know enough to decide whether they want to follow your advice or to try out another plan.

Proficient performer: Proficient performers are deeply involved in their task and although they still think analytically, they seem to understand intuitively what to do and how to go about doing it. They apply what they've learned in the past to new situations that are ever-evolving and ever-changing. A proficient driver, for instance, intuitively slows down for a curve on a wet road, then decides whether to brake or let up on the accelerator. For readers at this stage, you can discuss theory as well as practice.

The easiest way to make certain that your writing reaches the capability level of your audience is to ask a friend, colleague, or a typical reader to perform the process you explain and then to help you answer the questions in "A Checklist for Writing How-To Works," on page 237.

Even familiar processes can become confusing when you write about them. If you tell someone how to tie a shoe, using only words, not gestures, even the most experienced person will get all tangled up. Yet your readers, ever hopeful, will probably expect to accomplish the process you're explaining with ease and efficiency. If they can't, make sure their ineptitude is not caused by your directions. Explain the process aloud and ask your colleague to tell you which parts are clear and which aren't. To doublecheck your revised explanation, have a different reader try to follow your process.

Form and Variations

Most process writings follow a logical sequence from the beginning of the process to the end; they divide the process into steps according to what has to be done first, second, and so on. The more complicated the process, the more variations there may be in explaining how to perform it, even though the process itself may have to be performed in a fixed sequence ("You have to survey and prepare the building site before you can lay the foundation. . ."). There is no single right way to organize such a discussion; how you proceed depends on what you want to emphasize, which is determined by the order in which you discuss the steps and the amount of space you devote to each segment. Thus, although some books on swimming plunge right in with breathing and strokes, others do not.

Process in Sequence

A recipe provides an easy-to-remember format typical of short "how-to" writings. Most recipes consist of a descriptive title, a list of ingredients, a sequential explanation of the steps involved in preparing the food, and an indication of the outcome.

Nutritious Pack Snack

1/2 cup honey
1/2 cup peanut butter
3 T. butter
2 1/2 cups 100% bran cereal
1/2 cup dry milk
3 T. browned sesame seeds

Melt honey, peanut butter and butter over medium heat. Add cereal and dry milk. Mix and pack into an ungreased 8″ × 8″ pan. Sprinkle with sesame seeds.

Wait one hour, no longer, and cut into squares or bars.
Yields 16 bars.
A "good for you" cookie that needs no baking.

1. *Imply the recipe's objective in the title.*

2. *Identify any special equipment or unusual conditions that must be met before beginning the cooking.* None exist in this example.

3. *List the ingredients in the order they'll be used.* This order is easy to remember and logical to follow.

4. *Detail the steps in preparing the recipe, numbering the sequence in which they must occur, and concluding with the anticipated outcome.* In this case, 16 bars.

This is a simple explanation of a relatively simple process, yet it is written for cooks who already know how to "stand and face the stove." It omits some refinements that professionals might wonder about: does the kind of honey (clover, alfalfa, etc.) or butter (salted or unsalted) matter? Evidently not, or they would have been specified. The recipe also assumes that readers know how to brown sesame seeds, what "medium" stove heat is, when to remove the melted ingredients from the heat, and how to pack the mixture into the pan.

Even the simplest set of directions is likely to involve subprocesses. But where to put them? Should they be described where they would be performed in the overall process? Or would that be too distracting? Should they be explained at the end? Or not at all? Presumably the writer tried out alternative processes as well as alternative places to include subordinate information to arrive at the clearest, most efficient and effective way to perform the process and to explain it. Variations on the recipe could be presented at the end.

Process in Context

Another common format in process writings is to put a subject into context (historical, philosophical, theoretical, or some other relevant perspective) before getting down to the practical aspects. This format is particularly helpful when there is debate over either the aims or the methods of the process. Thus in "A Personal Note on Tone," Tim Payne discusses the disagreement between the "bright-siders" and the "dark-siders" before explaining how to produce the darker tone. In *Total Swimming*, Harvey Wiener spends the first five chapters justifying the benefits of regular swimming for the psyches and bodies of all swimmers. He then devotes another seven chapters on the relation of swimming to one's life style ("How To Find the Time and the Place," how to select a swim suit, at what age to start, before getting to the actual process of swimming, "Different Strokes for Different Folks." It is clear from

Wiener's emphasis and organization that the strokes are only one aspect of the total process and, in his view, not the most important.

Guidelines for Writing How-To Works

A successful piece of how-to writing is an expert balancing act. The writer, with the expert's graceful nonchalance, presents precisely the right amount of information to make a process—however simple or complex—crystal clear, with neither unnerving excess nor undue vagueness. If the writer strikes the right balance, the process will look easy and enjoyable, satisfying the readers' assumption that they can master the subject quickly. For American readers, ever optimistic, want to attain the expertise of a lifetime in the amount of time it takes to read the how-to work.

Be specific.   In how-to writings, be as specific as possible when giving measurements (lengths, weights, and quantities) so the finished product will emerge as close as possible to the ideal. If the reader is unfamiliar with the subject, it helps also to explain the rationale for those measurements. Thus in *Simplified Boatbuilding: The Flat-Bottom Boat,* Harry V. Sucher's discussion of "Fitting of Thwarts" is both precise and descriptive:

> The thwarts are fitted next. These, of course, function as seats for the occupants, but can add great structural strength to the hull if properly fitted. The ends of the thwarts are supported at their outer ends by longitudinal stringers fitted to the insides of the frame and extending from bow to stern. Thwarts vary in thickness from about 1/2 to 3/4 inches and are up to 12 or 14 inches wide in the average small boat. The height of the thwarts from the bottom depends somewhat on the size of the boat, but is generally from one-half to two-thirds of the distance of the depth of the sides of the boat. The average thwart is a plank of from 5/8 to 7/8 inches thick, and from 9 to 12 inches wide.

Margin notes, left: Identification of functions of thwarts
Identification of exact physical dimensions, but with allowance for variation

Margin notes, right: Identification of the relation of the part (thwarts) to the whole
Relative (rather than absolute) measurement accommodates varying boat sizes.

Sucher's directions are comprehensive, to accommodate boatbuilders of varying levels of skill. His measurements are flexible, to be adapted to standard sizes of lumber as well as to varying sizes of boats.

If your writing is intended for short-term reading such as a class paper or a newspaper, cite specific figures, such as prices. For works that may be read in the distant future omit such figures if you can; the numbers will change and date your writing.

Use illustrations.   Illustrations can be invaluable, especially a good diagram or a photograph. They can show what a part (say, a thwart) looks like, where it goes, and how big it is. They can indicate the relations among parts of a mechanism (say, an automobile engine) or a system (perhaps, the domestic plumbing). They can show where a part (such as a sleeve) fits into the whole. They can illustrate design and proportion (the layout of a vegetable garden). They can illustrate the steps in a process (how to make a soufflé). They can show right and wrong ways to do something (focus a photograph), before and after (house remodeling), simple and complicated alternatives to a process (a straight versus a flat fell seam). When in doubt, illustrate.

Use an appropriate organizational pattern.   How-to writings dealing with human relationships and emotions have to accommodate many variations and may be organized around issues or goals rather than steps in a process. In a brief essay, "You & Your Analyst," psychotherapist Dr. Douglas LaBier offers capsule advice on how prospective clients can choose a psychotherapist. He suggests that they ask the therapist two key questions, and arranges these to proceed from the more general to the more specific subquestions. Because the article is short, the kinds of answers the prospective clients should look for can only be suggested by key words; in a longer article the author could provide greater elaboration. LaBier lists each question and then suggests what to look for in the response:

> If someone wants help because of, for example, anxiety or depression, what kinds of reasons would you look for as possible causes?
> A good therapist will consider all possible sources of your problems. Childhood conflicts are the most obvious, but the therapist should also include possible biochemical disorders, personal values and external situations of work and love. A therapist who ignores or dismisses any of these is to be avoided.
> Another question is, What are your own [i.e., the therapist's] personal values and attitudes—about work, love, money and life in general?
> This not only helps you learn something about the therapist as a person, but also gives you some information to mull over regarding how his or her own outlook and values will affect the treatment. Does the therapist seem to enjoy his or her work, or sound bored or depressed? Be wary of therapists who sound extreme, either overly idealistic or overly self-centered. Does he or she seem interested in life in general, or strike you as a joyless, narrowly focused technician?

LaBier also suggests three criteria for interpreting the therapists' answers to these questions:

> Ask Yourself:
> Do I feel sufficiently challenged by this therapist to look at myself without feeling attacked or treated with disrespect?
> Do I think he or she is capable of understanding me?
> Do I think that he or she is sincerely interested in helping me, or views me as just a diagnostic category? Or as a big dollar sign?

The pattern here is general: ask the questions, look for crucial concepts in the answers, and make your decision. But there is no specific order in which these questions need to be asked or answered. And there is no single right answer; the questions point out dimensions of the issues as guides to enable readers to make their own decisions.

Adjust length by expansion or contraction.   If you're writing to a designated length, you will need to expand or contract the number and complexity of your recommendations. A short essay, such as LaBier's, will of necessity be brief. *Simplified Boatbuilding* doesn't sound so simple at 416 large, fully-packed pages. The obligation to fit a space format is why many "how-to" articles list "Five Steps to a Career Change" or "Ten Days to a Better Love Life." The steps they recommend are short and to the point. However, if you find that to accommodate the format you have to oversimplify the process or leave out too many essentials, change topics rather than perpetrate error or readers' unrealistic expectations.

Define terms and concepts.   When you first use a new term or concept, define it in language your readers can understand. You may need to break down the definition into its component elements, as in this definition of film speed from Tom and Michele Grimm's *The Good Guide for Bad Photographers.*

> What film speed means
>
> Lesson 1: A film's speed tells you how sensitive the film is to light. Some films are more sensitive than others. Their sensitivity is indicated by numbers, which are called *ASA numbers*. . . .
>
> Where to locate the film speed—in multiple places
>
> Lesson 2: You'll find a film's speed on its packaging box, the film cassette, its instruction sheet, and sometimes in the film name itself (Kodacolor 400, for example, has a film speed of 400). *Specific illustration*
>
> Range of film speeds that most nonprofessional readers will use
>
> Lesson 3: The speeds of popular 35mm films range from ASA 25 to ASA 400. The higher the number, the more sensitive the film is to light. *A useful rule to remember*
>
> The Important Lesson: For proper exposures with a 35 mm camera, you must set its *film speed dial* according to the ASA number of the film you are using. Unless you tell the camera how sensitive the film is, it cannot correctly make an automatic exposure or indicate the proper exposure with the camera's built-in exposure metering system. . . . *The most important point so-labeled: how to accommodate the ASA indication*
>
> Explanation provided of this significant point

Use consistent terminology and measurements.   In how-to writing readers will take what you say literally and explicitly; inconsistentcy (say, shifting between metric and English measurements) will be confusing. After he finished writing the manuscript for the first edition of *Baby and Child Care,*

Dr. Spock revised it carefully to make sure he didn't use confusing synonyms for key concepts, materials, or diseases:

> If I said to use "a mild soap" on page 50 and then on page 75 I said to use "a soap" I knew that an anxious mother might be driven into a slight panic wondering whether I meant a *mild* soap on page 75. It's important from a literary point of view to get the repetitions out, if possible. If not, then the repetition must sound *exactly* like the first statement so the advice will be unmistakably clear. (Bloom, 113).

Explain alternatives.   If there is more than one good way to perform a process and you have space to deal with more than the bare essentials, specify the alternatives and identify which one is preferable under what conditions.

In the extremely thorough *The Complete Book of Running,* James E. Fixx explains the four major ways for runners to train: (1) Intervals, consisting "of repeated hard runs over a measured distance, with recovery periods—the intervals—of relaxed jogging in between." This method, he explains, "is particularly versatile" because the duration, number, and total distance of fast runs can be varied, as can the time and activity between fast runs. (2) Fartlek, a term for "fast untimed runs over varied distances and terrains" to achieve a "good workout that is also fun." (3) LSD, running for a "long, slow distance." And (4) long, fast distance. Fixx explains that he approves of the first three alternatives because they can be adapted to the runner's temperament (highly disciplined versus more relaxed), the runner's purpose (for fun or to run races of various lengths), and to the time of year (running in the summer heat is different from running in the cold). But he rejects "long, fast distance" out of hand as a training method, on the grounds that "the body will eventually rebel and break down," and will not repair itself without the rest that this method denies.

Writing Good Directions: The American Red Cross Manuals

A comparison of the 1973 edition of the American National Red Cross *Standard First Aid & Personal Safety* with the 1992 edition of the same book, *American Red Cross First Aid and Safety Handbook,* reveals many changes that illustrate improvements in how to write good directions. Clear, accurate directions, easy for nonmedical readers to follow in moments of crisis, are of critical importance in dealing with the matters of life and death treated in this book. The discussion of how to provide first aid for heat illness typifies the changes made in clarifying directions between editions.

> The 1973 edition advises readers to cool the overheated body (105° F or higher) quickly down to 102°F, taking care not to "over-chill" the victim after that point is reached.

1. Undress the victim and, using a small bath towel to maintain modesty, repeatedly sponge the bare skin with cool water *or* rubbing alcohol; *or* apply cold packs continuously; *or* place the victim in a tub of cold water (do not add ice). . . . When the victim's temperature has been reduced enough, dry him off.

2. Use fans or air conditioners, if available, because drafts will promote cooling.

3. If the victim's temperature starts to go up again, start the cooling process again.

4. Do not give the victim stimulants.

The 1973 edition takes longer than the 1992 edition to get to the point. It begins with definitions of three conditions in which the body becomes seriously overheated and can't cool itself down, discriminating between heatstroke, heat cramps, and heat exhaustion. Then, in a single paragraph, it identifies the general causes of all three conditions. Following the causes are specific discussions of each condition, with signs and symptoms followed by first aid treatment. The treatment states the objective (*"immediate* measures to cool the body quickly") followed by the sequence in which the steps should proceed. Each step is numbered and broken out into a separate sentence or two of brief explanation.

In contrast, the 1992 edition is clearer. By using an appropriate organizational pattern, developing an extensive context, employing a clear graphic design and using a comfortable tone of language, the 1992 edition clearly outlines how to treat victims of heat illness.

Organizational pattern.   The 1992 edition is arranged in a more logical order than the 1973 edition. It begins with a general discussion of the causes of heat illness that opens with an explanation and proceeds to a warning: "If your body's temperature-regulating mechanisms are overwhelmed, your core temperature can skyrocket above a safe level." Then it explains the progression from the least (and probably the most common) to the most severe problems: heat cramps (muscle pains caused by salt loss), heat exhaustion (collapse caused by inadequate water intake), and heatstroke (sunstroke), "which can cause shock, brain damage, and death."

Context.   The 1992 edition provides a more extensive context to explain the causes of heat illness: external factors, such as being in a hot environment, either outdoors on a humid day or indoors in a hot, poorly-ventilated area; internal factors such as exposure to heat and sun after consuming alcohol or some medications; and physical factors such as age (children and older people are the most susceptible and more subject to "sudden collapse") and physical condition (people "out of shape and obese").

Graphic design.   The design of the 1992 edition lets readers *see* the main points immediately instead of having to hunt for them. *Example:* The most

significant difference between the two editions is the most conspicuous feature of the 1992 edition: a highlighted block that gives general directions for
"How to Cool a Victim of Heat Illness," no matter which kind. Because the
objective in all cases is to cool the victim quickly and immediately without
spending extra time deliberating over the diagnosis, the 1992 manual gets
right to the point. First, it emphasizes the general concern that the victim
"needs help right away." It then provides the first set of instructions (not present in the 1973 manual) to take the victim's temperature at the outset and
again a few minutes later. It provides clear explanations of why a given procedure must be done, in this case, to establish how serious the problem is
and whether or not the treatment is working.

The highlighted block then lists five different ways to cool the victim. The
ways are indicated by bullets but not numbered because they can be used in
combination rather than in sequence:

- Move the victim into the shade, into a cool room, or to an airconditioned
  building or car.
- Spray the victim with a hose, or pour a bucket of water over him or her
  (not in the face). Tell the person what you're going to do, and *do not use*
  these measures if the victim is confused.
- Wrap the victim in wet towels or sheets, then turn on a fan. . . .
- Place cold compresses on the victim's neck, groin, and armpits.
- If medical help is not immediately available and you suspect heatstroke,
  immerse the victim in cold water (bath, lake, stream), but only if you can
  carefully monitor his or her level of alertness and ABCs (airway, breathing, and circulation).

The highlighted block concludes with what to do after the victim's temperature drops below 100° F—two degrees lower than the 1973 edition recommends—"ease up on your cooling efforts" but continue to check the victim's
temperature at half-hour intervals for the next three to four hours in case it
should rise again.

On pages adjacent to the highlighted block is information that identifies
each of the three conditions, briefly listing and emphasizing each symptom
with a bullet. Heatstroke is identified this way:

Heatstroke

- Raised body temperature (above 102° Fahrenheit)
- Dry, hot, red skin. . . .
- Rapid, shallow breathing. . . .
- Unconsciousness

For each of the three conditions, the manual then provides specific first
aid instructions, all of which follow the same pattern:

- *First:* whether or not to call EMS: Yes, for heatstroke.

- *Second:* what NOT to do: "DO NOT give the [heatstroke] victim anything by mouth—not even salted drinks."
- *Third:* what to do: lists in the sequence in which the steps should proceed,
  with each step numbered and broken out into a separate sentence or two
  of brief explanation.

Language.   The orientation and language of the 1992 edition are reader-
friendly, much more so than those of the 1973 edition. The 1992 edition addresses the reader as *you;* both reader and victim are real people. It anticipates the reader's possible uncertainties ("Tell the victim in advance that
you're going to douse him or her."), misunderstandings ("Don't throw water into the victim's face."), and objections ("Don't worry about subjecting
the victim to extremes in temperature.").

In the 1973 edition the positive and negative instructions are intermingled, which makes them hard to sort out; the explanations of both symptoms
and first aid are long ("The victim may be unconscious" versus the 1992
"Unconsciousness"), which makes them harder to read; and calling EMS is
not mentioned.

In "What To Do in a Wilderness Medical Emergency," Dave Barry offers
a parody of this process, which might be called "Writing Bad Directions":

> Once the victim has been calmed, you need to obtain pertinent information
> by asking the following Standard Medical Questions:
>
> 1. Does he have medical insurance?
> 2. Does his spouse have medical insurance?
> 3. Was he referred to this wilderness by another doctor?
> 4. How much does he weigh? . . .
>
> Write this information down on a medical chart, then give the victim a 1986
> copy of *Fortune* magazine to read while you decide on the correct course of
> treatment.

Special Modes of Process Writing

There are many other ways to describe a process in addition to giving step-
by-step directions for how-to-do-it. Much of life, in fact, consists in learning
how to live it while we're immersed in the process of doing just that.
Sometimes writing while the experience is happening makes the ideas clear
and thereby helps both the writer and reader to understand the meaning of
a process that is still evolving. Unlike many how-to-do-it works, these special types of process writing do not lead to a completed product (assembling
a mountain bike) or a learned skill (mountain biking) or goal (ascending

Pike's Peak by mountain bike). Instead, they engage readers in the process of understanding or appreciating a process, whether abstract (drawing a picture of the essence of a room, being a good parent or child, functioning well as a college president or a farmer) or concrete (how to develop a potter's skill, how gristmills work, the rhythm of a farmer's day). Whatever specific skills these writings impart—how to make a pot or prepare comforting food for children or to do farm work—is incidental to the philosophy of life they convey—even in the self-mocking rendering of a disastrous attempt to play the saxophone ("Those record companies, I thought, You just can't keep them away"). Although some processes may be refined, some processes never end.

Process in Making Ideas Visible

Writing about the creation of an artwork or about bringing ideas to artistic reality is a very personal form of process writing that involves description of the artist/writer's thoughts, feelings, and motivations. Kathy Gorrell, a graduate student and artist, explains in "My Room" how she draws her own room: "I am not just creating my own room. I'm creating my own life. To me, both can be two ways of saying the same thing." In the paper that explores the drawing process she makes her ideas visible:

> Alone. No sounds but faint and distant ones outside. In pensive thought, I sit looking intensely into the room, making a conscious effort to mentally bring to reality the objects, surfaces, textures, colors, values as my memory will permit. I'm amazed at how much a part of this interior I have become.
>
> I walk over and take up a small piece of charcoal. Placing it on its side, I gently rub over the niche I have drawn behind the sofa, hiding it more thoroughly from the light that illuminates the rest of the room. Next to this niche is a small table on which nothing is identified—yet it all makes total sense.
>
> I am creating this room. Why do I make the choices I make? Not to inform viewers of the possessions it contains, for that would be both presumptuous and worthless. I draw to invite others into it. This room is my life and I share it with those who are obliged to see it or inhabit it. As I gaze into the room I've drawn I realize that it contains three worlds. The outside world that cannot be seen, only sensed by gazing out the windows. The world in my mind, accessible only to me. Then there is the room where I live, where others interact with me.

Then, in trying to explain her own creative process, Gorrell ponders the eternal dilemma of any artist: "Why is it that a single section is so successful, but when I approach the other challenges with the same intensity and zeal, I fall short in the end?" As with any work of art, she understands, "There are no set formulas to follow in order to obtain it. I've had to work through hours of making marks, rubbing in values, erasing it out again, to achieve this result." Then she reflects on the meaning of her process in relation to the piece of art she's working on:

> However, this little section is what makes it all worth it. The other areas become meaningful in relation to this one. When I begin, I never know how my drawing will conclude. There are so many choices. Each choice I make leads to a long list of others. I could be frustrated by this whole maddening process of being in constant flux and uncertainty.

Nevertheless, she says, if she—or any artist—knew what the end of life, of art would be, "then what would be the purpose in living it?" Even in this picture of the room

> there are many untold areas. What is around that corner? I have provided an open door, but what does that drawer contain? What is stored away in that cupboard? I choose what to expose and what to conceal. No one can open that drawer, unless of course they violate my space. They can only speculate by analyzing the parts of the room I have shown them.

What happens next, after the artist applies the "careful finishing touches"? "Shall I call it done now?" Gorrell wonders. She decides as most creators and inventors do at some point, "It is not finished, it's just time to stop so I can move on." Yes, "others will take it into their consciousness," teachers and other viewers from whom she has yet to learn new things. "I must," she concludes, "be willing to change, if necessary, for the drawing process is one of evolution. This drawing is only one view that has developed from past efforts. There will be many more." She's right. *Fait accompli*—but only for the moment.

Process in an Autobiographical Narrative Context

A compelling narrative about how to do something can provide a context that enhances both the teller and the tale. The narrative is structured, more or less, along the steps of the process, in sequence. It is told by an engaging narrator, who may or may not perform the process, but who characterizes those who do. There may be some drama in the production or completion of the process; there is always considerable color in the telling, which may be far more emotional or interpretive than conventional process writing. When the writer is deeply invested in the process, as we have seen in Kathy Gorrell's explanation of how she draws her room, the explanation may become a partial portrait of the artist—heart, soul, and mind, behavior and personality.

Consider, for instance, the work of M. F. K. Fisher, who writes elegant novels about food, and who also writes novelistically about food, elegant and plain. In "A Recipe for Happy Hens," she explains how to select a fresh egg:

An egg should be . . . SHOULD BE . . . fresh. But how is one to know the first subtle date, unless he has actually reached under warm feathers at the risk of a good protective peck and pulled out the fruit? Now, with refrigerating methods and computered chemical feeding and controlled hatching and all that, a graded government-inspected egg will remain edible for shameful lengths of time . . . and when in doubt, one can always float it gently in a bowl of water and see if it dances a little and bobs lazily toward the top.

Fisher then offers a nameless recipe involving a raw egg and a large dollop of personal philosophy:

> The quickest relationship between an egg and a man is when both are raw, the first perforce and the second from fatigue, weakness, or other hazards. . . . I used to revive my faltering offspring with a formula [seldom] printed, or perhaps never. I am afraid we never got around to naming it, but it is useful and good: a slice of dark bread, toasted or not, carefully spread with the yolk of one fresh egg and then patted generously with brown sugar and cut into little strips for little fingers. This would revive my girls as they grew, and growing is a hard job and needs plenty of encouragement. (I am past such hazards, but know that the same recipe, sprinkled generously with salt and freshly ground pepper instead of sugar, has worked timely miracles for me too. . . .)

If you wanted quick directions for how to determine the freshness of an egg, you'd probably consult a cookbook that didn't bury the process in the context of the hen on the nest and the author's views on current methods of poultry raising. But with Fisher's writing, more than half the fun is in encountering the author's original personality, which shines in every sentence and provides mosaic fragments of an autobiography. Her advice rings with the authenticity of experience; who but someone who has actually "reached under warm feathers" would be aware of the hazard of "a good protective peck"? She has enough self-confidence, as a cook and as a writer, not to give a fancy title to a plain, nourishing, nameless dish. And she has enough self-confidence to intermingle autobiography in her description of the process of making this food and feeding it to her daughters. We read this not for its efficiency or even for its recipe but for its evocative blend of style and substance, its recreation of the author and her milieu.

Process, Place, and Product

Sometimes a process and the resulting product(s) are so deeply embedded in a place and a historical context that to write about one is to write about the rest. The talents of Laura Brooks, baker, singer, student, and writer, coalesce in her essay, "Virginia Grist Mills." After identifying and describing various grist mills in Virginia, Brooks explains why they hold such fascination for her. Her identification with the subject began before she was born: "The fact that my grandfather was a miller may contribute to my inborn love

for the musical rushing of water over an overshot wheel or the noisy splash-
ing along a flume. Such steady rhythm of a grist mill is comforting to body
and spirits, no doubt therapeutic." On family vacations she not only stops
at "historic grist mill sites," but also purchases "odd flours—barley, buck-
wheat, bran, oat, dark rye, whole wheat pastry flour—by the ten and fifteen
pound bags" and freezes them "until the breadmaking urge arrives." Only
after a peroration on nineteenth-century "musical compositions that simu-
late milling themes" does Brooks explain how gristmills work:

> The stones for many early American mills were imported from Europe. Hence
> the word *buhr* for the French *buhr* stones, the costliest of all, cut in patterns
> of curved design to produce the finest flours. Later, Rhode Island granite and
> New York-Pennsylvania sandstone became highly prized for the 19th and early
> 20th century hard stones that are still dated by their straight furrowed grooves.
> An old mill can frequently be dated by the stone types and patterns which served
> as channels where heat and air passed as the stones rubbed together to grind
> the grain into flour or meal. Thus a miller's job of constantly adjusting the
> stones was a delicate one, affecting not only his reputation for a finely ground
> product, but also the very fact that his mill could go up in flames from the heat
> generated during operations. The task of "picking" the stones became a pre-
> occupation for the miller, who spent odd hours chiseling the grooves in the
> mill's stones to ensure finely ground flour.

Brooks explains that the difference between overshot and undershot mill
wheels depends "on whether the water is fed over or under the top of the
water wheel." She continues, "From the millpond or stream, a raceway or
flume controls the amount of water reaching the wheel," while a flood gate
"carries off the excess water, preventing the flume from overflowing." The
water wheel, she says, "is connected to the main gear by a rotating shaft,"
the "prized gears" being fashioned either of hard maple or oak or of metal
"handforged by 18th and 19th century blacksmiths." Then it's a straight shot
from the grinding process to the product:

> The grinding stones in old mills are connected to the series of operating gears
> by large vertical shafts; here, a turning upper stone [the "picked" stone] usu-
> ally sits on a stationary lower stone called a nether . . . Grain is fed into the
> mill through a hopper above the stones. After the grinding, the flour travels
> through the grooves between the stones and into the main chute where it is
> sorted by a sifter, separating the chaff from the fine flour. Thus the bran is sifted
> out. If the flour is used in baking, the final product is usually sifted several times.

Stone ground flour, says Brooks, buttressing her opinion with that of noted
food writer Alice Waters (including such reinforcement of one's own expertise is a good technique for anyone, novice or expert), is "far superior to
whole wheat flour ground in modern commercial mills, whose high speed
rollers generate heat that destroys vitamins and oxidizes oils present in the
whole grains that would otherwise enrich our breads." Before proceeding to

the recipes that supplement her account of the milling process, Laura concludes with:

> I encourage my readers to evoke a tie with the past that we all feel when we visit an old mill redolent with grain, foliage, sunlight against heart pine timbers, flowing water, sifting flour, and hand-forged iron. One of our natural links with history emerges through this system by which our forefathers fed themselves, bound up the power of the new world's resources, utilized industry, form, art, architecture and design, to create one of our oldest foods.

As Peter Conrad observes, "A recipe lovingly recited is also an evocation of the good life and a homage to the good earth."

Process and Portrait: Figure and Ground

Sometimes writers describe a process in great detail to focus either on the person performing it, or on the people affected by the process or the performance. The step-by-step account, the ground, in this figure-and-ground context tells the readers how-to-do-it and has its own interest and perhaps even instructional value, but that's not where the real emphasis lies. The portrait, the figure, is foregrounded. In student Craig Swanson's "The Turning Point," the portrait is the relationship between father and son interpreted against the background of pottery making.

> Dad lost his job last summer. They say that it was due to political reasons.   1
> After twenty years in the government it was a shock to us all. Dad never talked much about what he did at work, although it took up enough of his time. . . . I was impressed by his title, though he rarely seemed to enjoy himself. Just the same, it was a job. These days it's hard enough to support a family without being out of work.
>
> Apparently his co-workers felt so badly about the situation that they held   2
> a large testimonial dinner in his honor. People came from all over the east coast. I wish I could have gone. . . . It's a good feeling to know that your Dad means a lot to so many people. As a farewell present they gave Dad a potter's wheel. Dad says it's the best wheel he's ever seen, and to come from someone who's done pottery for as long as he has, that's saying a lot. . . .
>
> When I came home for Thanksgiving vacation the first thing I did was rush   3
> down to the basement to check it out. I was quite surprised. Dad had fixed the whole corner of the basement with a big table top for playing with the clay; an area set up for preparing the clay, including a plaster bat and a wedging board; the kiln Walt built for Dad one Christmas; one hundred and fifty pounds of clay; nine different glazes; hand tools for sculpting, and the brand new potter's wheel. It had a tractor seat from which you work the clay. It could be turned manually or by motor, and it offered lots of surface area, which always comes in handy. Dad was right, it was beautiful. He had already made a couple dozen pots. I couldn't wait to try it.

The next day I came down into the basement to find Dad in his old gray   4
smock preparing the clay. I love to watch Dad do art, whether it's drawing,
painting, lettering, or pottery. I stood next to him as he wedged a ball of clay
the size of a small canteloupe. He'd slice it in half on the wire and slam one
half onto the wedging board, a canvas-colored slab of plaster; then he'd slam
the other half on top of the first. He did this to get all the air bubbles out of
the clay. You put a pot with air bubbles in the kiln, the pot'll explode in the
heat and you've got yourself one heck of a mess to clean up. Dad wedged the
clay, over and over.

When he was finished he sat down, wet the wheelhead, and pressed the clay   5
right in the center of the wheel. Dad hit the accelerator and the clay started
turning. He wet his hands and leaned over the clay. Bracing his elbows on his
knees he began centering the clay. Steady right hand on the sides of the clay.
Steady left hand pushing down on the clay. Centering the clay is the toughest
part for me. The clay spins around and around and you have to shape it into
a perfectly symmetric form in the center by letting the wheel do all the moving. Your hands stay motionless until the clay is centered. It takes me ten or fifteen minutes to do this. It takes Dad two. I shake my head and smile in amazement.

Dad's hands cup the clay, thumbs together on top. He wets his hands again   6
and pushes down with his thumbs. Slowly, steadily. Once he's as far down as
he wants to go he makes the bottom of the pot by spreading his thumbs. His
hands relax and he pulls them out of the pot. Every motion is deliberate. If you
move your hands quickly or carelessly you can be sure you will have to start
again. Dad wipes the slip, very watery clay, off his hands with a sponge. It is
extremely messy.

To make the walls Dad hooks his thumbs and curls all of his fingers except   7
for his index fingers. Holding them like forceps, he reaches into the pot to mold
the walls to just the right thickness. He starts at the bottom and brings them
up slowly, making the walls of the pot thin and even all the way up, about
twelve inches.

Dad sponges off his hands, wets them, and then cups his hands around the   8
belly of the pot. Slowly, as the pot spins around, he squeezes his hands together,
causing it to bevel slightly. Dad spends five minutes on the finishing touches.
He's got himself a real nice skill.

It is a rare treat to watch Dad do something that he enjoys so much.   9

Ostensibly this is an essay about making a pot, which in fact occupies two
thirds of the text. Readers can follow the directions given here, and, with the
addition of a few more specific details (such as what Swanson's father uses
the "slip" for in paragraph 6 and what the "finishing touches" are in paragraph 8), they could probably learn how to do it. Swanson even defines unfamiliar terms such as *wedge* and *slip* when he uses them, to make sure that
readers will understand.

But the paper is about much more than potting; the process of making the
pot is the catalyst that draws Craig and his father together. The first two para-

graphs place Mr. Swanson's potting in its painful context; the potter's wheel is the consolation for the loss of his job and the potting itself is an activity in which he can engage because he has no formal claim on his time. Yet it is an activity he loves and is good at. Through Swanson's appreciation of his father's skill as a potter we recognize his respect, love, and concern for the man who performs this process so well. So we come to appreciate the pain and the pleasure as well as the process in this essay that focuses on "the turning point," epitomized in its wonderfully ambiguous title.

Process by Analogy

Analogies are so embedded in our culture and in our thinking processes that we regard them as natural and inevitable. The original, literal meanings of "grist for the mill," "open the floodgates," "separate the wheat from the chaff," even "millstone," which most contemporary readers understand only as analogies, are reinvigorated by Laura Brooks's essay on "Virginia Grist Mills."

The more abstract or unfamiliar the process, the more readers depend on analogies with what they know to help them understand what they don't. Writing for an audience of *New York Times* readers, Shirley Strum Kenny explains how she does her job as president of Queens College of the City University of New York, work that is difficult to interpret because of its breadth, depth, complexity, changeability, and vagueness. Parenthood, she says, was excellent career preparation. By using familiar key words that apply to both parenting and the presidency, Kenny's explanation of how she functioned as a parent allows the readers to make the implicit analogy between the two jobs. Thus the college presidency becomes far more understandable to readers, if no more manageable to the writer.

> *Time Management:* Drag out of bed, get kids up, make breakfast and [seven] school lunches . . . drive noisy children's car pool . . . teach, hold office hours . . . sit on committee du jour . . . fix dinner, supervise homework and lesson practice . . . tuck little ones in, tuck little ones in again, kiss them again, and again, drag out briefcase, grade papers or get back to research, stumble to bed in the wee hours . . . sleep a little. Start over.
>
> *Negotiation Skills:* Living with five teen-agers.
>
> *Endurance:* Surviving five teen-agers.
>
> *Controlled Emotions:* Learned mostly in hospitals. Or during midnight calls. Or lying [in bed] and waiting for the sound of a car coming up the driveway much too late.
>
> *Paperwork:* Administration . . . is a lot like housekeeping—one big general chore that consists of hundreds of little ones. If you don't keep after it every day it gets ahead of you. You're never finished; every day brings more of the same and then some: none of it very important in the abstract; all of it important in the concrete. . . .

> *Creativity:* Motherhood is the necessity of invention.
> *Tact and diplomacy:* Meeting Sarah's high school boyfriends.

Kenny continues with poise, immunity to embarrassment, organizational skills, delegation of authority, financial management, "communication skills, marketing skills, salesmanship, the art of persuasion and the ability to meet emergencies with a degree of sanity." Most importantly, Kenny says, "Family life gives you perspective. . . . You have to keep the big picture in mind while paying attention to details. And you have to make snap value judgments when dealing with competing needs." This list of characteristics also identifies the essential elements of the parenting process, a process in which the items are employed not in sequence, but as they are needed—a given issue on a given day may involve several or all. Kenny doesn't try to sort out the elements or identify a hierarchy. It's necessary to have all of them at the ready all the time if the family/college are to function well and if family/college members, including the mother/president, are to experience the process with effectiveness and enjoyment.

Process as Philosophy of Life

Most interpretive accounts of a process embed the author's philosophy in the process they explain or describe. There's a right way and a wrong way to do something, there are ways better and worse, elegant and clumsy, easier and more difficult. Some ways to work, to live are more satisfying than others, physically, intellectually, morally. Each account of a process that is satisfying to the author gives witness to the process's efficacy and argues implicit or explicit for its adoption.

Student Raymond Williams's "Farming" is such an account. To readers unfamiliar with the occupation, he explains what a typical day of summer farming is like, comparing it directly and indirectly with a typical day at college, where "my classes began at nine o'clock and ended at noon. For the rest of the day I was free to play, to study, or to socialize." In the course of interpreting the process, he justifies a way of life and expresses his own philosophy of how that life should be led.

> But at the farm, by nine o'clock, I have already bottle fed three calves, poured milk into buckets for six more, given grain and water to ten, and carried six bales and three fifty pound bags of feed to twenty young heifers. At noon all work stops, and I eat with the other workers; unlike at college, our day has just begun.
>
> After lunch we drive to the hay field where the alfalfa lies in windrows waiting for the baler to rake it up and compact it into tight seventy-pound bales. One person can handle the baling; it takes four to load and unload the hay

efficiently. Chris, by virtue of being the youngest and of being allergic to hay, drives the truck. Fred, the herdsman, and Vern, the farmer's oldest son, load the bales onto the truck, and I stack.

Stacking involves more than just setting one bale on top of another, for each layer must cross-tie the layer below, or when the truck hits a bump or goes uphill, the stack comes apart and spills hay to the ground. The first few layers are easy, but once the stack becomes taller than chest high, the job becomes more difficult. I heave two or three bales on top of the stack before climbing up to arrange them; once on top of the hay, I maintain a precarious balance as the truck jerks along traveling up and down the slopes of the field. Once I arrange the bales, I jump down to the truck bed, throw more bales to the top and begin the cycle again. This process continues until I have stacked one hundred and twenty-five bales in six layers.

Then Fred and Vern climb on the truck, and we take the hay to the barn to unload it. There is perhaps only one job which farmers hate worse than loading hay, and that is unloading it. The temperature in the barn is at least one hundred degrees, and dust fills the air; loud sneezes echo through the barn along with our grunts as we hurl each bale from one level to the next, until finally it is placed at the top of the stack, some thirty feet high. When Fred shoves the final bale into place, we all collapse for a short break; Chris hands us the water jug, and after the last person gulps his share, we reluctantly climb into the truck and return to the field.

One trip takes an hour and fifteen minutes, and today we make six trips. After four, we stop for supper and I am ready to quit. My shirt drenched with sweat, my arms green from the hay which has stuck to them, and my pants filled with scratchy hay particles, I desire a shower and sleep. But two hundred bales remain in the field, and the weather threatens rain, so sleep must wait. We gather the fifth load in the twilight, and we finish the final load by moonlight.

. . . I wonder why I choose to spend my summers working on a farm. Other jobs pay more and require fewer hours. . . . [But] carrying feed bags, throwing hay bales, hammering nails, and halter breaking heifers increases my muscle tone and the efficiency of my cardio-vascular system by one hundred percent of what they are during the school year. I enjoy the exertion, the sweat, and the sense of tiredness which a day of work brings. . . .

But the value and the appeal of farm work go beyond the physical benefits and the variety of tasks, for farming is conducive to reflection, and it offers experiences which college often fails to provide. Much of college centers around competition . . . for grades, for honors. . . . On the farm, cooperation replaces competition; the farmers help each other pick up hay, loan each other equipment. . . . [Moreover] the farmer must learn to cooperate with nature . . . which, even with numerous technological mechanisms, can be only partially controlled at best. Although veterinary medicine has improved greatly, animals still die with regularity. In one week I hauled away two calves which failed to respond to treatment that followed the prescribed steps perfectly. But on the farm prescribed steps do not always lead to their designated end. . . .

Working on a farm is valuable, because it allows me to feel and to experience rather than to think and to discuss. Although farming offers much time to think (one of the advantages of picking up hay is that it engages the muscles but not the mind), thought is tempered by experience in a way which college does not offer. This valuable function more than compensates for the long hours of hard work and the moderate pay of farm life; my true reward comes from my increased sense of the richness of life and of my place within that life.

Williams is not writing about farming to tell readers how to do it, but to explain to his readers and to articulate for himself why he does it. In this respect his essay is closer to Annie Dillard's reflections on nature and humanity's place in the universe (see page 126) than it is to conventional process writing. Yet his interpretation does provide an articulate analysis of what a farmer's life is like—body, mind, and soul. Williams is so thoughtful, so appreciative of the many benefits of farming while candidly acknowledging its limitations, that he makes readers want to experience farming for themselves. As with many well-written accounts of a process, to read about the process is to want to participate in it—even if you never contemplated it before. The integrity of Williams's understated narration reinforces the integrity of the way of life he explains.

Process as Parody

Almost any process, even lifesaving, can be parodied, as Dave Barry shows us (226). Although a parody may illustrate one or more possible methods of how-*not*-to-do it, we read parodies not for (mis)information, but for humor. Parodying one's own performance of a process is a particularly engaging sort of humor in which writers present themselves as the butt of their own jokes, evoking readers' sympathy along with laughter at the innocent, the klutz, the self-deluded, the vain, the pompous, the prideful, or whatever comic character they depict. This technique works especially well if the writer shares shortcomings with the readers early in the piece so that both writer and audience know they're laughing at the same flaws which cause the process to go astray.

In "Playing the Sax," student Ken Wunderlich presents himself as an egotistical character who believes he can "become a virtuoso overnight" through mastery of a single note or two. He borrows a friend's saxophone for the weekend to master the gentle art, "counting heavily on the fact that I once read a book about Charlie Parker, the legendary jazz saxophonist" to provide the necessary background.

I ran into some problems just setting up. For one thing, a tenor sax is too big to sit properly in your lap, so if you sit down and try to play it the mouthpiece ends up in your eyes. Also, all the reeds were either the wrong size or broken. I used one of the wrong size reeds, thus denying myself the sheer pleasure of splinters in my mouth. My final difficulty was the fact that my hands did not know where to go by themselves, as I had hoped they would. A piano is different: since a piano has eighty-eight keys, no one can begin to try to cover them all. But the way they put the sax together, it looks as if you ought to be able to push all the buttons down at once. It was a frustrating experience to seat my hands comfortably yet cover the necessary holes. Once I arrived at something feasible, I squatted on the floor to keep the oversized reed out of my eyes and got ready to play my first note. But my debut was delayed by a knock on the door [of my dorm room].

Those record companies, I thought. You just can't keep them away. The minute they hear about new and rising talent they hound you no end. But it was only Kevin. Kevin made a few ill-mannered queries about what in the world I thought I was doing, but I silenced him with my first note.

. . . I pranced up and down the hall playing note after note, all of which sounded pretty much the same, since I didn't know how to change notes just yet. Then I went back into my room and practiced my note for fifteen or twenty minutes, while Kevin sat sick with envy at my musical proficiency.

Checklist for Writing How-To Works

1. Do I understand the process I'm writing about well enough to explain it to others? Is my knowledge firsthand? derivative? up-to-date?

2. Who is my intended audience? people unfamiliar or familiar with the general subject area? with the specific process I'm discussing?

3. Is the purpose or objective of the process clear and stated at the outset?

4. How long can my explanation be? How much can I include? history, theory, philosophy of the subject? alternative methods? only the essentials?

5. Do I include all the crucial steps in the process? Do I explain them, clearly and unambiguously?

6. Do I explain all the essential terms, special equipment, concepts, and/or subprocesses at the appropriate places in the overall organization? Do I need to?

7. Do I need to use simpler, more precise, or more consistent language in my explanations?

8. Do I need to simplify instructions that are too complicated for my intended audience to understand?

9. Will a typical reader be able to follow my directions successfully? with relative ease?

10. Is my tone consistently positive and reassuring? Should it be?

A Selected Reference List of Writings About Processes

See also "Works Cited."

Cooking

Brody, Jane. *Jane Brody's Good Food Book: Living the High Carbohydrate Way.* New York: Norton, 1985.

Rombauer, Irma S., and Marion Rombauer Becker. *The Joy of Cooking.* Rev. ed. New York: Macmillan, 1985.

Etiquette

Martin, Judith. *Miss Manners' Guide to Excruciatingly Correct Behavior.* 1982. New York: Warner, 1988.

Finding a Job

Bolles, Richard Nelson. *The 1994 What Color Is Your Parachute: A Practical Manual for Job-Hunters and Career Changers.* Berkeley, CA: Ten-Speed, 1994.

Health and Fitness

Herbert, Victor, Ed. *The Mount Sinai School of Medicine Complete Book of Nutrition.* New York: St. Martin's, 1990.

Simmons, Richard. *Reach for Fitness: A Special Book of Exercises for the Physically Challenged.* New York: Warner, 1986.

Independence, Power, and Status

Corey, Stephen R. *The Seven Habits of Highly Effective People.* 1989. New York: Simon, 1990.

Dyer, Wayne. *Pulling Your Own Strings: Dynamic Techniques for Dealing with Other People and Living Life as You Choose.* 1979. New York: Harper, 1991.

Money

Porter, Sylvia. *Sylvia Porter's Your Finances in the 1990's.* New York: Prentice, 1990.

Parenting

Spock, Benjamin, and Michael B. Rothenberg. *Dr. Spock's Baby and Child Care.* 6th rev. ed. New York: Dutton, 1992.

Works Cited

American National Red Cross. *Standard First Aid & Personal Safety.* Garden City: Doubleday, 1973. 167–68.

American Red Cross Staff and Kathleen A. Handal. *American Red Cross First Aid and Safety Handbook.* New York: Little, 1992. 155–59.

Barry, Dave. *Dave Barry's Only Travel Guide You'll Ever Need.* New York: Fawcett, 1991. 164.

Bloom, Lynn Z. *Doctor Spock: Biography of a Conservative Radical.* New York: Bobbs, 1972. 113.

Conrad, Peter, "Arcadia: Last of the Head Trips," *New York Times Book Review* 6 June 1993: 11.

Dreyfus, Hubert, and Stuart Dreyfus. *Mind Over Machine: The Power of Human Interaction and Expertise in the Era of the Computer.* New York: Free, 1986.

Fisher, M. F. K. "A Recipe for Happy Hens." *With Bold Knife and Fork.* New York: Paragon, 1969. 111–12.

Fixx, James E. *The Complete Book of Running.* New York: Random, 1977. 85–87.

Grimm, Tom, and Michele Grimm. *The Good Guide for Bad Photographers.* New York: NAL, 1982. 55.

Half, Robert. *The Robert Half Way to Get Hired in Today's Job Market.* 1981. New York: Bantam, 1983. ix, 46–58.

Kenny, Shirley Strum. "From Parenting, a Presidency." *New York Times* 3 Nov. 1991, Education: 46.

LaBier, Douglas. "You & Your Analyst." *Washington Post* 28 June 1983: C5.

"Nutritious Pack Snack." *The Artist in the Kitchen.* Ed. Bebe Scott and Ann Maritz. St. Louis: The St. Louis Art Museum, 1977. 243.

Quinn, Jane Bryant. *Making the Most of Your Money: Smart Ways to Create Wealth and Plan Your Finances in the '90s.* New York: Simon, 1991. 21.

Sucher, Harry V. *Simplified Boatbuilding: The Flat-Bottom Boat.* New York: Norton, 1973. 213.

Wiener, Harvey S. *Total Swimming: How the Perfect Exercise Can Offer Rewards Both to the Body and the Inner Self.* New York: Simon, 1980. 20, 310, 324.

9

WRITING ABOUT SCIENCE

The important thing is not to stop questioning. Curiosity has its own reason for existing. One cannot help but be in awe when he contemplates the mysteries of eternity, of life, of the marvelous structure of reality. It is enough if one tries merely to comprehend a little of this mystery every day. Never lose a holy curiosity.

— ALBERT EINSTEIN

The most important factor [in invention] . . . is whether or not you could look at something and wonder, What makes it work? Could I make it better? Inventing takes curiosity; it takes drive; it takes an inability to be discouraged. An inventor is the kind of person who really doesn't get interested in a problem until it looks impossible.

— WILSON GREATBACH

[Because] 'perfection of the life and perfection of the work are irreconcilable,' I live and work in praise of imperfection.

— RITA LEVI-MONTALCINI

If you can't put it into English it means you don't understand it yourself.

— JERROLD ZACHARIAS

The Nature of Science Writing

Jerrold Zacharias's observation, "If you can't put it into English it means you don't understand it yourself," is especially true of writing on scientific subjects. Your main task as a writer about phenomena, concepts, and processes unfamiliar to your readers is to put them into English—to make others clearly see their nature. You will of course interpret your subject, to make others see it your way.

Although our culture is generally curious about what things are, how they work, and why they work, most Americans don't know much about the phenomena of science and technology. Americans rely on experts or interpreters to explain unfamiliar scientific and technical processes and phenomena of the physical, natural, and social sciences. As a researcher, a writer, a student, or an employee, you may have the need—or the desire—to provide scientific explanations for general readers or for a more specialized audience.

Subjects of Science Writing

Things.   You can discuss what water is—generally or more specifically, such as oceans (*The Sea Around Us*), acid rain (*Acid Rain: A Plague Upon the Waters*), or clouds (*International Cloud Album for Observers in Aircraft*). You can discuss what an animal is (*The Animal Kingdom*). Or, you can focus on a given genus, species, or variety of insect ("The Habits of 17-Year Periodical Cicadas"), amphibian (*The Case of the Midwife Toad*), mammal (*Of Wolves and Men*), or human (*The Human Animal*).

Phenomena.   Some phenomena are physical (*Child Growth*), physiological (*Stress*, "Alcohol: The Neutral Spirit"), social (*On Aggression, Coming of Age in Samoa*), psychological (*Forms of Ethical Development in the College Years*), or economic (*The Wealth of Nations, The Theory of the Leisure Class*).

Concepts and theories.   Some compelling considerations include aging (*Why Survive? Being Old in America*), language (*You Just Don't Understand: Women and Men in Conversation*), intelligence (*The Mismeasure of Man*), mathematics (*Principia Mathematica*), quantum mechanics (*The Dancing Wu Li Masters*), and time (*A Brief History of Time: From the Big Bang to Black Holes*).

Processes.   You may write about the process of evolution (*The Origin of Species, The Evolution of Useful Things*), the process of discovery (*The Double Helix: A Personal Account of the Discovery of the Structure of DNA, In Praise of Imperfection*), the process of exploration (*The Northwest Passage*), or the process of change (*The Structure of Scientific Revolutions*).

A thorough piece of science writing may include all of these categories—things, phenomena, concepts, theories, and processes.

Purposes of Science Writing

Whether you're discussing your own work or explaining the research of others, as a writer your fundamental question will be *What do I want to tell my readers about this discovery, invention, research, or scientific process?* In answering this basic question you'll focus on some of the following:

What is it?   Your focus may be a definition, a description, or an analysis.

How was it formed, created, or discovered?   Your focus may be process or narration.

How does it work?   Or, why did it fail to work? Your focus may be on process analysis.

Why is my version or variation of this subject better than other versions? What needs to be done to improve either my version or the existing state of the art? Your focus could be on analysis, comparison and contrast, or argument.

In what ways do scientists think about this subject or do work in this area? You may focus on process analysis or comparison and contrast.

What controversy exists concerning this subject?   Your focus could be a definition, an analysis, comparison and contrast, or an argument.

Why is my interpretation "right"?   You may focus on argument, buttressed by definition, description, or analysis.

Indeed, any or all of your answers to these questions could be considered an argument in favor of your point of view. How you answer these questions will depend on why you and your readers are interested in the subject and how much you know about it.

Audience of Science Writing

The readers of science writing are as diverse as its subjects. Although you can assume that most readers want to know about the subject, you'll need to identify other characteristics of your audience to make sure you write on a level that they can understand without writing down to them. You may find it helpful to ask the questions that follow.

What do my intended readers already know about the subject?   Perhaps they're innocents who, like James Thurber's grandmother, imagine that electricity is "dripping invisibly all over the house" from the wall sockets. At the other end of the continuum they may be highly specialized, making research contributions of their own to the field. Your readers may be anywhere along this continuum from novice to expert. You will need to adapt your presentation not only to what they know, but also to how they think about the subject.

Do I know as much as about the subject as my audience does?   You'll want to be at or above their level of knowledge. If you're writing as a student for a teacher, either shift to a subject you know better or to a less sophisticated audience.

Why do my readers want to know what I'm telling them?   Do they want to learn about the subject for its own sake, because, like the Himalaya Mountains, it's there? Do they want to learn about the subject because it is of current interest or because of a current controversy? Do they want to apply the knowledge to their professional work, hobby, special interest, or everyday life? Or do they want to satisfy the curiosity that your compelling lead, your other writings, or your reputation has aroused in them, even though they may not be particularly interested in the subject?

The Science Writer's Authority and Assumptions

If total, up-to-the-minute knowledge of a scientific subject were a prerequisite to writing on it, pens, typewriters, and word processors all over the world would whimper to a halt. The fact that scientific information is proliferating astronomically (in some medical and technical fields at the rate of more than 10,000 publications a month), implies that no one, however well-informed, can be familiar with more than a fraction of the material available. Fortunately, as a writer you're only responsible for a small segment of this expanding universe. Your training will lead you to the central research in a limited area; your interests will dictate still more specialized investigations in the laboratory, in life, and in the relevant professional literature. Over time, you should feel both comfortable and competent in the basic research in your specialty.

In general, the more you know about a subject the better qualified you are to write on it. For your purposes as a writer, you should know enough about your subject to write on it with sufficient authority to accommodate your intended readers' assumed level of knowledge, their expectations, and the writing's proposed length.

You'll probably write on scientific subjects from one of the perspectives that follow.

- student, undergraduate or graduate
- hobbyist (This does not connote a particular level of sophistication; it merely means you don't make your living from your hobby. Emperor Hirohito of Japan, for instance, is known in international scientific circles for his research in marine biology.)
- journalist, experienced or in training
- basic researcher, either the principal investigator or a member of an investigating team
- applied scientist, who uses the findings of basic research in the clinic, community, or other professional work

Dimensions to Consider

You'll need to know the major dimensions of the scientific or technical area you're discussing in a paper or longer work, no matter which perspective you hold or how naive or knowledgeable your audience is. These dimensions to consider follow.

Basic concepts.   Several basic concepts to address follow, each accompanied by a few examples.

- Commonly accepted definitions of fundamental terms (such as gravity, specific gravity, basal metabolism, molecular biology)
- Fundamental principles of the subject area (such as immune response, molecular orbital)
- Values and norms taken for granted by researchers in this field (such as parsimony, replicability)

Major and minor issues.

- What are these issues? (Is language a uniquely human phenomenon? If it is, then why can chimps be trained to "talk"? Or are they not really talking but just making conditioned responses to external cues and stimuli?)
- Agreements and disagreements over issues, principles. (Who agrees or disagrees? Over what? Why?)
- Historical issues. (Is the universe geocentric or heliocentric? Does the creationist, the evolutionist, or the big bang theory best explain the formation of the earth? Does evolution move in abrupt fits and starts or proceed gradually and progressively over time?)
- Current issues. (Is linguistic structure innate or learned through imitation and reinforcement? Is psychoanalysis, behavior modification, chemical

means, i.e., medication, or some combination of these methods the best way to treat neurotic behavior?)

Customary research designs, methods, and techniques.   Consider what these are in your field, and identify the advantages and disadvantages of each. Some common research designs in the social sciences, such as psychology and anthropology, include experimental/control group designs, surveys, single subject or case studies, and cross-sectional or longitudinal studies.

Interpretation of research results.   Interpretation of most facts, phenomena, statistics, graphs, and other collections of data is necessary for all readers. An I.Q. score of 110, a body temperature of 96.2 °F, an airspeed of Mach 1.5 mean nothing in the abstract; either writers or readers (or both) have to supply enough information to interpret the figures so they can assess the significance of each, preferably in a particular context, rather than in the abstract. To aid in interpretation you need to be able to answer the following questions.

- Under what conditions was the research conducted? How did these affect the results?
- With what other phenomena do these findings have to be linked in order to be intelligible?
- Is the research replicable? Why or why not?
- Does the research test/measure/study what it purports to? (i.e., Is it valid?) Does it do so with consistent (reliable) instruments?
- Are there other possible interpretations or explanations of the same phenomena or evidence? If so, what are they? Do they come from other researchers' work or your own? Are these equally reliable or valid? Why or why not?

How up-to-date is your knowledge?   If you write as an experienced scientist, which is a possibility for advanced students with research experience as well as for their mentors, you will also need to write from firsthand experience about the contributions you have made to the field in any of the following areas:

- theory
- research methodology or techniques
- basic research, discovering new information, material
- application of another's theory or basic research
- interpreting your own or others' research data
- making your findings (or another's) accessible to other scientists or to the general public

Writing for a General Audience

As a student, a hobbyist, or even an astute reader of scientific writing, you can learn most of what you need to know to write for a general audience. When you write for general readers, it helps to structure your writing as an inverted pyramid. Your writing will be clearest if you begin with the basics, even at the risk of repeating common information, which readers may have forgotten. Start with the single most essential piece of information that is fundamental to understanding the rest, and explain it in as much detail as you need to before introducing the second most essential piece of information. And so on. Gradually you'll build a foundation to help readers gain access to the higher reaches of the subject, its newer, more theoretical, more complicated, or more speculative implications. In the first two paragraphs of "Acid Rain," junior Kelly Shea, an English and biology major, demonstrates her knowledge of the fundamentals of the subject as well as an admirable ability to interpret a scientific phenomenon for a general audience. First, she defines the term, using a general chemistry textbook as her source.

At the outset, Shea clarifies a common misconception.

Although acid precipitation includes snow, hail, sleet, water vapor, mist, and even dew, it is often termed simply, "acid rain." Describing the "acid" portion of the phrase is more complicated. A general chemistry textbook defines an acid as a substance dissolved in water producing a solution of pH less than seven. So what does pH mean? The pH scale is one which describes the concentration of hydrogen ions in a substance. The more ions, the more "acid"; the less ions the more "basic." A lower pH value indicates high acidity, while a higher pH indicates high alkalinity (basicity). The pH scale goes from one to fourteen. One is highly acidic, fourteen is highly basic, and seven is neutral (neither acidic nor basic)—the ions are in balance.

Popular science writers often use rhetorical questions, and then answer them right away.

In the course of defining the central term, Shea includes a sub-definition, the following four sentences.

Shea assumes that even lay readers will have a general notion of acids and bases.

Normal precipitation has an average pH of 5.6, already on the acidic side of the scale, but not dangerously so. The various "rained on" substrates can handle this slight acidity, mainly because they possess a "buffering capacity." That is, they contain enough of certain materials which can, in effect, combine with the acids to produce harmless substances, and thus decrease the acidity. They buffer the medium (lake, soil, even a statue) against the acid by neutralizing the effects it can have.

Shea offers a general explanation of buffering, with some specific illustrations.

This information is so generally known that it's not necessary to identify the particular source.

Shea devotes the first third of her paper (most of it quoted above) to explaining the phenomenon of acid rain. This explanation becomes the basis for a comparison between the buffering that occurs with rain of "normal" acidity and the more devastating effects of acid rain, which are discussed in the next third of the paper. The last third of the paper contains an analysis of the causes of acid rain, the projection of more devastating long-term consequences, and an examination of possible solutions.

> Thus, an initially local problem [air pollution] has become a devastating phenomenon of global significance. Reports of ever-decreasing pH levels of rain come from all over the world. For example, a 1974 Scotland storm produced a rain of pH 2.4, the same pH as vinegar. And as the pH decreases, the deleterious effects increase.
>
> The most urgent question now is: What can we do about the problem? Devices called scrubbers have been installed in some smokestacks. . . .

Here Shea identifies a general phenomenon followed by a specific example. Although Shea could have cited the source of this information, it's not obligatory to do so in writing for a general audience. She then interprets the effect of decreasing pH. Indeed, throughout the essay, Shea is constantly interpreting (scrubbers, she explains, "are units which can trap most of the sulfur oxides and prevent their atmospheric getaway"). Thus an essay that explains one phenomenon, acid rain, involves explanations of other, related phenomena, including pH, excessive pH, buffers, and scrubbers. It includes comparison and contrast (of acid and not-very-acid rain), and it ends with an argument advocating cleaner air. Our world, she says,

> is slowly and silently falling apart and one day, when we do notice and wish we had done something about it sooner, it will be too late. We'll have lost much of the beauty, history, and integrity of nature and of man's creativity.

General readers may not have sufficient background to know or care how much the writer knows about the subject. If they themselves lack a research background or a knowledge of new discoveries or current controversies in the field, they may have no way of telling whether or not the writer is authoritative. So if they read for an overview or from casual interest, as long as the writing sounds credible, they'll probably take it at face value. Shea's paper on acid rain is credible because of its specificity and thoroughness.

In "A Fear of Pheromones," cancer researcher Lewis Thomas, M.D., uses a variety of literary techniques common to popular science writing to explain what pheromones do. He writes so that even readers with no scientific background can understand him:

> Most of the known pheromones are small, simple molecules, active in extremely small concentrations. Eight or ten carbon atoms in a chain are all that are needed to generate precise, unequivocal directions about all kinds of matters—when and where to cluster in crowds, when to disperse, how to behave to the opposite sex, how to ascertain what *is* the opposite sex, . . . how to mark our exact boundaries of real estate, and how to establish that one is, be-

yond argument, one's self. Trails can be laid and followed, antagonists frightened and confused, friends attracted and enchanted.

The messages are urgent, but they may arrive, for all we know, in a fragrance of ambiguity. "At home, 4 P.M. today," says the female moth, and releases a brief explosion of bombykol, a single molecule of which will tremble the hairs of any male within miles and send him driving upwind in a confusion of ardor. But it is doubtful if he has an awareness of being caught in an aerosol of chemical attractant. On the contrary he probably finds suddenly that it has become an excellent day, the weather remarkably bracing, the time appropriate for a bit of exercise of the old wings, a brisk turn upwind. En route, traveling the gradient of bombykol, he notes the presence of other males, heading in the same direction, all in a good mood, inclined to race for the sheer sport of it. Then, when he reaches his destination, it may seem to him the most extraordinary of coincidences, the greatest piece of luck: "Bless my soul, what have we here!"

In this essay, Thomas uses many literary techniques.

- Nontechnical vocabulary. Except for *bombykol,* every word is familiar.
- Simple explanations that readers recognize from their own experience or general knowledge. ("Trails can be laid and followed, antagonists frightened and confused.")
- Abundant illustrations. Ten short, examples indicate what kinds of "precise, unequivocal directions" pheromones provide, with one, "how to behave to the opposite sex," expanded into a lengthy paragraph about the male moth's sportive race toward the female.
- Explanations of nonhuman phenomena in human terms. ("Friends attracted and enchanted." Thus Thomas explains the moths' behavior, including the female who extends the invitation, "At home, 4 P.M. today"; the eager male, encouraged by this attractant to take some "exercise of the old wings," and "a brisk turn upwind"; and his extraordinarily good-humored companions "inclined to race for the sheer sport of it.")

Such anthropomorphic writing is risky. Done with less skill and wit, the attribution of language and human motives or perspective to nonhumans becomes cute or sentimental. This is known as the pathetic fallacy. It is usually unconvincing: "The skies wept, and the trees bowed down their heads as the dog, crying piteously, allowed the gentle earth to swallow up not only his mistress but also himself."

Writing for a Professional Audience

To maintain your credibility if you write for specialists, you'll need to know as much or more about the subject as they do. Only with this basis of knowledge will you be able to go beyond what is already known to make an original contribution however large or small, to the field. And unless you're writing a bibliography or a review of the existing literature, you have an obligation to say something new to an audience of specialists. Why should they bother reading what they already know? Any why should you tread again over familiar ground? That way lies weariness. If you know the field, whether it be astrophysics, color chemistry, or marine biology, you're probably well aware of the extent of your knowledge and limitations. You can check this by reading someone else's professional writing on the subject. If you understand it, you can probably write for your peers. If you don't, either the piece is poorly written or you need to learn more about the subject— or both. A common format for writing scientific papers and reports for a professional audience is described on pages 259–64.

The exception to this is writing for specialists who are your teachers. Unless you're writing a scientific or other research paper for an honors thesis, a doctoral dissertation, or other independent research, most teachers will not expect your knowledge to surpass theirs. Chances are that if you understand the major research in your subject and can synthesize, analyze, or critique the ideas sensibly, that will be sufficient for a course paper even if you don't contribute anything original. For instance, although Laird Bloom's biology term paper, "Methods of Pest Control Using Insect Pheromones," is essentially a synthesis of research presented in the professional literature and represents no original experimentation, it is a clear, accurate, articulate discussion of the issues, as the following excerpt indicates:

> The object of agricultural pest control is to minimize crop damage caused by insects, and this is usually achieved by reducing the insect population to a level where the damage is "economically acceptable"—less than one percent of the total crop (Siddall and Olsen, 1976). The two strategies employed to do this with pheromones alone are the direct elimination of the insect, through killing or physically removing it, and the prevention of reproduction (Shorey, 1977); other systems which combine pheromones and conventional control methods are also being investigated.
>
> The advantages of using pheromones are manifold. First, they are selective for one or a few closely-related species and presumably do not affect other species sharing the same range. Second, they are biodegradable. Third, they appear to be nontoxic. Finally and most importantly, they prompt *specific* patterns of behavior, and so calculated use of pheromones can in theory be used to manipulate species to man's advantage (Wood, 1977).

Bloom must draw on outside authorities for all of his information. He does not claim to be an expert; the instructor doesn't expect him, as an undergraduate, to present firsthand information on a subject that has required years of experimentation. His presentation is logical, well-organized, assured, and competent, with appropriate documentation for each instance where he consulted outside authorities. Because he's writing for a scientifically trained reader he doesn't have to use explanations as elementary as those in Thomas's "Fear of Pheromones," and it would be unseemly to anthropomorphize his subject, as Thomas did with the courting moths.

Experienced scientists can apply very sophisticated knowledge and research techniques to interpretations of others' research for a mixed audience of specialists and nonspecialists, as well. For instance, Edward T. Hall's *The Silent Language* is an enduring anthropological analysis of the powerful and pervasive elements of nonverbal communication, particularly the phenomena of space ("Beggars have beats, as do the policemen who try to get them to leave") and time (Americans consider "time a commodity. It can be bought, sold, saved, spent, wasted, lost, made up, and measured"). Although anthropologist Hall is writing for a general audience a book that he says "represents the cultural analogue of a musical primer," his comparative analysis of diverse animal and human cultures has proven of considerable significance to scientists as well as to general readers throughout the past thirty-five years. For instance, in the following excerpt, Hall explains one of the fundamental beliefs that pervades many of his analyses:

> Years of study have convinced me that the real job is not to understand foreign culture but to understand our own. I am also convinced that all that one ever gets from studying foreign culture [Hall has done fieldwork among the Hopi, Navajo, Hispanic-Americans, and the Trukese] is a token understanding. The ultimate reason for such study is to learn more about how one's own system works.

In *The Mismeasure of Man,* Harvard geologist and historian of science Stephen Jay Gould applies many scientific concepts in a highly critical examination of two centuries of what he considers misguided attempts by scientists, pseudoscientists, and their disciples to classify people according to their intelligence "through craniometry [measurement of skulls] and certain styles of psychological testing." Like other critics of others' work, Gould has the double obligation of proving why the others are wrong and why he is right. This he does with admirable methodology, care, and thoroughness; his manner of analysis provides an admirable model for researchers and for writers. The result of his complex but readable analysis is consequently of interest, as is Hall's work, to scientists and lay readers alike. For instance, Gould claims that through careful skull measurements, French anthropologist and surgeon Paul Broca (1824–1880) reinforced the views of other white male researchers:

> In general, the brain is larger in mature adults than in the elderly, in men than in women, in eminent men than in men of mediocre talent, in superior races than in inferior races. [Through Broca's manipulation of data, eminent Frenchmen were found to be superior to eminent Germans!]. . . Other things equal, there is a remarkable relationship between the development of intelligence and the volume of the brain.

Gould meticulously replicated Broca's research, remeasuring the very skulls Broca used, and concludes,

> . . . one cannot read Broca without gaining enormous respect for his care in generating data. I believe his numbers and doubt that any better have ever been obtained. . . . I spent a month reading all of Broca's major work, concentrating on his statistical procedures. [Despite his numerical accuracy, Broca] traversed the gap between fact and conclusion by what may be the usual route—predominantly in reverse. Conclusions came first and Broca's conclusions were the shared assumptions of most successful white males during his time—themselves on top by the good fortune of nature, and women, blacks, and poor people below. His facts were reliable . . . , but they were gathered selectively and then manipulated unconsciously in the service of prior conclusions. By this route, the conclusions achieved not only the blessing of science, but the prestige of numbers. Broca and his school used facts as illustrations, not as constraining documents. They began with conclusions, peered through their facts, and came back in a circle to the same conclusions. . . . they reflected their prejudices by another, and probably more common route: advocacy masquerading as objectivity.

Gould demonstrates how *a priori* conclusions led Broca to discard brain size as a criterion of intelligence in some cases where the evidence didn't support the thesis. Otherwise, Eskimos, Lapps, Malays, Tartars, and other Mongolian peoples "'would surpass the most civilized people of Europe. A lowly race may therefore have a big brain.'" But when the evidence supported his thesis, Broca used it. Thus he measured the brains of small people, including pygmies and old women, whom he had in advance determined to be less intelligent. This enabled Broca to conclude that small brains nonetheless "'belong exclusively to people of low intelligence.'" When Gould reanalyzed Broca's data according to multiple regression techniques that enabled him to assess the influence of height and age, the essential differences disappeared, including that of gender.

Important Characteristics of Science Writing

Definitions

No matter how naive or sophisticated your readers are, you'll need to make sure they understand each new term and concept at the time you introduce it. What *new* means will vary according to your readers' levels of expertise. If you're writing for a general readership, you'll probably be safest if you honor the unflattering journalistic assumption, "The readers know nothing." So that laypersons can understand, define every basic term in specific language. It won't help to make the definition more complicated than the term, as does lexicographer Samuel Johnson's famed definition of net: "Anything made with interstitial vacuities." If your readers are more knowledgeable than rank beginners, you'll still need to define new terms or familiar terms that you're using in a new or special sense.

There are a number of basic principles of definition that you can use in science writing. Some common ones are identified here; others are illustrated in the excerpt from Isaac Asimov's explanation of lasers, "Let There Be a New Light," that concludes this section (page 255).

Use synonyms for the subject.   In *The Dragons of Eden,* astronomer Carl Sagan uses two synonyms and dispels a common misconception (definition by negation) in defining "American sign language, known by its acronym Ameslan, and sometimes as 'American deaf and dumb language' (the 'dumb' refers, of course, to the inability to speak and not to any failure of intelligence)."

Identify the subject's components and/or structures.   Such definitions are common in chemistry and related fields; they could in some instances be considered capsule descriptions. In 1978, in a definition quite different from Sagan's, linguists Victoria Fromkin and Robert Rodman defined Ameslan as "a sign language of the deaf, which utilizes visual units of hand and body gesticulations as the building blocks of meaning-bearing signs. Nevertheless, all sign languages have rules of morphology, syntax, and semantics comparable to those of spoken languages."

Identify the subject's history, causes, or development.   In 1983 Victoria Fromkin and Robert Rodman supplemented their earlier definition of Ameslan or ASL with historical information: "ASL is an independent, fully developed language that historically is an outgrowth of the sign language used in France and brought to the United States by the great deaf educator [Thomas Hopkins] Gallaudet, after whom Gallaudet College for the Deaf in Washington, D.C. is named . . . "

Identify the effects or functions of the subjects.   In "The Wonder of Gravity," physicist Hans von Baeyer begins by discussing gravity's effects: "It dominates life. What triumph when the newborn infant first lifts his wobbly head from the mattress to peer around—the first victory over gravity. . . . Gravity, on the other hand, wins every time a pin drops, a plane crashes, a tower topples, an avalanche strikes and a baby rolls off the bed. . . . Gravity acts as a restraining, organizing, direction-giving principle in nature. Inexorably it draws form out of chaos."

Compare and contrast the subject with something else.   Hans von Baeyer observes, "Gravity, like space, is ubiquitous and, like time, it cannot be turned off. Electricity, another familiar force, can be switched off, magnetism can be shielded, even the strong force which holds atomic nuclei together can be counteracted by antimatter, but gravity passes through all materials, affects all matter equally, and has no opposing force, no shield, no anti-gravity."

Make an analogy between one or more properties of the subject and comparable properties of something familiar.   In explaining the functioning of gravity it is necessary to show how it operates over time. Hans von Baeyer does this through an analogy between time and a river: "The flow of time is represented by a flow of an imaginary medium. Time becomes a river. In the bleakness of the void . . . floats a vast and silent current of clear and subtle liquid which pervades every pore of the universe and bears everything within it inexorably forward. The current is time. Its motion cannot be stopped, its depth cannot be plumbed, its substance cannot be detected—because it is not real. Unlike a real river in real space, this current exists in the four dimensional space-time."

Use negation.   Identify what the subject isn't, as in Hans von Baeyer's negative comparison of gravity with space, time, electricity, and magnetism.

Isaac Asimov consistently uses these techniques of definition in his many popular science writings, which also follow the principle of beginning with a single essential fact and building to greater complexity. The first half of "Let There Be a New Light" presents information necessary to understand his main subject, the laser. He defines this first by its physical properties as "a thin beam of colored light."

Asimov begins at the beginning, with physical properties, and defines ordinary light as "a set of waves." He encourages readers not to ask, "Waves of what?" but "merely to imagine waves . . . as being broken up into tiny lengths, each of which contains just a few [another layperson's definition] ups and downs, or 'oscillations.'" These definitions in turn become the basis for the definition of "tiny lengths of waves, 'photons,'" to which Asimov devotes the next two paragraphs. He then uses the concept of "photons" to explain differences between red light, sunlight, ultraviolet light, x-rays, and gamma rays. He uses this discussion as the basis for explaining how photons are produced. And so on, step by step, until finally he is able to explain "how the light of this laser beam is different from every other form of light we know." The following explanation also depends on a series of interlocking explanations, proceeding from the basic to the more derivative, buttressed with definitions where necessary.

First, the laser beam is very intense. In every ordinary light-producing process, a vast range of photon frequencies is brought forth. Only a small portion of them are usually in the visible light range. In the laser beam, *all* the energy released can be in the form of visible light, and the beam is an unusually concentrated form of light, therefore.

The first component of the definition, a physical property

Note the comparison of the ordinary with the unusual.

Second, the laser beam is very uniform. Ordinary light is made up of photons of a variety of frequencies, while the laser beam is made up of identical photons. It is therefore all of one particularly tiny shade of one particular color. It is 'monochromatic' light (an expression that comes from Greek words meaning 'one color').

The second component of the definition, another physical property

A definition in terms of appearance

A definition based on etymology

Third, the laser beam is very compact. The photons of ordinary light are moving about every which way. It is difficult for that reason to keep a beam of ordinary light from spreading out. Laser beam photons, on the other hand, are all moving in the same direction. Ordinary light might be likened, therefore, to a vast mob with each member of it milling about in any direction he chose. The laser beam can, instead, be likened to a column of soldiers marching with absolute precision.

The third component of the definition, yet another physical property

A definition that identifies the constituent elements of the subject, again comparing the ordinary with the unusual

Illustrations

Trying to explain the configuration of a spiral staircase, the solar system, or DNA, or the workings of a telephone, a rocket, or a CAT scanner without using illustrations is like climbing a steep incline without using your arms and hands for balance. It can be done, but the ascent will be more difficult, less efficient, and more precarious than it would be with these perfectly natural aids. Physicist James Clerk Maxwell said, in an address to his peers,

> For the sake of persons of . . . different types, scientific truth should be presented in different forms, and should be regarded as equally scientific, whether it appears in the robust form and vivid coloring of a physical illustration, or in the tenuity and paleness of a symbolic expression.

Perhaps you're sufficiently expert to generate and interpret your own data or produce your own drawings or photographs with or without the help of computer programs. If you're not and you're doing original research, you may be collaborating with someone whose job it is to produce statistical analyses or scientific illustrations. If you're not already doing so, now's a good time to start. You may find supplementary illustrations, either in already published sources (such as tables of data) or in collections (such as the collections of photographs, drawings, and maps in the archives or public relations offices of universities, historical, and professional societies).

When illustrations are necessary.   Science writing is full of necessary illustrations, whether vivid photographs, drawings, diagrams, and charts or more pallid formulas, statistical tables, and graphs. If your verbal explanation will be clearer and more elegant with complementary illustrations, use what you need. Try out your text on one or two people whose level of knowledge is typical of your intended readers and ask them to tell you where and what illustrations will help to make the writing crystal clear.

Some types of illustrations are crucial to understanding the subject. It's impossible to understand the circuitry for house wiring, an implantable pacemaker, or random-access integrated circuit memory without diagrams; the stages of the Mercury (or other) space mission from launch to splashdown without drawings; or the sound modeling process for a Kurzweil synthesizer without a flowchart.

When illustrations are optional.   It is possible to understand without visual illustrations the conclusions reached in empirical research studies such as "Behavioral strategies for alcohol abuse prevention with high-risk college males," "The effects of revising with a word processor on written composition," and "The effects of a primary prevention program on Hispanic children." However, visual devices such as tables, graphs, charts, and summaries of statistical or other mathematical analyses enable knowledgeable readers to literally see—and perhaps evaluate for themselves—patterns in the raw data from which the researchers draw their conclusions.

If you have conducted the research you're writing about, your readers' scientific sophistication will determine whether you present the material in technical form and language or translate the raw data into words. For non-specialized readers, the physical illustrations should be simpler and accompanied by clarifying verbal explanations. In order to understand the research, such readers rely on the writer to function as a *translator.*

Interpretation and Translation in Science Writing

We rarely come upon facts and information in the raw without some context in which to interpret them. What is the meaning of the "fact" that the current population of the United States is around 250 million people? Is that a lot? too little? just about right? According to whose standards, whose point of view? "Objective" research is saturated with values, national, personal, stylistic. Even when looking through an electron microscope, what we see is not what we get but what we interpret in relation to what prior knowledge and our own predilections have taught us to expect. As Bertrand Russell has observed, our research—and our writing about it—will inevitably be imprinted with our national point of view:

One may say broadly that all the animals that have been carefully observed [in scientific research] have behaved so as to confirm the philosophy in which the observer believed before his observations began. Nay, more, they have all displayed the national characteristics of the observer. Animals studied by Americans rush about frantically, with an incredible display of hustle and pep, and at last achieve the desired result by chance. Animals observed by Germans sit still and think, and at last evolve the solution out of their inner consciousness.

In Russell's view, the facts don't simply exist "out there." Facts invariably become artifacts of the interpreter, the writer, in emphasis, arrangement, point of view, choice of language; and that is how writers and readers alike come to know anything. Clifford Geertz, an anthropologist who studies—among other things—other anthropologists and how they write, corroborates this. In "Blurred Genres," he observes that by the 1980s, social scientists had begun to use the methodologies and writing styles of other disciplines, and blurred genres and styles in the process. Yet even within a given discourse community that follows the same conventions there is considerable variation.

In *Works and Lives: The Anthropologist as Author,* Geertz analyzes the writings of four different anthropologists—Claude Lévi-Strauss, Edward Evans-Pritchard, Bronislaw Malinowski, and Ruth Benedict—to show how their very different literary styles reflect different worldviews, different styles of studying anthropology, and different ways of presenting the findings of their research. Japanese society, for instance, encapsulated in Benedict's metaphor of *The Chrysanthemum and the Sword,* would look very different to readers when viewed through the lenses of the other three anthropologists. Benedict uses the satirist's rhetorical strategy, Geertz says, to treat the societies studied as "fun-house mirrorings" of our own society, "this one elongated, that one squashed, the other twisted." None of the societies is presented "objectively," without interpretation or bias, and none of them can be. Contrary to popular impression, science writing isn't objective; it only looks that way to the innocent eye.

The *New York Times* characteristically publishes excellent science writings for nonspecialized readers. When focusing on a single study, the paper identifies *where the research was conducted,* the researchers' *professional affiliations* (though not always their names), the *size of the population studied,* and sometimes, information about *when the study was conducted and for how long.* As a rule in scientific papers, researchers *interpret* the *significance* of their research results. And *significance* is what the *Times* science writers focus on in *translating* research results for a lay readership.

Thus the *New York Times* of December 9, 1992, translates an article (whose authors are identified only as "researchers at the Minnesota Department of Public Health") from the *Journal of the American Medical Association,* compressing its findings into 150 words. The *Times* tells readers, "Cheese may be a bigger source of salmonella food poisoning than previously thought" and consequently caterers "might want to limit human hand contact with cold food items" to prevent the spread of "foodborne infections." From *Cancer Research*, a report of five years of research on 100 patients by Dr. Rakesh K. Jain of Massachusetts General Hospital and Harvard University, "a cancer biologist who is also a chemical engineer," the *New York Times* summarizes the information that "malignant tumor tissue in humans is under much greater pressure than normal tissue." Now breast biopsies can be more accurate, for "a rise in the pressure on the biopsy needle could show precisely when it entered the tumor."

In "For the Professional Mother, Rewards May Outweigh Stress," Jane Brody, a *New York Times* science writer specializing in research on medicine, health, and family issues, reports on the results of a "large" study of 1123 Canadian career women by Drs. Ethel Roskies and Silvie Carrier, two psychologists at the University of Montreal. Brody explains that the doctors found that career women:

> with husbands and children were happier and no less accomplished or financially successful than their counterparts without spouses or children who could devote much more time and attention to work. . . . The least satisfied were single profession women without children.

The researchers conclude, says Brody, quoting from the article and an interview with Dr. Roskies, "Our findings belie the popular belief that marriage and children are a barrier to career advancement, but they reinforce the belief that single status and/or childlessness are an impediment to personal well-being." Unless they wish to check out the original sources, *New York Times* readers must rely entirely on the reporter's understanding of the primary material.

As might be expected, examination of Roskies and Carrier's original paper, "Marriage and Children for Professional Women: Asset or Liability?" reveals that Brody was accurate. The original paper was presented at the APA/NIOSH (American Psychological Association/National Institute for Occupational Safety and Health) conference on "Stress in the 90's" two weeks before Brody's report appeared.

For a general readership, Brody concentrates on two aspects of the significance of the research results: the researchers' conclusions about "career patterns" and their relation to "personal well-being." She doesn't examine material that would interest Roskies and Carrier's professional peers, including:

- A review of the recent research literature. A review would place the research in context of the debate—and contradictory research findings—over whether marriage and children are "obstacles to career success" vs whether "single status and childlessness" are "harmful to personal well-being."

- An explanation of the research method. This includes Roskies and Carrier's population sample and how it was obtained. It also includes measures: career patterns were measured on the Index of Job Satisfaction and the Job Involvement Questionnaire; personal well-being was measured on one scale for physical health, and on three scales for psychological health. The method section also discusses the statistical procedures used to interpret these measures. "For scaled measures, univariate analyses of variance were performed separately for each dependent measure. . . ."

- Other aspects of the research results. These include sample demographics (66 percent of the final sample consisted of married women with children, 19 percent consisted of married women without children, 14 percent consisted of single, childless women) and a statistical measure of personal satisfaction—"there were almost twice as many single women in the high depression group" (28 percent) compared to married women with children (15 percent).

- Some of the discussion. Brody doesn't include the researchers' attempts to interpret certain aspects of the data, such as why the longer working hours of childless women aren't reflected in their income.

Special Forms of Science Writing

A Format for Scientific Papers and Research Reports

Whether you're writing a scientific or technical paper or a report for college, business, industry, or publication, you'll usually focus on a specific, limited problem or issue. Customarily, as in Roskies and Carrier's research, you will identify the issue and its dimensions and explain its background or review prior research on the subject. Then you will describe your own research methodology and, if necessary, justify your method and any innovations or changes you've made in the standard operating procedure. You'll then specify the results of the research and analyze and interpret them. You may conclude, space and imagination permitting, by showing the implications of your work and making suggestions for future research.

If your intended readers have a serious professional interest in the subject, you will probably want to use professional journal articles as models for the format and degree of technicality of your writing. Or, if you're writing a technical report for office use, you may wish to examine a current report as a model for organization and style. Here's a model that reflects the discussion in the preceding paragraph. It represents a common general format.

Statement of the problem.   This statement identifies a large issue or topic which you will eventually want to refine or narrow into one or more hypotheses—propositions that you can test and can prove correct or incorrect.

In benchmark research on racial discrimination reported in "Pygmalion Black and White," Pamela C. Rubovits and Martin L. Maehr begin with a brief review of the literature to show that teachers' expectations of their students affect the quality of student performance. They hypothesize that "it would seem probable that differential teacher expectation for black students and white students is related to differential school achievement," a view that their study is the first research to test. They then anticipate their findings, perhaps to prepare readers for what is to come, by saying that their study "yielded surprising results—results that can be interpreted as a paradigmatic instance of 'white racism.'"

Review of relevant research on the subject.   This review is not a series of book reviews but rather a survey of the major research articles and books pertinent to your topic, showing the current knowledge regarding your subject, your research method, or both. You won't want this survey to dominate your own work; if you're a student and simply synthesizing the research of others or replicating well-known experiments, you may not need a literature review at all except to cite the sources for your replication. If you're engaged in innovative research, however, you might include a more extensive literature survey to show the context into which your contribution fits.

In "Pygmalion Black and White," the authors reviewed much of the background literature in the opening paragraph to provide an intellectual context for the research identified in the statement of their hypothesis. In the second paragraph they refer in more detail to their earlier study with white students and teachers in which teachers called on and praised gifted students more than nongifted students. Their present study used the same procedure with one major difference; here the researchers wanted to consider "the interaction of white teachers with white students and black students," instead of exclusively with white students.

Step-by-step description of the research design, method, equipment, procedure, and measures.   You'll need to provide all this background information so your readers will know what you did, how you did it, where, when, and under what conditions. This knowledge will help them understand how you derived the evidence on which you based your conclusions and interpretations. A precise description of your design and method will also enable subsequent researchers to replicate your research to see whether your results were accurate.

Rubovits and Maehr discuss their experimental method in three sections: subjects, measurement procedures, and experimental procedure. Their subjects consisted of "66 white female undergraduates enrolled in a teacher training course" and "264 seventh and eighth graders attending three junior high schools in a small midwestern city." Neither the undergraduate student teachers nor the students were informed of the purpose of the study; the undergraduates simply thought they were participating in an ordinary classroom session as student teachers.

The principal instrument of measurement (validated in previous research) in this study is:

> An observational schedule that requires a trained observer to record the incidence of six different [student] teacher behaviors: (a) *teacher attention* to students' statements, subdivided into attention to requested statements and attention to spontaneous student statements [in presenting their results, the researchers consider these as two different behaviors] (b) *teacher encouragement* of students' statements; (c) *teacher ignoring* of students' statements; (d) *teacher praise* of students' statements; and (e) *teacher criticism* of students' statements.

The researchers also used a standard instrument, the Rokeach Dogmatism Scale, to measure the teachers' authoritarianism. In a questionnaire specially prepared for this research, they checked the credibility of their experiment and the student teachers' perceptions and interpretations of each student's behavior.

The experimental procedure is clearly explained. A week before teaching, each student teacher was given an instructional plan for a lesson on television, the same topic as in the earlier study, where it had stimulated a discussion that engaged all the students. Attached to each student teacher's lesson plan was "a brief general description of the students she would be meeting," an indication that she would be teaching "as heterogeneous a group of students as possible," and that teachers should be particularly alert to the differences between their students in terms of "verbal ability, interest, quality of comments, etc." A week later, each teacher was given a seating chart which identified each student by name, by IQ score, and by whether the student had been selected from the school's regular program or the gifted track. "The IQ score and track label had been *randomly* assigned," and therefore were not necessarily related to the student's actual ability or track assignment.

Each student teacher was assigned a randomly selected group of four students from "the same-ability-grouped class unit," two black and two white. "One black student and one white student were randomly assigned a high IQ (between 130 and 135) and the label 'gifted.'" The other black student and white student were "arbitrarily given lower IQ (between 98 and 102) and labeled 'nongifted.'" Before the class started each teacher was told to familiarize herself with this information on the grounds that "being aware of each student's ability level could help a teacher to deal with that student during the session."

An observer who did not know how the students had been labeled sat two rows behind them and tallied the teacher's behavior during the forty minute class session. After class, the observer discussed the session with the teacher, "attempting to start the teacher thinking about each student's performance in relation to his reported intelligence." The teachers filled out a questionnaire and two personality inventories; then the experimenters explained to the teachers what was really going on.

Statement of research results.   Ideally, this statement is an objective presentation of the data or other information obtained in your research and is accompanied by an indication of the research techniques by which the data were analyzed. It will answer such questions as: What happened? under what conditions? in what order? What did I discover or learn? To ensure clarity, you will want to present your evidence simply and unambiguously. Charts, graphs, diagrams, and other illustrations may be particularly helpful if your evidence includes extensive numerical data. Remember, though, that illustrations are not necessarily self-descriptive; they often require some written interpretation, as well.

Rubovits and Maehr present their results in a table, "Mean Teacher Interactions with Gifted and Nongifted Black Students and White Students" that gives frequency counts of teacher response to students classified as "Attention to unsolicited statements," "Attention to requested statements," "Encouragement," "Ignoring," "Praise," and "Criticism." The researchers also explain how they collected and analyzed the data. Each teacher met with four different kinds of students: gifted black, nongifted black, gifted white, and nongifted white and received a score for her interaction with each kind of student. These data were analyzed by a *multivariate analysis of variance—* a term familiar to professional readers of the article— with the nuances of this analysis explained in detail to clarify for the readers that the analysis did indeed measure what it purported to.

Analysis and/or discussion of the results.   The analysis or discussion is sometimes combined with the statement of the results. In your analysis you interpret the meaning of the data presented in your research results and state how they relate to the hypotheses tested. You may, for instance, focus on matters such as: Why did the events/phenomena occur? Why did the participants/subjects behave as they did? You'll also answer questions such as "What is the meaning of this deviation from the expected pattern of behavior?"

If your hypotheses are supported, your answers to these questions should explain why. If your hypotheses are not supported, you'll need to explain the unexpected or disappointing—and possibly embarrassing—results. Some possible explanations follow.

- The hypotheses involved testing concepts that were inappropriate or irrelevant to the issue you were trying to focus on.
- The research design or methods were inappropriate or inadequate to the task at hand.
- The data were incomplete.

If you have made mistakes, admit them but put them in perspective. Are all, or only a small portion, of your data suspect because of errors? Will you correct the problems of research design, method, and analysis in your subsequent research? Readers like to think you will learn from your mistakes, and a candid admission of the problems is the first step toward resolving them.

Rubovits and Maehr found that the data confirmed their hypothesis. They explain that, as they had also found in an earlier study, teachers paid the same *amount* of attention to gifted and nongifted students, but the *quality* of attention was quite different. Teachers criticized gifted students more than nongifted students, but this difference may have been because these students were black rather than because they were gifted. Whereas black students received most of the criticism, gifted white students received most of the positive attention. They were "called on more, praised more," and identified by teachers as the "most liked," "brightest," and leaders of the class.

In light of the researchers' earlier findings, these results are not surprising. But what Rubovits and Maehr find "disturbing" is the "evidence of white racism." They say, "Black students were given less attention, ignored more, praised less and criticized more"—especially the gifted black students, whom the teachers treated more negatively than they did the nongifted black students. The researchers take pains to explain why these findings are "not easily attributable to an experimental artifact of some kind," for the teachers were not responding to "any actual intellectual differences between black and white students or to any incongruity between label and actual potential." Nor were the findings an artifact of the observer's bias, because of the objective nature of the instruments. Dogmatic teachers (a quality of which the observer was unaware) were more discriminatory than less dogmatic teachers. Despite the fact that these young, idealistic student teachers expressed generally liberal beliefs, they did not carry these over to their treatment of black students by being particularly ingratiating.

Conclusion and suggestions for further research.   Because science is cumulative, in your conclusion you will want to identify the results of your research and to integrate these with the existing theory or larger body of knowledge of which it is a part, including your own earlier research, if any. If your results support your hypotheses, you might consider matters such as the following:

- How does my research illustrate or validate the larger issue?
- What does my hypothesis add to previously existing theory?
- How do my research results contribute to previous knowledge? surpass it?
- What does my research imply for subsequent investigation of the topic?
- How could my research be improved on? modified to investigate related issues?
- What, if anything, have I had to omit from this study that warrants further investigation? How does it bear on the research at hand?
- What resources (time, money, research population, equipment, or design) that weren't available this time would enhance future research?

The authors of "Pygmalion Black and White" do not make suggestions for future research or for application of their findings, though the implications are obvious. Rubovits and Maehr do say that these student teachers were inexperienced in the classroom and with blacks, and that their teaching might benefit from more experience. In another article, if not this one, these authors or others using their research could apply these results by making specific suggestions for how teachers can avoid racism and stereotyping, and how student teachers can be taught to do so before they assume charge of the classroom.

Interviews

The general principles of interviewing (pages 105–12) apply to interviewing scientists, inventors, and naturalists as well. But there are some special considerations with such interviews because they are rarely written for an audience of the scientist's peers. In interviewing scientists, inventors, or naturalists, the interviewer is likely to function as a translator of information from the scientist's specialized field—with its technical and esoteric knowledge, conventions and technical language—to the readers' generalized and nontechnical knowledge.

Consequently, in conducting the interview you're likely to ask your subject to address one or more of the following:

- Explain her motivations, and why she does what she does.
- Identify her "style" of working in science, and why it suits her and her research.
- Define key terms and concepts.
- Explain how scientists in her field typically do their work, what they investigate, and why.

- Explain in what ways her research builds on that of her peers and in what ways she's breaking new ground.
- Identify and explain her major research contributions, or focus on her current work.
- Interpret a scientific controversy of current or historical interest, take a stand, and defend it.
- Show how her research can be used to solve practical or theoretical problems.
- Identify research needed in the future and explain why it's needed.

Don't hesitate to ask your subject to slow down, spell unfamiliar words, or repeat or amplify explanations. Although you'll have done some homework in advance, you may need to ask for other sources of information to consult after the interview.

When you write the interview, you'll do what the *New York Times* reporters (pages 257–59) did in translating the essence of scientific papers from a scientific context to a popular one. A good example is journalist Kenneth A. Brown's *Inventors at Work,* a readable and informative collection of long but fast-paced interviews with sixteen contemporary inventors. Brown typically provides several paragraphs of introduction in which he focuses on the subject's major invention, how it came about, and gives a bit of biographical information. Brown then lets the subject talk, interrupting with a few telling questions. Here's a typical question and answer from Brown's interview with Wilson Greatbach, inventor of the implantable pacemaker:

> INTERVIEWER: *Are carefully planned experiments more important to inventors than the sudden burst of inspiration that sends you to your lab at four in the morning?*
>
> GREATBACH: I'm a proponent of the big jump. I like to throw something together, see if it works, and go on from there. Later I might go back and fill in the gaps, but I might even let someone else do that.
>
> One problem I have with the people I work with at universities is that they like to work step by step by step. And in their view, you don't start one step until you've finished the last one. But, there's usually a place in any project where you can say, "Well, maybe if I just built this thing, I could jump way over here."
>
> In the pacemaker, for example, throwing a bunch of parts together and touching the wires to a dog's heart to make it beat—that was a big jump.
>
> After that jump, I could go back and fill in different details: What kind of materials can be used in the body? What kind of circuitry can be used? A pacemaker is nothing more elaborate than a flasher that you see on a highway construction site. But you've got to redesign that flasher so that it will work off its battery for ten years instead of only a few nights. You've got to wrap it in something that the body won't reject, like silicon rubber or platinum or stainless steel. You have to find what's right and what isn't.
>
> All those details are important, but if I've at least made the big jump, I know that I can make the heart go with a tiny pulse of electricity.

Natural History Writing

General characteristics.   Many of the characteristics of natural history writing and natural history writers, that hardy and closely observant breed, have been discussed in Chapter 4, Writing About Places (pages 83–114). Except for scientific research papers, which emphasize the data and the precise issue at hand and subordinate the persona as well as the presence of the researcher, other natural history writings represent a conspicuous blend of the writer's persona and personality with the subject under investigation. However, natural history writers are invariably teachers, if not preachers; what they emphasize depends on their interests, their readers, and current political or social issues that bear on their subject.

Focus.   If you're writing as a natural historian you'll invariably begin by *describing, explaining,* and consequently *interpreting* a natural phenomenon. You'll ask and answer one or more of the basic questions identified at the beginning of this chapter—What is a given phenomenon, species, organ, form of behavior, whatever? How does it work? and so on (see pages 243–46). If you're extremely thorough, or your focus is very restricted, that may be all you'll do. Many works, whether brief articles or long books, maintain a singular focus and emphasis. These include Charles Darwin's *On the Origin of Species by Means of Natural Selection* (which devotes 457 pages to his discovery of natural selection), and Jane Goodall's *The Chimpanzees of Gombe: Patterns of Behavior* (which in 673 pages presents an exhaustive description and analysis of her subject, ranging from "The Mind of the Chimpanzee," "Relationships," and "Grooming," to "Hunting," "Aggression," "Territoriality," and "Social Awareness").

You might, however, expand your focus to examine the consequences of the information you've presented, as many contemporary ecological writers do. Such writers identify and address problems that are usually caused by the encroachments of "civilization"—a dubious term—and the meddling if not direct interference of human beings. Thus Barry Lopez begins *Arctic Dreams* with both a defense of the arctic landscape and a statement of prospective problems:

> As temperate-zone people, we have long been ill-disposed toward deserts and expanses of tundra and ice. They have been wastelands for us; historically we have not cared at all what happened in them or to them. I . . . think, however, that their value will one day prove to be inestimable to us. It is precisely because the regimes of light and time in the Arctic are so different that this landscape is able to expose in startling ways the complacency of our thoughts about land in general. . . .
>
> If we are to devise an enlightened plan for human activity in the Arctic, we need a more particularized understanding of the land itself—not a more refined mathematical knowledge but a deeper understanding of its nature, as if it were, itself, another sort of civilization we had to reach some agreement with. . . .

At the heart of this narrative, then, are three themes: the influence of the arctic landscape on the human imagination. How a desire to put a landscape to use shapes our evaluation of it. And, confronted by an unknown landscape, what happens to our sense of wealth.

Themes such as these are not, nor are they ever, neutral. The message of Darwin's subtitle, *The Preservation of Favoured Races in the Struggle for Life,* could be and was indeed used by British empire builders to justify the nineteenth-century spread of imperialism under the guise of assuming "white man's burden." But in the moral vision of twentieth-century nature writers, to know nature is to love it, and to be committed to preserving it.

Thus Lopez tips his moral hand at the outset by asking, "What does it mean to grow rich? Is it to have red-blooded adventures and to make a fortune, which is what brought the whalers and other entrepreneurs north?" "Hiss, boo," Lopez implies. This is a very wrong answer. The subtitle of his book, *Imagination and Desire in a Northern Landscape,* implies that the right answer lies in these not-so-rhetorical questions: "Is it to retain a capacity for awe and astonishment in our lives, to continue to hunger after what is genuine and worthy? Is it to live at moral peace with the universe?" The answer can only be a resounding, "Yes."

The message for prospective natural historians is clear: If you don't love your natural subject, don't write about it. You'll only offend your readers, who expect you to take the moral high road. Thus Jane Goodall's confession is right on the mark: "I readily admit to a high level of emotional involvement with individual chimpanzees—without which, I suspect, the [25 years of] research would have come to an end many years ago."

Authorial stance.   The author's message for prospective readers is equally clear: "Love the subject as I do. Or leave it alone." For many of these hard-edged moral realists of the natural world, there can be no compromise. "Come," they say, "let me take you by the hand and lead you into the woods the arctic the wild the jungle. If you were not convinced of these truths before reading my work, you will emerge utterly committed to my cause." And so they invite their readers to enter the realm where none before have ever gone, precisely as the naturalist has and to participate fully with all their senses. "I would draw you," says Lopez,

> simply to walk across the tundra; to watch the wind stirring a little in the leaves of the dwarf birch and willows; to hear the hoof-clacket of migrating caribou. Imagine your ear against the loom of a kayak paddle in the Beaufort Sea, hearing the long, quivering tremolo voice of the bearded seal. Or feeling the surgical sharpness of the Eskimo's obsidian tool.

Motion, sight, hearing, touch, heart and mind, total involvement. Yes. From this moral perspective contemporary natural history writing has become, like travel writing, according to Anatole Broyard, "a quintessentially modern thing, the present regretting the past. We travel like insurance appraisers, assessing the damage." From this point of view Goodall concludes *The Chimpanzees of Gombe:* "Are the chimpanzees at the end of their evolutionary trail?" The question can never be answered, for "the days of the great African forests are numbered." Soon the only chimpanzees will be "in laboratories and zoos," the only evolution possible " will be *un*natural selection." So we must "learn about chimpanzee behavior in the wild," she urges, "before it is too late." Her sermon continues with the hope that "this new comprehension of the chimpanzees' place in nature will bring some relief to the hundreds who presently live out their lives as prisoners in our laboratories and zoos," the "innocent victims" of human torturers. Goodall, like fellow naturalists, is deeply ashamed of "the behavior of our own species—our arrogant assumption that *our* needs, *our* pleasure, *our* wishes must inevitably come first." Her message implies a clear call to social action, though exactly what to do is left up to the readers, who by the end of the book should be thoroughly committed to the cause.

Aesthetic issues.   Putting your readers on the scene, whether crossing open ground, rising from the plains, or entering Walden woods, requires that your writing appeal to the senses (see page 117). It follows naturally that most writers of natural history have considerable aesthetic appreciation for their subject. In the course of imparting *Mortal Lessons,* surgeon Richard Selzer dramatizes and personifies his subjects: bones, gallstones, skin, the liver. He defends, for instance, the liver's aesthetic appeal by showing us what it looks like, "that great maroon snail, whose smooth back nestles in the dome of the diaphragm, beneath the lattice of the rib cage." Complaining "I think it altogether unjust that as yet the liver has failed to catch the imagination of modern poet and painter as has the heart," he says, "the heart is purest theatre." "Let danger threaten, and the thrilling heart skips a beat or two and tightrope-walks arrhythmically before lurching back into the forceful thump of fight or flight." With the dramatic, beating overtones of Poe's "Telltale Heart," he concludes, "And all the while we feel it, hear it even— we, its stage and its audience."

Structure.   Writings about natural history often reflect an overall organization by *major topics,* as in Goodall's emphases on areas of chimpanzee behavior, with each major division subdivided on the basis of *time* (such as historical development or change), *process* (such as research sequence), *progress, evolution, change in the subject,* or *flow of events.* Often, the message is embedded in a narrative account that meanders at times, but inevitably the writing proceeds toward the concluding ecological message.

Scientific Narrative

Narratives abound in science writing. They may be *accounts of explorations* in the lab (James Watson's *Double Helix*), across the tundra (Barry Lopez's *Arctic Dreams*), or on the high seas (Charles Darwin's *Voyage of the Beagle*). Narratives can be embedded in accounts of the research process, formal (as in many scientific papers) and informal (as are many sections of Goodall's *Chimpanzees of Gombe*). Narratives are used in scientific definitions (by Richard Selzer, for example), in explanations (by writers such as Lewis Thomas), and in autobiographies (by Rita Levi-Montalcini, for example). There are even scientific detective stories, such as Berton Roueché's long-running "Medical Detective" series in *The New Yorker,* in which scientific sleuths—health officers, physicians, epidemiologists—gather evidence, painstakingly check out clues, and, voilà, finally determine the cause of a mysterious illness, death, or epidemic.

To write a scientific narrative, you'll need to pick a subject whose research, detection, or investigation makes a good story.

Focus on a clear central issue.   A central issue is embodied in the question, "What is the structure of DNA?" asked by James Watson in the research that his account, *The Double Helix,* details.

Describe some impediments to the conclusion.   A narrative about elusive scientific phenomena with some drama inherent either in the research or resolution is compelling to read. Will it be possible to determine the structure of DNA? What impediments are there to this? What difficulties are there in the research process? facilities? materials? funds? conflicting personalities? One critic has observed of *The Double Helix,* "If you see scientists as superhuman altruists, patiently working together in brilliant teams for the betterment of mankind, James Watson's account will come as a revelation." Indeed, in the opening line Watson fires the first salvo, "I have never seen Francis Crick in a modest mood."

Structure a distinct time line.   The narrative should have a specific time frame which to structure and build suspense in a story that seems psychologically, if not literally, to take a long time. Which researcher will discover DNA first, racing against time and rivals? Will it lead to a Nobel Prize? for whom?

Depict vigorous or colorful personalities.   If the principal characters have flamboyant personalities, the narrative will be that much more interesting, though as Barry Lopez demonstrates in *Arctic Dreams,* a powerful narrative can come from the force of the events. Watson pits himself, whom he portrays as a zealous and unscrupulous researcher, against various other individual temperaments. He plays out the research process against a background of "typical" postwar British research:

> In England, if not everywhere, most botanists and zoologists were a muddled lot. Not even the possession of University Chairs gave many the assurance to do clean science; some actually wasted their efforts on useless polemics about the origin of life. . . . What was worse, it was possible to get a university degree in biology without learning any genetics.

In compelling their readers' interest, such writers can impart a great deal of scientific information, whether or not they emphasize it. As readers recall the story, they remember and understand the science as well.

Checklist for Writing About Science

1. Do I have a clearly delimited topic?

2. Do I know enough to write on it from firsthand experience or research? from the research or writings of others? Is my information up-to-date? Does it represent the state of the art in research methodology and gathering of data?

3. How general or specialized is my intended audience? How does their level of sophistication affect the terminology and background of my presentation? Will my readers understand what I'm talking about?

4. Do I define each unfamiliar term at the point where I first use it? Do I need to or is its meaning clear from the context?

5. Do I explain the significant processes and subprocesses that are essential to understand my subject?

6. Is my writing clearly organized according to the logical pattern of a process, a research sequence, or the development of a natural phenomenon? or according to the narrative thrust of an exploration, an autobiography, or a detective story?

7. Does my interpretation of the subject accommodate all (or the bulk of) the salient information? How does it relate to the interpretations of my predecessors, if any?

8. Do I use supporting information (facts, figures, graphs, statistics) responsibly to buttress my interpretation?

9. Although my writing will, perforce, involve considerable explanation, is it primarily expository? an extended definition? a narrative? an argument in

favor of my view of the subject and in opposition to others' views? or some combination of these?

Selected Reference List of Writings About Science

Attenborough, David. *Discovering Life on Earth*. Boston: Little, 1982.

Bronowski, Jacob. *Science and Human Values*. 1956 rev. ed. New York: Penguin, 1964.

Brown, Roger. *Words and Things*. New York: Free, 1958.

Carson, Rachel. *The Sea Around Us*. 1950. New York: Oxford UP, 1978.

Chomsky, Noam. *Syntactic Structures*. Cambridge, MA: MIT, 1958.

Darwin, Charles. *The Descent of Man*. 1871. Many reprints.

Dyson, Freeman. *Disturbing the Universe*. 1979. New York: Harper, 1981.

Eiseley, Loren. *The Unexpected Universe*. New York: Harcourt, 1972.

Ferris, Timothy. *Galaxies*. San Francisco: Sierra, 1982.

Gamow, George. *One, Two, Three . . . Infinity*. 1947. New York: Viking, 1975.

Gilligan, Carol. *In a Different Voice: Psychological Theory and Women's Development*. Cambridge, MA: Harvard UP, 1982.

Gould, Stephen Jay. *Ever Since Darwin: Reflections in Natural History*. 1977. New York: Norton, 1979.

———. *The Panda's Thumb: More Reflections in Natural History*. New York: Norton, 1982.

Kuhn, Thomas S. *The Structure of Scientific Revolutions*. 1962. rev. ed. Chicago: U of Chicago P, 1970.

Lopez, Barry. *Of Wolves and Men*. New York: Scribner's, 1978.

Lueders, Edward. *Writing Natural History: Dialogues with Authors*. Salt Lake City: U of Utah P, 1989.

McPhee, John. *Rising from the Plains*. New York: Farrar, 1986.

Petroski, Henry. *The Evolution of Useful Things*. New York: Knopf, 1992.

Terrace, Herbert S. *Nim: The Chimpanzee Who Learned Sign Language*. New York: Knopf, 1979.

Thomas, Lewis. *The Youngest Science: Notes of a Medicine Watcher*. New York: Viking, 1983.

Watson, James D., and Francis H. C. Crick. "Molecular Structure of Nucleic Acids." *Nature*. 25 Apr. 1953 171:737–38.

Selected Reference List of Writings About Science Writing

See also the bibliographies in the works listed here.

Bazerman, Charles. *Shaping Written Knowledge: The Genre and Activity of the Experimental Article in Science*. Madison, WI: U of Wisconsin P, 1988.

Fritzell, Peter A. *Nature Writing and America: Essays upon a Cultural Type*. Ames: Iowa SUP, 1990.

Halloran, S. Michael. "The Birth of Molecular Biology: An Essay in the Rhetorical Criticism of Scientific Discourse." *Rhetoric Review* 3 (1984): 70–83.

Myers, Greg. *Writing Biology: Texts in the Social Construction of Scientific Knowledge.* Madison, WI: U of Wisconsin P, 1990.

Works Cited

Asimov, Isaac. "Let There Be a New Light." *Is Anyone There?* Garden City: Doubleday, 1967. 102–14.

Brody, Jane E. "For the Professional Mother, Rewards May Outweigh Stress." *New York Times.* 9 Dec. 1992: C16.

Brown, Kenneth A. *Inventors at Work.* Redmond, WA: Microsoft, 1988. 29.

Broyard, Anatole. "Being There." *European Travel & Life.* Rpt. in *The Bread Loaf Anthology of Contemporary American Essays.* Ed. Robert Pack and Jay Parini. Hanover, N.H.: UP of New England, 53–58.

Darwin, Charles. *On the Origin of Species by Means of Natural Selection: or The Preservation of Favoured Races in the Struggle for Life.* London, 1859. 6th ed. 1876. Rpt. in *The Works of Charles Darwin.* Ed. Paul H. Barrett and R. B. Freeman. 16 vols. New York: New York UP, 1987.

Fromkin, Victoria, and Robert Rodman. *An Introduction to Language.* New York: Holt, 1978, 1983. Harcourt, 1993. 415–17.

Geertz, Clifford. "Blurred Genres: The Refiguration of Social Thought." *Local Knowledge: Further Essays in Interpretive Anthropology.* 1983. New York: Basic Books, 1985. 21–22.

———. *Works and Lives: The Anthropologist as Author.* Stanford, CA: Stanford UP, 1988. 115–16.

Goodall, Jane. *The Chimpanzees of Gombe: Patterns of Behavior.* Cambridge: Harvard UP, 1986. 59, 593–94.

Gould, Stephen Jay. *The Mismeasure of Man.* New York: Norton, 1981. 20, 83–88, 103–07.

Hall, Edward T. *The Silent Language.* 1959. New York: Anchor, 1973. xviii, 30, 43, 45.

Hawking, Stephen. *A Brief History of Time: From the Big Bang to Black Holes.* New York: Bantam, 1988.

"Higher Pressure in Human Tissue." *New York Times.* 9 Dec. 1992: C16.

Levi-Montalcini, Rita. *In Praise of Imperfection: My Life and Work.* New York: Basic Books, 1988.

Lopez, Barry. *Arctic Dreams: Imagination and Desire in a Northern Landscape.* 1986. New York: Bantam, 1989. 12–13.

Roskies, Ethel, and Sylvie Carrier. "Marriage and Children for Professional Women: Asset or Liability?" APA/NIOSH Conference. Washington, D.C., 19 Nov. 1992.

Rubovits, Pamela C., and Martin L. Maehr. "Pygmalion Black and White." *Journal of Personality and Social Psychology.* 25. 2 (1973): 210–18.

Russell, Bertrand. *Philosophy.* New York: Norton, 1927. 29–30.

Sagan, Carl. *The Dragons of Eden: Speculations on the Evolution of Human Intelligence*. New York: Random, 1977. 9.

Selzer, Richard. "Liver." *Mortal Lessons: Notes on the Art of Surgery*. 1976. New York: Touchstone, 1987. 62–77.

Thomas, Lewis. "A Fear of Pheromones." *The Lives of a Cell: Notes of a Biology Watcher*. 1974. New York: Bantam, 1975. 17–21.

von Baeyer, Hans. "The Wonder of Gravity." *The Alumni Gazette* (College of William and Mary) 46 (1979): 22–28.

Watson, James. *The Double Helix: Being a Personal Account of the Discovery and Structure of DNA*. 1968. New York: Macmillan, 1980. 19, 63–64.

10

~ .·✓

WRITING ABOUT
CONTROVERSY

The opposite of a correct statement is a false statement. But the opposite of a profound truth may well be another profound truth.

— NIELS BOHR

Where there is much desire to learn, there of necessity will be much arguing, much writing, many opinions, for opinion in good men is but knowledge in the making.

— JOHN MILTON

My starting point [in writing] is always a feeling of partisanship, a sense of injustice. . . . I write because there is some lie that I want to expose, some fact to which I wish to draw attention, and my initial concern is to get a hearing.

— GEORGE ORWELL

All journalism is subjective; . . . fairness, not some unattainable notion of 'objectivity,' is the reporter's obligation.

— CARL BERNSTEIN

Purposes for Writing About Controversy

As the epigraphs to this chapter indicate, the world is full of potential arguments. You can argue over the meanings of words and concepts (*love, beauty, justice,* for instance), the truth of interpretations (Were Sacco and Vanzetti guilty of murder or not?), the merits and demerits of policies (school integration) or issues (the drafting of women). Every time you express your attitude toward something you raise the possibility of controversy, of debate with someone who may disagree with you.

It is not the purpose of *Fact and Artifact* to discuss how to argue or debate a subject formally; as an experienced writer, you've probably already encountered a great deal of advice on formal argumentation. But as a writer of reviews, portraits, interpretations of processes, places, and scientific phenomena, you've been arguing anyway. Directly and indirectly your point of view, persona, tone, and selection of details conspire to make a case for the point of view you favor: "*The Revenge of the Killer Tomatoes* is a witty postmodern satire of the horror film genre." "For a more powerful backhand hit the ball *this* way, not *that* way—and not *the other way,* either."

Joan Didion's explanation reinforces the view that writing is an aggressive act:

> You can disguise its aggressiveness all you want with veils of subordinate clauses and qualifiers and tentative subjunctives, with ellipses and evasions—with the whole manner of intimating rather than claiming, of alluding rather than stating—but there's no getting around the fact that setting words on paper is the tactic of a secret bully, an invasion, an imposition of the writer's sensibility on the reader's most private space.

Taking a stance on a controversial matter, whether overtly or by implication, can serve a number of purposes. You can *call attention to a problem* (Should college athletes use steroids?); *identify and analyze a problem's new or neglected aspects* (What is the relation of steroids' exaggeration of aggressive tendencies to athletic strategies? to military training?); *investigate a problem* (Are athletes on our campus using steroids? If so, with what consequences?); *defend, attack, or modify the status quo* (What price victory?); or *argue for reform* (Stop steroid use immediately!). A complicated piece of writing may perform all of these functions simultaneously.

Critical Thinking

Critical thinking, as Peter Elbow defines it in *Embracing Contraries,* is logical thinking whereby we "examine our premises and assess the validity of each inference" while striving for accuracy and control. Elbow contrasts critical thinking with the free-flowing intuitive, creative thinking we use when we get hunches, see gestalts, "sense analogies or ride on metaphors or arrange the pieces in a collage." Critical thinking and intuitive thinking are complementary. Intuitive thinking can quickly generate "a rich array of insights"; critical thinking (being analytic) can focus, shape, and perhaps restrain the random and erratic aspects of the intuitive process.

Some Principles to Sharpen Critical Thinking

As an advanced student, you've probably become accustomed to this interplay of critical and intuitive thinking not only in composition courses, but also in advanced courses in other disciplines. Indeed, without bothering to label them or sort them out, you've probably been using both processes in generating then revising many of the types of writing discussed in *Fact and Artifact*. Nevertheless, it is appropriate to make some of the principles explicit because of their importance in constructing arguments, both direct and implied.

Dispel stereotypes and stereotypical thinking.   Do men or women come to mind when you think of *soldier, doctor, nurse, prime minister, soccer player, gymnast, Supreme Court justice, elementary school teacher?* Your first, and automatic, choice will probably be the typical—and stereotypical—male for all but the roles of nurse, teacher, and possibly gymnast. However, you can easily break out of the stereotype by simply telling yourself to think of the other gender and naming specific people who fulfill these roles: Margaret Thatcher as former prime minister, Sandra Day O'Connor as Supreme Court justice, and a male nurse or schoolteacher you know personally.

Much of anyone's thinking is automatic. It has to be to be efficient. You don't spend time reassessing judgments and decisions that have already proven effective, just as you don't think about putting one foot in front of the other after you've learned to walk. However, when faced with a new issue, a new person on the scene, or a novel situation, your initial reaction may depend on stereotyping. "Well, it's about time a Democrat/Republican got elected. He's got to do a better job than the Republicans/Democrats did during the past four years." "I know I should 'Buy American,' but Japanese/German/Swedish cars are so much better-engineered." "I'm uneasy about leaving Grandma with that male nurse. Women are so much more compassionate and nurturing." The list could be endless. While there may be some truth in such generalizations, stereotypical thinking also masks differences, unique and individual features, and alternative possibilities. Because it's automatic, stereotypical thinking is so easy that you'll have to be ever-vigilant in guarding against it. Here are some ways to reinforce your conscious choice to stop stereotyping and to think critically and originally.

Look for contradictions.   Embrace contraries. Peter Elbow elaborates: "Good writing is hard because it means trying to be creative and critical . . . good intelligence is rare because it means trying to be intuitive and logical." To get contraries to interact productively rather than to impede each other, you can either "heighten the opposition between them and promote an alternation back and forth" or blend or merge the two.

Play with alternative and multiple points of view.   You can consider political, economic, religious, social, intellectual, aesthetic, national, or sexual points of view. (The first letters of these views spell *Persians,* a useful mnemonic device.) The most natural way to "embrace contraries" is to pause when you have reached a conclusion or decided that a generalization is true and test your result from an alternative point of view.

For instance, "wealth is the best measure of success" is axiomatic in America's business-oriented society. However, your own awareness of other measures should make you uncomfortable with simple assertions. What would *wealth* or *success* mean from a religious point of view? (the accumulation of good deeds? freedom from a multitude of sins? the absence of ill-gotten gain?) What would *wealth* or *success* mean from a political standpoint? (good will among voters? international esteem? winning elections and, consequently, the ability to control or spend vast sums of money?) A quick way to identify alternatives is to look up the keywords in *Bartlett's Familiar Quotations* or *The Harper Book of American Quotations,* which often present a myriad of possibilities cheek by jowl. For instance, the 62 quotations on *wealth* in the *Harper Book of American Quotations* are themselves often expressed in oppositions, ranging from Benjamin Franklin's "He does not possess wealth; it possesses him"; to Henry David Thoreau's "A man is rich in proportion to the number of things which he can afford to let alone"; to William James's "The opposition between the men who have and the men who are is immemorial." If such quotations don't provoke enough oppositional thinking, you could also look up *money* (65 entries), or embrace some contraries— *poverty* (49 entries), *charity* (20 entries), or *love* (100 entries).

In "The Scholar's Obligations to Native Peoples," historian James Axtell, who specializes in Eastern Woodland Indians, addresses some of the complicated agendas and multiple viewpoints operating in scholars' attempts to understand the truth about North American Indians:

> "The truth" has many faces, or rather one face that appears different according to the vantage point and eyesight of the observer. To further complicate matters, the ethnohistorian of North America quickly discovers that his Indian constituents left numerous descendants who care passionately about the treatment their ancestors receive in "the white man's" history books. In combination these two circumstances—the protean quality of historical truth and

the pressure exerted by ethnic heirs—pose special problems for the ethnohistorian and raise vital questions about the scholar's obligations to native peoples. . . .

Axtell includes the viewpoint of fellow historian Francis Jennings, who suggested "that one of the most important things a non-Indian scholar could do for the Indian people today is to 'attempt to write an accurate history' of Indian-white relations, 'a history of real human beings' with all their warts and wonderfulnesses, rather than a farce about cardboard stereotypes." Historians, says Axtell, like other scholars, have an obligation "not to please their readers but to educate and enlighten them." Consequently, scholars must resist censorship or pressure from any groups—"whether by Indian politicians, or government agencies, publishers or lawyers"—to promote a single viewpoint. Indeed, there is no single generic Indian tradition, for "all native traditions are *tribal* traditions, not generically Indian . . . one tribe's tradition often contradicts that of another. Traditions have to be evaluated and used as carefully as any other historical source. . . . It is crucial to collect the viewpoints of many different native people, representing different ages, genders, statuses, and political and religious persuasions, just as it is in the study of any other group. And it is vital to remember that their views of the distant past are likely to be uninformed and warped by the intervening centuries, for the simple reason that history has to be relearned by every generation and is not a genetic inheritance." These observations and cautions can be generalized to each and every subject under the sun that depends on human interpretation for its meaning. Are there any exceptions?

Another way to envision multiple perspectives is to play off the literal against the figurative. Play off the practical against the theoretical, the concrete against the abstract, one set of connotations against another. Using different points of view can help you to look at the issue from multiple perspectives, some of which are bound to represent unforeseen dimensions. Another way to "re-see" your subject is to imagine how someone quite different from yourself, or how any pair of quite different people, might look at it—an engineer versus an artist, a physician versus a writer, a parent versus a child, someone who "owns" the problem versus someone who doesn't. Make parallel lists of opposite or antagonistic ways of perceiving aspects of the subject, and when you can, another list that reconciles the oppositions. Consider the connotations of each list and play with the possibilities of embellishment.

oppositions		reconciliation
black	white	gray (or plaid, tweed, checked)
black	white	brown (interracial, with many variations)

This type of thinking is obvious in the way Shelley M. Smith begins a letter to her campus newspaper:

> How did I, a short, overweight, arthritic, mixed-race woman, suddenly become a vertically challenged, gravitationally disadvantaged, alternatively capable, Native/European American person of gender? I didn't even notice that I had gotten so complex. I still feel like the same old me.

These alternative sets of labels embody the essence of her argument, that "the adherents of politically correct newsspeak and many others miss the whole point of trying to eradicate discrimination. Putting new labels on people doesn't eliminate their differences and ignoring the differences won't make them go away."

Smith continues, taking issue with the conventional view that "discrimination and some attempts to eradicate it are based on the notion that differences are bad." "Not so!," she says,

> Differences are great and I certainly don't want to be just like everyone else. . . . Changing what one calls the differences doesn't accomplish anything unless the underlying attitudes are changed first. Changing those negative attitudes is what eradicating discrimination is all about.

"But how," she concludes, alluding to the competing labels with which she began her letter, "can those attitudes be changed if one can't even discuss the differences . . . without fearing attacks by 'word police'?"

Write one text against another text.   Because your current reading is embedded in your past reading, you often read one text against another, whether or not you intend to. Although a particular commentary on, say, the Vietnam War or a biography of Eleanor Roosevelt may be new to you, what you've read previously about the subject will influence your current reading. So will more general reading—about other wars, other presidents, other presidents' wives—whether or not you can call it specifically to mind. Your past thinking and reading look over your shoulder as you read any current text and inevitably influence how you interpret what you read and consequently, how you write about it. The extent of the influence may depend on how secure you are in your knowledge of the subject and in your ability to think creatively (and therefore independently) about it.

When you cite sources, you make this influence explicit; you and your readers expect the ethos and ideas of your sources to resonate with your own. In "Letter from Birmingham Jail" (1963), a classic defense of using nonviolent protest to end racial segregation, Martin Luther King, Jr. clearly associates himself with the great tradition of principled protest:

> . . . I am in Birmingham because injustice is here. Just as the prophets of the eighth century B.C. left their villages and carried their "thus saith the Lord"

far beyond the boundaries of their home towns, and, just as the Apostle Paul left his village of Tarsus and carried the gospel of Jesus Christ to the far corners of the Greco-Roman world, so am I compelled to carry the gospel of freedom beyond my home town. Like Paul, I must constantly respond to the Macedonian call for aid.

King's range of references throughout this fifty-paragraph essay begins as early as Socrates. It encompasses Christian history from the early prophets to Christ himself, to Paul, to Aquinas, Augustine, Martin Luther, and John Bunyan; and embraces the views of contemporary Protestants (Reinhold Niebuhr and Paul Tillich) and Jewish (Martin Buber) theologians. By this means, King, writing from a jail cell and under suspicion as an outside rabble-rouser, establishes his character as quite different from that of a criminal. Although he is ostensibly addressing the eight Southern clergy who had published a statement urging him to "go slow" with his protests, he actually intends his letter for the worldwide audience his civil rights activities commanded. King's allusions reveal him to be educated, wise, deeply religious, widely read, and highly principled—and thus a fit moral leader.

In other instances, the sources that influence you may be generalized to norms of a field or conventions of a genre. Although you won't necessarily cite them explicitly, these sources influence your choice of form, language, perhaps even your argument itself. Thus in "When We Dead Awaken: Writing as Re-Vision," Adrienne Rich explains how her consciousness as a woman grew in tandem with her development as a poet. As a Radcliffe undergraduate, defining herself by her "relationships with men," her "style was formed first by male poets." As with any newcomer to a field, Rich had to learn from what already existed. But as she grew in sophistication and self-knowledge, she angrily rejected the masculine canon, concluding that she, like other women, had been victimized by the male environment, "society, language, and the structures of thought." To write as a woman, she has to explore and exploit what lies in "'the new space'" beyond "the boundaries of patriarchy," space that women can claim for their own.

Question authority.   Peter Elbow, Martin Luther King, Jr., and Adrienne Rich encourage us in their personal examples to question the validity and application of laws, principles, assumptions, and definitions. The motto "question authority" lives in everyone who refuses to accept the status quo, the obvious example, the pat answer, the argument from precedent ("This is the way we've *always* done it."), the simplistic explanation, or the cliché view of life.

Some Strategies to Sharpen Critical Thinking

The strategies that follow can help you focus quickly on your subject, on the stance you'll take in constructing an argument about it, and on the sources you'll use and how you'll use them.

Identify the issue.   What is the subject, the main issue (drafting women into the armed services)? Are there related subissues (the existence of peacetime draft, inequities in the drafting process)? You can't anticipate all of the related issues at the outset; many, in fact, may appear as you dive further beneath the tip of the iceberg that initially attracted your attention.

Determine your attitude toward the issue.   Are you for or against the matter at hand, or uncertain about it? (Women should/should not be drafted.) Or do you favor some aspects of it and oppose others? (I'm in favor of drafting unmarried women, but not pregnant women or mothers.) You'll write a stronger argument if you pick a subject about which you feel strongly, whether positively, negatively, or with a mixture of attitudes; anger's cutting edge hones many an argument's sharpest points. If you're indifferent toward your subject, why should your readers care about it?

Define the controversy's key terms.   Establishing clear, specific, reasonably objective definitions eliminates many of your readers' objections to your arguments. Defining terms to your own advantage also gives you considerable control over the argument, as Shelley Smith's alternative definitions (page 280) reveal. If you're debating the drafting of women, for instance, your argument will be more focused if you specify the group of women you're talking about: all women? women between the ages of 18 and 21? 18 and 25? unmarried women only? women without children? mothers with dependent children? But beware of highly personal or idiosyncratic definitions; they're bound to be self-serving and consequently call your motives or your credibility into question.

Pick an arguable issue.   Choose an issue that has a proposition which is objectively definable and uncertain. Some issues cannot be argued. It's futile to debate a proposition that is certain according to either absolute standards or the values of the culture that's discussing it. In Judeo-Christian cultures "Sin is evil" is not arguable. However, what constitutes "sin" may vary from one group or individual to another. Lying, a sin according to the Ninth Commandment ("Thou shalt not bear false witness"), may not be a sin to people who would condone white lies, lies to deceive enemies, or lies intended to comfort the sick and dying. Yet in *Lying: Moral Choice in Public and Private Life,* philosopher Sissela Bok argues that all such lies are evil because of the liar's intentional attempt to mislead those lied to.

Be sure of the facts.   Although you may want to argue about the *interpretation* of facts, your writing will be far more convincing if you include specific details such as precise facts and figures to provide a convincing "solidity of specification." You'll depend on primary and secondary sources for most of your information.

Use sources appropriately.   Primary sources include yourself—what you know from common sense, specialized knowledge, and an understanding of the relevant contexts in which evidence or information appears—and other people with intimate firsthand knowledge of the subject or the controversial matter. Other primary sources of controversial information may be photographs, documents, or records (financial statements, wills, letters, research reports) that identify problems or furnish evidence about them. Sometimes such sources, singly or in combination, show the existence of problems (manufacturing defects, sexual or professional harassment, discrimination) that the perpetrators are inclined to ignore or deny.

Secondary sources include people: friends, associates, and perhaps, enemies of your primary sources; experts on the subject at hand or specialists who can help interpret tricky points of law, financial records, medical evidence, or other technical matters. Other secondary sources of information can be found in places: revealing settings that provide significant contexts for controversy—sites of pollution or nuclear tests, politicians' offices, scientists' laboratories, corporate boardrooms, suburban shopping malls, the street where you live. Take a good look.

Publications, databases, and other sources of printed or electronically retrievable information are obvious secondary sources. Unless you know precisely what you're looking for, it's wise to start your search with more general sources before consulting the more specialized.

If the subject is of national significance, there's likely to be information on it in national publications, such as the *New York Times,* the *Washington Post,* major newsmagazines, and perhaps U.S. government documents. The latter are listed in the *Monthly Catalog of U.S. Government Publications,* with annual compilations and indexes. Good indexes to help you locate articles about your subject are the *New York Times Index,* the *Readers' Guide to Periodical Literature,* Farber's *Classified List of Periodicals for the College Library,* and the *Essay and General Literature Index* (EGLI), which indexes individual essays that are compiled in books.

To find books or articles on a particular subject, consult the *Library of Congress Subject Headings,* which lists topics by various key words and cross-references, before you look up the topic headings in the card or microfiche catalog. You can create a computerized bibliography of recent sources using your library's CD-ROM bibliographies and indexes to magazines, journals, and newspapers (such as *Art Index, Applied Science and Technology Index, InfoTrac II-Academic Index,* Modern Language Association *International Bibliography, Sociofile* (social sciences), and *Medline* (medicine, nursing, psychiatry). Or you could use the same topic headings or combinations of key words to make more extensive online database searches.

A library reference room will have collections of general and specialized encyclopedias (*Encyclopedia Americana*), bibliographies (Eugene P. Sheehy, *Guide to Reference Books*), biographical directories (*Who's Who in America,*

American Men and Women of Science), atlases (*National Geographic Atlas of the World*), almanacs (*Facts on File, Statistical Abstract of the United States*), and many other works.

If the subject is of local or regional significance, try current or back issues of the local papers. Local libraries and historical societies may have not only a wealth of books, pamphlets, and other publications on hometown history, industries, and public citizens, famous and infamous, but also collections of letters, maps, and privately printed documents. Church, police, and courthouse records can also help.

Other useful sources of specialized information are professional journals, and trade (business and organizational) publications intended for employees, customers, or members. Such journals often report controversies in related articles in the same or successive issues. See *Writer's Market* (pages 324–27) listings of 4000 "Consumer Magazines" and "Trade, Technical, and Professional Journals," or ask specialists what they read and what the level of technicality and emphasis is in the publications they recommend. To evaluate the usefulness of a reference material, ask:

- *How up-to-date is it?* The copyright date is one clue; the edition number is another. Unless you're writing on a historical subject, you'll probably want to begin with current materials and work backward chronologically because recent material often supercedes earlier information.
- *How general or specialized is the work?* What degree of specialization do you want? Is the coverage skimpy or thorough?
- *Is the source accurate, as far as you can tell?* Is it documented with reliable sources that readers can check?
- *Is the source biased?* Does it emphasize one point of view over another? Can you recognize the viewpoint? Are there other materials available that will provide alternative views and divergent interpretations of the same event or phenomenon?

If you're trying to interpret conflicting information, pick the most objective source. Assuming that all the sources have equal access to the evidence, the least biased source should be the most accurate because those who produce, release, or interpret the information have little or no vested interest in its use. Because "inside" sources are closest to the origin of the information and may have the biggest stake in how the information is used, they may also be the most biased interpreters.

If you're trying to interpret conflicting information from sources with equal bias, pick the source with the most authoritative reputation, and corroborate everything with at least two reliable sources.

But what if there are many authoritative sources, each with a different opinion, and you don't have firsthand access to any information? Suppose you're trying to determine whether the Iraqis have a secret cache of nuclear weapons that was not detected in the 1991 Gulf War. Look first for the least biased source. But maybe everyone is partisan—Americans, Iraqis, Israelis, and representatives of the United Nations and other nationalities, whether or not their citizens were directly involved. Who has the most unlimited access to the facts? Perhaps the opposing military commanders or national leaders do. But are they without bias? Can you find any uncensored information? Whose evidence most fully answers the question? You'll have do the best you can in such an all-too-common situation, weighing the alternatives and admitting your uncertainties if the information is not solidly substantiated. If your sources are unreliable or uninformative or too many doubts remain, you may have to switch to a topic with evidence that is less ambiguous.

Arguments: Assertive, Informal, and Implied

The preceding suggestions for finding and selecting evidence to support an arguable, manageable thesis imply that writing—and reading—about controversy is a cool, intellectual process that explores all the evidence and rationally comes to the most sensible conclusion. Yet you have only to think of your last debate over an issue—small (Do we buy a real or an artificial tree for Christmas?), medium (Should the United States adopt a national health care system?), or large (What are the most important national priorities: debt reduction, full employment, military security, support for education, social security and pension protection, tax relief?) to realize that arguments often generate more heat than light and that arguers often make their points through emotional means, with or without a rational underpinning of demonstrable facts and confirmed evidence.

By whatever kind of argument you use to make your point, formal or informal, direct or implied, intellectual or emotional, or some combination of these, your aim in writing about controversy will be to convince your readers that the subject is indeed a problem, that the causes or effects are what you say they are, and that your solutions, if you offer any, are the right ones. If you choose to make your point through amassing incontrovertible evidence, logically arranged, your argument will probably be direct, straightforward, perhaps even low key. *Fact and Artifact* assumes that you're already experienced in writing formal arguments that have an antagonistic context in which the writer debates two or more points of view and ultimately judges one as superior to the other(s). If your memory needs refreshing, you can read books on rhetoric and argumentation, some of which are cited in "A Selected List of Writings about Controversy" (see pages 306–7).

Assertive Arguments

Not all books on formal logic address assertive arguments, which are particularly common in some types of professional writing where the object is not to defeat an opponent but to reach a consensus of understanding among the members of one or more discourse communities. This is sometimes called "Rogerian persuasion" to acknowledge the influence of humanistic psychologist Carl Rogers. Unlike Aristotelian argument, assertive argument is dialogic, nonconfrontational, keeps communication open, respects the opposition, and allows for multiple truths. Consequently, this kind of argument, an embodiment of the Golden Rule ("Do unto others . . . "), is particularly useful for calmly addressing inflammatory subjects or hotheaded antagonists. The following material describes its structure.

Introduction.   Begin by sending conciliatory signals, state the subject as a problem to be solved, rather than as a controversial issue to be argued over.

Fair statement and interpretation of the opposing position.   To demonstrate that you understand the opposing position(s) and to show what you find of value in these views, summarize the principal points your readers would be likely to make in opposition to yours, even if these appear to contradict or undermine your own arguments. Let readers know that you recognize the basis of their reasoning, whether it be commitment to a particular philosophy or tradition, or a concern for morals, ethics, values, or laws.

Show where you and the opposition agree and why.   To maintain the meeting of minds you establish at the outset, include these points of agreement early in the discussion, perhaps intermingled with your acknowledgment of the merits of contradictory views.

Fair statement and interpretation of your own position.   Here you're after reciprocity. To encourage your readers to understand your position as fairly as you've understood the opposition's, identify the significant ways in which your views differ from the other viewpoint. Specify on your own behalf, as you did earlier for your opponents, comparable moral, ethical, legal or other bases for your position.

In an assertive format, you may begin your own argument with a fairly nonthreatening point or an objection of low intensity and build toward more controversial issues as your argument gains momentum. An easy way to tell which are the least controversial points and which are the most debatable is to see which points require the most development. The more evidence required to make a point, the more likely it is to be either unfamiliar to readers or uncongenial, or both. This is especially true if strangeness provokes resistance—and it often does. So the most highly debatable points will be the most fully developed and will probably come at the end.

A conclusion that indicates the benefits of adopting some features of your position.   If you can sincerely reconcile opposing viewpoints and can transform your position from an impediment to an opportunity, so much the better. If you can't, your position should nevertheless appeal to some aspects of your readers' self-interest.

Informal Arguments

Persuasion, friendly or otherwise, overt or more subtle, is likely to involve one or more of the following types of support. Unlike formal proof, which is subject to refutation and counterproof, informal means of persuasion are often judged credible and consequently acceptable within the readers' discourse community because of the author's authority and manner of expression, through the power of supporting testimony and examples, including imagery, scenarios, wit, and humor.

Author's reputation, expertise, and authority.   If an author could simply say "Trust me" and compel conviction, most arguments would be brief indeed. If you have a reputation for expertise in a field, your readers will probably already be aware of it and will respond prejudgmentally, prepared before they even read a word either to accept your views or to debate them. If readers don't know you at the outset, your comfortable use of the discipline's discourse conventions (language, syntax, stylistic conventions, format) and your references to works by peers will quickly establish your membership in that community. By including a review of relevant literature early in a scientific or technical paper, you not only embed your argument in the context of an ongoing dialogue, but signal your wide knowledge of the field, as well.

An easy way to establish your authority, and consequently your credibility, is to provide specific details or information that only an "insider" would know. Jane Ballard's recitation of her duties as the assistant manager of a chain drugstore compels not only our belief in her expert understanding of the job, but also agreement with her view that all such employees are "automatons programmed to perform mindless task after mindless task":

> All over the nation employees such as I would come in before the store opened, turn off the alarm, open the safe, make sure the register drawers each held forty dollars, sweep the floor, straighten the shelves, turn on the lights, let the other employees in, unlock the video cabinets, open the doors for the day, go to the bank, unload the supply truck, stock the shelves, answer inane and mundane questions from the customers, do the daily paperwork, count the money in the safe, make up the daily deposit, do the price markups, do the item changes, give the other employees their breaks, let them go home, run the register, count down the drawers to forty dollars, call in the daily figures, straighten the shelves, sweep the floors, lock the doors at closing time, turn off the lights, set the alarm, lock the door after stepping outside, go to the bank to make the night deposit.

Jane's argument for quitting to return to school is embedded in the job description.

Sometimes simply "being there" invests the writer with authority, limited by whatever boundaries are established. In her ambiguously titled "Meaning Well in the Third World," student Christine Ennulat describes her novice status:

> I am in Haiti for six weeks as a member of a work team sent by an interdenominational Christian mission organization with lots of rules. We are going to build the second floor of an orphanage. I think to myself that it's got to be better than the two weeks of boot camp training I have just endured in the swamps of Florida—even if we're not allowed to go barefoot because of parasites. . . . Even if we have to wash our hands after we touch the orphans.

At other times, a writer claims total authority on the subject, as does *New York Times* reporter Jeffrey Schmalz, right from his opening sentence of "Covering AIDS and Living It": "Two years ago tomorrow, I collapsed at my desk in the newsroom of The *New York Times,* writhed on the floor in a seizure and entered the world of AIDS." Who among Schmalz's readers would question his authority?

But what if you have neither reputation nor expertise on a subject but write essentially to express your opinion? You can still establish a credible ethos and persona (pages 23–25) if you treat your subject with appropriate seriousness—even reverence—or with humor or satire (Chapter 7). Or you can support your claims with others' testimony, conventional wisdom, or examples.

Testimony.   The testimony of others—experts, respected public figures, commentators and analysts, "the man in the street" or peers, or satirists—doesn't necessarily have to be fair, but it does have to be on your side. In using it to buttress your point of view, you imply the existence of a community of like-minded people, perhaps a consensus.

In a three-page argument titled "Should Drugs Be Legal?" *Newsweek* reporter Tom Morgenthau, like many writers without special expertise on a subject, uses the testimony of a variety of commentators, pro and con, including an editor, mayors and U.S. Representatives, professors of public health and public affairs, a criminologist, a U.S. Attorney, and the former head of the National Institute on Drug Abuse. Morgenthau concludes with commentary that both reinforces and complicates his resounding "No." "Legalization," he says, "is an inequitable trade-off that is based on a failure of empathy for society's victims: all those who are addicted (or who will become addicted in the drug-filled future) would be condemned to a brutal struggle with their dependency." Morgenthau uses the testimony of psychiatrist Mitchell Rosenthal, president of Phoenix House Foundation, a New York–based network of drug treatment centers, for a summary conclusion:

"Such reasoning is immoral, elitist, and racist—a case of 'writing off hundreds and hundreds of thousands of people, their families, and their children.'"

Examples.   *Fact and Artifact* abounds in examples ranging from an explanatory word or phrase to paragraph- or page-long quotations from student writings and published works. They illustrate, clarify, demonstrate the truth of—and thereby assert merits of—the points to which they refer. See the examples in "Techniques of Direct and Implied Arguments," (pages 293–98).

Implied Arguments

An implied argument makes a case for or against a given point primarily through indirect means, unlike the direct argument where indirect means, such as tone and persona, are subordinate. The real thesis of an implied argument is implicit, in contrast to the usually explicit thesis of the direct argument. If you choose to make your point primarily through an implied argument, you may decide to use emotional and rhetorical techniques that reinforce or sometimes circumvent rational means and objective evidence. Here, for instance, are two stanzas from a war protest song of American skytroopers in Vietnam in the late 1960s, "Napalm Sticks to Kids":

> Napalm sticks to kids, Napalm sticks to kids,
> When'll those damn gooks ever learn?
> We shoot the sick, the young, the lame,
> We do our best to kill and maim,
> Because the "kills" all count the same,
> Napalm sticks to kids. . . .

> Blues [helicopter gunships] out on a road recon,
> See some children with their mom.
> What the hell, let's drop the bomb,
> Napalm sticks to kids. . . .

The implied argument of this satire has an explicit pseudothesis that states the opposite of what the author really means. This song explicitly states that because the innocent and disabled are easy targets, the skytroopers should "drop the bomb." The implicit thesis is just the reverse: War is evil because it callously slaughters the innocent—the "'kills' all count the same."

To make its point memorably, an implied argument may draw on a variety of literary techniques commonly associated with fiction—a narrative persona who may be a participant in the activities, a point of view that shifts among various participants and the narrator, dialogue, character conflict, the setting of scenes, symbolic use of objects and natural phenomena, and careful attention to tone, including irony and satire. These techniques make implied arguments compelling to read, even though at times they may violate the principles of sound direct argumentation.

Advantages of implied arguments.   Because of their engaging literary techniques, implied arguments can express their points in varied, attractive, shocking, or otherwise memorable ways not as likely to be found in direct arguments. They count on the readers' personal associations and emotions to supplement the literal and objective meanings of the evidence.

Reconfigure familiar or problematic topics.   An implied argument may appeal to an audience that is either bored with the familiar or hostile to the explicit point. If the antiwar thesis of "Napalm Sticks to Kids" were spelled out directly, saying that war kills the innocent, people might read it and shrug their shoulders, not because the point is false or because they're inhumane, but because the thesis is a truism so obvious that it doesn't bear stating explicitly. Yet any thesis, however commonplace, is worth debating if the argument can be stated in a fresh, vivid way calculated to compel interest. The cynically satiric tone and unusual perspective of "Napalm Sticks to Kids" are as grim as the subject: "See some children with their mom./What the hell, let's drop the bomb." The cynical satire reinforces the readers' predictable sympathy for victimized mothers and children and thus for the implied thesis. The song is a sardonic commentary on a war that symbolized a host of military, political, and social mistakes. Yet even in 1968, when it was sung as a commentary on the My Lai massacre, the hawks who endorsed the Vietnam War might have been moved to acknowledge the merit of the doves' position more readily through this example than if they were harangued by an explicit argument. A hard sell often irritates or antagonizes— impelling clergy and others to argue by using more subtle parables and analogies.

Discuss taboo topics.   An implied argument may address a point that a writer cannot express overtly. Satires (Jonathan Swift's "A Modest Proposal"), allegories (stories that personify virtues such as charity and vices such as pride), and fables (moralistic stories that personify animals, as in *Animal Farm*), become a means of criticism when a powerful ruler or political repression curtails a free press or makes people afraid to speak out. Soldiers in Vietnam couldn't publicly criticize military policy, but they could sing "Napalm Sticks to Kids" among themselves. When you depict a political leader as a fox, as satirists have been doing since the Renaissance, you show that person to be wily and crafty and deceptive; but even if you never name the leader openly, readers will know who you mean and, with luck, you'll escape the penalties of being critical.

Appear impartial.   An implied argument may help a writer maintain the appearance of impartiality. Journalists and others who wish to provide more interpretation of a person, idea, or phenomenon than their medium customarily permits often use implied arguments. In such a context, you organize objective facts in a revealing sequence or juxtapose them in such a way that the details comment on one another, thereby enabling the facts to "speak for themselves" without direct analysis. Thus in "38 Who Saw Murder Didn't Call the Police," *New York Times* reporter Martin Gansberg presents what on the surface is an apparently objective narration of an hour's events relating to a murder. However, through his choice and arrangement of details, even in the first two paragraphs, Gansberg provides a searing commentary on this occurrence:

> For more than half an hour 38 respectable, law-abiding citizens in Queens watched a killer stalk and stab a woman in three separate attacks in Kew Gardens.
> Twice their chatter and the sudden glow of their bedroom lights interrupted him and frightened him off. Each time he returned, sought her out, and stabbed her again. Not one person telephoned the police during the assault; one witness called after the woman was dead.

The irony of Gansberg's tone is unmistakable, even in the first sentence. It is the duty, the writer implies, of every "respectable" citizen to aid people in trouble; however "law-abiding" people may be, they are accomplices if they observe a murder in progress without trying to aid the victim. As a reporter, Gansberg must stick to the facts; convention frowns on editorializing in news articles. As a humane writer, however, Gansberg can recite certain facts ("not one person telephoned the police during the assault") and emphasize them by putting them first to call attention to people's inhumanity.

Conciseness.   An implied argument is concise, partly because it is elliptical and not comprehensive. The writer sketches a particular line of argument and counts on the readers to corroborate it with their own, equally compelling, supplementary information. For instance, in thinking about "Napalm Sticks to Kids," readers may reinforce the title refrain with connotative images of the terrors of the Vietnam (or any) war, such as the widely reprinted photograph of a naked, napalmed child running in terror down a road, burning.

Elliptical emotional appeal.   An implied argument hints at more than it actually states and often makes its point through emotional rather than intellectual means. Yes, "napalm sticks to kids" and to women and to sick people—as stated in the song. By simply saying this, the author expects listeners to react emotionally to the suggested horror and to reject its cause, the war. Having controlled the subject and the tone, the author leaves the logical extension of the argument up to the listener.

Evade direct confrontation.   Because an implied argument does not necessarily proceed logically, it can evade issues that a direct argument has to face. Napalm also sticks to enemy soldiers, a point the song ignores. As such, it may be a more effective (devastating) weapon than bullets, grenades, or other alternatives. A direct argument with the same antiwar thesis would have to consider the assets as well as the liabilities of napalm as a weapon, even if it ultimately rejected using napalm. A direct argument would require the writer to do more research and more work than an implied argument.

Disadvantages of implied arguments.   Are implied arguments the lazy writers' way out? Do they place the real burden of the argument on the perceptive reader? *Au contraire.* To write an effective implied argument requires exceptionally tight control over structure, point of view, tone, and emphasis. Without this control, readers may simply miss the point.

Indeed, in spite of its many advantages, implied argument has a number of limitations. Except for some burlesques and parodies, which make their point obvious by exaggeration, implied arguments usually understate their case. A subtle argument, direct or implied, gambles its potential effectiveness against the risk that readers will miss the point if they do not understand its allusions or its techniques. Moreover, if the argument is concise, and elliptical, it may not cover all the points the author wants to make, as an overt, point-by-point argument would do. The more allusive and incomplete it is, the greater the risk that the readers will fill in the blanks in their own way, independently of what the author intends. Readers' interpolation or imagination can quickly undermine the author's argument.

Suppose listeners to "Napalm Sticks to Kids" had relatives killed in Vietnam and could supplement the poem's argument with their own memories. Their image of the war might be dominated by the deaths of their relatives rather than by the deaths of napalmed native children, or by the stark Vietnam war memorial in Washington, D.C., inscribed with the names of thousands of casualties. If so, they might decide that the song meant what it said explicitly and agree with it. Because the song deals with only part of the argument, it, like other implied arguments, is particularly vulnerable on the issues it ignores, the evidence it omits, and the loopholes in its reasoning.

Implied arguments aren't generally used in contexts where the writer needs to get to the point immediately. Such contexts include typical examination answers (Why Keynesian theory is right/wrong?), campaign speeches or letters to one's legislators on a public issue ("Ten reasons why you should support tough drunk driving laws"), formal debates (Resolved: "That the United States should/should not remove its troops from the Middle East"), laboratory or research reports ("The Effects of Sensory Deprivation on Infants"), critical or analytic essays ("Autobiographers in Their Own Rite: Self-Constructed Artifacts"). Any argument that presents a straightforward logical case supported by accurate, representative, verified evidence will essentially be direct, although the writer may also use indirect means to reinforce the direct point. Thus a letter of job application, though presenting the direct argument of "Why I am qualified for the job at hand," will likely reinforce its overt point through implied means, as well. A positive tone, correct spelling and mechanics, an attractive layout, a clear typeface, and crisp paper will all enhance the writer's intentionally positive image.

In many instances, you will have the choice of conducting your argument by emphasizing either direct or implied means, or perhaps by using a combination of both. Indirect means can help to make the familiar memorable. They can revive a neglected or forgotten issue. Or they may serve as a prelude or supplement to a direct argument. The following techniques of argumentation—implied connections, single case, narration, and combining vignettes—are common to both direct and implied arguments.

Techniques of Direct and Implied Arguments

The techniques discussed below have applications to both direct and indirect arguments.

Implied Connections Between Items in Sequence

A statement is known by the company it keeps. Two or more statements in juxtaposition can become an implied argument, an understatement similar to an analogy in the way they work. Locating A next to B (next to C . . .) will cause each to cast its aura on the other. In "The Clan of One-Breasted Women," Terry Tempest Williams writes:

> I belong to a Clan of One-Breasted Women. My mother, my grandmothers, and six aunts have all has mastectomies. Seven are dead. The two who survive have just completed rounds of chemotherapy and radiation.
>
> I've had my own problems: two biopsies for breast cancer and a small tumor between my ribs diagnosed as a "borderline malignancy."
>
> This is my family history.
>
> Most statistics tell us breast cancer is genetic, hereditary, with rising percentages attached to fatty diets, childlessness, or becoming pregnant after thirty. What they don't say is living in Utah may be the greatest hazard of all.
>
> We are a Mormon family with roots in Utah since 1847. The "word of wisdom" in my family aligned us with good foods—no coffee, no tea, tobacco, or alcohol. . . . Traditionally . . . Mormons have a low rate of cancer.

Before 1960, only one of Williams's relatives had faced breast cancer. Her mother died at thirty-eight. The year after, Williams told her father of a recurring dream; for years she "saw this flash of light at night in the desert." It so "permeated my being," she said, "that I could not venture south without seeing it . . . illuminating buttes and mesas."

> "You did see it," he said.
>
> "Saw what?"
>
> "The bomb. The cloud. We were driving home from Riverside, Califor-

nia. You were sitting on [your mother's] lap. . . . It was an hour or so before dawn. . . . We not only heard it, but felt it. I thought the oil tanker in front of us had blown up. We pulled over and suddenly, rising from the desert floor, we saw it, clearly, this golden-stemmed cloud, the mushroom. The sky seemed to vibrate with an eerie pink glow. Within a few minutes, a light ash was raining on the car."

I stared at my father.

"I thought you knew that," he said. "It was a common occurrence in the fifties."

Flash! Williams hits her readers with the connection between the nuclear explosions and breast cancer with the same powerful impact that the recognition exploded in her own consciousness. This simple juxtaposition convinces us utterly—but partly because we can bring external information to bear on the subject that an audience of the 50s, 60s, or even 70s would not have known.

Argument by a Single Case

In an argument by a single case, the writer treats a single example or group as a unit to represent all other cases of its kind, even while focusing essentially on the case at hand. An argument that uses a single case as the central or entire example is implicitly an argument by analogy. Arguments in advertisements for humanitarian causes do this when they tell the case history of an appealing victim (of racial discrimination, of starvation, of political persecution), often accompanied by a pathetic photograph, conclude and indicate how much the victim was helped by donations to the philanthropy in question. The single case, it is implied, is representative of hundreds or thousands, and analogous to them all in significant ways. Another argument by analogy is implied in the same ads when the funds appear to have been contributed by someone just like—you guessed it—yourself, the intended reader. Appeals such as these are likely to depend heavily on emotion; often, they don't attempt to present a balanced account of the factual or other supporting evidence, though as a potential donor you can subject the evidence to the same scrutiny you would use in examining other types of arguments.

Generalizations on the basis of analogies and single cases hold up as long as the points of comparison remain valid, significant, and relevant. Under these conditions you and your readers can assume that because A and B share qualities C, D, and E, they probably also share quality F. Therefore, because a given phenomenon pertains to A, it will also pertain to B, or because A produces certain effects, so will B. And so on. The analogy or the single case example will break down when the points of comparison, overt or implied, cease to be meaningful or relevant, and when you can generalize no further. It's better to stop while you're ahead.

Argument by a single case: narrative.   Arguments by a single case are often made through narration of an incident focusing on a central character or typical group. Often the central character, perhaps the writer, learns something significant about the issue at hand or the way of the world, and generalizes about it, implicitly or explicitly. This is the technique used by various personal essayists and by writers of fables and other stories with morals. "Don't count your chickens before they hatch"—and James Thurber's variation, "Don't count your boobies before they hatch"—are intended to apply not only to other instances of eggs, chickens, and boobies, but also to all situations in which the apparently certain expectations of individuals, groups, and even nations have been disappointed.

In some narratives the characters remain unenlightened, but the narrator's critical consciousness provides insight for the readers. We have discussed in other chapters how the narrative techniques of plot, theme, characterization, action, settings, and dialogue can be used to make a point, directly or implicitly. In "Soup, Hugs, and Pity Parties," student Cathy Lafferty uses all of these techniques to present readers with the collective folly of a pity party. Her account shows this party to be a social event with a moral purpose that leaves its do-gooder participants feeling smugly satisfied, but without either enlightening them or changing the social problem that is its focus. Lafferty's critical perspective is juxtaposed with the characters' obtuseness right from the start.

> The topic for the evening at Cooper House was hunger and everyone was curious to know what dinner would be. The week before the campus pastor had fed them "radioactive chili" and led them in a discussion about nuclear war, but he was out of town this week so Tom, a student, was in charge of the meeting.
>
> Tom had just come back from a month in Haiti so he considered himself an expert on the subject of hunger. He was full of self-importance as he put the last touches on his authentic Haitian dinner of beans, plantain, and a small amount of shredded chicken heavily spiced with garlic. There wasn't much to go around, but Tom said that was what made it really authentic.
>
> Dinner didn't last long and after a quick prayer, interrupted several times by growling stomachs and the ensuing giggles, the slide show began. "These are some of the pictures I took during my trip to Haiti." Click. Three naked children play in the street. . . . Click. Cane workers, gritty with soot and sweat, dip their fingers into the meager scoop of beans served to each on a leaf. . . . Click. A young boy, belly protruding from malnutrition, stares blankly at the camera while flies suck at the oozing sores on his pathetic face. . . .
>
> [After the light went on] reactions, first softly whispered and then more boldly spoken, began to form on the quivering lips of the newly enlightened. "Do people really live like that?" "How can the dictator live in a palace when children are starving?" "Why doesn't our government do something?" "I feel so guilty for being so well off." "What can we do?" . . .

Tom led off, "I believe you have to go there yourself to really feel the needs of the people. You have to know where they're coming from before you can help them. I plan to go back there and throw myself into the lifestyle for a while. You know, live off the land like they do and maybe do a little fishing and snorkeling. Maybe I'll even buy a burro and a couple of chickens. The day I learn to eat beans and lizard will be the day that I can really begin to understand the people and their problems."

Bruce, an aspiring engineer, broke in. "But how is your eating lizards going to solve world hunger? . . . I think we need to go in and teach them a better way of life—our way of life. We need to introduce our industries so that the Haitians can raise their standard of living. It would be good for us, too. The labor costs there would be cheaper 'cause the cost of living is lower."

The dialogue continues in this vein, with all the speakers characterizing themselves as naive or insensitive.

Tom spoke again, "I've learned from experience that you don't need particular skills. Look at me. I don't know anything and I went down to Haiti. I really think I did some good. You really don't have to know anything to help. You just have to show the people that you care and give them a hug every once in a while. It makes them feel good and it makes you feel good, too."

"You can do that sort of thing here in this country, too," replied Phil. "I spent my Labor Day weekend up in New York working in the soup lines. Of course by the time I flew up and back I only had time to really get into it once or twice, but I got a lot out of it."

"This is all great," said Brian, "but I'm hungry. Can we adjourn now?"

"Yeah! Let's go get a pizza and some beer at Buddy's Pizza Palace," said Jim as he seconded the motion. Within minutes the place was empty. Some had gone for pizza. Others went back to the dorms to do their homework and break into their stashes of junk food sent from home. A couple of girls grabbed diet milkshakes and went jogging to try to lose fifteen pounds before the dance on Saturday.

And people starve.

The other students' comments underscore their lack of understanding of the problem, their superficial attempts to understand it, and their simplistic and ineffective solutions (such as the inappropriateness of trying to apply the values of an industrialized America to an agrarian culture). They unwittingly reveal their own selfish motives (they try to help because it makes *them* feel good or because it will profit American businesses), their own shortcomings, and their tendency to forget the problem as soon as the discussion is over. The narrator, omniscient and omnipresent, recognizes these difficulties and expects readers to understand the problems and the implied solutions, even if the participants don't. Lafferty provides occasional ironic interpretations in her own authorial voice, in labeling the slide show watchers as "newly enlightened," for instance, while their own innocent remarks manifest their continued ignorance—"The day I learn to eat beans and lizard will be the day that I can really begin to understand the people. . . .".

Argument by a single case: combined vignettes.   Sometimes an extended narrative of a single incident makes the point, as in "Soup, Hugs, and Pity Parties." At other times the point or an aspect of it is implied through a series of vignettes which combine like mosaic pieces to make a compelling case stronger than the sum of its parts. George Orwell uses this technique in "Marrakech," an essay that illustrates, and implicitly corroborates, his claim that all colonial empires are sustained by dehumanization of the poor, non-white natives. Among the many vignettes that, when combined, reinforce the thesis is this pungent illustration:

> I was feeding one of the gazelles in the public gardens.
> Gazelles are almost the only animals that look good to eat when they are still alive, in fact, one can hardly look at their hindquarters without thinking of mint sauce. The gazelle I was feeding seemed to know that this thought was in my mind, for though it took a piece of bread I was holding it obviously did not like me. It nibbled rapidly at the bread, then lowered its head and tried to butt me, then took another nibble and then butted again. Probably its idea was that if it could drive me away the bread would somehow remain hanging in mid-air.
> An Arab navvy working on the path nearby lowered his heavy hoe and sidled towards us. He looked from the gazelle to the bread and from the bread to the gazelle, with a sort of quiet amazement, as though he had never seen anything quite like this before. Finally he said shyly in French: "*I* could eat some of that bread."
> I tore off a piece and he stowed it gratefully in some secret place under his rags. This man is an employee of the Municipality.

In this vignette the *characters* are Orwell-as-character, the gazelle, and the navvy. The *setting* is the Marrakech public gardens. The *theme* is hunger, of beast and man. The *plot* involves a man who feeds a gazelle (*action*) and is approached by a laborer who himself wants to eat gazelle's food (*conflict*). The man feeds the navvy (*resolution of conflict*). The *dialogue* is "I could eat some of that bread."

Orwell as narrator expects his readers to understand the irony of the fact that the healthy, aggressive gazelle, which itself looks good enough to eat, is better fed than its keeper, a municipal employee. Orwell expects his readers to add this bit of evidence to illustrations of comparable points he supplies throughout the essay: fields of unmarked graves; "a frenzied rush" of ghettoized Jews scrambling for cigarettes; "very old women . . . bodies reduced to bones and leathery skin, bent double under the crushing weight" of enormous loads of firewood. Readers must integrate the messages of each vignette to make the essay's unified thesis. In so doing, they should be moved to understanding, to indignation, and perhaps to action on behalf of underpaid, underfed, oppressed peoples everywhere.

Other ways to make an argument by a single case are through *analysis* or *case history,* presenting the evidence and results of a single case study or experiment in scientific research and drawing general conclusions from it. In these instances, the single case will usually be treated as a *symbol* for all others like it, even though it is dealt with individually. Although a single case may be memorable, interesting, and intrinsically significant, as are the examples of the pity party and gazelle-feeding at the Marrakech public gardens, are the authors justified in expecting readers to make the necessary leap from the particular to the general?

Asking yourself the following questions of the case in point should help you judge its suitability for use in an argument by a single case.

1. Is the case sufficiently typical or representative to warrant the heavy load of generalization I place on it? Does it allow for exceptions? alternatives?

2. If the case is atypical, will this be clear to the reader? Can I generalize about it at all? to what extent?

3. Is the case presented in enough detail so the readers can understand its significance? its implications?

4. Are all the aspects of the case at hand relevant to the points I wish to make? If not, is the case suitable for my argument?

5. Can I demonstrate the truth of my argument convincingly on the basis of only a single example or do I need other examples to accompany it?

6. Is my generalization (and thesis) explicit? implicit? If the latter, do I make my point clear?

7. Do I control the tone and point of view to reinforce my real opinion, whether stated directly or implied?

8. Are my readers likely to agree with my generalizations? If not, what must I use to be convincing?

Intensive Research: Extensive and Extended Argument

Long-term research projects include term papers, articles, theses, dissertations, books, or other open-ended research of the sort involved in investigative reporting. Although not every research effort is fraught with controversy, every research report is an argument not only for the research findings, but also for the legitimacy—even superiority—of the questions the researcher asks, of the researcher's premises and investigative process, and of the researcher's judgments and interpretations every step of the way.

The general process discussed here is typical of scholarly research in the sciences, social sciences, and humanities and of investigative reporting, although scholarly researchers profess, at the outset, anyway, to be more open-minded than investigative reporters. It is beyond the scope of this book to discuss discipline-specific applications of research techniques or the theoretical or philosophical orientations particular to specific fields. The illustrations in this section focus on the general process of investigative reporting, though applications to other fields should be readily apparent.

The subjects discussed here are within the scope of students working individually or in teams, perhaps with more independence and a variety of research methods than would be possible in projects assigned for regular course work. All of these require the investigator to expend extensive time, effort, and, perhaps, resources, often in collaboration with others because the work is so painstaking and labor-intensive. If you are a member of such a team, interpret *you* as plural in the discussion that follows.

Choosing a Subject

It's not wise to leap into the sea of an intensive investigation, no matter how alluring the tips of the icebergs floating therein. You'll need to decide, "Is the project right for me? And am I right for the project?" Answering the questions that follow can help you determine whether there's a "goodness of fit" between you and the proposed research.

Do you find the subject fascinating?   You know you have a compelling subject when, like the love of your life, it haunts your waking hours, your reveries, your dreams. If you're only mildly interested in the subject to begin with, it will be hard to sustain the energy that your investigation will require. But if you're intrigued by it right from the start, you'll have a reservoir of interest to draw on during the rough spots in your investigation. As with a close friendship or a marriage, the greater your commitment, the greater your chances of success, in this case, of completing your investigation, writing it up, and calling your findings to public attention.

You know you have a compelling subject when you find yourself giving a higher priority to investigating it than to pursuing other forms of fun and games, perhaps even, at times, to eating and sleeping at regular intervals. You know your subject is compelling when you're willing to go well beyond the extra mile in pursuit of crucial evidence and elusive details; to "run half over London, in order to fix a date correctly," as James Boswell did in writing the masterpiece biography of a subject dear to his heart, Dr. Samuel Johnson. "But no subject is worth this madness," your friends may exclaim. They're missing the point of what you could consider a more-or-less rational obsession.

In fact, if you're not invested in your subject at the outset, stop! Search until you find another issue, a cause that makes all your efforts seem worthwhile. Then you'll have a strong likelihood of sticking with your research, and of convincing others of its importance.

Is the issue worth your time and effort to investigate?   Ultimately, the issue will have to be meaningful to a specific external audience in order to write about it—for *public disclosure* of your findings is essential in intensive research. Sometimes a question that appears fairly simple and straightforward can have fascinating ramifications, while sometimes it can be a dud. The questions "What is the truth of a life?" and "How do you know?" have generated for this writer thirty years of research on autobiography, producing enough exciting possibilities to explore for a lifetime.

The legacy of the Watergate investigation, begun in 1973 by two junior *Washington Post* reporters, Bob Woodward and Carl Bernstein, set the standard for countless campus and local newspapers to emulate. If your subject is current, your investigation will set forces in motion to bring about social or institutional change or political reform. You'll write in the hope that your pursuit of truth will lead to justice for one and all. If your subject is historical, you may write to rehabilitate a reputation or to correct errors, omissions, or injustices perpetuated through generations of biased ignorant, partial, or self-serving accounts (as shown in James Axtell's analysis on pages 278–79). No subject is too exalted for the investigative writer's examination; the emperor can always be scrutinized to see whether he's wearing new clothes— or any clothes at all. No subject is too trivial for investigation if it leads to discoveries of great significance.

Student newspapers, for instance, have investigated student alcoholism; substance abuse by school athletes (sometimes with encouragement from their coaches); differential allocation of athletic funds to men's and women's sports; fraternity and student government misappropriation of general student funds; fraternity hazing and pledge deaths; student government election fraud; unauthorized grade changes and fraudulent degrees; cheating and plagiarism; harassment of minorities by students; sexual harassment of students by faculty; and challenges to the free speech code. As at the University of South Carolina, news of these investigations has not only reached the national press, but also caused major changes in the campuses where they occurred. As a consequence of the *Daily Bruin's* investigation of gross underrepresentation of student and employee minorities at UCLA, the university has attained a minimum of 30 percent minorities throughout the institution.

The *Gamecock* of the University of South Carolina asked what at the outset seemed like a simple, though potentially loaded question. What salary was Anwar Sadat's widow, Jihan el-Sadat, paid in 1984–85 to teach one course, in her special appointment as a lecturer? The administration of President James Holderman refused to answer for a number of months, but, as a public institution, was finally forced to acknowledge that the figure was $330,000. You can imagine the repercussions on a campus where the annual salaries for full-time faculty averaged less than $40,000 and had been frozen for some years because of chronically low state funding. This disclosure resulted in a five-year full-scale legislative and newspaper investigation of the president's fund-raising practices and expenditures. Holderman ultimately resigned because the investigation exposed his costly house refurbishing, gifts, and travel expenditures which averaged $7,400 a month—paid from university bookstore profits (see Cook, Watts).

How original is your question?   And, in turn, how original does it have to be? If the point of the investigation is to teach a relative newcomer how people do research in an academic subject, scholarly investigation may plow familiar ground. If the point is to make an original contribution, you'll need first to understand the existing research, perhaps through a literature search (pages 283–85), before staking your claim. Investigative reporters, on the other hand, always look for new territory—or the truffle beneath familiar turf. A quick survey of writing on a controversial issue or of recently published papers on your subject can tell you what's been done.

Conducting the Investigation

Conducting a research investigation, like embarking on any other indeterminate, indefinite process, involves making a number of hopeful assumptions: that it's doable, that you and your associates can do it in the time you have allocated, and that you'll come up with some worthwhile results. If you're determined to learn from the process, and to have fun, as well, you can consider your research a partial success even if you run out of time or energy with results at variance with your great expectations.

Devise an appropriate research method.   Like styles of writing, methods of research investigation are as varied as the researchers themselves, as Clifford Geertz's *Works and Lives* illustrates. Yet, contrary to popular myth, researchers seldom go where no one has ever trod before. You'll save a great deal of time if you examine the research methods of others who have done comparable work. Read their work to learn what you can from them. If you can serve as an apprentice on a project, you'll learn on the job. If not, hang around the lab, the office, or the newsroom and see what you can pick up. Feel free to ask questions, even naive or trivial ones, if you are new to the field. In some areas, computer simulations can help you to conceptualize quickly an astonishing variety of models. It's crucial to play with the myriad possibilities of research design until you come up with one or two that might work best. Time spent at this stage is effort saved later. Consider the following questions in examining your subject:

- What method is most appropriate to the task?
- What method is most efficient—in time, effort, personnel, materials? Or is efficiency in one category worth greater expenditure in another? What, for instance, are the costs and benefits of spending money to save time?
- All in all, is your research process as elegant as you can make it?

After you've planned your research procedure step by step, pretest it on a small scale, if possible, to see what works and what doesn't, as well as where the glitches and potential pitfalls are. With foresight—and luck—trial can prevent error.

Find a sponsor.   To start an investigation you have to have good reason—preferably with evidence—to believe that a problem actually exists. If your work promises to be costly or time-consuming, a sponsor—most likely a professor, newspaper, or organization whose principles your investigation reinforces—is invaluable. The sponsor will not only help to provide a context for your research, but also to pay for it—if you're lucky, perhaps your tuition, and a salary, in addition to the costs of the investigation.

Do those who pay the investigator call the shots? To an extent, they do, as James Axtell makes clear (page 279), just as the editorial policy of the *Washington Post* would determine whether or not they'd send Woodward and Bernstein out to do a story on the Watergate burglary and continue to pay for the investigation thereafter. Sponsors also provide protection for the investigator.

Ask a manageable question.   Your choice of subject, or of a specific aspect of your subject, may be partly determined by your available research time. Controversial or novel subjects need to be explained thoroughly enough to enable unfamiliar readers to understand the background, the issues, and the larger implications. You need to include enough details to satisfy skeptical readers that you know what you're talking about, even if they don't agree with you; a solid case can compel belief, even forestall libel suits. So you may need to write about a smaller segment of your subject than you had anticipated, to have room for sufficient support for your assertions.

If the question is complicated, break it into smaller subquestions and pursue one of those. Suppose, for instance, that you are distressed by great variations in penalties for drunken drivers who cause fatalities. One drunken driver is jailed for a year and ordered to pay $150,000 restitution to the victim's family. Another is fined $500 and sentenced to a weekend program of public service for six months. Another is acquitted, largely because the driver holds a responsible position as a nurse, despite incontrovertible evidence of having consumed six beers just before hitting and killing a teenage pedestrian. Because of limited time and space for writing, you may decide to focus on variations in penalties for drunken drivers who cause fatalities in your local police jurisdiction rather than nationwide.

If you start your investigation from scratch, be sure to allow enough time to do it thoroughly. A realistic way to calculate your research time is to come up with a generous estimate of how long it will take you to do each step—then double it. With luck, that figure will approximate the time you'll actually need to spend. For example, even investigating a subject as seemingly simple as a sudden rise in prices at your college bookstore might require an interview with the bookstore manager, another interview with the manager of a rival bookstore for comparison, and calls to several publishers to verify what the bookstore managers have told you, before you can begin to write. Even the most carefully planned investigation has to be flexible enough to accommodate schedules of people you're interviewing and repeated phone calls if people aren't available or you need to follow up or verify your initial contacts. Often, one lead suggests another; your own sense of completion (or a deadline) will tell you when to stop.

Case histories lend themselves to manageable investigation in a limited time. If you know someone whose situation seems reasonably typical of a common plight, you can interview the person and use the case history as a specific example about which you can generalize. Student Denise Butler used the case history of Ann and Roger (not their real names) to make her readers aware of the widespread problem of spousal abuse. Their life together, Butler says, was typical. Roger had been beaten throughout childhood by "an alcoholic father who demanded strict adherence to the laws he set down." After an early, shotgun marriage, the wife beatings began almost immediately; "Roger was always sorry but said it was the only way to control Ann." For the first five years Ann covered up for him, "There was always the promise and the belief that this was the last time." She then left him, returned when he promised to reform, and for the next fifteen years she and their children lived "in silent fear of the beatings, sexual abuse, and midnight walks at gunpoint." Roger's acknowledgement of his "numerous affairs" finally drove Ann to a therapist, and ultimately to a divorce. She was willing to tell her story to Butler because, as Ann said, "'I hate for children to grow up believing it's O.K. to stand a woman in a corner and beat her until she's unconscious, when she misbehaves.'"

Butler expands on Ann's case with information gained from reading:

> Ann's story is not unlike the 27 million other cases reported yearly in emergency rooms across the country. 4.7 million of these cases result in serious injuries similar to Ann's broken ribs and concussion. Still other women are literally beaten to death. The statistics are appalling but the truth is that there are probably twice that number of unreported instances of wife beating.

You might devote a limited amount of time (several hours, a week, a whole semester or longer) to a trial investigation of an apparently simple question. Try using whatever primary or secondary sources of information (pages 283–85) are appropriate to the issue, and see what you come up with. If one source doesn't work, try another.

Persevere. If you've ever tried to trace the lineage of an ancestor, you're undoubtedly aware of the need for painstaking perseverance. Records may or may not exist; you won't know until you search in obvious and more obscure places. Those records that you do find may not be complete, or they may be in handwriting or a language you can't understand. Even when the birth record or the flyleaf in the family bible corroborates the existence of "Jane Smith," what other evidence do you have that she's the Jane Smith you're looking for? Could her name have been changed by marriage? And so on. (Laurel Thatcher Ulrich's Pulitzer prize-winning *A Midwife's Tale* is an exemplary model of this type of research, in its sophisticated, seven-year investigation of a Revolutionary War midwife's diary.)

When the subject of your investigation is controversial—or might be if new information about it were to be revealed, it may be even harder to find obscure or concealed evidence or other salient information. You will write more responsibly on any subject if you corroborate each bit of information with at least two sources independent of each other, to try to avoid problems that individual, biased, or self-serving sources might create.

Be willing to take risks.   It's hard to determine in advance what these will be. But you can bet your ballpoint that if your research threatens the status quo, you're going to put people on the defensive who have a vested interest in keeping things as they are. They may respond, politely or otherwise, by trying to block your investigation ("Confidential. For official use only.") or by questioning the accuracy and completeness of your information. They may question your fitness to write on the subject ("Too complicated for an undergraduate to understand. Trust me.") or your competence in so doing. They may haul out precedent ("No one has ever complained about this before!") or policy ("Channel all complaints through the Grievance Committee.") to try to keep you quiet. They may attack you personally to try to discredit your work. They may ostracize, shun, reprimand, or fire you. If the stakes are high enough, or your opponents angry enough, they may carry out their threats. If you're crusading for a cause, you may decide that principle overrides any personal considerations. But if you can't stand the heat, as Harry Truman was fond of saying, get out of the kitchen.

Student Kenneth Via's essay, "A Bark With a Bite," recounts the efforts of Marin County, California student reporters of the award-winning high-school newspaper, *Bark,* to investigate the ease with which underage teenagers could buy liquor without proof of age. The project was carefully planned. The reporters questioned their fellow students to get some sense of the extent of the problem. Their advisor insisted that the reporters, aged fifteen to seventeen, get permission slips from their parents. She consulted the Student Law Center in Washington, D.C., and followed up on its advice by discussing the proposed investigation with a local libel lawyer. Even though the actual investigation took only four days, the advance preparations required nearly a month.

The reporters spent four days trying to buy liquor without showing proof of age. In ten of twenty-four attempts, they succeeded. Wrote student Karen

Gliebe in *Bark,* "A Redwood [High School] junior enters a Corte Madera liquor store. She is just five feet tall, wears braces, has freckles, and looks about 14 years old. She exits with a six-pack of beer. 'No problem,' she says." Although some students, fearing an end to easy liquor purchases, called the reporters traitors, their efforts were commended by the Marin County Board of Supervisors and the local papers. Predictably, however, there were some potentially serious negative repercussions. Sylvia Jones, the faculty advisor, was reprimanded by the principal for encouraging the students to break the law, and thereby placing "not only yourself but the school and district in serious legal risk." When the *Bark* defended Ms. Jones, the superintendent remarked ominously, "We control the printshop and I don't see how the school papers, the *Bark* in particular, can have the audacity to attack the administration when we can wipe them out."

Be prepared for surprise, failure, or fizzle.   Can you cope with the possibility of lack of evidence, dead ends, or defeat after weeks or months of hard work? Can you cope with knowing that any day your investigation could blow up in your face? Or that you could be wrong? Or that if your research generates controversial findings, people with power may try to suppress them? Consider the difficulties Galileo and Freud, among other notable investigators, faced before their controversial ideas were accepted in the scientific community.

Be prepared for success.   Reaching and influencing an audience, causing them to see an issue your way, making contributions to the field, changing the world in some way, small or large, are an investigator's ultimate rewards. (Well, there's always fame and money, but don't count on either.) How and where you can present your findings is the subject of the next chapter. As you may have surmised by now, publication of controversial material is not necessarily easy.

In *Poison Penmanship,* Jessica Mitford explains the difficulties she faced in publishing her investigation of the fraudulent Famous Writers School, whose advertising encouraged naive aspiring writers to enroll in an extremely expensive correspondence course under the mistaken belief that their work would be critiqued personally by Rod Serling, Bennett Cerf, Faith Baldwin, or other Famous Writers. "If you want to write and see your work published," chorused Baldwin and Cerf in practically identical sales pitches, "my colleagues and I would like to test your writing aptitude." Mitford's international reputation as a tough and thorough investigator gave her access to all fifteen of the Famous Writers, and a tour of the school itself, where fifty-five nonfamous nonwriters composed canned paragraphs of criticism for some 50,000 manuscripts a year. But fear that the Famous Writers School would retaliate by withdrawing their lucrative advertisements caused the editors of *McCall's, Life,* and the *Atlantic* to refuse to publish Mitford's article, despite initial commitments to do so. Finally the *Atlantic* not only relented but canceled its advertising contract with Famous Writers School.

One final word of caution. By the time you've finished a long-term investigation, you'll have an enormous investment in it, heart and mind, body and soul. Nevertheless, keep your reader's attention focused on your subject, not on yourself. Hard work should look easy and read well. Lillian Ross advises, "Do not, in effect, say, 'Look at me. See what a great [writer] I am! Do not, if you want to reveal that the Emperor is not wearing any clothes, write, "I am showing that the Emperor is naked." If you look intently at your subject rather than into the mirror, you may, indeed, create a new aspect of the universe.

Checklist for Writing About Controversy

1. Do I find the subject fascinating? significant?

2. How meaningful is it to others—either on its own merits or through my writing? Who will read this—people likely to agree with me on the issue? prospective opponents? people receptive to change? or people with a vested interest in the status quo?

3. How much effort am I willing to spend to write about it? Is it worth the effort?

4. Can I cover the subject in the amount of space I have for writing? in the amount of available time?

5. Do I have a realistic strategy for investigating my subject? What, for instance, are the main issues and important subissues? What research process will I use?

6. What and who are my key primary sources? secondary sources? Where will I find them? Do I have access to them?

7. Am I willing to take the necessary risks to write about a controversial subject?

8. How will I write about it? as a straightforward presentation of the facts? as a narrative? as an implied or direct argument? as a research paper or report? as an investigative article or series? What will I emphasize? What will I select to include? exclude?

Selected Reference List of Writings About Controversy
(see also Works Cited)

Bazerman, Charles, and James Paradis, Eds. *Textual Dynamics of the Professions: Historical and Contemporary Studies of Writing in Professional Communities.* Madison: U of Wisconsin P, 1991.

Bloom, Lynn Z., Karen Coburn, and Joan Pearlman. *The New Assertive Woman.* 1974. New York: Dell, 1975.

Clifford, James. *The Predicament of Culture: Twentieth-Century Ethnography, Literature, and Art.* Cambridge, MA: Harvard UP, 1988.

Cooper, Marilyn M., and Michael Holzman. *Writing as Social Action.* Portsmouth, N.H.: Heinemann. 1989.

Corbett, Edmund P. J. *Classical Rhetoric for the modern Student.* 3rd ed. New York: Oxford UP, 1990.

Deakin, James. *Straight Stuff: The Reporters, the Government, and the Truth.* New York: Morrow, 1984.

Elbow, Peter. *Writing Without Teachers.* New York: Oxford UP, 1973.

Hohenberg, John, ed. and commentator. *The Pulitzer Prize Story II, 1959–1980.* New York: Columbia UP, 1980.

Horowitz, Gideon. *Sadistic Statistics: An Introduction to Statistics for the Social and Behavioral Sciences.* Wayne, NJ: Avery, 1981.

Kinneavy, James L. *A Theory of Discourse.* 1971. New York: Norton, 1980.

Kuhn Thomas. *The Structure of Scientific Revolutions.* Rev. ed. Chicago: U of Chicago P, 1970.

Mitford, Jessica. *The American Way of Death.* New York: Simon, 1968.

Scholes, Robert. *Textual Power: Literary Theory and the Teaching of English.* New Haven: Yale UP, 1985.

Scholes, Robert, Nancy R. Comley, and Gregory L. Ulmer. *Text Book: An Introduction to Literary Language.* New York: St. Martin's, 1988.

Seldes, George. *Even the Gods Can't Change History. The Facts Speak for Themselves: An Investigation of Truth in Reporting.* Secaucus, NJ: Stewart, 1976.

Steffens, J. Lincoln. *The Autobiography of Lincoln Steffens.* 1931. New York: Harcourt, 1968.

Tompkins, Jane. "'Indians': Textualism, Morality, and the Problem of History." in *Race, Writing, and Difference.* Ed. Henry Louis Gates, Jr. Chicago: U of Chicago P, 1986, 101–19.

Woodward, Bob, and Carl Bernstein. *All the President's Men.* New York: Simon, 1974.

Works Cited

Axtell, James. "The Scholar's Obligations to Native Peoples." *After Columbus: Essays in the Ethnohistory of Colonial North America.* New York: Oxford UP, 1988. 244–53.

Bok, Sissela. *Lying: Moral Choice in Public and Private Life.* New York: Pantheon, 1978.

Cook, Alison. "Magna Cum Fraud." *Gentleman's Quarterly.* 62.8 (Aug. 1992): 184–192, 197–201.

Didion, Joan. "Why I Write." *New York Times Book Review* 6 Dec. 1976. 2.

Elbow, Peter. *Embracing Contraries: Explorations in Learning and Teaching.* New York: Oxford UP, 1986. 55–57, 234.

Gansberg, Martin. "38 Who Saw Murder Didn't Call the Police." *New York Times* 17 Mar. 1964: B1.

Geertz, Clifford. *Works and Lives: The Anthropologist as Author.* Stanford, CA: Stanford UP, 1988.

Harper Book of American Quotations. Comp. Gorton Carruth and Eugene Ehrlich. New York: Harper, 1988.

King, Martin Luther, Jr., "Letter from Birmingham Jail" 1963. rpt. *The Essay Connection: Readings for Writers.* Ed. Lynn Z. Bloom 3rd ed. Lexington MA. 1991, 592.

MacDonald, Susan Peck. "The Literary Argument and Its Discursive Conventions." *The Writing Scholar: Studies in Academic Discourse.* Ed. Walter Nash. Newbury Park, CA: Sage, 1990, 31–62.

Mitford Jessica. *Poison Penmanship: The Gentle Art of Muckraking.* 1975. New York: Knopf, 1979.

Morganthau, Tom. "Should Drugs Be Legal?: *Newsweek* 30 May, 1988, pp. 36–38.

Orwell, George. "Marrakech." *An Age Like This 1920–1940.* Vol. 1 of *The Collected Essays, Journalism and Letters of George Orwell.* Ed. Sonia Orwell and Ian Angus. 4 vols. New York: Harcourt, 1968. 187–93.

Rich, Adrienne. "When We Dead Awaken." *On Lies, Secrets, and Silence, Selected Prose 1966–1978.* New York: Norton, 1979. 32–49.

Ross, Lillian. *Reporting.* 1964. New York: Dodd, 1981. 3.

Schmalz, Jeffrey. "Covering AIDS and Living It: A Reporter's Testimony." *New York Times* 20 Dec. 1992, sec. 4: 1,5.

Ulrich, Laurel Thatcher. *A Midwife's Tale: The Life of Martha Ballard, Based on Her Diary, 1785–1812.* New York: Knopf, 1990.

Watts, Tige. "USC can't shake off Holderman ghost." *The Gamecock* [U. of South Carolina], 24 Aug. 1992, 1, 6–7.

Williams, Terry Tempest. "The Clan of One-Breasted Women." *Refuge: An Unnatural History of Family and Place.* New York: Random, 1991. 281–90.

11

PUBLISHING: REACHING A WIDER AUDIENCE

He does not write at all whose poems no man reads.

— MARTIAL

Publish or perish.

— ACADEMIC MOTTO

No place affords a more striking conviction of the vanity of human hopes than a public library.

— SAMUEL JOHNSON

The Three R's of Publishing: Rewards, Risks, Responsibilities

Rewards

Seeing your name in print is like seeing your name in lights on a theater marquee. Publication represents just what the word implies: *public* recognition of your writing, an external validation of your work, acknowledgment that other people want to read what you write. Lord Byron, who "woke one morning and found himself famous" upon the publication of *Childe Harold's Pilgrimage* acknowledged, "'Tis pleasant, sure, to see one's name in print." That's the happy side of publishing. However, as Samuel Johnson's quotation on the chapter opening implies, literary renown and money are neither synonymous nor certain.

Risks

Publication is also risky, and that may or may not be exhilarating, depending on how much of a risk-taker you are. When you publish, you make a public commitment to your ideas, your research, your way of seeing the familiar and the unfamiliar. The more original you are—in subject, point of view, or style—the greater your opportunity to contribute significantly to your field. However, you are also more likely to risk offending readers who can't cope with the new and different. Consider the difficulties that James Joyce, D. H. Lawrence, and Gertrude Stein had in publishing works that had innovative styles, unconventional content—books such as *Ulysses* and *Lady Chatterly's Lover,* which are now considered classics.

Other works are rejected because publishers are afraid of stylistic innovations, unconventional or immoral subjects, or commercial failure. Among notable writings that were initially rejected are Walt Whitman's *Leaves of Grass,* George Orwell's *Animal Farm,* Julia Child's *Mastering the Art of French Cooking* (twice), James Joyce's *Dubliners* (twenty-two times), and William Faulkner's *Sanctuary,* which, according to *Rotten Rejections,* received the publisher's comment, "Good God, I can't publish this. We'd both be in jail." Alex Haley was an accomplished author before he finished *Roots,* having collaborated with Malcolm X on the latter's best-selling and widely respected *Autobiography of Malcolm X.* Nevertheless, *Roots* was rejected thirteen times before Haley had even an encouraging reaction from an editor. He said he wept in gratitude, though his reward—and revenge—was the book's enormous commercial success.

Such cautionary tales, and they are legion, reinforce the point that when you write you run the risk that your writing may take a great deal of effort without returning an immediate or eventual reward. Although instant success occasionally happens, the odds of attaining fame and a livable income with one's first works are about the same as the chances of an aspiring actor becoming a Broadway star without first performing in local acting companies and summer stock. But the process is not mysterious, as Judith Appelbaum's candid, comprehensive, and reassuring *How to Get Happily Published* makes very clear. Her book gives a good strategic overview of the publishing process.

Responsibilities

Writing is a performing art, with an audience actual or implied, waiting to read your work. When you decide to publish, you make a public commitment to accuracy and to excellence. To err in print is to undermine your competent authorial persona, so before submitting a manuscript for publication, you will need to take the following extra precautions.

Double-check your information.   Check all facts against two sources that are up-to-date and reliable. If they're biased—and almost everything, statistics, graphs, and photographs included, has a slanted point of view—you'll need to acknowledge and account for the bias. If you find your sources tilting more to one side than you wish, you'll need to incorporate other sources that right the balance.

Quote sources accurately.   Whether your sources are written or oral, make sure you represent both the words and the music accurately. Identify the context if necessary to convey the essence of the quotation. Suppose you quote a newspaper headline that reads: "The Economy Falters, a President Falls/Voters Lose Faith and Choose Change." But which president? George Bush? Jimmy Carter? Herbert Hoover? the president of another country entirely? You need to specify the president, the country, the paper's date, or all three, depending on how much information would make the reference clear.[1]

Edit and proofread.   Polish your prose until it shines. The prospect of publication is a considerable incentive to revise and revise again, and to finetune your work until the content, organization, style, and form approach your ideal. Even if you have already done considerable revision, a final, cleareyed look at a manuscript is likely to reveal infelicitous word choices and errors of spelling, punctuation, and mechanics, which undercut the writer's professional image.

Editing and Proofreading a Manuscript: Final Copy

In "Red and Black, or One English Major's Beginning," student Ning Yu explains the difficult circumstances of how he learned English while living in Communist China. Final changes in the manuscript appear in brackets and follow the boldfaced, bracketed words and punctuation from the previous version. The boldfaced material was omitted in the final copy and the text here is abridged slightly.

Red and Black, or One English Major's Beginning

I have always told my friends that my first English teacher was my father. 1
That is the truth, but not the whole truth. It was a freezing morning more than twenty years ago, we, some fifty odd boys and girls, were shivering in a poorly heated classroom when the door [was] pushed open and in came a gust of wind and Comrade Chang Hong-gen, our young teacher. Wrapped in an elegant army overcoat, Comrade Chang [strolled] strode in front of the blackboard and began to address us in [what was then to us] outrageous gibberish. His [stride, his] gestures, his facial expressions, and his [vocal resonance] [loud voice] unmistakably communicated that he was lecturing us as a People's Liberation Army captain would address his soldiers before a battle—in revolutionary war movies, that is. Of course we didn't understand a word of the speech until he translated it into Chinese later:

Comrades, red-guards, and revolutionary pupils: The Great Revolutionary Teacher Marx teaches us: "A foreign language is an important weapon in the struggle of human life." Our Great Leader, Great Teacher, Great Supreme-Commander, and Great Helmsman, Chairman Mao, has also taught us that it is not too difficult to learn a foreign language. "Nothing in the world is too difficult if you are willing to tackle it with the same spirit in which we conquered this mountain."

Now, as you know, the Soviet Social Imperialists and the U.S. Imperialists have agreed on a venomous scheme to enslave China. For years the U.S. Imperialists have brought war and disaster to Vietnam. . . . Their evil purpose is obvious—to invade China . . . from the south through Vietnam.

. . . As intellectual youth, you must not only prepare to sacrifice your lives for the party and the Motherland, but also learn to stir up our people's patriotic zeal and to shatter the morale of the enemy troops. . . . to crush the enemy, you must learn your English lessons well with me.

Then Comrade Chang paused, his face red and sweat beading [out] on the 2
tip of his nose. Though nonplused, we could see that he was genuinely excited, but we were not sure whether his excitement was induced by "patriotic zeal," [his grandiose utterance of nonsensical sounds in such a long chain,] or the [mere] pleasure of hearing [those] grandiose sounds issued from his own lips. [Somehow] For my part, I [intuited] [suspected] that verbal intoxication [was more likely the true cause of] [caused] his excitement. [, for] Scanning the classroom, he seemed to bask in our admiration rather than to urge us to sacrifice our lives for the Party. He then translated the speech into Chinese and [impressed us with] [gave us] another dose of [his] eloquence:

From now on, you are not pupils anymore, but soldiers. Young, intellectual soldiers fighting at a special front. Neither is each English word you learn merely a word anymore. Each new word is a bullet shot at the enemy's chest, and each sentence is a hand grenade.

Comrade Chang was from a "red" family. [, as] His name [suggests—] *hong*   3
means red in Chinese, and *gen* means root, so literally, [this young teacher of
ours] [he] was "Chang of Red Root." [They] [Students] said that his father was
a major in the People's Liberation Army. . . . When the Great Proletariat Cultural Revolution started, Mr. Chang had just graduated from the Beijing Foreign
Languages Institute, a prestigious university in the capital [of Red China] where
some thirty languages were taught to people "of red roots." . . . We understood that Comrade Chang would work only for a token period in our ghetto
[neighborhood] middle school, but as soon as the "movement" was over and
everything back to normal, Comrade Chang [, we knew,] would leave us and
begin his diplomatic career.

[One of the conclusions drawn by the Revolution] In the later 1960s [was   4
the word] [the Revolution defined] "intellectual" [was really] [as] "subversive."
So my father, a university professor educated in a British missionary school in
Tianjin, was regarded as a "black" element, an enemy of the people. [In 1967,]
our family was driven out of the university faculty apartment [early in 1967],
and I found myself in a ghetto [neighborhood] middle school, an undeserving
pupil of the red expert Comrade Chang.

[It was] In [that] [a] shabby and ill-heated schoolroom [we] [I] began [our]   5
[my] first English lesson, not "from the very beginning" by studying the alphabet, but with some powerful "hand grenades."

Drop your guns!
Down with Soviet Neo-Czarists!
Down with U.S. Imperialism!
Long live Chairman Mao!
Victory belongs to our people!

These sentences turned out to be [almost] more difficult and more danger-   6
ous to handle than real grenades, for [very] soon the words became mixed up
in our heads. So much so that not a few "revolutionary pupils" reconstructed
the slogans to the healthy satisfaction of themselves but to the horror of
Comrade Chang.

Long live the Soviet Neo-Czarists!
Victory belongs to your guns!

Upon hearing this, Comrade Chang turned pale and shouted at us, "You idiots! Had you uttered anything like that in Chinese, young as you are, you could
have been thrown into jail for years. Probably me too! Now you follow me
closely: "Long live Chairman Mao"!

"Long live Chairman Mao"! We shouted back.
"Down with the Soviet Neo-Czarists!"
"Down with the Soviet Neo-Czarists!"

Comrade Chang decided that those two sentences were enough for idiots to   7
learn in one lesson, and he told us to forget the other sentences for the moment.
Then he wrote the two sentences on the chalk board and asked us to copy them
on our English exercise books [which of course we didn't have. None of us

knew what an English exercise-book was at that time]. [Alas, how could any-body in our school know what that was!]

I wrote the two sentences on my left palm and **[remembered to avoid]** 8 [avoided] putting my left hand in my pocket or mitten for the rest of the day. I also remembered [**well**] what Comrade Chang said about being thrown into jail, for as the son of a "black, stinking bourgeois intellectual," I [**intuitively**] grasped the truth in his warning. The two English sentences were [**but**] a long series of meaningless [**sounds**], [**unheard of and**] unutterable [**. I can't register them accurately in my mind simply because Teacher Chang had assigned them some Chinese meaning.**] [sounds. Comrade Chang had the power to impose some Chinese meaning on my mind.] So, before I forgot or confused the sounds, I invented a [**sort of**] make-shift transliteration in Chinese for the phonetically difficult and politically dangerous parts of the sentence. I put the Chinese words *gie, mian,* and *mao* (cut, noodle, hair) under "Chairman Mao," and *nju za sui* (beef organ meat) under "Neo-Czarists." "Down with" were bad words ap-plied to the enemies; "long live" were good words reserved for the great leader. These were easy to remember. So I went home with a sense of security, [**because I thought my crude**] [thinking the] device helped me distinguish the Great Leader from the enemy.

The next morning, Comrade "Red Roots" asked us to try our [**new**] weapons 9 before the blackboard. Nobody volunteered. Then Comrade Chang began [**to**] call[ing] us by name [**s and**]. . . . [**However, though my classmates obediently stood up one after another**] [in fact,] none [of my classmates] remembered the sentences.

My fellow pupils were all "red" theoretically. But they were not Comrade 10 Chang's type of red. Their parents were coolies, candy-peddlers, or bricklay-ers. Poor and illiterate. Before the 1949 revolution, these people led miserable lives. [**After**] [Even] the revolution [**the parent's lives were not much improved**] [didn't improve their lives much], and [**they would rather have had**] [parents preferred] their children [**to**] do chores at home [rather] than [**allowed them to**] fool around with books, especially after the "Great Proletariat Cultural Revolution" started in 1966. Books were dangerous. Those who read books [**were persecuted.**] [often ran into trouble for having ideas the Party didn't want them to have.] "Look at the intellectuals," they said. "They suffer even more than us illiterates." . . .

[**So**] [Thus] my friends didn't waste [their] time in remembering nonsense. 11 [**But**] [Still] Comrade Chang's questions had to be answered. Since I was the only one in class [**who was**] not from a red family, my opinion was always [the one] asked last [**for**], if asked at all. I stood up when Comrade Chang called my name. I had forgotten the English sounds too . . . I glanced at my left palm and [**a sudden**] [an] inspiration lit up my mind. "Long live gie mian mao!" "Down with nu za sui!" My friends stared, and Comrade Chang glared at me. "Say that again." He couldn't believe his ears. I did. This time my classmates burst into a roar of laughter. "Cut noodle hair!" "Beef organ meat!" they shouted again and again.

"[**You**] Shut up!" Comrade Chang yelled, trembling with anger and point- 12 ing at me with his right index finger. "What do you mean by 'cut noodle hair'?

That insults our great leader Chairman Mao." [**Upon**] Hearing that, the class suddenly became silent. The sons and daughters of the "Chinese working people" knew how serious an accusation like that could be. But Calf stood up and said: "Comrade Teacher. . . . Ning Yu didn't [**seem to**] mean any harm[.] [**, for all**] He was trying to [**to do is**] throw [**the**] [a] hand grenade at the enemy [.] [,] [**However, didn't**] He also call[ed] the Soviets 'beef organ meat.' He said one bad thing (not enough respect for Chairman Mao) but then said a good thing (condemning the Soviets). One take away one is zero. So he didn't really do anything wrong, right?" [Again] the room shook with laughter.

Now Comrade Chang flew into a rage and began to lecture us about how 13
class enemies often say good things to cover up evil intentions. . . . He said that in the "urgent state of war" what I said could [**neither**] [not] be forgiven [n]or overlooked. [**I must seriously**] [He told me to] examine my [**own**] mind and conduct [a] severe self-criticism before being [**ruthlessly**] punished. "The great proletariat dictatorship," he said, "is all powerful. All good will be rewarded and all evil punished when the right time comes." [**This young teacher of ours**] [He] left the classroom in anger without giving us any new [**bullets or**] hand grenades [**that day**].

I felt ruined. Destroyed. Undone. I [**almost felt the**] [could feel] icy steel 14
handcuffs [closing] around my wrists. I could hear the revolutionary slogans that the [**revolutionary masses**] [mobs] would shout at me when I was [**taken away to be crushed by the iron fist**] [dragged off by the iron hand] of the Proletariat Dictatorship. My legs almost failed me on my way home [**after the school was over**].

[**But**] Calf knew better. "You [**really**] have nothing to worry about. . . . [**All**] 15
Words are empty shells. It's the feeling that people attach to a word that counts."

"I'll be crushed like a rotten egg by the iron fist of the Great Proletarian 16
Dictatorship," I said.

"No way. Red Rooty is not going to tell on you. Don't you know he was 17
more scared than you? He was responsible. How could you [**utter those sounds had**] [say such things if] he [had] not taught you? You get it? You relax. *Gie mian mao*! You know, you really sound like Rooty." Calf grinned.

[**With the help of**] [Although] Calf's wisdom [**I did**] [helped me to] "get it," 18
[but] relax I could not. My legs were as stiff as sticks and my heart beat against my chest so hard that I could hardly breathe. For many years I had [**been trying**] [tried] to get rid of my "blackness" by hard work and good manners. But I could not succeed [**because however**]. [No matter how] hard I tried I could not change the fact that I was not "red." . . .

The next morning, I went to school with a faltering heart, expecting to be 19
called out of the classroom and cuffed. [**Yet**] [N]othing happened. Comrade Chang seemed to have forgotten [**the episode of yesterday**] [my transgression] and gave us [**about**] three handfuls of [**new**] "bullets." He slowed down [**considerably**] too, placing more emphasis on pronunciation [**of the individual words**]. He cast the "bullets" into hand grenades only after he was sure that we could shoot the "bullets" with [**some**] certainty.

Nothing happened to me that day, or the next day, or the week after. Calf 20
was [**apparently**] right. As [**days and**] weeks passed, my [**hatred**] [dislike] of

Chang [**began to**] dwindle[d] and I began to feel something akin to gratitude toward him. Before [learning] his English tongue twisters, [**all**] we [**did was to**] [only] recite[d] Chairman Mao's thirty-six poems. We did that for so long that I memorized the annotations together with the text. I also memorized how many copies were produced [**respectively**] for the first, the second and the third printings. I was bored, and [**the new sounds**] Teacher Chang[**'s tongue twisters**] brought me relief . . . .

Forty hand grenades were as many as the Party thought proper for us to 21 [**have**] [hold]. Before I mastered [**my newest explosive**] [the fortieth] tongue twister—"Revolutionary committees are fine"—our "fine" revolutionary committee ordered Comrade Chang to stop [**his**] English lessons and to make us dig [**deep**] holes for air raid shelters. Comrade Chang approached [t]his new task with just as much "patriotic zeal" as he taught English[.] [**, seemingly**] [In truth he seemed] content to let our "bullets" and "hand grenades" rust at the bottom of the holes we dug.

But I was not willing to let my only fun [**to**] slip away [**that**] easily. When 22 digging [**the air raid shelter**] hole[s] I repeated the forty slogans silently [**again and again**]. I even said them at home in bed. One [**evening**] [night] I [**unwittingly**] uttered a sentence as I climbed onto my top bunk. Reading in the bottom bunk, my father heard me and was surprised. He [**wanted to know**] [asked] where I learned the words. Then for the first time I told him about Comrade Chang's English lessons.

Now it may seem strange for a middle school boy not to turn to his family 23 [**for help**] during a "political crisis[.] [,]" [**B**] [b]ut at that time it was not strange [**for me**] at all. [**By then**] my mother, my sister, and my brother had already been sent to the countryside in two different remote provinces. [Getting help from them was almost impossible for] [**and**] they had enough pressing problems themselves. Help from my father was even more impractical; he was already an "enemy of the people," and therefore whatever he said or did for me could only [**further**] complicate my problems rather than resolve them. So I left him in the dark. Since we only had each other in the huge city of eight million people, we shared many things, but not [**each other's**] political problems.

Our home in the working class neighborhood was a single seventeen-square- 24 meter room. Kitchen, bathroom, sitting room, study, bedroom, all in one. There was no ceiling, so we could see the black beam and rafters [**lying**] [when we lay] in bed. The floor was a damp and sticky dirt, which defied [**any**] attempt[s] at sweeping and mopping. The walls were yellow and were as damp as the dirt floor. To partition the room was out of the question. Actually, my parents sold their king-sized bed and our single beds, and bought two bunk beds in their stead. My mother and sister each occupied a top bunk, my father slept on one bottom bunk, and my brother and I shared the other. [**The**] Red Guards had confiscated and burned almost all of my father's Chinese books, but miraculously they left his English books intact. The English books were stuffed under the beds on the dirt floor. We lived in this manner for more than a year [un]til the family members were scattered all over China, first my siblings to a province in the northwest, and then my mother to southern China. They were a thousand miles from us and fifteen hundred miles from each other. After they left,

I moved to the top bunk over my father, and we piled the books on the other bed. Thanks to the hard covers, only the bottom two layers of the books had begun to mold.

That evening, after hearing me murmuring [**to myself**] in English, my father gestured [**for**] me to sit down [**in**] [on] his bunk [**and**] [.] [He] asked [me] whether I knew any [**other English**] sentences [other] than the one he had [**just**] heard. I jumped at [**this**] [the] opportunity to go through the [**complete**] inventory of my English arsenal. [After] [**Having patiently**] listen[ed] [ing] to my forty [odd] slogans my father said: "You have a very good English teacher. [**I mean**], [He] has an excellent pronunciation, standard Oxford pronunciation. But the sentences are not likely to be found in any [**English**] books written by native English speakers. Did he teach you how to read?"

"I can read all those sentences if you write them out."

"If I write them [**out**]? But can't *you* write them by yourself?"

"No."

"Did he teach you grammar?"

"No."

"Did he teach you the alphabet?"

"No."

My father looked amused [**and**] [.] [S]lowly [**shaking**] he shook] his head, [and then] [**he**] asked [**again**]: "Can you recognize the words, the separate words, when they appear in different contexts?"

"I think so, but I'm not sure."

He re-opened the book that he was reading and turned to the first page and pointed with his index finger at the first word in the first sentence, signaling me to identify it.

I shook my head.

He moved his finger to the next word. I didn't know that either. Nor did I know the third word, the shortest word in the line, the word made up of a single letter. My father traced the whole sentence slowly, hoping that I could identify [**any**] [some] words. I recognized the bullet "in" and at once threw a hand grenade at him: "Beloved Chairman Mao, you are the red sun in our hearts." Encouraged, my father moved his finger back to the second word in the sentence. This time I looked at the word more closely but couldn't recognize it. "It's an 'is,'" he said. "You know 'are' but not 'is'! The third word in this sentence is an 'a.' It means 'one.' It is the first letter in the alphabet and you don't know that either! What a teacher! A well-trained one too!" He [then] cleared his throat and read the whole sentence aloud [**to me**]: "It is a truth universally acknowledged, that a man in possession of a good fortune, must be in want of a wife."

The sounds he uttered reminded me of Chang's opening speech, but they flowed out of my father's mouth smoothly. I asked my father to repeat it several times because I liked [**its**] [the] rhythm. Pleased with my curiosity, my father began to explain the grammatical structure of the sentence. [**But**] His task turned out to be much harder than he expected, for he had to explain [the] [such] terms as "subject," "object," "nouns," "verbs," and "adjectives." To help me understand the structure of the English sentence, he had to teach me Chinese grammar first. . . .

[That night,] our English lessons started [that night]. He taught me the let- 39
ters A through F. By the end of [that] [the] week, I had learned my alphabet.
Afterward he [began to teach me] [taught] the basics of [English] grammar,
sometimes using my hand grenades [as examples] to illustrate the rules. He also
taught me the international phonetic symbols and the way to use a dictionary.
For [my] reading materials, he excerpted [grammatically] simple passages from
whatever books [that were] available. We started our lessons at a [fairly] manageable pace, but after a couple of months, for reasons he didn't tell me till the
very last, he speeded up [the lessons] considerably [. and] [.] The new words
that I had to memorize increased from twenty words per day to fifty [words].
To meet the challenge, I wrote the new words on small, thin scraps of paper
and hid them in the little red book of Chairman Mao, so that I could memorize them during political study hours at school. In [the] hole-digging afternoons I recited the sentences and sometimes even little paragraphs—aloud when
I was sure that Chang was not around.

Before the sounds and shapes of English words became less [slippery,] elu- 40
sive, before I could confidently [learn more of English] [study] by myself, my
father told me that I would have to continue [my English study] on my own.
He was going to join "the Mao Tsetung Thought Study Group" [in] [at] his
university. . . . [a] euphemism for imprisonment. [It had happened to him]
[He had been imprisoned] once when my mother and siblings were still in
Beijing. Now it had come again. [So] I [simply] asked, "Are you detained or
arrested?" "I don't know." He said, "It's just a Study Group." "Oh," I said,
feeling the [full] weight of the [two] words. Legally, detention couldn't be any
longer than fifteen days; arrest [must] [had to] be followed by a conviction and
a sentence, which [also] had a definite term [too]. "Just a Study Group" could
be a week or a life-time. I was [to be] [left] on my own in a city of eight million people, my English lessons indefinitely postponed. What['s] [was] worse,
some people never returned alive from "Study Groups."

"When are you joining them?"   41
"Tomorrow."   42
I [was] [pretended to be] "man" enough not to cry, but my father's eyes were 43
wet when he made me promise to finish [Austen's] *Pride and Prejudice* by the
time he came back.

After he left for the "Study Group," bedding roll [and all] on his shoulder, 44
I took my first [good] [careful] look at the book he thrust into my hands. It was
a [fairly] small book with dark green cloth covers and gilt designs and letters
on its spine. The frontispiece had a flowery design and a woman figure on the
upper right corner, . . . [holding] a scroll [like a baby in her arms]. . . . [In]
[On] the unrolled scroll, there were some words. I was thrilled to find that I
could understand all the words in the top two lines with no difficulty except
the last word: EVERYMAN, / I WILL GO WITH THEE. . . .

Two months after my father entered the "Study Group," I stopped going to 45
his university for my monthly allowance. The Party Secretary of the bursar's
office [had worn] [wore] me out by [repeatedly] telling me [how poorly] [that]
my father and I [didn't] deserve[d] to be fed by [the] "working people." "Your
father [had] [has] never done any positive work," meaning the twenty [odd]

years my father [**had**] taught at the university undermined rather than contributed to [**the**] socialist ideology. To avoid starvation, I picked up horse drop-
pings in the streets and sold them to the farming communes in the suburb [**of
Beijing**]. Between the little cash savings my father left to me and what I earned
by selling dung, I managed [**a malnourished but**] [**an**] independent life.
Meanwhile, I didn't forget my promise to my father. When I saw him again
nineteen months later, I boasted of having thumbed his dictionary [**in**]to shreds
and [**crawled**] [struggled] through Austen's novel [**by sheer will power,**] from
cover to cover. I didn't understand the story, but I [**did**] learn[ed] many [**English**]
words.

My father was not surprised to find that I took pleasure in [**such**] drudgery. 46
He knew that looking up [**new**] English words [**from**] [in] a dictionary and
wrestling with an almost incomprehensible text could be an exciting challenge.
It [**was an**] [provided] an intellectual relief for [**people**] [a teenager] living at a
time when the entire country read nothing but Chairman Mao's works [**and
uttered nothing but revolutionary slogans**]. "Don't worry whether you are red
or black," my father said. "Just be yourself. Just be an ordinary everyman.
Keep up with your good work, and when you learn [**your**] English well enough,
you'll be sure of a guide 'in your most need'."

[**Now doing research on Henry David Thoreau at a major university in New** 47
**England, I often feel surges of gratitude toward my father, and, well, even to
Comrade Chang.**]

Most of Ning's changes are small alterations, mainly of words and phrases
in the earlier draft, to make the final version read more smoothly. The following principles guided Ning's text editing:

1. Make the style fit the subject and context. In this case, many stylistic revisions involve substituting simpler language, which Ning as a schoolboy
would have used at the time of the events he narrates, instead of complicated
expressions that he could only have learned as a sophisticated adult, fluent
in English at the time he wrote the essay. Thus he revises "vocal resonance"
in the fifth sentence to "loud voice," much more in keeping with the general
language level of his tale. *Note:* Subject, style, and context are interrelated.
If Ning had decided to write his entire essay in an elevated, formal style, then
"vocal resonance" would have been appropriate.

2. Be brief. In paragraph 2, Ning pares away most of the words from "his
grandiose utterance of nonsensical sounds in such a long chain," leaving only
"grandiose sounds." Likewise, in the next sentence he replaces "was more
likely the true cause of" simply with "caused."

3. Avoid unnecessary qualifiers. In paragraph 20 Ning deletes "apparently"
from "Calf was apparently right."

4. Don't state the obvious. In this revision, Ning deletes "what was then to
us" from the fourth sentence in paragraph 1, leaving the final version to read
". . . Comrade Chang . . . began to address us in outrageous gibberish."
The context makes obvious the fact that Chang's—or anyone's—English

would have been unintelligible to Chinese children who, at the time, having never studied or even heard the language, wouldn't have a clue as to its meaning. Likewise, because there is only one *Pride and Prejudice* (paragraph 43), it is unnecessary in this context to identify the book's well-known author.

5. Use precise words. Do not settle for close substitutes or vague alternatives. Sometimes Ning, whose native language is Mandarin Chinese, mistakes one English word for another word of similar sound and close—but not exact—meaning. This is the case in paragraph 1, where Ning originally said, "Comrade Chang *strolled* in front of the blackboard. . . ." The revision, "*strode* in front of the blackboard," substitutes for a word connoting casual ambling one that implies the vigor and thrust appropriate to Chang's address to "his soldiers before a battle."

In paragraph 10 Ning wisely substitutes "parents preferred" for the vague original, "they would rather have had," which leaves readers wondering who the *they* is and what they wanted.

6. Vary your vocabulary. To make your writing interesting, unless repetition is necessary for emphasis, try not to overuse certain words. In paragraph 20 Ning deletes words he's used fairly often—"the new sounds"—and uses "Teacher Chang's tongue twisters" instead. The witty alliteration makes the new version itself sound somewhat like a tongue twister, thereby reinforcing the point.

7. Use a point of view compatible with the narrator's character. Throughout the essay Ning deletes from his writing expressions that indicate an adult perspective rather than the child's viewpoint he's trying to recreate. Thus in paragraph 13, Ning substitutes the simple "he" for "this young teacher of ours" because the teacher's youth is more fully apparent to Ning as an adult looking back on the scene than it is to the schoolchildren at the time.

8. Show, don't tell. Ning deletes the essay's last paragraph (47); its meaning is clear enough from the rest of the narrative.

Checklist for Editing

See also "Checklist for Style," (page 48), and "Checklist for Revision," (pages 80–81).

Word choice
1. Do I use strong, emphatic verbs?
2. Do I use the active voice primarily, and save the passive voice to imply passivity?
3. Are verb tenses congruent? (i.e. Are there any shifts between present and past tenses? Should there be?)

4. Are pronoun referents clear? (If I say *it* or *that* will readers know what I'm referring to?)

Sentences

1. Do my sentences have an emphasis and variety that reinforces their meaning?

2. Do I combine groups of sentences that are too short or choppy?

3. Do I break up long or cumbersome sentences?

4. Do I occasionally use parallel construction of sentences or phrases (the same types of words in the same order—"I came, I saw, I conquered.")?

5. Do I use sentence fragments? Can they really stand alone, or should they be incorporated into other sentences?

Spelling and mechanics

1. Do I check the spelling of all words of which I am doubtful? (A computer spell-check will catch many problem words and typos, but it will not discriminate among homonyms—*their, they're, there.*)

2. Do I use punctuation conventionally? If not, do I have good reasons for breaking the rules?

3. Do I acknowledge sources accurately? with appropriate note and bibliographic form?

Types of Publications

Any type of writing discussed in this book is potentially publishable. Fortunately for aspiring writers, there are many places to try your luck. There are over 50,000 magazines and sponsored publications and 40,000 new books published in the United States each year (85 percent of which are nonfiction), not to mention newspapers, campus publications, corporate bulletins, organizational newsletters, art museum catalogs, and fundraising cookbooks. Many of these publications are for specialized audiences and have smaller readerships than the better-known journals. Often these specialized publications pay little or nothing for the material they publish, but they're good places to start to build your reputation as a writer. Publications with large readerships often pay very well, but the competition is enormous. Few writers can meet it when they're just beginning, and many never do. John McPhee, who writes regularly for the *New Yorker*, says he routinely sent all his essays to that magazine for the first eleven years of his career, and each essay was just as routinely rejected. "When The *New Yorker* finally started taking them, they were ready—and so was I."

Some common types of publications follow, identified from the less to the more highly selective.

Class publications.   Some writing classes or other courses put out their own publications. Contributing to these publications is a good way for students to share their best work with each other, with other comparable classes, with prospective majors, and with interested professionals or community groups. All it takes is a computer— preferably with desktop publishing capability—and a printer, some paper, and an energetic student or teacher to organize the manuscripts and production.

Campus publications.   Campus publications include literary or humor magazines, newspapers, law school reviews, publications of various colleges or schools within a university, and those of alumni groups. Unlike classroom publications, these are usually published according to a regular schedule. The opportunity for campus publication is always present, as is the opportunity for constructive criticism from student editors, who are your peers and classmates. Indeed, many of these publications serve as laboratories for the kinds of writing, or editorial or production work, that you might do after graduation.

Special-interest group publications.   Groups with special interests often publish their own bulletins, newsletters, or magazines either for their own members or for a wider readership. Such groups include religious and political organizations; scouting, hosteling, hiking, and other sports and outdoor groups; neighborhood or apartment-complex associations; garden clubs; hobbyist associations; and a host of civic, philanthropic, and self-help groups. Many of these groups have affiliates at local, regional, state, or national levels, with publications for each division. If you're a member of any such group, you may already read their publications, and you may find that they welcome volunteer writing, editorial, and production help.

Company magazines, trade journals, specialized consumer magazines. Some company magazines— such as corporate bulletins, trade journals, and consumer magazines—are usually written by paid staff members. Others, such as airline, computer, and entertainment magazines, accept freelance articles pertinent to the consumers' interests. Unlike the publications of the kinds of groups mentioned earlier, these magazines often pay their contributors. Some students are now publishing state-of-the-art computer manuals and computer software programs; expertise in this new field is often independent of age.

Journals of professions and learned societies. From archaeology to zoology, from economics to physical education to literary criticism, learned journals abound. Some are very specialized (*African-American Review, American Literature,* The *Journal of Sports Psychology*) and some are more general (*Science, Southern Review, Signs*), but all are for scholarly readers. Science students, often participate in laboratory research that results in joint publication with senior researchers and a team of colleagues; graduate students in many fields publish articles, individual or collaborative, in which they make use of their newly specialized knowledge. Publication in these journals helps to establish the writer's scholarly reputation.

General interest magazines and newspapers. Depending on their quality and pay scale, general interest magazines and newspapers may be more or less selective, in choosing articles than learned journals. A great deal of the writing on which *Fact and Artifact* focuses is suitable for magazines and papers of general interest. Newspapers often accept op-ed articles, interviews, reviews from freelance writers or from part-time stringers who report regularly on local or regional news, such as educational developments, sport events, civic issues, or human interest stories.

Publish it yourself. Personal computers with capabilities for desktop publishing enable everyone to publish attractive, professional-looking booklets, monographs, bulletins, even entire magazines or book-length works. Because such publications are relatively inexpensive to produce, businesses and organizations often publish their own work, or produce a master copy to be sent to a copying service or commercial printer.

When you publish a work on your own, it is important to remember the audience for which you intend to distribute your work so you can target them very specifically. Organizations are easy to focus on if the members are the readers. But if you're publishing, say, a church cookbook or a guide to hometown entertainment, you may want to enlist local businesses and bookstores to help sell it. Large sales can be both a blessing and a curse, if the details of production, advertising, selling, and mailing take a great deal of time away from other writing you may want to do.

Appelbaum's discussion of "The Self-Publishing Option" in *How to Get Happily Published* provides a useful overview of the subject. For more extensive guides to the strategic, practical, and technical aspects of self-publishing you'll find the following particularly helpful:

Parker, Roger C. *Looking Good in Print: A Guide to Basic Design for Desktop Publishing.* 2nd ed. Chapel Hill, NC: Ventana Press.

Poynter, Dan. *The Self-Publishing Manual: How to Write, Print & Sell Your Own Book*. Santa Barbara, CA: Para Publishing.

Ross, Tom and Marilyn. *The Complete Guide to Self-Publishing*. Cincinnati: Writer's Digest Books.

Because the books cited throughout this chapter are often updated annually, look for ones with the most recent publication date.

Beware of vanity presses that will publish anything—as long as the author subsidizes the cost. These are the presses that advertise "Manuscripts Wanted!" or send circulars to doctoral students, offering contracts on the basis of half-written dissertations. The scanty, if any, editorial help they provide is matched by their meager sales—usually to the author's friends and relatives; rarely do these sales return more than 25 percent of the author's initial investment. These publications are not treated seriously by reviewers or other professionals.

Writers' Guides

Be sure you are familiar with the publication to which you submit your writing. This cannot be emphasized too strongly, because editors are looking for articles compatible with their publication's subject matter, format, and style. If your writing has been successful in class, on campus, or in publications of other limited groups, you might wish to try to place other writings with publications having a wider readership. Because you already know the territory, you might start with your hometown papers, local magazines, or publications which address your special interest.

If you are a regular reader of the publication to which you wish to submit your work, it should be easy to answer the following questions you need to ask when targeting your writing for any publication:

1. What are the purposes of this publication? Does it promote any particular values, philosophy, or point of view? If so, what are they?

2. Who reads it and for what purposes? to gain professional knowledge or general information? for entertainment? for other reasons?

3. What sorts of articles (essays, features, editorials, reviews, others) does it ordinarily publish? Do these have a characteristic format, length, and organizational pattern?

4. What is the prevailing tone, level of language (formal or informal), and type of specialized language or jargon in the publication?

5. Do photographs, charts and graphs, statistics, or other illustrations commonly accompany the written text? Can I provide these or arrange for someone else to do so?

6. Are my abilities, viewpoints, interests, and literary style compatible with this publication? Could I write for it and would I want to?

For detailed information about which publications pay their writers and which don't, the writers' guides in the following list offer a variety of incidental information on how and where to start publishing. Two of the guides, *Publisher's Weekly* and *Writer's Market,* are particularly comprehensive for general writers, though any journal or magazine will send, on request, its current preferences and editorial specifications. Because publications are born and die, change addresses and editors, and adapt their contents to changing tastes and interests, make sure you consult the *current* volumes or issues of those listed below. These and others should be available in your library.

Ayer Directory of Publications. Philadelphia: Ayer. A directory of daily and weekly newspapers, including college publications; and of consumer, business, technical, trade, and farm magazines arranged by state and city or town of publication.

Directory of Literary Magazines. Mt. Kisco, NY: Moyer Bell Ltd. Sponsored by the Council of Literary Magazines and Presses, this directory lists 500 American periodicals that publish fiction, poetry, and nonfiction.

Gale Directory of Publications and Broadcast Media. Eds. Karen E. Koek and Julie Winklepleck. Detroit: Gale. Thousands of annotated listings of newspapers, magazines, trade publications, radio and television stations. The arrangement, by geographic location, makes it easy to target work with a local focus.

International Directory of Little Magazines and Small Presses. Ed. Len Fulton. Paradise, CA: Dustbooks. This lists all sorts of literary magazines with limited circulations and transient editorial staffs; the contributors' pay is often in prestige rather than cash.

Knowing Where to Look: The Ultimate Guide to Research. by Lois Horowitz. Cincinnati: Writer's Digest. How and where to find information, including addresses and statistics.

Literary Market Place. New Providence, NJ: R. R. Bowker. This partly annotated, exceptionally useful volume lists names and addresses of book and newspaper publishers, literary agents, book manufacturers, and a wealth of other information, arranged by field of activity and subject matter. It also includes literary prizes and writers' conferences.

Publishers' Trade List Annual. New Providence NJ: R. R. Bowker. This large assemblage of publishers' current book catalogs reveals the "personalities" of particular publishing houses and imprints—their specializations and idiosyncrasies.

Publishers Weekly. New York: Publishers Weekly. This is an invaluable comprehensive source of information about publishing facts, figures, ideas, and people, such as the names of editors and literary agents. Announcements of new magazines, often eager for copy, are particularly useful.

Standard Periodical Directory. New York: Oxbridge. This identifies over 65,000 publications by title, previous title, publisher's name, address, editor's name, descriptions of editorial content, circulation figures, and other information.

The Writer. Boston: The Writer. A monthly publication full of upbeat and generally reliable articles by professional writers, on how to write and market various kinds of fiction and nonfiction for general and special fields.

Writer's Digest Handbook of Magazine Article Writing. Cincinnati: Writer's Digest. Similar to *The Writer.* The publisher also offers tapes, correspondence courses, a criticism service, and speakers' kits.

Writer's Market: Where and How to Sell What You Write. Cincinnati: Writer's Digest. This thoroughly annotated annual guide covers over 4000 publications to which a wide variety of freelance writers might wish to submit their work. It is organized by types of publications, subdivided by categories. Thus it lists "Consumer Magazines," including Art and Architecture, Business and Finance, Humor, Personal Computers, Photography, Sports, Women's. Its list of "Trade, Technical, and Professional Journals" includes the categories of Auto and Truck, Aviation and Space, Business Management, Farm, Government and Public Service, Law, Medical, Real Estate, and Travel. *Writer's Market* also provides extensive information on book publishing, and on the business of writing.

A typical listing in *Writer's Market* gives the magazine's address, editor's name, circulation, intended readers (such as the readership of *Equal Opportunity,* "90% college juniors and seniors; 10% working graduates"), focus ("an understanding of educational and career problems of minorities is essential"), manner of distribution ("distributed through college guidance and placement offices"), and sorts of articles wanted: "how-to (job-hunting skills, personal finance, better living, coping with discrimination); humor (student or career related); interview/profile (minority role models); . . . personal experience (professional and student study and career experiences)." The entry also specifies the timing and content of special issues; the number of manuscripts purchased annually; the length, type and nature of illustrations (if any); payment; whether or not the writer should inquire about the prospective submission ("Query first"); and the length of decision time ("Reports in 6 weeks.").

Entries may include the manuscript slant, specifying topics and literary types that are wanted and those that would be rejected: *Sierra* wants "Exposé (well-documented on environmental issues of national importance such as energy, wilderness, forests, etc.) . . . photo feature (photo essays on threatened or scenic areas"). But "No 'My trip to . . . ' or 'why we must save wildlife/nature' articles; no poetry or general superficial essays on environmentalism." *Mad Magazine* eschews "TV or movie satires, . . . articles about Alfred E. Neuman . . . ." *New Mexico Magazine* says, "No generalized odes to . . . the Southwest. No sentimentalized, paternalistic views of Indians or Hispanics."

Entries also advise on style: *Tennis* seeks "conversational, informal writing styles"; *Mad* advises, "Have fun! . . . Think visually! . . . We like outrageous, silly and/or satirical humor." *New Mexico Magazine* wants "good style, good grammar" but "No glib, gimmicky 'travel brochure' writing." While specifying a "narrative, anecdotal style" for historical articles, *Virginia Cavalcade* warns, "Too many submissions are written for an academic audience or are simply not sufficiently gripping."

Entries include the manner of manuscript transmission. Although all publishers now assume that submissions will be written on computers and laser or letter-quality printed, some indicate whether they want discs or will accept electronic transmission.

These publications are only some of the general guides and guidelines. Many specialized fields have their own guides to their numerous publications. There are over 2000 journals in the social sciences alone, many of which are identified in Alvin Y. Wang's *Author's Guide to Journals in the Behavioral Sciences* (Hillsdale, NJ: Erlbaum, 1989). Over 3200 scholarly journals in American, British, and international literature and languages are identified in the continually updated *MLA Directory of Periodicals* (New York: Modern Language Association). And so on. You can construct a bibliography of publications on specialized topics by feeding a cluster of relevant key words into a computerized information retrieval system; ask your librarian for help.

But first and foremost, keep your eye on the prize—the writing itself, transformed through revising and editing into work that you'll be proud of and that others will want to read. As you revise and edit to transmute that shimmer in the mind's eye to words that gleam golden on the page, you'll experience the pleasure, and the power, that emerge when fact becomes artifact.

How to Submit Writing for Publication

Polishing the appearance of a manuscript may be like polishing a car; the car may not run any better, but it certainly looks more impressive. You can increase the chances that your manuscript will be treated with respect if you make it look professional by adhering to the conventions that follow.

Identifying Potential Publishers

Look for a good fit between your writing and where you wish to publish it, as previously discussed (pages 324–26). As you browse in libraries or newsstands, list appropriate publications in the order in which you intend to submit your manuscript to them. Then write to the editor-in-chief of, say, your top three choices—more if you intend to send out a lot of queries—for writer's guidelines and submission requirements such as length, format, whether the editor wants to see queries or partial works first, and in form (disk? how many hardcopies?). Enclose a self addressed stamped envelope (SASE), phone and FAX numbers, and an E-mail address if you have one, for prompt answers.

Query Letters

Before sending a manuscript, it's advisable to query the editor in a letter of not more than one single-spaced page. Sending a brief letter of inquiry rather than the whole piece will enable you to submit your manuscript where it's most likely to be received with interest. Advance queries will save you potential rejections, postage, and time, for your work won't languish in an editorial office where it isn't wanted.

The ostensible purpose of a query letter is to find out whether your topic and approach fit the publication's current needs. However, its major purpose is, as *Writer's Market* says, "to convince the editor that your idea would be interesting to the publication's readership and that you are the best writer for the job." Your query letter should provide the following information.

State your specific idea.   Don't simply suggest a general subject. If you can encapsulate your idea in a catchy title, so much the better.

Show your enthusiam.   Explain your idea in a way that conveys your enthusiasm for the project. Will it be a first person narrative, a how-to-article, a summary of opinions? From what angle or point of view? What will your style be? Some query letters demonstrate these by beginning with a paragraph that resembles the lead of their proposed article.

Sketch the article's structure.   Give enough information to show how you will proceed, and on what evidence.

Mention your special expertise or experience.   Tell the publisher why you are qualified to write on the subject. Previous experience, such as working for a newspaper or other publications, can help; if you have no experience, don't call attention to this. If an editor wants to see clippings of your work, submit something related in subject or style to your current proposal.

Identify your sources.   Tell the publisher where you'll get the information to write about your idea. Sources include interviews, case histories, personal experience, published materials, letters, videotapes, and knowledge of the territory. If you plan to use photographs or other visual materials, identify their sources as well.

Specify the length.   Give the number of words counted by your word processor—somewhere between 220 and 300 words on a typed page. Your estimate should reflect the importance of the subject and the magazine's format; some publishers adhere to strict word limits. There's no point in sending long articles to journals that publish pieces with short formats unless you plan extensive revision.

Indicate a realistic completion date for the manuscript.   Unless you've already finished locating all the information and corroborating each piece of evidence, the project will take longer than you think.

Don't discuss fees or request editorial advice at this stage.

A sample query letter might look like this:

Mr. Jonathan F. King, Editor-in-Chief
Sierra
730 Polk St.
San Francisco, CA 94109

Dear Mr. King:

I have recently completed a 5000-word article titled "Our Vanishing Beaches: Citizens and Survival." The article's thesis is that the natural ecology and recreational potential of many of America's best beaches are being destroyed by overuse; private citizens must act now to preserve these natural treasures for current and future generations. Would you be interested in considering this article for publication in *Sierra*?

Although the problem addressed is perennial, my article takes a new slant on the subject, that of the involvement of private citizens in public policy specifically aimed at beach preservation. It begins with some horror stories documented with evidence obtained by the Sierra Club (I'm president of the U.C.L.A. student branch) and the Wilderness Society on the effects on the ecology of oil spills, dumping of toxic wastes, and beachfront condominium complexes. Then, using projections derived from information provided by the Environmental Protection Agency, the article demonstrates the potential destruction of the beaches and of marine life in 1995, 2000, and 2005. The potential consequences are horrifying, even by conservative estimates; they imply the destruction of 50 percent of the existing usable beachfront and a comparable destruction of marine life. The article will conclude with a threefold plan for action by concerned citizens. In general, the focus is on action and on prevention of future problems.

Although the manuscript is completed, if you like the idea but have suggestions for changes, I can try to incorporate these and have the article to you within two weeks of receipt of your letter. I write a weekly ecology column for the *Daily Bruin,* which is also reprinted in my hometown paper, *The Orange*

County Weekly. Considering the paper's conservative slant, I have been grati-fied by the readers' responses to my articles, two of which I enclose because of their relevance to "Our Vanishing Beaches."

Thank you for considering my proposal. I look forward to hearing from you.

Sincerely,

Boyd Bradley

This query letter follows the suggested format. It is straightforward, suffi-ciently specific to convey the argument of the article, the research method-ology, and supporting evidence. Bradley has had experience both with the subject and as a writer; his writing style is apparent from the query letter and from the clippings of articles he encloses.

But will this letter, however well-written and authoritative, be sufficiently intriguing for the editor of *Sierra* to want to see "Our Vanishing Beaches: Citizens and Survival"? Without knowing what other submissions on the subject King has received lately, this is impossible to predict. If the article strikes King as original, imaginative, and he hasn't published others like it in recent months, he's likely to be interested. If the idea too strongly resembles submissions recently published, waiting in the wings, or rejected, King is less likely to be attracted, but at least Bradley should get a quick answer—in a SASE—at minimum cost of time and expense to himself.

Submitting Work for Consideration

If an editor says, "Yes, send along the article," follow the suggestions un-der "Responsibilities" (page 311) to make the manuscript as accurate and elegantly written as you can, and use the suggestions that follow to prepare a clean, crisp copy of your manuscript for editorial scrutiny.

Choose appropriate paper. Use plain white, heavy weight (20-pound) standard-size paper, 8-1/2″ × 11″, unless computer software disks or print-outs are acceptable. Avoid erasable paper; one swipe of an editor's elbow and you lose half a page.

Print out the manuscript in distinct black ink. Double space the article and print on one side of the paper only. Send the specified number of copies and disk, if requested.

Identify your article by title and author. Include your institutional affil-iation, if relevant, on the first page, or on a separate sheet if the article will be read blind—when an editor or manuscript reader is not shown author's name. On author-identified submissions, put your name next to the page number on each page (Bradley, 4, or Bradley, 4 of 8). Leave a four-inch top margin on the first page only. Triple space between the last line of the title/author identification and the first line of the text of the article.

Use standard margins.   Use a 1-1/2″ margin at the left and top, 1″ at the right and bottom. The left-hand margin should be even; the right-hand margin should be ragged. It's better not to justify (align text at) the right-hand margin because you want the spacing within your text to be reproduced in type exactly as it is in the manuscript. Justification defeats this aim by altering the internal spacing to make the right-hand margin even. Indent each new paragraph five character spaces.

Number each page.   Use Arabic numerals (1, 2, 3) in the upper right-hand corner. Indicate on the first page, above the pagination, the total of the number of words in the article.

Don't end line with hyphens.   End each line with an entire word rather than breaking the word across two lines. A word processor with "justification off" does this automatically. Because your manuscript guides the typesetter, hyphens could get reproduced by mistake when the article is set into type. If the paper is to be reproduced from a disk, you'll be all set.

Proofread for typing errors.   Check also for misspellings, missing words or lines, and misquotations—compare your version with the original source.

Clip the pages together.   Don't staple or otherwise bind them.

Make a copy.   Photocopy the final, corrected version and make a backup disk to keep for yourself in case the original goes astray in the mail or in an editor's office. If the original is returned with editorial comments and you agree with them, incorporate them in your subsequent rewriting. If the original is returned in pristine condition, you can send it out again as is.

Always enclose a SASE.   This is for your own protection so you'll get the manuscript back in case it's rejected. If you're likely to move within six months, indicate an alternative address and the date after which it should be used; manuscripts sometimes sit around in editorial offices longer than you'd like them to. Use first-class postage (paper-clipped, not stuck, to the return envelope and supply a return envelope big enough to hold your manuscript without folding, so it will look crisp when you send it out again. If your manuscript returns from the rounds of several editors' offices limp and smudged, mail a fresh printout; editors are far more receptive to professional-looking manuscripts than to those that exude authorial weariness or naivete. In these days of inexpensive copying, some editors don't return manuscripts anymore, but you should send a SASE unless editorial guidelines say not to.

Enclose a short, simple cover letter.   If you've sent the manuscript in response to a favorable query letter, you have a better chance of getting a thoughtful reading of your article if you refer to the editor's invitation. At this point, however, you won't need to say much about the article itself; the manuscript should be self-evident and should not require additional explanation. Some professional journals request a one-paragraph abstract to be submitted with the article; you can determine this in advance. To refresh the editor's mind, you may wish to include a sentence or two of any biographical information that is relevant to your authorial expertise. A sample cover letter might read:

Mr. Jonathan F. King, Editor-in-Chief
Sierra
730 Polk St.
San Francisco, CA 94109

Dear Mr. King:

At your invitation, in response to my initial query about "Our Vanishing Beaches: Citizens and Survival," I enclose the article for possible publication in *Sierra*. In accord with your suggestions, I revised the manuscript to include more firsthand information about the ecological activities of student groups in the Los Angeles area and have included quotations from interviews with several student leaders to reinforce this material.

As you may recall, I have been active in student ecology groups for some years; the article grew out of my experience and my convictions on the subject. I write an ecology column for the U.C.L.A. *Daily Bruin,* which is reprinted in the *Orange County Weekly.* Thank you for considering the article. I look forward to hearing from you soon.

Sincerely,

Boyd Bradley

Keep track of where you send the manuscript, and when.   The safest way is to keep a copy of your cover letter to the editor. As a routine matter, keep copies of all business correspondence for later reference. If you keep a separate computer file or manila file folder for each manuscript, you can file the related correspondence in the same place. If you haven't heard from an editor after three months (six months for scholarly journals), write a brief letter inquiring whether your manuscript is still under consideration. Enclose a SASE for this reply, also.

Don't submit the same article simultaneously to more than one publication. If you feel you need to do this, ask for permission from the editors in question. It's appropriate to send out multiple query letters concerning the same article. But don't submit the article to more than one publisher unless their readerships are essentially different (say, your hometown newspaper and a national magazine) and the editors agree to multiple submissions. Multiple submissions abuse editorial time and goodwill. If your manuscript should be accepted simultaneously by two editors, you'll have to reject one offer of publication, an embarrassment if you wish to maintain cordial relations with both.

After Work Is Accepted

Once your article is accepted by a publisher, you will need to get permission to reprint direct quotations totalling more than 300 words of prose from any single copyrighted published source or even a single line of a poem or a song, the latter often prohibitively expensive, if available at all. You can usually obtain permission to quote by writing to the publishers of the prose works in question, and paying the appropriate fee, if any. However, to save the time and expense of obtaining permission, you can often transform direct quotations into paraphrases so that the quoted material comes under the "fair use" word limit—three hundred words.

Whether or not you will be charged a permissions fee depends on the original publisher's general policy, the date and context in which the work appeared originally, and the context in which it will be reprinted. The rule of thumb is, if reprinting portions of someone else's writing will help the reprinter make money, then the original author or author's publisher usually requests a fee. If the reprinting is not for profit, then the fee may be waived.

A writer who has submitted a manuscript has to fight the natural inclination to linger by the mailbox, waiting with moist palms and palpitating heart for an answer. There are two good remedies for this. One is to keep several different manuscripts in circulation at a time, as a way to avoid putting all your emotional investment into one editor's basket. The other is to continue to write new manuscripts, which may require such concentration that those out in the mail will occupy only your peripheral vision.

Writing that hides in a cozy desk drawer or file folder is safe, snugly and securely tucked away. But, there in the dark, no one can read it. Writing needs exposure to the light of public scrutiny, however revealing, however risky this may be. Such illumination is necessary for you to gain your place in the sun, as a real writer, where you belong.

Note

[1]In this case, the reference is to former president George Bush, in the *New York Times* of November 4, 1992, A1.

Works Cited

Appelbaum, Judith. *How to Get Happily Published*. 4th ed. New York: Harper, 1992.

Bernard, André, Ed. *Rotten Rejections: A Literary Companion*. 1990. New York: Penguin, 1990.

McPhee, John. Spring Writer's Conference. The College of William and Mary. March 1981.

Writer's Market 1993: Where and How to Sell What You Write. Ed. Mark Kissling. Cincinnati: Writer's Digest, 1993. 19, 342, 412, 445, 511, 560, 669.

INDEX